FRONTIERS OF JUSTICE

THE TANNER LECTURES ON HUMAN VALUES

FRONTIERS OF JUSTICE

DISABILITY, NATIONALITY, SPECIES MEMBERSHIP

Martha C. Nussbaum

THE BELKNAP PRESS
OF HARVARD UNIVERSITY PRESS
CAMBRIDGE, MASSACHUSETTS
LONDON, ENGLAND

First Harvard University Press paperback edition, 2007

Library of Congress Cataloging-in-Publication Data
Nussbaum, Martha Craven, 1947–
Frontiers of justice : disability, nationality, species membership /
Martha C. Nussbaum.
p. cm. — (The Tanner lectures on human values)
Includes bibliographical references and index.
ISBN-13 978-0-674-01917-1 (cloth: alk. paper)
ISBN-10 0-674-01917-2 (cloth: alk. paper)
ISBN-13 978-0-674-02410-6 (pbk.)
ISBN-10 0-674-02410-9 (pbk.)
1. Social justice.   2. People with disabilities—Civil rights.
3. Minorities—Civil rights.   4. Animal rights.
I. Title.   II. Tanner lectures on human values.
HM671.N87 2005
320′.01′1—dc22   2005050240

In Memory of John Rawls

ACKNOWLEDGMENTS

This book began as the Tanner Lectures in Human Values at the Australian National University, Canberra, in November 2002. The lectures were subsequently presented as the Tanner Lectures in Human Values at Clare Hall, Cambridge University, in March 2003. The first debt of gratitude I owe is thus to the Tanner Foundation, for their great generosity in enabling me to deliver the lectures twice and thus to receive an unusually large amount of valuable commentary and discussion. I then owe thanks to the seven commentators, for their close reading of my draft and their extremely valuable input: Lenore Manderson, Leslie Francis, and Eva Kittay on issues of disability, Zoya Hasan and Amartya Sen on issues of transnational justice, and Peter Singer and David DeGrazia on the entitlements of nonhuman animals. I am also grateful to others present at the seminars and discussions for their valuable input, and especially to Robert Goodin and Michael Smith.

The material on disability was also the subject of a symposium at the American Philosophical Association's Pacific Division; I am deeply grateful to Lawrence Becker, Eva Kittay, Andrews Reath, and Anita Silvers for their extremely helpful input. The same lecture was also delivered at the School of Criticism and Theory at Cornell University, where I received valuable comments from many participants, especially from Dominick La Capra, Mary Jacobus, Magda Romanska, and Michael Steinberg.

The material on transnational justice was presented as the Olaf Palme Lecture, sponsored by Queen Elizabeth House, Oxford. I am grateful to Frances Stewart for this wonderful invitation, and to Frances Stewart, Sudhir Anand, Barbara Harriss, and others for their stimulating comments.

Finally, the material on animals was presented at a symposium honoring the ninetieth birthday of Alan Gewirth; sadly, this symposium was less than a year before his death in the spring of 2004. I am grateful to Gewirth, to Michael Kremer, and to Michael Green for their challenging comments on that occasion.

For reading drafts and offering me valuable feedback, I am exceedingly grateful to John Deigh, Craig Duncan, Elizabeth Emens, Chad Flanders, Leslie Francis, Sherri Irvin, Charles Larmore, Martha Minow, Henry Richardson, Cass Sunstein, and Candace Vogler. I know I have not answered all their questions.

Joyce Seltzer has done her usual superb job of editing, and I am unusually grateful to Ann Hawthorne for her meticulous copy-editing and to Jennifer Johnson and Rachel Goodman for proofreading and indexing.

Earlier versions of the material have appeared in print as follows:

- Early versions of all three sections of the argument appear in the *Tanner Lectures on Human Values*, volume 24 (Salt Lake City: University of Utah Press, 2004), pages 413–508.
- An early version of material from Chapters 2 and 3 appears as "Capabilities and Disabilities: Justice for Mentally Disabled Citizens," *Philosophical Topics* 2 (2002): 133–165.
- An early version of material from Chapters 4 and 5 appears as "Beyond the Social Contract: Capabilities and Global Justice," *Oxford Development Studies* 32 (2004): 3–18.
- An early version of material from Chapter 6 appears as "Beyond 'Compassion and Humanity': Justice for Non-Human Animals," in *Animal Rights: Current Debates and New Directions*, ed. Cass R. Sunstein and Martha C. Nussbaum (New York: Oxford University Press, 2004), pages 299–320.

All material is printed here by courtesy of the Tanner Foundation. None of the earlier versions is in any way final; indeed, my formulations in this volume are on many points very different from the earlier ones, and, I hope, more nearly adequate.

My project is critical of John Rawls. I have singled out Rawls's theory for critical examination because it is the strongest political theory in the social contract tradition that we have, and, indeed, one of the most distinguished theories in the Western tradition of political philosophy. I focus on areas that Rawls himself regarded as unsolved problems, problems that challenge his theory in ways that he was not altogether certain it could meet. That focus is appropriate because he solved so many other problems so well. My ultimate purpose is to extend the core ideas of his theory to deal with these new issues. Although I believe that this extension cannot be done without serious alterations in the parts of his theory that derive from the social contract tradition, I believe that the theory itself, its principles and its intuitive underpinnings, provides excellent guidance as we pursue these new and difficult questions. With greatest respect, friendship, and sadness, I dedicate this book to his memory.

CONTENTS

ABBREVIATIONS

Throughout this book, works by John Rawls are abbreviated as follows:

DL   "Kantian Constructivism in Moral Theory" (Dewey Lectures), *Journal of Philosophy*, 77 (1980): 515–571

IPRR   "The Idea of Public Reason Revisited," in *The Law of Peoples, with "The Idea of Public Reason Revisited"* (Cambridge, Mass.: Harvard University Press, 1999)

JF   *Justice as Fairness: A Restatement,* ed. Erin Kelly (Cambridge, Mass.: Harvard University Press, 2001)

LHE   *Lectures on the History of Ethics,* ed. Barbara Herman (Cambridge, Mass.: Harvard University Press, 2000)

LP   *The Law of Peoples, with "The Idea of Public Reason Revisited"* (Cambridge, Mass.: Harvard University Press, 1999)

"LP"   "The Law of Peoples," in *On Human Rights: The Oxford Amnesty Lectures, 1993,* ed. Stephen Shute and Susan Hurley (New York: Basic Books, 1993)

PL   *Political Liberalism,* enl. ed. (New York: Columbia University Press, 1996)

TJ   *A Theory of Justice* (Cambridge, Mass.: Harvard University Press, 1971)

Here then is a proposition, which, I think, may be regarded as certain, that 'tis only from the selfishness and confin'd generosity of men, along with the scanty provision nature has made for his wants, that justice derives its origin.

—David Hume, *A Treatise of Human Nature*

And it is rather peculiar to think of the happy person as a solitary person: for the human being is a social creature and naturally disposed to live with others.

—Aristotle, *Nicomachean Ethics* IX.9

INTRODUCTION

Theories of social justice should be abstract. They should, that is, have a generality and theoretical power that enables them to reach beyond the political conflicts of their time, even if they have their origins in such conflicts. Even political justification requires such abstraction: for we cannot justify a political theory unless we can show that it can be stable over time, receiving citizens' support for more than narrowly self-protective or instrumental reasons.[1] And we cannot show that it can be stable without standing back from immediate events.

On the other hand, theories of social justice must also be responsive to the world and its most urgent problems, and must be open to changes in their formulations and even in their structures in response to a new problem or to an old one that has been culpably ignored.

Most theories of justice in the Western tradition, for example, have been culpably inattentive to women's demands for equality and to the many obstacles that stood, and stand, in the way of that equality. Their abstraction, though in some ways valuable, concealed a failure to confront one of the world's most serious problems. Attending adequately to the problem of gender justice has large theoretical consequences, since it involves acknowledging that the family is a political institution, not part of a "private sphere" immune from justice. Correcting the oversight of previous theories is therefore not a matter of simply applying the same old theories to a new problem; it is a matter of getting the theoretical structure right.

Today there are three unsolved problems of social justice whose neglect in existing theories seems particularly problematic. (No doubt there are still other such problems, which as yet we do not see.) First, there is the problem of doing justice to people with physical and mental impairments. These people are

people, but they have not as yet been included, in existing societies, as citizens on a basis of equality with other citizens. The
problem of extending education, health care, political rights and
liberties, and equal citizenship more generally to such people
seems to be a problem of justice, and an urgent one. Because
solving this problem requires a new way of thinking about who
the citizen is and a new analysis of the purpose of social cooperation (one not focused on mutual advantage), and because it also
requires emphasizing the importance of care as a social primary
good, it seems likely that facing it well will require not simply a
new application of the old theories, but a reshaping of theoretical structures themselves.

Second is the urgent problem of extending justice to all world
citizens, showing theoretically how we might realize a world
that is just as a whole, in which accidents of birth and national
origin do not warp people's life chances pervasively and from
the start. Because all the major Western theories of social justice
begin from the nation-state as their basic unit, it is likely that
new theoretical structures will also be required to think well
about this problem.

Finally, we need to face the issues of justice involved in our
treatment of nonhuman animals. That animals suffer pain and
indignity at the hands of humans has often been conceded to be
an ethical issue; it has more rarely been acknowledged to be an
issue of social justice. If we do so acknowledge it (and readers of
this book will have to judge for themselves whether the case for
so doing has been well made), it is clear, once again, that this
new problem will require theoretical change. Images of social
cooperation and reciprocity that require rationality in all the
parties, for example, will need to be reexamined and new images
of a different type of cooperation forged.

There are many approaches to social justice in the Western
tradition. One of the strongest and most enduring has been the

idea of the social contract, in which rational people get together, for mutual advantage, deciding to leave the state of nature and to govern themselves by law. Such theories have had enormous influence historically, and have recently been developed with great philosophical depth in the distinguished work of John Rawls. Such theories are probably the strongest theories of justice we have. At any rate, Rawls has powerfully made the case that they do better than the various forms of Utilitarianism in articulating, probing, and organizing our considered judgments about justice.

A theory may, however, be truly great and yet have serious limitations in some area or areas. Classical theories that rested on the public-private distinction had severe problems when it came to confronting the equality of women, and even Rawls's very astute approach to this problem has shortcomings.[2] Rawls himself acknowledged that the three problems I have just described are especially difficult ones for his contractarian theory to solve. He believed that the second might after all be solved, and he devoted much of his work at the end of his life to solving it; the first and third he called problems "on which justice as fairness may fail" (*PL* 21). He suggested that the issues needed further examination so that we could see how serious these problems were and what it might take to solve them (*PL* 21). Although my project in this book did not begin with Rawls's self-critical statement, that statement is a useful way of articulating its intentions.

I begin from the conviction that these three problems are indeed serious unsolved problems of justice. I argue that the classical theory of the social contract cannot solve these problems, even when put in its best form. It is for this reason that I focus throughout the book on Rawls, who to my mind expresses the classical idea of the social contract in its strongest form and makes the strongest case for its superiority to other theories. If

Rawls's distinguished theory has serious shortcomings in these three areas, as I hope to show, *a fortiori* other, less developed or less appealing forms of the contract doctrine are likely to have such problems.[3] I hope to show that the type of difficulty we shall encounter cannot be handled by merely applying the old theoretical structure to the new case; it is built into the theoretical structure itself, in such a way as to lead us to search for a different type of theoretical structure, albeit one in which major elements in Rawls's theory will survive and provide valuable guidance.

These problems are not simply problems in academic philosophy. Doctrines of the social contract have deep and broad influence in our political life. Images of who we are and why we get together shape our thinking about what political principles we should favor and who should be involved in their framing. The common idea that some citizens "pay their own way" and others do not, that some are parasitic and others "normally productive," are the offshoots, in the popular imagination, of the idea of society as a scheme of cooperation for mutual advantage. We could challenge those images in practical politics without identifying their source. It is actually quite helpful, however, to go to the root of the problem, so to speak: for then we see much more clearly why we got into such a difficulty and what we must change if we wish to advance. Thus, although this book engages with philosophical ideas in detail and with attention to the complexities and nuances of the theories in question, it is also intended as an essay in practical philosophy, which may guide us back to some richer ideas of social cooperation (old as well as new) that do not involve such difficulties. Although people can certainly engage in practical politics on all these issues without such a detailed philosophical investigation, I believe that the detailed investigation is helpful, both because it shows respect for the people one is criticizing and because it is always helpful to see exactly where the problem kicks in, so that one can change the right thing rather than the wrong thing. In fact, I am skeptical that a less detailed philosophical investigation has much practical relevance, when the questions are complex and the theoretical structures elaborate. If we go too quickly to the "bottom line," we lose the characteristic type of illumination that philosophy is able to provide. Certainly the great practical works in political philosophy are not great because of lack of detail. John Stuart Mill's *On Liberty* is great despite its frustrating lack of detail, and would have been even better had it spent more time working out foundational issues, such as the account of harm, or the relationships between liberty and preferences, liberty and rights. Rawls's two great books supply especially valuable practical guidance because they do try to answer hard foundational questions with rigor and pleasing detail.

My project here is both critical and constructive. For I shall argue that, with respect to all three of the problems under consideration, the version of the "capabilities approach" that I have long been developing suggests promising insights, and insights superior to those suggested, for those particular problems, by the social contract tradition. (As we shall see, I also hold that my approach converges in large measure with a different type of contractarianism, one based purely on Kantian ethical ideas without the idea of mutual advantage.) My previous account of the capabilities approach in *Women and Human Development* outlined the view, spoke about issues of method and justification, and discussed in detail its treatment of two particularly difficult problems, the problem of religion and the problem of the family. It also commended the approach as superior to preference-based Utilitarianism, in a detailed confrontation with that theory.

The next logical step, in the process that may over time lead to "reflective equilibrium,"[4] is to compare the approach to another strong theoretical approach, arguing that it is also superior to that approach, at least in some areas. This book supplies a part of that next step, by showing that with respect to the three unsolved problems the capabilities approach does better. I do not claim to have shown that it is better overall, since there may be other issues on which it does worse than contractarian theories. I focus on the theory of John Rawls in large part because I believe that it delivers answers that are basically right for the questions it does consider (though I differ in some details concerning the articulation of the theory of primary goods), and it is thus of some interest to try to figure out why, by Rawls's own account, it has difficulty with the three unsolved problems. Whether the capabilities approach could indeed be shown to do better than Rawls's theory overall is thus a question I shall not address; it must await a further, and lengthier, examination; for now, the decision rests with each reader (as, indeed, it always does in the end).

Readers will see that in articulating my own capabilities approach, here, as in *Women and Human Development,* I take over some central ideas from John Rawls: the idea of political liberalism (a form of liberalism not grounded in divisive religious or metaphysical principles) and the idea of overlapping consensus (the idea that people with different metaphysical and religious conceptions can accept the core of the political conception). Rawls always stressed, and stressed increasingly at the end of his life, that *Political Liberalism* concerned not his own conception of justice, but rather a family of liberal conceptions of which his own conception was only one. I hope that it will be seen that my capabilities approach is another member of this family, and thus that my proposal to add it to the Rawlsian conception advances, rather than displaces, Rawls's larger project.

In the process of arguing that the capabilities approach can handle the three specific problems of justice, I also extend the approach and modify it—most obviously in Chapters 5 and 6, where I extend it to deal with issues of transnational justice and to questions of justice involving nonhuman animals. Throughout, however, there are other more subtle modifications and elaborations of the approach for which readers interested in the development of the approach might want to be on the alert:

1. The intuitive starting point of the approach, and the way in which it argues that a given capability ought to be on the list, is discussed in Chapters 1, 3, and 5; see especially the treatment of the example of education in 5.i.

2. The notion of human dignity used in the approach is discussed in 3.iv and 3.ix, and see also 5.iii. The role of the species norm in thinking about dignity is discussed, and it is argued that dignity does not rest on some actual property of persons, such as the possession of reason or other specific abilities; this account represents a shift from some earlier discussions of "basic capabilities." It is also argued that dignity is not a value independent of the capabilities, but that the articulation of the political principles involving capability are (partial) articulations of the notion of a life with human dignity.

3. The relationship between the capabilities approach and Utilitarianism is discussed (again) in Chapter 1, and also in 5.ii and 6.iii. None of these discussions contains surprising material, but there are some new arguments, and new organizations of old arguments.

4. The relationship between capabilities and rights is discussed in 5.iii. It is made clear that the capabilities approach is one species of a human rights approach, and an improved account is given of why the language of capabilities seems superior to the (bare) language of human rights.

5. The relationship of the capabilities approach to issues of pluralism and cultural variety is discussed (again, but perhaps more concisely) in 5.v and 1.vi.

6. The role of the concept of equality in the capabilities approach is discussed in 5.iv and in 6.ix. Because these arguments are both new and complex, I do not attempt to summarize them here.

7. The Rawlsian idea of "overlapping consensus," in relation to the capabilities approach, is discussed in 3.iv, 5.vi, and 6.xi. I address concerns about whether there can be an overlapping consensus among nations with diverse histories and traditions, and the even more difficult question whether we can expect an overlapping consensus on extending some basic rights to animals.

8. The relationship between capabilities as entitlements (rights) and duties to secure those entitlements is discussed in 5.i.

Thus the book does not simply recapitulate the constructive account given in *Women and Human Development*, extending it to the new areas. It breaks new ground in a number of areas, frames old distinctions more adequately, and tries to address a number of questions that readers and critics have raised. This is not surprising, both because of the imperfect nature of the previous articulations of the approach and because of its world-responsive character: new problems lead to alterations in the theoretical structure itself. My arguments should therefore be of interest to people who are not particularly interested in the three problems that are the book's focus, although it seems to me that it would be odd for a person concerned with issues of justice not to be interested in them all.

1

SOCIAL CONTRACTS
AND THREE UNSOLVED PROBLEMS
OF JUSTICE

> Men being, as has been said, by Nature, all free, equal and inde-
> pendent, no one can be put out of this Estate, and subjected to
> the Political Power of another, without his own *Consent*. The only
> way whereby any one devests himself of his Natural Liberty, and
> *puts on the bonds of Civil Society* is by agreeing with other Men to
> joyn and unite into a Community, for their comfortable, safe, and
> peaceable living one amongst another, in a secure Enjoyment of
> their Properties, and a greater Security against any that are not
> of it.
>
> —John Locke, *Second Treatise of Government*

i. The State of Nature

Imagine a time without political government, with no sovereign, laws, courts, established property rights, or contract. Human beings could live in such a condition, but life would not
go well. As Thomas Hobbes famously put it, in the text that
stands at the beginning of the classical Western social contract
tradition:

> In such condition, there is no place for Industry; because the
> fruit thereof is uncertain: and consequently no Culture of the
> Earth; no Navigation, nor use of the commodities that may be
> imported by Sea; no commodious Building; no Instruments of
> moving, and removing such things as require much force; no
> Knowledge of the face of the Earth; no account of time; no Arts;
> no Letters; no Society; and which is worst of all, continuall feare,

and danger of violent death; And the life of man, solitary, poore, nasty, brutish, and short.[1]

So people make a contract with one another, agreeing to give up the private use of force and the ability to take another man's property, in exchange for peace, security, and the expectation of mutual advantage. By considering the contract that would be made in an initial situation in which people are imagined as "free, equal, and independent,"[2] as John Locke put it, we gain insight into the justification of political principles. Thinking about the structure of political society as the outcome of a contract made in an initial situation that is in some crucial respects fair, evenly balanced, we gain a deeper understanding of what justice requires.[3] Thus, through a procedure that assumes no antecedent advantages on the part of any individual, we extract a set of rules that duly protect the interests of all.

The idea of basic political principles as the result of a social contract is one of the major contributions of liberal political philosophy in the Western tradition. In its various forms, the tradition makes two signal contributions. First, it demonstrates clearly and rigorously that human interests themselves—even if we begin with an artificially simplified conception of such interests—are well served by political society, a society in which all surrender power before law and duly constituted authority. Second, and even more significant, it shows us that if we divest human beings of the artificial advantages some of them hold in all actual societies—wealth, rank, social class, education, and so on[4]—they will agree to a contract of a certain specific sort, which the theories then proceed to spell out. Given that the starting point is in that sense fair, the principles that result from the bargain will be fair. The tradition thus bequeaths to us a procedural understanding of political society[5] in which the equal worth of persons and the value of reciprocity among them are central features.

This understanding of political society is a prominent part of classical liberalism's assault on feudal and monarchical traditions.[6] From the fact that we are all rough equals in the state of nature follow some profound criticisms of regimes that make wealth, rank, and status sources of differential social and political power. The idea of the contract made in the state of nature thus provides not only an account of the content of political principles but also a benchmark of political legitimacy. Any society whose basic principles are far from what would be chosen by free, equal, and independent persons in the state of nature is to that extent called into question.

Because the tradition provides a vivid, rigorous, and illuminating way of thinking about justice among equal persons, it has remained philosophically fertile. The most powerful and influential theory of justice in the twentieth century, that of John Rawls, sets itself squarely within this tradition; Rawls has pursued the implications of the contract idea more rigorously and completely, perhaps, than any thinker yet.

Rawls emphasizes his allegiance to the social contract tradition from the very beginning of *A Theory of Justice*, saying, "My aim is to present a conception of justice which generalizes and carries to a higher level of abstraction the familiar theory of the social contract as found, say, in Locke, Rousseau, and Kant."[7] "The guiding idea is that the principles of justice . . . are the principles that free and rational persons concerned to further their own interests would accept in an initial position of equality" (*TJ* 11). Defending his use of the term "contract" against potential objections, he concludes, "Finally there is the long tradition of the contract doctrine. Expressing the tie with this line of thought helps to define ideas and accords with natural piety"

(16; cf. 121). (The odd remark about "natural piety" is an example of Rawls's lifelong respect for the theories of his predecessors, a hallmark of both his teaching and his writing.)

Rawls's historical connections are more complex than these remarks suggest. For one thing, he draws heavily on David Hume's view about the "Circumstances of Justice" to flesh out elements that are less explicit in classical contractarian thinkers, although Hume is not a social contract thinker. This source of complexity poses no problems, however, since Hume's ideas on these issues dovetail well with those of Locke and Kant. Rawls explains his choice of Hume by saying that Hume's account of the Circumstances of Justice is "especially perspicuous" (*TJ* 127), more detailed than those of Locke and Kant.

In two crucial respects, however, Rawls's theory is different from all preceding social contract views. Because Rawls's aim is to generate basic political principles from a very spare set of assumptions, and because it is an example of what Rawls calls "pure procedural justice," in which the correct procedure defines the correct outcome, Rawls diverges from the historical tradition by not assuming that human beings have any natural rights in the state of nature. His view thus departs more radically from the natural law views of Grotius and Pufendorf than do the theories of Locke and Kant.

A second difference involves the role of moral elements in the contract procedure. Rawls's choice situation includes moral assumptions that Hobbes, Locke, and even Kant (in his political writings) eschew.[8] The Veil of Ignorance supplies a representation of moral impartiality that is closely related to the Kantian idea that no person should be used as a mere means of the ends of others.

Rawls's dual allegiance—to classical social contract doctrine and to the core ideas of Kant's moral philosophy—is a source both of illumination and of profound tension in Rawls's theory.

There is no doubt, however, that, despite his deep commitment to moral ideas of equal respect and reciprocity, Rawls never diverges from understanding his project as a part of the social contract tradition, as he reconstructs and interprets it.[9] Even where there are, apparently, important divergences, Rawls points the reader to underlying similarities. Thus, although he appears not to use the fiction of a state of nature, he informs his readers that in fact he does so. "In justice as fairness the original position of equality corresponds to the state of nature in the traditional theory of the social contract" (*TJ* 12). And in general, as we shall see, there is a great deal in his view that can be well understood only by focusing on these connections. Through Rawls's work, the tradition has made its most sophisticated contribution to our thinking about what justice requires when we begin from the idea of equal persons, their worth and their capacities.

The critical part of my argument will focus on Rawls and, to a lesser extent, on other modern social contract thinkers (David Gauthier, for example). My argument will not address more purely Kantian forms of contractarianism that detach themselves altogether from the social contract tradition, with its focus on mutual advantage—although in Chapter 2 I shall discuss the potential for convergence between my capabilities approach and such contractarian doctrines (for example those of Thomas Scanlon in ethics and Brian Barry in politics). In our time, the social contract tradition has assumed a distinctive shape, in part through the pervasive influence of economic ideas of bargaining on our political culture as a whole. Contractarians in philosophy criticize these ideas, but they are also in some ways influenced by them as they interpret and recast the classical idea of the social contract. Rawls argues against the Utilitarianism so dominant in economics and, through economics, in public policy; but he uses the classical idea of the social contract to convince his reader (prominently including the economically oriented reader) that the correct way of thinking about political principles is a richer, more moralized way.

Thus the influences shaping modern contractarianism are complex. With the exception of Rawls I shall not be offering a detailed exegesis of any particular historical figure, although I shall try to show the main lines of influence that connect each major thinker to the Rawlsian framework. I think it is fair to say, however, that, whatever the subtleties and complexities of each individual thinker, the tradition has bequeathed to us a general image of society as a contract for mutual advantage (people getting something by living together that they could not get each on their own) among people who are "free, equal, and independent." It is this idea, deeply embedded in our political culture, that will be the target of my scrutiny.

ii. Three Unsolved Problems

1. *Impairment and disability.*[10] Despite the tradition's major contributions and ongoing value, its modern exemplars prove insufficient to address three of the most pressing problems of justice in today's world. The classical theorists all assumed that their contracting agents were men who were roughly equal in capacity, and capable of productive economic activity. They thus omitted from the bargaining situation women (understood as non-"productive"), children, and elderly people—although the parties might represent their interests.[11] These omissions, already striking in the seventeenth and eighteenth centuries, have to some extent been rectified in contemporary contract doctrines, though the idea that the family is a private sphere immune from law and contract has not always received the thoroughgoing criticism it deserves.[12]

No social contract doctrine, however, includes people with severe and atypical physical and mental impairments in the group of those by whom basic political principles are chosen. Of course in most modern societies, until recently, such people were simply not included in society. They were excluded and stigmatized; there was no political movement to include them. People with severe mental impairments, in particular, were not even educated. They were hidden away in institutions or left to die from neglect;[13] they were never considered part of the public realm.[14] So it was not surprising that the classical social contract thinkers failed to imagine them as participants in the choice of political principles, nor, indeed, that they were willing to sign on to foundational assumptions (for example, a rough equality of power and physical and mental ability) that ensured that they would not be included at the initial, foundational stage.

For many people with impairments and disabilities, who are fully capable of participating in political choice, this omission from the situation of basic choice already seems to be a defect from the point of view of justice. They are not being treated as full equals of other citizens; their voices are not being heard when basic principles are chosen. This problem seems all the graver when we recognize that many of the factors that sometimes exclude people with impairments from participation in political choice are social and far from inevitable. Thus there is no principled reason why they could not have been included in a choice situation that is not supposed to assume any particular design of social institutions. Some people with severe mental impairments, however, could not be included in the group of political choosers directly, however generously we assess their potential for such a contribution. For those people, the failure to include them in the role of chooser does not seem like an injustice, so long as there is some other way to take their interests into account.

The omission of people with impairments and disabilities from the contract situation becomes more damaging still, however, once we take account of a striking structural feature of all social contract theories. The social contract tradition conflates two questions that are in principle distinct: "By whom are society's basic principles designed?" and "For whom are society's basic principles designed?"[15] The contracting parties are imagined to be one and the same as the citizens who will live together and whose lives will be regulated by the principles that are chosen. The core moral idea in the tradition is that of mutual advantage and reciprocity among people who need to make such a contract. The chosen principles regulate, in the first instance, their dealings with one another. Other interests and persons (or other creatures) may be included either derivatively, through the parties' own cares and commitments, or at a later stage, after the principles are already chosen. But the primary subjects of justice are the same ones who choose the principles. Thus when the tradition specifies certain abilities (rationality, language, roughly equal physical and mental capacity) as prerequisites for participation in the procedure that chooses principles, these requirements also have large consequences for the treatment of people with impairments and disabilities as recipients or subjects of justice in the resulting society. The fact that they are not included in the group of choosers means that they are not included (except derivatively or at a later stage) in the group of those for whom principles are chosen.

Rawls's theory is more subtle at this point, because he does explicitly distinguish the parties in the Original Position from citizens in the society that they will ultimately design. (Citizens lack the informational limitations of the Veil of Ignorance; in their place they have an extensive moral education designed to engender sentiments that render the society stable.) But so far as our questions about disability and species membership are concerned, this difference is not significant. The parties choose principles as if for a society in which they themselves are going

to live, advancing their plans. The citizens live with the principles those parties have chosen, under that thought experiment.
Thus, though they may make practical arrangements for the
needs of human and animal beings who were not included in the
original contracting group, they are not at liberty to redesign
the principles of justice themselves in the light of their awareness
of these issues. In *Political Liberalism,* Rawls puts things in a
slightly different way that makes his basic attachment to the historical tradition clear: the parties in the Original Position are
now envisaged as "representatives" of or trustees for citizens.
The characterization of the citizens for whom they are trustees,
however, now explicitly incorporates just those features of *TJ*'s
characterization of the parties that causes problems from the
point of view of disability issues: their mental and physical abilities, like those of *TJ*'s parties, are said to lie all within the "normal" range. So, in the end, the parties are designing principles
for citizens who, like themselves, are human beings possessed of
no serious mental or physical impairments.

But the "by whom" and the "for whom" questions need not
be linked in this way. One might have a theory that held that
many living beings, human and even nonhuman, are primary
subjects of justice, even though they are not capable of participating in the procedure through which political principles are
chosen. One might have strong reasons for seeking such a theory and separating the two questions, if one starts from the idea
that many different types of lives have dignity and are worthy of
respect. If one thinks that way, one would acknowledge from
the start that the capacity to make a contract, and the possession
of those abilities that make for mutual advantage in the resulting
society, are not necessary conditions for being a citizen who has
dignity and deserves to be treated with respect on a basis of
equality with others.

Thus the omission of people with disabilities from the initial choice of basic political principles has large consequences for their equal citizenship more generally, through the structure that is characteristic of social contract theories. Today, when the issue of justice for people with disabilities is prominent on the agenda of every decent society, the omission of all of them from participation in the situation of basic political choice looks problematic, given the evident capacity of many if not most of them for choice; and their omission from the group of persons *for whom* society's most basic principles are chosen is more problematic still. Even if their interests can be taken into account derivatively or at a later stage, we naturally wonder why this postponement is necessary, and whether it is not likely to affect the fully equal treatment of such citizens—even if it is not in and of itself a form of unequal treatment. Rawls, as we shall see, acknowledges a gap in his theory at this point and worries about it. I shall argue that Rawls's treatment of the problem of disability is inadequate, and yet not easy to rectify. The full inclusion of citizens with mental and physical impairments raises questions that go to the heart of the classical contractarian account of justice and social cooperation.

2. *Nationality.* A second area of difficulty in the social-contract tradition concerns the role of nationality or place of birth in influencing people's basic life chances. In this increasingly interdependent world, we need to consider issues of justice raised by inequalities between rich and poor nations that affect the life chances of their citizens. The contract model is typically used to construct a single society, which is imagined as self-sufficient and not interdependent with any other society. Both Kant and Rawls do recognize the importance of confronting issues of justice between nations. But the logic of their theories leads them to pose this question at a second stage, and derivatively. They imagine that after states are established, relations among them still resemble a state of nature; so further

principles must be chosen to regulate their dealings with one another.

Thus, in this two-stage approach, states are treated as isomorphic with "free, equal, and independent" persons in the first stage of the argument. Once again, then, if we are to think in terms of a contract to depart from the state of nature at this second stage, we will have to ask who gets included in the group that makes the contract, and what conditions of independence, freedom, and rough equality must be assumed in order for the contract model to get off the ground. It may be doubted whether assuming the independence and rough equality of states makes any sense at all in a world in which a powerful global economy makes all economic choices interdependent and often imposes on poorer nations conditions that reinforce and deepen existing inequalities. Moreover, such assumptions entail that nations that are very unequal in power to the dominant nations, especially those whose developmental stage is pre-industrial or partly so, will have to be left out of the initial contracting group. Their needs will have to be dealt with later, after basic principles that profoundly affect the lives of their people are already chosen and fixed, and these needs will be addressed out of charity, not as a part of basic justice. (The situation of poorer nations in this sense resembles that of persons with impairments in the first stage of the social contract.)

Already in the seventeenth century, Hugo Grotius had developed a nuanced account of the interdependence of nations, arguing that moral norms constrain the actions of all nations and individuals in "international society." Grotius held that the human rights of individuals in some circumstances justify interference in the internal affairs of another nation. Even more significantly, he argued that the very determination of who owns what property awaits a full scrutiny of need and surplus, the poor in one nation having in some instances ownership rights to another nation's surplus.[16] But Grotius was no social contract theorist, and he could not have come to these conclusions had he started from the ideas that later became standard in the social contract tradition. For the very logic of a contract for mutual advantage suggests that one would not include in the first place agents whose contribution to overall social well-being is likely to be dramatically lower than that of others. When we are speaking of a contract between nations, extremely needy nations are in that position: why would prosperous nations pursuing mutual advantage want to include them in the contracting group, when they can handle relations with them in other ways, after basic principles are already chosen? Since, moreover, the states concerned have defined entitlements to property long before they enter the second-stage contract between nations, and those principles are understood as fixed, no radical proposal such as Grotius' idea about ownership and need could even be entertained.

The issue of justice between nations was in one sense unavoidable in the world of the classic social contract doctrines. The major theorists were very well acquainted with wars between states and with the phenomena of trade and colonial expansion. But it seemed possible to adopt a thin approach to international relations, focusing on issues of war and peace and refusing to discuss economic redistribution or protection for basic human rights. (Notice, however, that Grotius had already argued that peace would not be lasting if it did not take account of the need for economic redistribution.) Today this thin approach, entrenched in the practices of wealthy nations and in our systems of international law, is proving increasingly inadequate to the world in which we live. There are staggering differences between rich and poor nations in all the areas most central to basic life chances: mortality, health, education, and others. Even if we bracket the questions of retrospective justice created by the legacy of colonialism, there are urgent forward-looking issues of justice on the table as people think critically about the operations of the global economic system, which is controlled by a small number of nations but has a decisive impact on all. Even the best attempts by the social contract tradition to solve these problems—John Rawls's *The Law of Peoples* and related work by Thomas Pogge and Charles Beitz—prove insufficient guides to the complexities of the issues we face. The capabilities approach, which in many ways revives the Grotian natural law tradition, provides more useful guidance.

3. *Species membership.* When we think about the concept of global justice, we typically think of extending our theories of justice geographically, so that they include more of the human beings on the Earth's surface. We also often think of extending them temporally to take account of the interests of future people—although that set of issues will be only briefly mentioned in these pages, for reasons that I shall shortly discuss. What less often comes to mind—although we think about it more often now than people did in former generations—is the need to extend our theories of justice outside the realm of the human, to address issues of justice involving nonhuman animals. In this area theories of the social contract have obvious defects. Because their core image for the origin of principles of justice is that of a contract made among rational human adults, they have no room, at least in their account of basic social justice, for the interests of nonhuman creatures (even those that are in some ways rational). Once again, the fact that such theories conflate the question "Who frames the principles of justice?" with the question "For whom are these principles framed?" means that they cannot include animals in the group of subjects for whom the theory is devised, given that animals do not partake in the making of contracts.

Theorists in this tradition typically hold either that we have no direct moral duties to animals (Kant) or that, if we do, they are duties of charity or compassion rather than justice (Rawls). This stance seems insufficient (although I shall need to do more to distinguish questions of justice from questions of charity and to say why the wrongs suffered by animals should be seen as raising issues of justice). Our choices affect the lives of nonhuman species every day, and often cause them enormous suffering. Animals are not simply part of the furniture of the world; they are active beings trying to live their lives; and we often stand in their way. That looks like a problem of justice, not simply an occasion for charity. So it is another large shortcoming in a theory if it cannot even frame the relation between humans and animals as the sort of relation it seems to be, involving the problems it clearly seems to involve.

The three issues of justice I have mentioned are all different. Each requires separate treatment, and each puts pressure on the contract doctrine in different ways. All, however, have one important feature in common: they involve a serious asymmetry of power and capacity between the creatures whose entitlements will be my focus and some dominant group. That asymmetry will play a role in explaining, in each case, why the traditional contract approach cannot deal with the issues well.

All three of these issues are now widely recognized as important, although formerly they were not. Thus shortcomings in the social contract tradition that used to seem minor now begin to look major. They prompt us to look beyond the social contract, to see what other ways there might be of articulating the grounds of a truly global justice.

iii. Rawls and the Unsolved Problems

Rawls himself recognizes that his theory runs up against some difficult problems in just these areas. In *Political Liberalism* he mentions four problems that are difficult for his conception of justice to handle: what is owed to people with disabilities (both temporary and permanent, both mental and physical); justice across national boundaries; "what is owed to animals and the rest of nature" (as we shall see, Rawls does not grant that these are issues of justice); and the problem of saving for future generations. Of all these he concludes, "While we would like eventually to answer all these questions, I very much doubt whether that is possible within the scope of justice as fairness as a political conception" (*PL* 21). He goes on to say that his conception can be extended, he believes, to give plausible answers to the problem of future generations (I agree, and therefore I have not treated that problem here). Similarly, he claims, his conception may be extended to deal with the problem of international justice; *The Law of Peoples,* his last book, represents his attempt to make good on that claim. It does not in fact, however, give a satisfactory account of those issues. As for the other two problems, Rawls says that they are "problems on which justice as fairness may fail." With regard to those cases where justice as fairness "may fail," he sees two possibilities. One is "that the idea of political justice does not cover everything, nor should we expect it to." The other possibility is that the problem is indeed one of justice "but justice as fairness is not correct in this case, however well it may do for other cases. How deep a fault this is must wait until the case itself can be examined" (21).[17]

Although my project did not in fact begin from this remark of Rawls's, it is useful to think of my argument as an attempt to take up the challenge that Rawls poses here to himself and to others. I do so by working through these problems one by one, in order to see to what extent a theory of his type (both Kantian and social contract) can handle them. I shall argue that Rawls's theory cannot in the end deliver satisfactory answers to any of these three problems, and in particular (as he himself says) cannot deal with them as problems of basic justice; a version of the capabilities approach, as I have developed it in *Women and Human Development*,[18] can deal with these issues better.

This conclusion is of particular interest because Rawls's theory of justice is, I believe, the strongest theory of political justice we have. On the topics with which it deals, it offers conclusions that are extremely powerful and appealing. The two principles of justice that it advances are plausible. Although I shall make some criticisms of the theory of primary goods in terms of which the principles are framed, I believe that they are basically correct, and the theory that I shall develop from different starting points converges very largely with them. It is important to see from the start, however, that on all three of the unsolved problems, Rawls's theory of justice *offers no principles whatsoever.* Rawls does indeed take up the international case later, using separate principles. But the assumptions of his theory entail that our other two questions are simply not covered, and are not meant to be covered, by the principles of justice as presented. Rawls invites a further examination of these two cases, suggesting that if this further scrutiny makes it clear that these are unsolved problems of justice, some supplementation and/or reassessment of his theory will be required. I hope to provide the examination and the supplementation that he invites.

Rawls mentions at the outset of *TJ* that all contract doctrines have two parts, which may be assessed independently. One part is the design of the initial choice situation; the other is the resulting set of principles. "One may accept the first part of the theory (or some variant thereof), but not the other, and conversely" (*TJ* 15). My conclusion will be that the principles themselves, or something very like them, are good principles—not only for those cases to which Rawls applies them, but for other cases concerning which he advances no principles at all (see Chapter 3, section ix). Moreover, the ideas of fairness and reciprocity that these principles embody and render concrete are themselves deeply attractive ethical ideas (apart from certain difficulties inherent in the specifically Kantian form that Rawls gives them). It would be good to extend those principles and those ideas to our unsolved problems of justice. The initial choice situation, though, contains grave problems when we grapple with the three particular problems that are my focus, however well it may do in the areas to which Rawls applied it. If we can arrive at principles related to those of Rawls by another route, as I shall do, drawing on suitably enlarged conceptions of reciprocity and dignity, we shall be able to extend those principles to cases that he believed a theory like his own could not reach. My conclusion is not that we should reject Rawls's theory or any other contractarian theory, but that we should keep working on alternative theories, which may possibly enhance our understanding of justice and enable us to extend those very theories.

iv. Free, Equal, and Independent

The social contract tradition is complex. It includes some figures, such as Jean-Jacques Rousseau, who do not conceive of the social contract as a contract among independent individuals. My argument has nothing direct to say about the type of nonliberal theory exemplified by *The Social Contract,* with its concept of the General Will and its relative lack of concern for the liberties of individuals. Insofar as Rousseau's theory does influence Rawls and other modern contractarians, I believe the materials of that influence are present, as well, in the liberal theorists Locke and Kant; what is *sui generis* about Rousseau in this particular area would take us away from the examination of a distinctively liberal tradition. The historical figures who provide the materials for this liberal tradition are Locke and in some respects Kant. A major precursor is Thomas Hobbes, who also has importance for contemporary social contract doctrines, especially in the work of David Gauthier.[19] But Hobbes is not a liberal, and consideration of his doctrine of sovereignty would take us far from our theme; moreover, the details of his views are notoriously obscure. So I focus on Hobbes only to the extent that he offers a perspicuous account of some features of the social contract that are made much of by others who are more directly in the tradition I have in mind. David Hume is important to the project, too, although he is not a contractarian, because Rawls borrows Hume's account of the Circumstances of Justice and builds important features of his own contractarian account around it.

This book is not a historical project, and I do not claim to offer an exhaustive or even a detailed interpretation of any precontemporary figure. I address a very general set of presumptions that have profoundly shaped thinking about justice in the Western tradition, not only in philosophy but also in public policy and international relations. Nonetheless, since I speak of a tradition, and allude often to the views of its main proponents, it seems important to isolate in an abstract way the constitutive elements of the sort of theory with which I shall be concerned.

These include an account of the Circumstances of Justice, the situation in which making a contract for political principles makes sense; a related account of the attributes of the parties to the contract; an account of what they hope to gain by making the contract—the point of social cooperation; and an account of the moral sentiments of the parties to the contract. Seeing these features more clearly will help us, later, to identify and contrast the corresponding elements of the capabilities approach.

1. *The Circumstances of Justice.*[20] The search for basic political principles, the social contract theorist holds, does not arise in any and every circumstance. For people to think that it makes sense to get together on principles of political society, they have

to find themselves in a particular type of situation. The description of this situation is absolutely central for Rawls, who introduces the description right at the beginning of his discussion of the Original Position. Following the tradition, he holds that these circumstances embody "the normal conditions under which human cooperation is both possible and necessary" (*TJ* 126); unless these circumstances obtained, "there would be no occasion for the virtue of justice, just as in the absence of threats of injury to life and limb there would be no occasion for physical courage" (128).

Following Rawls (who draws on Hume here), we can divide these circumstances into two types: objective and subjective. The objective circumstances of the parties to the bargain are, basically, those that make cooperation among them both possible and necessary. Rawls stipulates that they must coexist together "at the same time on a definite geographical territory" (*TJ* 126). They are roughly similar in physical and mental powers, in such a way that no one can dominate the rest. They are vulnerable to aggression, and the united force of all the others can block the enterprises of any one. Finally, there are conditions of "moderate scarcity": resources are not so abundant that cooperation is superfluous nor "are conditions so harsh that fruitful ventures must inevitably break down" (126–127).

Subjectively, the parties have roughly similar needs and interests, or at least complementary interests, so that cooperation among them is possible; but they also have different plans of life, including differences of religion and comprehensive social or ethical doctrine, that potentially give rise to conflicts among them. They have weaknesses of knowledge and judgment, although it is important to Rawls that these are stipulated to fall within the "normal range" (*PL* 25).

Theorists in the social contract tradition believe that human beings do typically find themselves in such circumstances—at least if we subtract the artificial advantages of wealth and social class and the influence of existing political structures. Thus the fiction of the state of nature, which is explicitly said to be an imaginary hypothesis, not an account of a remote historical time,[21] is nonetheless held to be a veridical account of some especially important properties of human interaction in the real world. But the description excludes people whose mental and physical powers are very unequal to those of "normal human beings"; for related reasons, it seems bound to exclude nations, and their inhabitants, whose powers and resources are very unequal to those of the dominant nation or nations; finally, and obviously, it excludes nonhuman animals. Theorists in the tradition are aware of these omissions. They simply judge that the omissions are not a major problem for the theories at the stage where basic principles are being chosen.

2. *"Free, equal, and independent."* Included in Rawls's account of the Circumstances of Justice are three attributes of the parties to the contract that are particularly salient for the tradition; these features are prominent even when a thinker does not offer a systematic account of the Circumstances of Justice, as does Rawls. I therefore isolate them for special study. The parties to the social contract are, first of all, *free:* that is, nobody owns anyone else, nobody is the slave of anyone else. The postulate of natural liberty is a very important part of the tradition's assault on various forms of hierarchy and tyranny. Locke is not alone in insisting that it entails that nobody may be subjected to the power of another but by consent.[22] Kant, who gives perhaps the most detailed account of this condition, understands it to mean that people have rights to pursue their own conceptions of happiness, so long as they do not infringe upon "the freedom of others to pursue a similar end which can be reconciled with the freedom of everyone else within a workable general law."[23] In other words, it is wrong to force people to be happy in accor-

dance with your way of being happy, even if you are a benevolent despot. What can be required is that each person limits his freedom by the freedom of others. This right is understood by the tradition to be prepolitical. "This right of freedom belongs to each member of the commonwealth as a human being, in so far as each is a being capable of possessing rights."[24] (As we shall see, Rawls does not accept the tradition here, since he does not assert that there are prepolitical natural rights. He does, however, hold that equality is grounded in natural capacities, in particular in the capacity for a sense of justice; *TJ* 504 ff.)

This feature of the tradition looks unexceptional, and indeed it does have striking moral and political importance. But it becomes potentially problematic when we ask what capacities such natural freedom presupposes, confronting it with the lives of citizens with severe mental impairments and, in a quite different way, with the lives of nonhuman animals. There is a suggestion in the tradition that certain positive abilities are prerequisites of having the right not to be someone's slave, and that those abilities include, at least, the capacity for rational moral choice. Does this mean that a being without these capacities can be enslaved? Not necessarily, but we cannot easily find in the contract doctrine as classically developed any reason to say that slavery, in such an instance, would be a violation of natural liberty. Nor do theorists question the enslavement of animals. (Already in Kant's lifetime, Bentham famously compared the treatment of nonhuman animals to slavery.) So we should be aware that we may require a new and more expansive conception of freedom and its prerequisites, in order to deal adequately with such questions.

Second, and a feature of particular importance, social contract doctrines hold that their parties begin the bargain in a situation of rough *equality*—not just moral equality, but a rough equality of powers and resources. All the advantages and hierarchies among human beings that are created by wealth, birth, class, and so on are imagined away, and we are left with the naked human being, so to speak. As thinkers in the tradition often remark, there are no very great differences among human beings in basic powers, capacities, and needs. Hobbes influentially observes:

> Nature hath made men so equall, in the faculties of body, and mind; as that though there bee found one man sometimes manifestly stronger in body, or of quicker mind then another; yet when all is reckoned together, the difference between man, and man, is not so considerable, as that one man can thereupon claim to himselfe any benefit, to which another may not pretend, as well as he. For as to the strength of body, the weakest has strength enough to kill the strongest, either by secret machination, or by confederacy with others, that are in the same danger with himselfe.
>
> And as to the faculties of the mind . . . I find yet a greater equality amongst men, than that of strength . . . That which may perhaps make such equality incredible, is but a vain conceipt of ones owne wisdome, which almost all men think they have, in a greater degree, than the Vulgar.[25]

Similarly, Locke insists that in the state of nature it is obvious "that Creatures of the same species and rank promiscuously born to all the same advantages of Nature, and the use of the same faculties, should also be equal one amongst another without Subordination or Subjection."[26] This insistence that the great differences among men are artifacts of current social conditions becomes a pervasive theme in eighteenth-century philosophy. Adam Smith, for example, stresses that the difference between a philosopher and a street porter consists primarily in their habits and education; Rousseau suggests that reflection on the common weaknesses and vulnerabilities of human beings would reveal a profound similarity beneath distinctions of class and rank.[27]

It is important to distinguish this sort of rough equality in power and capacity from moral equality, although the thinkers of the tradition seldom make this distinction with any clarity. One might hold that beings are moral equals without holding that they are rough equals in power and capacity. One might also hold the converse. We can see a way of connecting the two equalities: if human beings really are more or less equal in power and capacity, then it looks rather arbitrary for some to be given vastly greater authority and opportunity than others. (Locke, in particular, relies on some such connection.) But one could concede this without conceding that natural inequality of power and capacity would actually entitle human beings to differential treatment in essential moral areas of human life (and *mutatis mutandis* for other sentient beings). Thus it is to the great credit of Rawls that he carefully distinguishes these two types of equality. Nonetheless, we should not forget that he requires both in order to get his theory off the ground.

The assumption of equality (in powers and capacities) is supposed to show us something important and true about human beings, which should lead to the criticism of existing hierarchies. But it also does crucial work inside each social contract theory, explaining how political principles come out the way they do. The rough equality among the parties is crucial to understanding how they contract with one another, why they would make a contract in the first place, and what they hope to gain from the social contract. It is thus important to see how such an equality assumption requires us to put some important issues of justice on hold. In particular, justice for people with severe mental impairments and justice for nonhuman animals cannot plausibly be handled within a contract situation so structured. As we shall see, Rawls grants this, with problematic consequences for his theory of justice as fairness in those areas.

It is not surprising that the classical social contract thinkers willingly put these problems on hold. Whether they even cared about them may be doubted. But even if they had cared about them, the urgent need to undermine the basis of monarchical and hierarchical conceptions of politics explained and to a great extent justified the decision to focus on those human beings who are roughly equal in power and resources. We do not live in the same world now, and we have no such excuse for not facing these problems head on, in the course of designing basic political principles.

As for the poorer nations, there is a sense in which the hierarchy of wealth and power that now exists among nations is just as artificial as the hierarchies of birth and wealth that the contract tradition is designed to undermine. Thus the contract tradition contains an important insight that is highly relevant to thinking critically about global inequalities. And yet, adequate criticism of the hierarchy among nations requires a kind of radical rethinking of national boundaries and basic economic arrangements that cannot be achieved if we simply imagine the contract doctrine applied a second time over, as nations already constituted, and imagined as virtual persons who are rough equals, contract for the best cooperative deal among them.

Third, the parties to the social contract are imagined as *independent*, that is, individuals who are not under the domination of or asymmetrically dependent upon any other individuals. In some versions this assumption includes the idea that they are interested only in fostering their own conceptions of happiness, not those of others. In some they are assumed to have benevolent interests, or even (in Locke) natural duties of benevolence. But the central point is that each is imagined to be similar with respect to independence, and each is a separate source of claims and projects. Locke gives his opponents examples of people who have lived like this: he thinks the Native Americans are such people. Each is also an independent source of social cooperation, or, as Rawls puts it, a "fully cooperating member of society over a complete life." Rawls models this feature of the tradition by the assumption that the parties in the Original Position have no interest in one another's interests. They are not necessarily egoists, but they are concerned to advance their own conceptions of the good, not those of others (*TJ* 13).

One might begin by noting the absence of children and elderly people from the account of the political domain in such theories—and even of adult women, whom most of these thinkers understood as dependents of men (since they did not count work performed in the home as productive work). Even if we assume that those omissions are not a serious problem for the theories, we then notice that such theories make no place for those who for long stretches of a life, or even the whole of a life, are markedly unequal to others in their productive contribution or who live in a condition of asymmetrical dependency. Such people are clearly absent from the contracting group—and, given the conflation I have emphasized, they are *ipso facto* absent from the group of citizens for whom the principles of justice are framed. Their interests might possibly be handled at some later stage. But their needs do not shape the parties' choice of basic political principles, or even their conception of the primary goods of a human life, since they are imagined as contracting for mutual advantage with others similarly placed. Thus issues that seem extremely important for social justice—issues about the allocation of care, the labor involved in caring, and the social costs of promoting the fuller inclusion of disabled citizens—fail to come into focus or are explicitly deferred for later consideration. (Rawls allows his parties to represent continuing lines, in order to be able to grapple with issues of saving for future generations. But he does not in any other way relax the assumption of mutual disinterest *in the Original Position*.)

Like the assumption of equality, the assumption of independence is not easily altered without altering the entire conception of the social contract and what it is for. For the picture is that each of the parties is a productive individual who will be willing to sacrifice some prerogatives in order to reap the rewards of mutual cooperation.

3. *Mutual advantage as the purpose of social cooperation*. The parties are imagined as cooperating with one another in order to secure a mutual benefit, something they could not get without social cooperation. Rawls eschews any assumption of altruism or benevolence on the part of the parties to the social contract—although he models it in other ways in the larger structure of his doctrine. Because this complexity leads to difficult questions about Rawls's relationship to the idea of mutual advantage, I defer this issue for examination in section vi. Other modern contractarians, such as Gauthier, leave altruism out completely. Even Locke, who focuses on benevolence, describes the point of the social compact itself as "for their [the parties'] comfortable, safe, and peaceable living one amongst another, in a secure Enjoyment of their Properties, and a greater Security against any that are not of it."[28] Thus far, though not in other respects, he is similar to Hobbes, who holds that the only thing that would lead a person to forgo an advantage he enjoys in the state of nature is some sort of advantage in regard to his own well-being.[29] No attachment to justice for its own sake is required, and also no intrinsic, noninstrumental regard for the good of others.

4. *The motivations of the parties*. Here there is little to add to what has been already observed. The parties to the social bargain are imagined as having motives that fit well with their pursuit of advantage: they want to advance their goals and proj-

ects, whatever they are. This hypothesis of the pursuit of advantage by one's own lights does not imply that the philosophers in question are egoists about the moral sentiments, although Hobbes surely is. The parties may have many different conceptions of their own advantage, and in some cases (Locke in particular) this may include a robust concern for the good of others. Moreover, in some cases (for example David Gauthier), including only self-goal-directed motives and sentiments in the bargaining position may be simply a device to extract other-regarding results from a parsimonious starting point. Rawls omits benevolent motives for a related reason. But we should raise questions here. It is uncertain that this parsimonious starting point will even lead in the same direction as a more sympathetic and other-committed starting point. The pursuit of mutual advantage and the success of one's own projects is not less than a compassionate commitment to the well-being of all human beings; it is just different. It goes in a quite different direction—unless one stipulates that all the parties take the well-being of all others to be a part of their own pursuit of their own well-being. Locke does assume something like this, though with results that leave us in some doubt about the overall consistency of his theory. Rawls and most other contractarians feel that a strong assumption of benevolence is to be avoided; political principles should be extracted from a starting point that is both less demanding and more determinate.

v. Grotius, Hobbes, Locke, Hume, Kant

Now that we have before us a schematic outline of the features of the social contract tradition on which the arguments of subsequent chapters will focus, it seems useful to add a somewhat fuller account of the pertinent contributions of each thinker, since these historical matters will not figure in later arguments. I shall focus on the parts of each thinker's views that seem most salient as we assess modern contractarian theories, proceeding in chronological order.

I begin with Hugo Grotius, since his natural law approach to basic principles of international relations is the one I shall attempt to revive; but Grotius' approach suggests a general template for thinking about domestic issues as well, although he does not so apply it. In *On the Law of War and Peace* (1625), Grotius gives an account of the basic principles of international relations, tracing it to the Greek and Roman Stoics (Seneca and Cicero above all). Put very simply, this approach holds that the way to begin, when we think about fundamental principles, is to think of the human being as a creature characterized both by dignity or moral worth and by sociability: by "an impelling desire for fellowship, that is for common life, not of just any kind, but a peaceful life, and organized according to the measure of his intelligence, with those who are of his kind." Grotius thinks of these features as deeply natural; he connects them to a metaphysical theory of human nature. We may, however (with Cicero, who was agnostic in metaphysics), view these claims as freestanding ethical claims out of which one might build a political conception of the person that can be accepted by people who hold different views in metaphysics and in religion.

The general idea of Grotius' natural law theory is that these two features of the human being, and their ethical value, suggest a good deal about the treatment to which every human being is entitled. Thus political theory begins from an abstract idea of basic entitlements, grounded in the twin ideas of dignity (the human being as an end) and sociability. It is then argued that certain specific entitlements flow from those ideas, as necessary conditions of a life with human dignity.

Grotius does not ask how one might use these insights to think about the just structure of an individual state. His focus, instead, is on the relations among states. Here he holds that, although the space between nations is a space without a sovereign, it is nonetheless a morally ordered sphere, in which a number of very specific principles shape human interactions. (He argues strenuously against the proto-Hobbesian idea that the space between nations is a space of power and force only, where it is legitimate for all nations to pursue their national security above all else.) From these ideas Grotius derived his famous neo-Ciceronian account of both *ius ad bellum* and *ius in bello*.[30] War is rightly undertaken only in response to a wrongful aggression; all preemptive and preventive war is banned, as a way of using human beings as tools of one's own interests. In war, very strict limitations on conduct are also entailed by these same ideas: no excessive or harsh punishments, as little damage to property as possible, a prompt restitution of property and sovereignty at the conclusion of war, no killing of civilians. (Cicero added a ban on deception in war, as a way of violating human dignity by using others as a means; Grotius does not follow him this far.)

What I want to bring out about Grotius' theory is that it begins with the content of an outcome, in the sense of an account of basic entitlements of human beings whose fulfillment is required by justice; if these entitlements are fulfilled, then a society (in this case, "international society") is minimally just. The justification of the entitlement set is not procedural, but involves an intuitive idea of human dignity and argument to the effect that a certain entitlement is implicit in the idea of human dignity. Grotius argues explicitly that we must *not* attempt to derive our fundamental principles from an idea of mutual advantage alone; human sociability indicates that advantage is not the only reason for which human beings act justly. Grotius evidently believes that a society based upon sociability and respect rather than upon mutual advantage can remain stable over time.

There are some features of Grotius' view that I shall not be emulating. In particular, his political conception of the person is strongly rationalistic, relying, like the Stoics', on a very strong distinction between humans and animals. I shall later criticize such ideas. But the basic structure of his view is similar to the one that I shall defend.

Notice that for Grotius the important kind of equality among persons is moral equality, which entails equality of respect and entitlement. Equality of powers plays no significant role in his argument. A person whose physical powers are very different from those of "normal" human beings gets treated exactly like every other human being. (Because his theory is so rationalistic, inequality in mental powers may get differential treatment: Grotius does not comment on this question. Thus we do not know whether there are empirical prerequisites for equal dignity or whether Grotius holds, as I shall, that any child of human parents has the fully equal dignity that belongs to every human being.) There is thus no analogue in his theory to Hume's Circumstances of Justice or to the similar assumptions in the theories of Hobbes, Locke, and Kant. Wherever human beings are alive, there are already Circumstances of Justice between them, just because they are human and sociable.

Grotius' theory was enormously influential, as was the related natural law theory of Samuel Pufendorf.[31] I shall not discuss Pufendorf's theory here, because the main features I want to bring out are already present in Grotius' theory, and it is Grotius' theory, closely derived from Roman Stoic models, that is a major source for my own thinking.

As we approach social contract theories, we must be careful not to make an overly simple contrast between the two sorts of theories. Although modern contract theories do attempt to dispense with all ideas of natural rights or natural law, classical contract doctrines all contain prominent natural law and natural-right elements, thinking of the state of nature as including binding moral norms and morally justified entitlements of persons, whether or not these suffice to organize conduct. The need for a contract arises because entitlements are insecure, not because there are no prepolitical and preprocedural entitlements. Moreover, the two types of views do not differ greatly in their assessment of human insecurity in a situation without law. Pufendorf, for example, describes the state of nature in a way that is very close to Hobbes's pejorative description, stressing the baneful influence of competition. From the vantage point of the modern debate, the overlap of theory-types in the classical period is striking.

Thomas Hobbes's *Leviathan* (1651) might be treated as the antitype to everything Grotius stands for, but such a presumption would clearly be mistaken. Indeed, what is most striking to someone who examines the social contract tradition beginning from the natural law tradition is how much these theorists agree with Grotius and his fellow natural law thinkers. That is to say, Hobbes holds that there are natural moral laws that enjoin "*Justice, Equity, Modesty, Mercy,* and (in summe) *doing to others, as wee would be done to*" (XVII). But he believes that these moral laws can never give rise to a stable political order, because they are "contrary to our naturall Passions, that carry us to Partiality, Pride, Revenge, and the like" (ibid.). Natural sociability can be observed among bees and ants, but in human beings there is no reliable sociability without coercion. Because our natural passions are fundamentally competitive and egoistic, with fear playing a central motivating role, the state of nature—the state of human relations in the absence of a strong coercing sovereign—is a state of war. Hobbes famously describes this state as a very miserable one indeed.

In this state of war, there is a rough equality of powers and resources. Where bodily strength is concerned, the weakest can kill the strongest by stealth; where mental capacity is concerned, this rough equality will be doubted only by those who have a "vain conceipt" of their own wisdom (ibid.). (Hobbes includes no discussion of people with disabilities.) Although Hobbes appears to think humans are moral equals as well (the natural law part of his theory suggests this strongly, at any rate), it is equality of power and ability that plays the salient role in his argument. Equality of ability plays a large role in making the state of nature as bad as it is: for it generates an equality of hope, which in turn spurs people on to further competition.

Given this natural equality of power, our passions incline us to make peace with one another, so that we can get on with our lives in tolerable security. "The Passions that encline men to Peace, are Feare of Death; Desire of such things as are necessary to commodious living; and a Hope by their Industry to attain them. And Reason suggesteth convenient Articles of Peace, upon which men may be drawn to agreement" (XIII).

Hobbes does not portray his social contract as generating principles of justice. He speaks of justice in ways that are hard to reconcile, sometimes arguing that there is no justice where there is no coercive power (XV), and sometimes arguing that there are natural principles of justice, albeit ineffectual ones, given our natural passions.[32] But the social contract does generate the fundamental principles of political society. The contract is a reciprocal agreement to transfer natural rights (XIV). Its object is for every man a "good to himselfe", for the group of human beings a mutual advantage, "that Is to say, of getting themselves out from that miserable condition of Warre" (XVII). Envisaging the foundation of political society on the contract model causes Hobbes to make the fundamental move to which I have drawn attention: he conflates the group of the contract-makers with the group of those for whom and about whom contract is made. (In the process, he remarks that a contract with "bruit Beasts" is impossible; XIV). People contract for a secure existence with one another.

In Hobbes's view, unlike those of his liberal successors, the only plausible form such a contract can take is one that grants all power to a sovereign, with the subjects reserving no rights of their own. The role of the sovereign is, by fear of punishment, to keep people's passions in check and thereby preserve the security in which they can live together. Wherever there is no such strong sovereign—as in the space between states—the state of war prevails. Unlike modern international-relations realists, who in many ways follow his lead, Hobbes holds that the state of war is immoral as well as insecure and unfortunate. There are binding moral norms in nature, and those are violated in the state of war. But in his view morality is an utterly impotent force in human relations. It cannot be the basis for political principles for a stable and workable political society.

John Locke's theory of the social contract, the tradition's most influential theory, is also its most exasperating. It contains heterogeneous elements that are difficult to combine into a single coherent picture—both because Locke's ideas about contract and rights occur in works of different dates, and it is not clear to what extent he changed his mind, and because within the *Second Treatise of Government* itself, our main source for his account of the social contract, there are heterogeneous elements, as well as many difficult problems of interpretation. Moreover, it is ultimately impossible to understand Locke's doctrines fully without close attention to his polemical context. Thus what I shall say here will be little more than a set of conjectures. Nonetheless, I hope it may bring out aspects of his contract theory that are significant for us in what follows.

Locke's central concern is to establish that in the state of nature, that is to say, a hypothetical situation without political society, human beings are naturally "free, equal, and independent." Free, in the sense that none is the natural ruler of any, and each is naturally entitled to rule himself; equal, in the sense that none is entitled to rule over the others, and all jurisdiction is "reciprocal, no one having more than another" (4); and independent in the sense that all are, as free, entitled to pursue their personal projects without being in a hierarchical relation with anyone else. Locke clearly holds, with Hobbes, that human beings have roughly similar powers of body and mind. Unlike Hobbes, he connects this equality closely to moral entitlements: "being furnished with like Faculties, sharing all in one Community of Nature, there cannot be supposed any such *Subordination* among us, that may Authorize us to destroy one another, as if we were made for one another's uses, as the inferior ranks of Creatures are for ours" (6). Locke appears to hold that similarity of power is sufficient for the reciprocal status of ends-in-themselves, and for the wrongness of treating another as a means. It may also be necessary for that status, since Locke does seem to think that our (allegedly) superior faculties give us a license to use animals as mere means.

In Locke's polemical context, arguing, as he is, against people who ascribe a natural right of rule to certain individual human beings, the connection he makes between equality of power and moral equality is understandable; but it leaves us with difficult problems to resolve. Certainly we should not agree with Locke that greatly unequal powers license treatment as mere means. Whether we should grant that equal powers entail moral equality is profoundly unclear. The right way to ground moral equality almost certainly does not involve reliance on a putative power-equality.

Not surprisingly, Locke does not discuss the question of people with disabilities; given his polemical context, their presence in the argument would simply blur its outlines.

In Locke's state of nature there are binding moral duties, including a duty of self-preservation and, given natural equality and reciprocity, a duty to preserve others, a duty not to take the life of another, and a duty not to do what tends to destroy others by impairing their liberty, health, or property. (These duties seem to be derived from the fundamental law of nature, which is the preservation of humankind.)[33] Citing Richard Hooker's views, Locke holds that the recognition of moral equality also gives rise to positive duties of benevolence and beneficence. Seeing that others are my equals, I see that I have a duty to love them as myself. This means that if I have a desire, I cannot claim its satisfaction without at the same time willing the satisfaction of like desires in other human beings (5). In that sense moral reciprocity and the sentiments that undergird it do not need the social contract for their establishment. They are imagined as present already in nature. (Locke's views about the subordination of women are difficult to reconcile with the overall nature of his argument.)

Combined with these ideas about our natural duties is another idea that is closely related to the Grotian natural law tradition. We have a natural dignity. Made by God, we have been invested with "Dignity and Authority" (I.44); we are "curious and wonderful" pieces of "workmanship" (I.86).[34] This being the case, we rightly want a life "fit for the Dignity of Man" (15, Locke quoting Hooker), a life "suitable to the dignity and excellence of a rational creature."[35] Each one of us is, however, also needy; we cannot stably achieve such a life on our own. Therefore, "we are naturally induced to seek Communion and Fellowship with others, this was the Cause of Mens uniting themselves, at first in Politick Societies" (ibid., Hooker again). In other words, our dignity is a legitimate source of entitlement, and those entitlements can be achieved only by cooperation; fortunately, we have cooperative moral sentiments that make a productive common life possible, and the main job of such a life should be to ensure that we all have the opportunity to live in accordance with human dignity.

Locke does not discuss the relationship between natural sentiments that lead people to form political societies and the duties of reciprocity that derive from natural equality. The former are connected to need and weakness, together with the desire for a life commensurate with human dignity; the latter with the natural rights associated with natural equality. Since in any case Locke is borrowing from Hooker in some of the crucial passages here, he never makes it fully clear how all these different concepts are to be interrelated. But it would seem that Locke, especially where he is closest to Hooker, has many elements of a Grotian natural law theory of the origins of political society: we join together out of positive sentiments of benevolence and positive moral duties of reciprocity that derive from a mutual recognition of human dignity in one another; we join society seeking a life commensurate with human dignity. If this were the primary focus of Locke's theory, it would strongly resemble Grotius' theory and the one that I shall develop.

Locke, however, turns in a different direction when he actually articulates the idea behind the social contract. Although he does not concede that the state of nature is a state of war—he insists that it is much richer than that—nonetheless, absent political society there is really nothing to prevent it from turning into a state of war. And thus his account of the contract focuses on mutual advantage as the goal with which the parties agree to accept the authority of laws and institutions. They agree to accept limits to their freedom "for their comfortable, safe, and peaceable living one amongst another, in a secure Enjoyment of their Properties, and a greater Security against any that are not of it" (95). Again, "The great and *chief end* therefore, of Mens uniting into Commonwealths, and putting themselves under

Government, *is the Preservation of their Property*" (124). We hear nothing in such passages about benevolence and mutual support for human dignity.

Locke, then, is an important antecedent for both the theory I shall defend and the one that I shall criticize. Had he further developed his (and Hooker's) ideas about society as based on a shared desire to produce a life worthy of human dignity, his theory might have been an entitlement-based theory with no need (or at least not the same need) for a social contract based on the idea of mutual advantage. The account of entitlements based on human dignity would be the source of political principles, and the contract fiction would be unnecessary. Instead, the argumentative move for which his political theory is best known relies on mutual advantage, linked to natural equality and insecurity, for its generation of political principles. On the other hand, the ultimate shape of his society, strongly protective of individual entitlements to life, liberty, property, and religious freedom (which are taken to have a prepolitical foundation in natural rights), certainly shows the influence of the entitlement-based aspect of his view, as he utterly rejects a Hobbesian account of the state as both inappropriate and unnecessary.

It cannot be emphasized enough that modern contractarians draw from only one aspect of Locke's theory, namely the fiction of a contract for mutual advantage in the state of nature, leaving aside both his doctrine of natural rights and his related emphasis on benevolence and human dignity.

David Hume's *Treatise of Human Nature* (1739–40) and *An Enquiry Concerning the Principles of Morals* (first edition 1751; posthumous edition 1777) are very important sources for Rawls, who says that they state what he takes to be the conditions under which justice is possible and necessary (*TJ* 127). Hume is not a contractarian; his account of justice bases it on convention. But he has a good deal in common with the contractarians (especially the modern contractarians, who in any case have dropped Lockean natural rights) in his thinking about why justice emerges from a state without justice, and what makes it attractive. (Rawls is able to combine Hume with the social contract tradition because his own account of justice has no role for natural rights and in that sense is close to Hume's conventionalism.) Like the contractarians, Hume relies on mutual advantage as the key to the emergence and maintenance of justice. And he lays out with exceptional clarity the conditions under which mutual advantage is to be expected. Moreover, he applies his insights explicitly to the case of disability. I shall focus on the *Enquiry* (III.1), which articulates the relevant factors more explicitly.

Hume begins by imagining the classical Golden Age, in which there is no scarcity, no need for work, and no occasion for competition, since every individual has whatever he or she needs to satisfy even the most "voracious" desires. In such a situation, there would be no need for justice, he argues, since there would not even be any need for distribution of goods among persons: everything could be held in common, as we now hold water and air.

Imagine, next, a situation in which scarcities are as they are now, but human beings are different: their generosity is unlimited, and each person "feels no more concern for his own interest than for that of his fellows." Such an "extensive benevolence" would, once again, render justice unnecessary, since all would be delighted to supply the needs of all.

Now Hume examines the opposite extremes of these two situations. Suppose the situation of human beings is so miserable, with such extreme want, that nothing can be gained from cooperation. In such a state, once again, justice has no toehold: each will reasonably snatch what he can to stay alive. If, a fourth possibility, we imagine that human beings are utterly wicked and rapacious and utterly lacking in the ability to conform their conduct to morality and law, here, too, justice will achieve nothing.

In short, justice has a point only when there is a moderate but not a desperate scarcity of possessions and when human beings are selfish and competitive, with bounded generosity, but also capable of limiting their conduct. That Hume believes to be our actual situation (see also *Treatise*, III.II.ii). He stresses that selfishness is not all-powerful: indeed, in most people, "the kind affections, taken together, over-balance all the selfish," even though it is "rare to meet with any one, who loves any single person better than himself" (*Treatise*, ibid.).[36] But kindness is uneven and partial, felt most strongly toward one's own family, and only sporadically to people at a distance. This all means that justice can play a useful role in human affairs. "Thus, the rules of equity or justice depend entirely on the particular state and condition in which men are placed, and owe their origin and existence to that utility, which results to the public from their strict and regular observance" *(Enquiry)*.

Once rules of justice are in place, new sentiments become attached to them, as people see the utility of those rules in a pleasing light, and as "the artifice of politicians" produces "an esteem for justice, and an abhorrence of injustice" *(Treatise)*.

Justice, then, is a convention whose utility is directly related to the circumstances, physical and psychological, in which we are placed. And Hume further stresses that among those circumstances is a rough equality of power among human beings. In a passage of great importance for my subsequent discussion, he observes:

> Were there a species of creatures intermingled with men, which, though rational, were possessed of such inferior strength, both of body and mind, that they were incapable of all resistance, and could never, upon the highest provocation, make us feel the ef-

fects of their resentment; the necessary consequence, I think, is that we should be bound by the laws of humanity to give gentle usage to these creatures, but should not, properly speaking, lie under any restraint of justice with regard to them, nor could they possess any right or property, exclusive of such arbitrary lords. Our intercourse with them could not be called society, which supposes a degree of equality; but absolute command on the one side, and servile obedience on the other. Whatever we covet, they must instantly resign: Our permission is the only tenure, by which they hold their possessions: Our compassion and kindness the only check, by which they curb our lawless will: And as no inconvenience ever results from the exercise of a power, so firmly established in nature, the restraints of justice and property, being totally *useless,* would never have place in so unequal a confederacy.

Hume goes on to say that this is in fact our situation with regard to animals: they may have some intelligence, but they are markedly inferior to us. Some, he adds, have thought this our situation, as well, with respect to the people of colonized parts of the world, but Hume at least implies that this was an error resulting from the temptation of greed. As for women, Hume notes that their very unequal physical weakness seems to entail that they are not subjects of justice; nonetheless, women do manage by seductive wiles to get men to allow them "to share in all the rights and privileges of society."

Because Hume is not a contractarian, he does not assume that the framers of rules of justice must be the same group of people as those for whom the rules are framed. His exclusion of people with severe disabilities, and of women (who never get *justice,* though they may seduce their way into certain advantages), derives solely from his focus on rough equality of power as among the Circumstances of Justice. Despite his emphasis on the kindly affections in human beings, he believes that the behavior of the much stronger to the much weaker must always be lacking in basic decency: a mere despotism of force, unless the seductions of sexuality intervene to prevent force from being used. (And of course Hume must be well aware that women's sexual attractiveness does not always supply men with a reason not to use force against them; indeed, it often gives men an additional incentive to use force.)

In short, the much weaker, whether in body or in mind, are simply not part of political society, not subjects of justice. Even to the extent that women receive certain advantages, they are not members who are protected as equals under rules of justice, any more than are household pets, who may also escape ill treatment because of their pleasing traits. Hume's reliance on rough equality of power has very strong consequences for his theory of justice. There is no basis for just and decent treatment of people with disabilities, or of women. Indeed, where the former are concerned, the account seems to entail that we would exercise despotism over them. As for animals, the despotism that we currently exercise—which was being vigorously challenged at the time of the *Enquiry* by Bentham and by the budding movement against cruelty to animals—is simply validated as inevitable, unless humane sentiments intervene in a particular case. But Hume has already said that these sentiments are likely to be partial, uneven, and unreliable. (Thus his theory predicts that we would continue to treat our pets reasonably well, but have no regard for the animals we eat; no conventions would ever arise to change this situation.) It would appear that the classical theorists of the social contract are bound to draw the same conclusion, insofar as they rely on rough equality as a necessary condition of justice between persons.

Although Rousseau's version of the social contract is in many ways not a liberal theory, and I have said that I shall there-

fore not deal with it in my argument, except insofar as it converges with the theories of Locke and Kant, it is worth noting
that in *The Social Contract* (1762), nearly contemporaneous
with Hume's *Enquiry,* Rousseau accepts the premise of rough
equality that figures both in Hume and in the social contract
tradition. Although he holds that the social contract substitutes
a "moral and legitimate equality" for "whatever physical inequality nature may have been able to impose upon men" (I.ix),
immediately, in a footnote, he qualifies this statement, saying
that "the social state is advantageous to men only insofar as
they all have something and none of them has too much." And
although he does not comment further on this question, he
clearly holds that women are not to be citizens on account of
their physical difference from men.

Kant's theory of the social contract is most prominently discussed in the essay "Theory and Practice" (1793) and in *The
Metaphysics of Morals* (1797). The relationship of Kant's political philosophy to his moral philosophy is complex and disputed;
thus any sketch of features that are for our purposes salient
must be especially sketchy. John Rawls evidently draws primarily
on Kant's moral philosophy, with its core idea that human beings should always be treated as ends, never merely as means.
This idea of human inviolability is an intuitive starting point for
Rawls's entire theoretical enterprise (see *TJ* 2), although Rawls
makes it clear that political principles are required to give this
idea determinate content. But Kant's political philosophy is not
simply the working out in the political domain of that key moral
idea. Instead, Kant firmly links himself to the classical theory
of the social contract. Thus his political theory has a mixed character: his treatment of natural freedom does link the political
philosophy strongly to the moral philosophy, but there are other
elements that lead in a somewhat different direction. (The tensions one could find in a more systematic analysis of Kant's polit-

ical philosophy are not unlike those that I shall find in John Rawls's mixed theory, which mingles Kantian ethical notions with classical social contract doctrine.)

In essence, Kant's theory of the social contract is very similar to Locke's—without the role that God plays in Locke's theory, which in any case my own sketch has not discussed. Natural liberty, construed as equal liberty, is the key attribute of human beings in the state of nature, and the social contract comes about when human beings choose to exit from the state of nature (which is more Lockean than Hobbesian, not always a state of war) and "enter, with all others, a juridical state of affairs, that is, a state of distributive legal justice" (*MEJ*, Akademie, p. 307). Once again, then, Kant's theory involves natural entitlements, and is not in the modern sense a pure contractarian theory or a "pure procedural" theory; the contract is required because entitlements are insecure in the state of nature.

Kant seems to hold that it is not only advantageous but also moral for all persons to join the contract. On the one hand, encroachment on the possessions of others is not wrong in the state of nature (ibid.); on the other hand, Kant appears to hold that it is wrong of people to want to remain in a condition where nobody is secure against violence (308). The reason he holds this seems to be that the choice to remain in the state of nature is a choice to "hand over everything to wild violence . . . and so subvert the rights of human beings altogether" (308 note). Is there a difference between Kant's contract and Locke's on this point? There may be, although Locke's own attitude to the contract is complex. Nonetheless, both do also stress the mutual advantageousness of the contract, and mutual advantage provides a sufficient motive for entering into it.

In Kant's contract, the group of contracting parties, imagined as free, equal, and independent, is the same as the group of citizens for whom political principles are chosen. Nonetheless, unlike Locke, Kant acknowledges that there will be citizens in the society who are not active contracting parties and who are not characterized by independence. Such people are women, minors, and anyone else who cannot support himself by his own industry, including people in the employ of other individuals and dependent upon those individuals for subsistence—for example sharecroppers, as contrasted with farmers. All such people "lack civil personality" because they are not independent. This thought leads Kant to distinguish between "active" and "passive" citizens. Active citizens (whom I understand to be the group who are also framers of the social contract) have the right to vote on account of their independence. Members of the other group still retain certain rights as human beings; they have freedom and equality as humans, but they are only "underlings of the commonwealth" (315). They have no right to vote, to hold political office, even "to organize, and to work for the introduction of particular laws" (ibid.). So Kant clearly holds that ongoing dependency is a condition that does not pertain to most adult males in a society, and one that rightly disbars one from most political rights. Only his doctrine of prepolitical rights yields any rights for these individuals.

In this way, the rough equality of parties in the state of nature enters Kant's theory, creating two tiers of citizenship. The inequality in power of certain people dooms them to passive status: they cannot support themselves by their own industry. Kant's category is complex: some of the members of the "passive citizen" group can in time perhaps exit from that status, and he stresses this fact (315). It is clear, however, that women and people with disabilities[37] are permanently in the passive category. That does not mean that their needs are not taken care of in some way; but they are not fully equal participants in the creation of political institutions—even after these institutions are created by the initial contract.

We have now concluded this sketchy survey of the formative ideas in the historical tradition. Such a sketch can hope only to have highlighted some areas of difficulty for the tradition: its equation of the group of framers with the group of eventual citizens; its reliance on an idea of rough equality of power and force, oddly run together at times with the very different idea of moral equality; its focus on mutual advantage as the point of the contract; its consequent difficulty in handling the citizenship of women and people of unequal physical and mental powers. These difficulties remain in modern contractarian theories. On the other hand, we can also see that the tradition contains sources of strength and illumination that are discarded by modern contractarians: in particular its idea of moral entitlements and duties in the state of nature, its idea that all human beings ought to acknowledge and respect the entitlement of others to live lives commensurate with human dignity. These ideas are omitted in the starting points of modern contractarian thinking, which attempts to derive political principles procedurally, from the contract situation itself. (Rawls restores some of these moral elements in procedural form through the Veil of Ignorance.)

One more feature of the tradition remains to be discussed, since it runs through all these texts: its strong rationalism. The contracting parties—hence, the citizens in the resulting society—are imagined as characterized by rationality, and by roughly equal rationality. Obviously enough, one cannot make a contract without rationality of some sort, and so there is good reason for the tradition to focus on rationality as an attribute of citizenship, given the way citizenship has already been linked to the ability to enter into a contract. But there was no corresponding reason to link rationality with being a primary nonderivative *subject* of justice: it is only the conflation on which I have focused that leads the tradition to that position. Only Hume, because he does not employ the device of a contract, is able to entertain the possibility that other creatures possessed of awareness or intelligence, such as nonhuman animals, might be primary beneficiaries of justice—but then his views about mutual advantage end up ruling out that possibility. When we discuss mental disability, we will see that the equation of citizen status with (prudential and moral) rationality is a hurdle that even the best contemporary theories cannot surmount, without losing their formative link to the social contract tradition.

vi. Three Forms of Contemporary Contractarianism

We now turn to the contemporary versions of social contract doctrine, or, more broadly, of contractarianism, that are the real focus of this account. The recent philosophical tradition contains several distinct forms of contractarianism, which have very different implications with regard to the problems that concern us.[38] I shall now describe three forms of contractarianism. One is a purely egoistic form, in which political principles with a moral content are derived from mutual advantage alone, with no moral assumptions. David Gauthier's political theory is the salient example of this sort of view. John Rawls's theory is a mixed theory, combining classical social contract elements with Kantian moral elements that supply important constraints on the political principles that will be chosen. Finally, there are modern contractarianisms of the pure Kantian type, which work from the Kantian ideas of fairness and mutual acceptability alone, without the idea of mutual advantage. Such theories are developed by Thomas Scanlon in ethics, and by Brian Barry, using Scanlon's moral theory for the purposes of political theory.

All three types are procedural theories: that is, they imagine an initial choice situation that is structured in a certain way, and that structure is supposed to generate principles that are by definition adequate. The principles are not to be tested against any prior or independent account of rights or entitlements. (In that way, they all depart rather strikingly from the historical social contract tradition.)

Gauthier's *Morals by Agreement* imagines that the parties to the social contract are surrogates for real human beings and that the point of social cooperation, for both real human beings and the parties, is mutual advantage, advantage being understood in a rather narrow way, as focused on one's own property and security. This sort of contract doctrine has some real strengths, if it can be made to work: for it operates with very parsimonious assumptions. If reasonable principles of justice can emerge from a starting point that involves only prudential and no moral assumptions or goals, then one might reason that *a fortiori* we could get similar or even stronger such principles if we did incorporate moral assumptions. Thus the choice of a purely prudential, indeed egoistic, account of the goals of social cooperation seems to put the theory of justice on a stronger footing than the choice of a thicker, more moralized starting point. That, at any rate, is what some of the people who reason this way, and certainly Gauthier, believe.

Thus we should not criticize even such theories for assuming, implausibly, that human beings are egoistic or merely self-interested—at least not without further evidence that the theorists in question believe that people are like that. For they may simply be trying to see how far we can go on the basis of a small number of uncontroversial assumptions. And yet there is some danger in so proceeding. Apart from the question whether the gambit works—which Rawls and other critics deny—such a strategy surely gives salience, within the theory of justice, to whatever political principles *can* be justified by appeal to rational self-interest. Thus it does not come as a complete surprise that Gauthier thinks the problem of physical and mental impairment is a difficult one for a political theory to solve. He has, after all, framed the starting point and the goal in such a way that it will indeed be difficult to solve it. At this point, he might have said, "Well of course real people are not like this, and real societies will include principles dictated by other goals." And yet, the fact that his fundamental structuring principles come from the picture of social cooperation that focuses on mutual advantage makes it difficult for him to backtrack: wouldn't he have to say that other, quite different principles, perhaps equally fundamental, will be involved in this area? And wouldn't this upset the theory's claim to have generated a relatively complete set of political doctrines out of uncontroversial materials?

Moreover, it cannot be assumed that the starting point of self-interest really is less, so to speak, than a different, more moralized set of assumptions. That is, we cannot assume safely that if we can get principles X and Y and Z out of prudence, then a richer moral starting point will give us X and Y and Z, plus more than that. For the richer moral starting point might actually cast doubt on X or Y, or suggest a wholly different way of thinking about society. So it seems best not to begin with such a thin account of social cooperation unless one means it—unless, that is, one does believe, with Hobbes, and possibly with Gauthier, that people really will not agree to political principles unless they can foresee some advantage to themselves—in a rather narrow material sense of advantage—from the cooperation.

For such reasons John Rawls designs his starting point very differently. The parties in Rawls's Original Position are themselves prudential seekers of their own advantage. They do not pursue justice as an end in itself; they are imagined as concerned to advance their own conception of the good, and there is no stipulation that such a conception need include any altruistic elements. But as Rawls repeatedly points out, the account of the parties is only one part of a two-part model of the person in the Original Position. The other part is supplied by the Veil of Ignorance, with its informational restrictions on the parties: they do not know their own race, or class, or birth, or sex, or conception of the good. The informational restrictions are intended to model the moral impartiality that real people can attain if they work at it. Rawls concludes *A Theory of Justice* by stating that the position characteristic of the parties under the Veil of Ignorance can be assumed by real people at any time, and that it is a model of moral purity: "Purity of heart, if one could attain it, would be to see clearly and to act with grace and self-command from this point of view" (*TJ* 587). Citizens in the Well-Ordered Society are understood to endorse the society's principles from a point of view that includes both the interest in their own happiness and the sense of fairness modeled by the Veil of Ignorance. Thus a commitment to impartiality as a good in itself enters the picture of the social contract. The parties want to pursue their own advantage; but the Veil ensures that they do so only on terms that are fair to all.

This seems to be the best way to deploy the social contract tradition if principles of justice are what one is seeking. I focus on Rawls's theory throughout this book because I think it is the strongest and most convincing theory in the tradition, in large part because of the richer moral character of its original choice situation (and of the moral intuitions that this situation embodies). I think it is implausible to suppose that one can extract justice from a starting point that does not include it in some form, and I believe that the purely prudential starting point is likely to lead in a direction that is simply different from the direction we would take if we focused on ethical norms from the start. Nonetheless, Rawls is still a member of the social contract tradition, and I shall argue that his account of social cooperation is in many respects constrained by his very deep adherence to the contract idea.

Rawls's theory has a hybrid character. On the one hand, the

shared moral judgments that his theory is intended to capture, especially in the design of its initial choice situation, are profoundly Kantian, prominently including the intuitive idea that "Each person possesses an inviolability founded on justice that even the welfare of society as a whole cannot override" (*TJ* 3). This is very similar to the intuitive starting point from which my own capabilities approach will begin. Once the hypothetical process of contract formation is under way, then, considerations of fairness dictate that each person be respected as an equal and an end within it. On the other hand, Rawls's allegiance to the classical social contract tradition, with its emphasis on mutual advantage as the goal of social cooperation, plays a large role in setting up the initial contract situation and determining who gets included within it—as framers of principles, but also, given the structure of contract doctrine, as the people for whom, in the first instance, the principles are framed. My treatment of Rawls throughout this book will be aimed at documenting the tensions that these heterogeneous elements of his theory create for the problems on which I shall focus. Why should people form a social compact with others? Love of justice on its own does not and cannot answer this question for Rawls. Although love of justice is present in the intuitive underlying ideas of the theory, it enters the choice situation only once the project is under way, in the form of the formal constraints on the parties' knowledge shaping and limiting their choices.[39] But as to why there should be such a compact at all, the answer is still, basically, mutual advantage, not benevolence or love or justice.[40]

Because this question is so complicated, and because Rawls's ways of talking about social cooperation shift subtly over time, a bit more focus on the text seems required at this point. In *TJ*, Rawls defines society as "a cooperative venture for mutual advantage" (4, 126). He elaborates on this point by saying that "social cooperation makes possible a better life for all than any would have if each were to live solely by his own efforts" (4; almost identical wording at 126). Characterizing the main idea of his theory, he states, "The main idea is that when a number of persons engage in a mutually advantageous cooperative venture according to rules, and thus restrict their liberty in ways necessary to yield advantages for all, those who have submitted to these restrictions have a right to a similar acquiescence on the part of those who have benefited from their submission" (112). In other ways, as well, he depicts the parties as pursuing a mutual advantage through their decision to cooperate together (see, for example, 128, denying prior moral ties among the parties; and 119, noting that their ability to get what they want is limited by the existence of others). Rawls also connects his own theory closely to the familiar theory of rational choice, insisting that what is distinctive about his own theory is its incorporation of moral assumptions.

In *Political Liberalism,* however, the locution "a cooperative venture for mutual advantage" is replaced by "society as a fair system of cooperation over time" (14 and elsewhere), and mutual advantage is not mentioned. Indeed, in one very odd passage, Rawls looks back at *TJ* and simply denies that mutual advantage is the right way of thinking about his earlier theory: "Finally, it is clear from these observations that the idea of reciprocity is not the idea of mutual advantage" (17, referring to a dispute about *TJ* between Gibbard and Barry). So it is not only the new work that is in question: it is Rawls's understanding of his own earlier work. The passage is odd because one might have thought that Rawls either would say that he had misspoken in the prominent passages of *TJ* that I have just mentioned, or would say that he had changed his view; but he is simply silent about the apparent contradiction.

I believe that in fact there is no contradiction, and that therefore it is not a failing in Rawls not to have noted and unraveled the problem. This is so because Rawls is talking about two different questions. In the *PL* passage, Rawls is talking about the attitudes of citizens in the Well-Ordered Society: they do not expect that each and every person gains from fair cooperation, when they compare the fair scheme to schemes of unfair cooperation that they may imagine. (They do not expect this because they have had the moral education that the Well-Ordered Society provides.) Rawls says that if we were to imagine that a person in a society not well ordered by the principles of justice made a transition to the Well-Ordered Society, we could not show him that he would gain, for he might not gain; he would have to have an understanding of reciprocity that did not involve the idea that each and every person should gain by entering the Well-Ordered Society from his own society.

This is quite a different point from the point made in *TJ*, with reference to the classical social contract tradition. There, the point is that cooperation is preferable *to noncooperation* for reasons of mutual advantage. The comparison is between some reasonable set of principles and no principles, not between any existing society (the parties do not know their own society) and some other. To see that cooperation is preferable to noncooperation, the parties do not have to have any particular moral education. They need only know that the Circumstances of Justice obtain between them.

What Rawls is saying in *PL,* then, is that *ex post,* the citizens in the Well-Ordered Society have to develop and maintain an understanding of reciprocity that supports their continued attachment to principles that are not as personally advantageous for some of them as other, less egalitarian principles might be. But that does not mean that the formation of the initial choice situation does not involve considerations of mutual advantage as compared with the situation of noncooperation. Rawls does not show as much interest in the social contract doctrine in *PL* as in

TJ. But he insists that he is building on the arguments of *TJ*, and changing them only where he explicitly says so.

As all the classical theorists emphasize, the goal of mutual advantage is closely connected to the restriction on the initial group of contracting parties that Hume so eloquently discussed. As Hume says: if there is a group that is grossly unequal in power and resources to the majority group, it is not very clear that cooperating *with those people* on fair terms is advantageous—as opposed either to dominating them or to dealing with them by personal charity. I see no reason to think that Rawls has diverged from Hume on that point. He insists repeatedly that his understanding of the Original Position and its restrictions is unchanged from *TJ* to *PL*, and *PL* itself explicitly reaffirms the Humean restrictions in its insistence that citizens have "normal" capacities. I conclude that mutual advantage in the sense in which the classical theorists use it has not been displaced from the theory, even though the Kantian idea of reciprocity will prove dominant in the Well-Ordered Society once principles of justice are chosen.

But the initial choice situation is a fiction. People never actually face the choice between cooperation and noncooperation. So what does it mean to say that there is reciprocity between citizens in the Well-Ordered Society and yet an affirmation of the Humean Circumstances of Justice in thinking about the origin of society's basic principles? The reality to which the fiction corresponds was well captured by Hume: namely, we do not *need* to cooperate with people who are much weaker than the normal case, because we can simply dominate them, as we now dominate nonhuman animals. Domination does not entail cruelty: we may treat them kindly, as we sometimes do. Moreover, such a theory can even hold that cruelty is morally bad: other moral virtues and their principles enter in at this point. Nonetheless, *justice* is not the appropriate relation to them, given their great weakness by comparison to the "normal" case. For Rawls as for Hume, the idea of justice remains linked to the idea that there is something we all gain by cooperation rather than domination.

In terms of the citizens of the Well-Ordered Society and their knowledge, there are limits to the commitment to reciprocity that is demanded of citizens. They are asked to accept, on grounds of justice, a situation that may be less advantageous to them than one that they might find in a nonegalitarian society. But they accept these "strains of commitment" secure in the knowledge that their fellow citizens are all "fully cooperating members of society over a complete life." They do not accept the additional strain of extending their commitment to citizens who are not similarly productive, and who might therefore be dominated (although other ethical virtues may suggest that they should not be). Within the confines set up by the Humean conditions, they are prepared to give everyone strict justice.

This starting point makes it very difficult for Rawls to include fully the interests of people with unusual physical and mental impairments, at the point where basic principles of justice are being designed. He is perfectly aware of this fact, and emphasizes it, as we have seen, although he does not believe that this problem should lead us to reject his theory. Similarly, his understanding of social cooperation also causes difficulties when one tries to use the theory in thinking about transnational justice and about what we owe to nonhuman animals. And although Rawls states that on account of the Veil of Ignorance the parties have no basis for "bargaining in the usual sense" (*TJ* 129), he never denies—and this remark suggests—that they do bargain, albeit in an unusual sense. Each is "forced to choose for everyone" (140) by the constraints of ignorance, which are unusual; but their purpose is still mutual advantage, albeit within the constraints of fairness.

Despite these limitations, however, the ideas of reciprocity and fairness embodied in Rawls's characterization of citizens in the problematic passage from *PL* do important work in showing us why *we* might want to solve these problems, extending Rawls's theory through further development of his ideas of inviolability and reciprocity. To be sure, these intuitive ideas, for Rawls, do not stand independently of the principles of justice, and he offers no principles of justice for the three cases that concern us (apart from the approach to international issues in *The Law of Peoples*). But we may, still keeping the intuitive ideas in close relation to the principles of justice, try to extend both the principles and the intuitions while questioning the other part of the theory (which Rawls says is independent), the original choice situation. If we start from the bare idea that each person has "an inviolability founded on justice that even the welfare of society as a whole cannot override," we see strong reasons why we should seek principles of justice that accord full justice and equality to people with disabilities, to citizens of all nations, and to nonhuman animals (who can count as persons in an extended sense, although Rawls did not so count them). Rawls's intuitive starting points, and the principles that emerge from them, will turn out to be good guides to these unsolved problems, helping us to see why it is important to solve them despite the economic burden that solving them might require the "normally productive" citizen to bear.

So far as the moral sentiments go, Rawls's theory, once again, is subtle and complex. On the one hand, the Veil of Ignorance is intended as an abstract model of benevolence. He explicitly says that, by combining self-interest with ignorance, he hopes to get results that approximate to what we would get from benevolence with full information (*TJ* 148–149, to be discussed more fully in Chapter 2). Why, then, not include benevolent sentiments directly? Rawls says that doing so would lead to a more indeterminate result: by introducing the informational restrictions instead, he hopes to get precise and specific political principles. So benevolent sentiments, although they do not belong to the parties in the Original Position, still belong to the model as a whole; and the citizens in the Well-Ordered Society are imagined as having such sentiments. In fact, the section of *TJ* that deals with the moral sentiments and their education is among its richest and most fascinating. Nonetheless, the reason the parties get together to frame political principles at all is not benevolence, which only constrains how they operate once the exercise is under way.

Four aspects of Rawls's initial choice situation need to be kept in view in what follows, since I shall find difficulties with all, and since they are to some extent independent of one another. I believe that we need to modify all of them in order to extend his principles and the intuitive ideas behind them to the new cases I shall consider. First, we must scrutinize Rawls's account of primary goods, with its commitment to measuring relative social positions (once the priority of liberty is fixed) with reference to wealth and income, rather than by some more heterogeneous and plural set of indices, such as capabilities. That commitment is important to Rawls; it forms a key element in his argument for the Difference Principle (the principle stating that inequalities will be acceptable only if they raise the level of the least well-off), and he resolutely defends it against Sen's insistence on capabilities. But such a commitment is not essential to a Kantian/contractarian theory of Rawls's type. Thus the problems that I shall identify in this area of the theory do not pose serious problems for contractarianism, though they do (I shall argue) pose problems for Rawls.

The second problem area is Rawls's Kantian political conception of the person, which is key to many aspects of his theory; his analyses of freedom and reciprocity are related to that, as is the account of the role of primary goods. Because in this conception personhood is seen as requiring a rather high degree of rationality (moral and prudential), it becomes impossible to conceive of the equal citizenship of people with severe mental impairments, or of the rights of nonhuman animals. The conception also poses problems, I argue, for an adequate understanding of "normal" people as they go through growth, maturity, and decline.

Although these Kantian elements of Rawls's theory are especially prominent in *PL*, the idea that certain actual natural capacities are the basis for the equality of citizens is present already in *TJ*. In the important section titled "The Basis of Equality" (504–512), Rawls argues that many accounts of the basis of human equality in political philosophy have gone wrong by holding that different degrees of intelligence or moral capacity ground different political entitlements. Instead, without giving up on the project of using natural capacities to provide an account of the basis of equality, one may argue that the relevant property is a "range property": that is, it does come in degrees, but the possession of some essential minimum degree of it is sufficient for equality. "We are not directed to look for differences in natural features that affect some maximand and therefore serve as possible grounds for different grades of citizenship" (509). We do, however, look for some minimum degree of the capacity, understood as the capacity for a sense of justice, or the capacity "to take part in and to act in accordance with the public understanding of the initial situation" (505). This condition is not stringent. "I assume that the capacity for a sense of justice is possessed by the overwhelming majority of mankind, and therefore this question does not raise a serious practical problem . . . There is no race or recognized group of human beings that lacks this attribute. Only scattered individuals are without this capacity, or its realization to the minimum degree" (506).

People with severe mental impairments, however, are exactly those "scattered individuals" that Rawls has in mind. It is not clear why the fact that they are a relatively small minority means that there is no serious problem here. Rawls says only that possession of the minimum degree of the capacity is sufficient for equality, not that it is necessary. But later, discussing animals, he does say, "While I have not maintained that the capacity for a sense of justice is necessary in order to be owed the duties of justice, it does seem that we are not required to give strict justice anyway to creatures lacking this capacity" (*TJ* 512). In this important discussion (recapitulated at *PL* 19), Rawls makes it clear that he links the idea of political justice very closely to the ability to make and abide by an agreement. There may certainly be moral duties where this basic capacity is absent, but not duties of justice.

This conception of the person, like the emphasis on income and wealth, is important to Rawls but is not required by contractarian theories in general. All contractarian theories must rely on some account of rationality in the bargaining process, and all assume that the framers of the social contract are the same group as the citizens for whom principles are being framed. Thus no theory of this kind can fully include people with severe mental impairments as people for whom, in the first instance, principles are being framed. Nonetheless, a social contract thinker might have adopted an account of the person that saw rationality as more thoroughly embedded in need and animality than Kant does. Such a conception would not solve all the problems I shall identify, not without a thoroughgoing redesign of the social contract approach. Nonetheless, it would at least lead in the direction of a solution.

Finally, however, there are two commitments that lie at the heart of the entirety of the social contract tradition: the idea that the parties to the social contract are roughly equal in power and ability, and the related idea of mutual advantage as the goal they pursue through cooperating rather than not cooperating. Much though Rawls adds moral elements to his theory, rendering it richer and more adequate, he never gives up the social contract starting point. For this reason, as he himself states, he has difficulty with the problems that are our focus. These are the commitments that, above all, I think we need to jettison in order to extend the intuitive ideas of his theory and the principles it generates to our new cases.

There is another form of contemporary contractarianism[41] that does not have these two problematic features. Starting from the Kantian idea that principles, in order to be fair, must be rationally acceptable to all who are affected, the approach develops a systematic Kantian account of the acceptability of moral principles. Thomas Scanlon's *What We Owe to Each Other* is the most important recent example of such an approach.[42] Scanlon's book deals with ethical principles and does not discuss questions of political theory. Thus it has no need to elaborate a theory of the good things that politics distributes, or to face questions of pluralism and religious or cultural difference. If it did face such questions, the theory would need to adopt some relatively determinate account of basic goods, much as Rawls's theory has done; only at that point could it really be compared with the theory that I shall consider.

The arguments I develop in this book have nothing to say in criticism of Scanlon's theory—although the questions I raise about the Kantian conception of the person might also apply to his theory, especially to its critique of desire.[43] Scanlon makes no assumptions about the circumstances (rough equality, for example) that bring people together in search of political principles, since he is not discussing the framing of such principles. Nor does he assume that people who frame principles are framing them for themselves—indeed, he asks good questions about the role that guardianship would play in the case of people with severe mental impairments, whose interests need not be in any way postponed. Finally, he does not assume that mutual advantage is the goal of ethical contracting, and of course it would be most implausible to offer such an account of the point of all ethical choice. Thus his enterprise, illuminating in its own right, is not vulnerable to the criticisms that I shall raise against the social contract tradition and against the aspects of Rawls's theory that display an allegiance to it.

Scanlon's approach to ethics has been developed as a source of political principles by Brian Barry in *Justice as Impartiality*.[44] Barry explicitly criticizes the reliance on mutual advantage both in classical social contract doctrine and in Rawls. He points to the treatment of people with disabilities as one problem that makes the defects in such approaches particularly vivid, although he does not develop the point in any detail. I shall discuss Barry and Scanlon at the end of Chapter 2, suggesting that in principle such forms of contractarianism are attractive as sources of political principles, and that they have much in common with the approach that I favor—which, however, focuses in the first instance on the articulation of a theory of the good (as fundamental entitlements), and locates rational acceptability at a rather different, and later, point in the theory. In any case, we have at this point moved very far from classical social contract doctrine and its modern exponents. Although the Scanlon/Barry form of contractarianism shares the commitment to the *moral* equality of persons that animates the classical doctrines, it does not share an emphasis on similar abilities and power in the state of nature, and it therefore does not have the problems entailed by this focus.

Social contract models of justice have great strengths. Their conception of political principles as the outcome of a contract among rational independent adults rightly emphasizes the worth of each human being and the irrelevance, for (normative) political purposes, of the artificial advantages of class, wealth, status, and existing hierarchies of power. Rawls's moralized version of the starting point avoids some of the pitfalls of thinner versions, building impartiality and mutual respect into the basis from which political principles will be generated. My arguments begin from the assumption that theories of justice in the social contract tradition are among the strongest theories of justice we currently have. Nonetheless, I shall suggest that they provide inadequate solutions to our three pressing problems. In order to extend the theories to these cases we need to question some of their central assumptions.

vii. The Capabilities Approach

But of course it is not very productive to criticize a tradition, especially one that is fertile and deeply entrenched, without offering an alternative. The second, constructive purpose of my project is to argue that there is an approach to issues of basic justice that can take us further than social contract doctrines can, particularly in the three areas under discussion. Because this alternative approach shares some intuitive ideas with the Rawlsian version of contractarianism, and because the principles it generates have a close family resemblance to the principles of justice, we may view it as an extension of or complement to Rawls's theory, with these new problems in focus. I believe we should recognize that the alternative approach has significant strengths; we should pursue it and develop it further, thus resurrecting older political theories in the Grotian natural law tradition— while we also continue to pursue and develop orthodox contractarian theories. Nothing would be less in the spirit of this project than the wholesale rejection of theories that have illuminated so much about core issues of social justice. The hope would be that if we keep working on both types of theories and they generate related results across a wide range of areas, this harmony will give us confidence that we are on the right track.

But in the three areas under discussion, I believe it will become clear that the capabilities approach supplies sounder guidance for law and public policy.

The alternative, then, is the "capabilities approach," an approach that has been developed in somewhat different ways by me in philosophy and by Amartya Sen in economics. Sen's use of the approach focuses on the comparative measurement of quality of life, although he is also interested in issues of social justice. I, by contrast, have used the approach to provide the philosophical underpinning for an account of core human entitlements that should be respected and implemented by the governments of all nations, as a bare minimum of what respect for human dignity requires. In *Women and Human Development* and elsewhere, I argue that the best approach to this idea of a basic social minimum is provided by an approach that focuses on *human capabilities,* that is, what people are actually able to do and to be, in a way informed by an intuitive idea of a life that is worthy of the dignity of the human being. I identify a list of *central human capabilities,* arguing that all of them are implicit in the idea of a life worthy of human dignity.

The capabilities are then presented as the source of political principles for a liberal pluralistic society; they are set in the context of a type of political liberalism that makes them specifically political goals and presents them in a manner free of any specific metaphysical grounding. Presented and commended by argument in this way, the capabilities, I argue, can become the object of an overlapping consensus among people who otherwise have very different comprehensive conceptions of the good.[45]

I argue, further, again relying on the intuitive idea of human dignity, that the capabilities in question should be pursued for each and every person, treating each as an end and none as a mere tool of the ends of others. (This aspect of the approach has obvious application to the area of sex equality, since women have all too often been treated as the supporters of the ends of others, rather than as ends in their own right.) Finally, my approach uses the idea of a *threshold level of each capability,* beneath which it is held that truly human functioning is not available to citizens; the social goal should be understood in terms of getting citizens above this capability threshold. (That would not be the only important social goal: in that sense I aim only to provide a partial and minimal account of social justice.)

I shall be contrasting the capabilities approach with modern contractarian approaches, especially Rawls's. But really these approaches are close relatives and allies of the capabilities approach. The capabilities approach was originally designed above all as an alternative to the economic-Utilitarian approaches that dominated, and to some degree still dominate, discussions of quality of life in international development and policy circles, especially approaches that understand the point of development in narrowly economic terms. We need to pause to fill in, briefly, that part of the background.

The most prominent approach to quality-of-life assessment in development economics and international policymaking used to be simply to rank nations in accordance with gross national product (GNP) per capita. It has by now become obvious that this approach is not very illuminating, because it does not even ask about the distribution of wealth and income, and countries with similar aggregate figures can exhibit great distributional variations. South Africa used to shoot straight to the top of the list of developing countries by this measure, despite its gross inequalities. Unlike both the capabilities approach and Kantian forms of contractarianism, these approaches do not consider each person as an end, but are willing to promote an overall social good in ways that may in effect use some people as means to the enrichment of others.

As the example of South Africa also reveals, the GNP approach goes wrong in another way as well. It fails to inquire about key elements of a human life—involving key entitlements, the capabilities approach will say—that are not always well correlated with wealth and income, even as distributed: elements such as life expectancy, infant mortality, educational opportunities, employment opportunities, political liberties, and the quality of race and gender relations. Countries that do very well on GNP per capita have often done egregiously badly on one of these other distinct goods, as the *Human Development Reports* of the United Nations Development Programme make clear when they index nations on a wide variety of parameters.

Sometimes economists in the Utilitarian tradition focus instead on the total or average utility of the population, as measured by expressions of satisfaction. Here again, we run into the problem of respect for the separate person—for an aggregate figure does not tell us where the top and the bottom are. In that sense, it shows no more respect for each separate person than does the crude GNP approach. Average utility is an imprecise number, which does not tell us enough about different types of people and their relative social placement. This imprecision makes it an especially bad approach when we are selecting basic political principles with a commitment to treat each person as an end.

What is more, Utilitarian economists typically aggregate not only across distinct lives but also across distinct elements of lives. Thus, within the total or average utility will lie information about liberty, about economic well-being, about health, about education. But these are all separate goods, which vary to some extent independently of one another.[46] Moreover, there are reasons to think that they all matter, and that we should not give up one of them simply in order to achieve an especially large amount of another. A central argument used by John Rawls against Utilitarianism has been that because of its commitment to trade-offs among diverse goods, it offers insufficient protection for political and religious liberty. It encourages trade-offs between those goods and others in order to produce the largest social total (or average).[47] But this sort of point seems true more generally: similarly, we should not give up on emotional health to achieve a great deal of employment opportunity, or on self-respect in order to achieve a great deal of health. Once again, Utilitarianism's commitment to aggregation creates problems for thinking well about marginalized or deprived people, for whom some of the opportunities that Utilitarianism puts at risk may have an especially urgent importance.

There is a further problem with the reliance on utility: it does not even include all the relevant information. One thing we want to know is how individuals feel about what is happening to them, whether they are dissatisfied or satisfied. But we also want to know what they are actually able to do and to be. People adjust their preferences to what they think they can achieve, and also to what their society tells them a suitable achievement is for someone like them. Women and other deprived people frequently exhibit such "adaptive preferences," formed under unjust background conditions. These preferences will typically validate the status quo.[48] Satisfaction is one thing that is important; but it is surely not the only thing.

Finally, by focusing on the state of satisfaction, Utilitarianism shows a deficient regard for agency. Contentment is not the only thing that matters in a human life; active striving matters, too. Robert Nozick introduced at this point the famous example of the "experience machine": a person is hooked up to a machine that produces pleasant experiences, while he or she actually does nothing.[49] Most people would agree that being hooked up to the machine does not suffice for well-being. It would be better to be active in the world, even if one encountered some frustration. This thought has political importance: for there are choices to be made about how people will be active in a nation. Some forms of government promote satisfaction without allowing people much scope for choice and activity; others promote choice and activity, even if it is likely that people who are left free to choose will make mistakes and incur frustrations. It seems that Utilitarianism leads the mind away from the importance of democratic choice and personal liberty.

Thinking about the defects of Utilitarian approaches to development pushes us, then, in the direction of a substantive account of certain central abilities and opportunities, prominently including opportunities for choice and activity, as the relevant space within which to make comparisons of quality of life across societies, and as the relevant benchmark to use in asking whether a given society has delivered a minimal level of justice to its citizens. Our critique suggests that such a list will contain a plurality of distinct items, and that it will not treat these items as simply offering different amounts of a single homogeneous good. Nor will the assessment focus solely on how people feel about their relation to these goods; it will ask, as well, what they are actually able to do and to be.

The basic intuitive idea of my version of the capabilities approach is that we begin with a conception of the dignity of the human being, and of a life that is worthy of that dignity—a life that has available in it "truly human functioning," in the sense described by Marx in his 1844 *Economic and Philosophical Manuscripts.* (I use the Marxian idea for political purposes only, not as the source of a comprehensive doctrine of human life; Marx makes no such distinction.) Marx speaks of the human being as a being "in need of a totality of human life-activities," and the approach also takes its bearing from this idea, insisting that the capabilities to which all citizens are entitled are many and not one, and are opportunities for activity, not simply quantities of resources.[50] Resources are inadequate as an index of well-being, because human beings have varying needs for resources, and also varying abilities to convert resources into functioning. Thus two people with similar quantities of resources may actually differ greatly in the ways that matter most for social justice. This issue will become especially salient when we confront the theory with issues of impairment and disability.

With this basic idea as a starting point, I then attempt to justify a list of ten capabilities as central requirements of a life with dignity. As with Rawls's principles, so here: the political principles give shape and content to the abstract idea of dignity (cf. *TJ* 586). These ten capabilities are supposed to be general goals that can be further specified by the society in question as it works on the account of fundamental entitlements it wishes to endorse. But in some form all are held to be part of a minimum account of social justice: a society that does not guarantee these to all its citizens, at some appropriate threshold level, falls short of being a fully just society, whatever its level of opulence. And although in practical terms priorities may have to be set temporarily, the capabilities are understood as both mutually supportive and all of central relevance to social justice. Thus a society that neglects one of them to promote the others has shortchanged its citizens, and there is a failure of justice in the shortchanging.

The capabilities approach is not intended to provide a complete account of social justice. It says nothing, for example, about how justice would treat inequalities above the threshold. (In that sense it does not answer all the questions answered by Rawls's theory.) It is an account of minimum core social entitlements, and it is compatible with different views about how to handle issues of justice and distribution that would arise once all citizens are above the threshold level. Nor does it insist that this list of entitlements is an exhaustive account of political justice; there may be other important political values, closely connected with justice, that it does not include.[51]

The list itself is open-ended and has undergone modification over time; no doubt it will undergo further modification in the light of criticism. But here is the current version.

The Central Human Capabilities

1. *Life*. Being able to live to the end of a human life of normal length; not dying prematurely, or before one's life is so reduced as to be not worth living.

2. *Bodily Health*. Being able to have good health, including reproductive health; to be adequately nourished; to have adequate shelter.

3. *Bodily Integrity*. Being able to move freely from place to place; to be secure against violent assault, including sexual assault and domestic violence; having opportunities for sexual satisfaction and for choice in matters of reproduction.

4. *Senses, Imagination, and Thought*. Being able to use the senses, to imagine, think, and reason—and to do these things in a "truly human" way, a way informed and cultivated by an adequate education, including, but by no means limited to, literacy and basic mathematical and scientific training. Being able to use imagination and thought in connection with experiencing and producing works and events of one's own choice, religious, literary, musical, and so forth. Being able to use one's mind in ways protected by guarantees of freedom of expression with respect to both political and artistic speech, and freedom of religious exercise. Being able to have pleasurable experiences and to avoid nonbeneficial pain.

5. *Emotions*. Being able to have attachments to things and people outside ourselves; to love those who love and care for us, to

grieve at their absence; in general, to love, to grieve, to experience longing, gratitude, and justified anger. Not having one's emotional development blighted by fear and anxiety. (Supporting this capability means supporting forms of human association that can be shown to be crucial in their development.)

6. *Practical Reason.* Being able to form a conception of the good and to engage in critical reflection about the planning of one's life. (This entails protection for the liberty of conscience and religious observance.)

7. *Affiliation.*

   A. Being able to live with and toward others, to recognize and show concern for other human beings, to engage in various forms of social interaction; to be able to imagine the situation of another. (Protecting this capability means protecting institutions that constitute and nourish such forms of affiliation, and also protecting the freedom of assembly and political speech.)

   B. Having the social bases of self-respect and nonhumiliation; being able to be treated as a dignified being whose worth is equal to that of others. This entails provisions of nondiscrimination on the basis of race, sex, sexual orientation, ethnicity, caste, religion, national origin.

8. *Other Species.* Being able to live with concern for and in relation to animals, plants, and the world of nature.

9. *Play.* Being able to laugh, to play, to enjoy recreational activities.

10. *Control over One's Environment.*

    A. *Political.* Being able to participate effectively in political choices that govern one's life; having the right of political participation, protections of free speech and association.

    B. *Material.* Being able to hold property (both land and movable goods), and having property rights on an equal basis with others; having the right to seek employment on an equal basis with others; having the freedom from unwarranted search and seizure. In work, being able to work as a human being, exercising practical reason and entering into meaningful relationships of mutual recognition with other workers.

The basic idea is that with regard to each of these, we can argue, by imagining a life without the capability in question, that such a life is not a life worthy of human dignity.[52] The argument in each case is based on imagining a form of life; it is intuitive and discursive. Nonetheless, I believe that the process, and the list, can gather broad cross-cultural agreement, similar to the international agreements that have been reached concerning basic human rights. Indeed, the capabilities approach is, in my view, one species of a human rights approach, and human rights have often been linked in a similar way to the idea of human dignity.

The capabilities approach is fully universal: the capabilities in question are held to be important for each and every citizen, in each and every nation, and each person is to be treated as an end. The approach is in this way similar to the international human rights approach; indeed I view the capabilities approach as one species of a human rights approach.[53] Arguing in favor of a set of cross-cultural norms and against the positions of cultural relativists has been an important dimension of the approach.[54] But it is also crucial to stress that the approach builds in an important place for the norm of respect for pluralism, and this in six ways.[55]

First, I consider the list as open-ended and subject to ongoing revision and rethinking, in the way that any society's account of its most fundamental entitlements is always subject to supplementation (or deletion).

I also insist, second, that the items on the list ought to be specified in a somewhat abstract and general way, precisely in order to leave room for the activities of specifying and deliberating by citizens and their legislatures and courts. Within certain parameters it is perfectly appropriate that different nations should do this somewhat differently, taking their histories and special circumstances into account. Thus, for example, Germany's interpretation of the free speech right, according to which there can be a good deal of legal regulation of antisemitic speech and political organizing, is rather different from the U.S. interpretation, which protects such speech unless there is an imminent threat of public disorder. Both interpretations seem right, given the different histories of the two nations.

Third, I consider the list to be a freestanding "partial moral conception," to use John Rawls's phrase: that is, it is explicitly introduced for political purposes only, and without any grounding in metaphysical ideas of the sort that divide people along lines of culture and religion. As Rawls says, we can view this list as a "module" (*PL* 12, 145) that can be endorsed by people who otherwise have very different conceptions of the ultimate meaning and purpose of life; they will connect it to their religious or secular comprehensive doctrines in many ways.

Fourth, if we insist that the appropriate political goal is capability and not functioning, we protect pluralism here again.[56] Many people who are willing to support a given capability as a fundamental entitlement would feel violated were the associated functioning made basic. Thus, the right to vote can be endorsed by religious citizens who would feel deeply violated by mandatory voting because it goes against their religious conception. (The American Amish are in this category: they believe that it is wrong to participate in political life, but they appear happy that citizens have the right to vote.) The free expression of religion can be endorsed by people who would object to any establishment of religion that would involve dragooning all citizens into some type of religious functioning. Where health is concerned, advocates of a capabilities approach differ about whether the appropriate goal is capability or functioning. My own view is that people should be given ample opportunities to lead a healthy lifestyle, but the choice should be left up to them; they should not be penalized for unhealthy choices.[57]

Fifth, the major liberties that protect pluralism are central items on the list: the freedom of speech, the freedom of association, the freedom of conscience. By placing them on the list we give them a central and nonnegotiable place.

Sixth and finally, I insist on a rather strong separation between issues of justification and issues of implementation. I believe that we can justify this list as a good basis for political principles all around the world. But this does not mean that we thereby license intervention with the affairs of a state that does not recognize them. It is a basis for persuasion, but I hold that military and economic sanctions are justified only in certain very grave circumstances, involving traditionally recognized crimes against humanity. So it seems less objectionable to recommend something to everyone, once we point out that it is part of the view that state sovereignty, grounded in the consent of the people, is a very important part of the whole package.

This is the core of the approach. It has close links with contractarian theories, especially Rawls's theory, and its critique of Utilitarianism is in key respects the same. In particular, the ideas of human dignity and the inviolability of the person are core intuitive ideas in both theories, and generate the arguments of both against certain types of social aggregation that neglect the separateness of each life. Both approaches are united in opposition to the pursuit of a glorious total or average in ways that subordinate certain groups or individuals; one person's exceeding well-being is not permitted to compensate for another person's misery. In both approaches, furthermore, ideas of mutual respect, reciprocity, and the social bases of self-respect play a central role.

The capabilities approach and Rawlsian contractarianism are allies across a wide space of the terrain of justice, and it seems welcome that theories with somewhat different assumptions and procedures generate closely related results. In *Women and Human Development* I argue that convergence between the best informed-desire approaches and the capabilities approach should give us confidence that we are on the right track. So, too, in this case: if two approaches that share some deep intuitive starting points but differ greatly in procedure and structure should converge across a wide range of recommendations, that convergence should be a source of confidence. Another way of putting the same point is that the capabilities approach can help us extend the Rawlsian approach to three areas that Rawls was unsure his theory could cover. In that spirit, let us now examine more closely some of the differences between the capabilities approach and modern contractarianism.

viii. Capabilities and Contractarianism

The deepest difference between the capabilities approach and Rawlsian contractarianism lies in its basic theoretical structure. Rawls's approach, like most social contract doctrines, is a procedural approach to justice. In other words, it does not go directly to outcomes and examine these for hallmarks of moral adequacy. Instead it designs a procedure that models certain key features of fairness and impartiality, and relies on these procedures to generate an adequately just outcome.[58] Given an adequate design of the original situation, whatever principles emerge will be by definition just. To illustrate this feature of his conception, Rawls uses the example of dividing a cake (*TJ* 85). In an outcome-oriented conception of justice, we identify a correct outcome (let us stipulate that equal shares is that outcome); we then design a procedure that will achieve this result.[59] Similar is our approach to designing a criminal trial. We begin with the correct outcome (the guilty, and only the guilty, are convicted), and we design procedures that will generate that outcome as often as possible. In Rawls's conception, by contrast, there is no independent criterion for the right result: "instead there is a correct or fair procedure such that the outcome is likewise correct or fair, whatever it is, provided that the procedure has been properly followed" (86). All the controversial moral work goes into the design of the procedure itself. (As our historical sketch has shown, classical social contract doctrines are only partly procedural: Locke's, in particular, contains a robust account of human dignity and natural rights against which the resulting outcome will rightly be measured.)

The capabilities approach is like the criminal trial. That is, it starts from the outcome: with an intuitive grasp of a particular content, as having a necessary connection to a life worthy of human dignity. It then seeks political procedures (a constitution, various allocations of powers, a certain type of economic system) that will achieve that result as nearly as possible, although it seems likely that such procedures will change over time and may also vary with the circumstances and history of different nations.[60] Justice is in the outcome, and the procedure is a good one to the extent that it promotes this outcome.

Defenders of procedural accounts of justice often feel that outcome-oriented views are not complex enough, don't have enough moving parts. Defenders of outcome-oriented views are likely to feel that procedural views put the cart before the horse: for surely what matters for justice is the quality of life of people, and we are ultimately going to reject any procedure, however elegant, if it doesn't give us an outcome that squares well with our intuitions about dignity and fairness. (Rawls's theory is so front-laden, so to speak, has so much moral content packed into the procedure itself, that it avoids this criticism to some extent; but it still seems odd that we should have more confidence in the procedure than in the outcome it generates.)[61] Although the following analogy may strike some fans of procedural justice as a bit unfair, it seems to the outcome-oriented theorist as if a cook has a fancy, sophisticated pasta-maker, and assures her guests that the pasta made in this machine will be by definition good, since it is the best machine on the market. But surely, the outcome theorist says, the guests want to taste the pasta and see for themselves. They will be inclined to decide for or against the machine on the basis of the pasta it produces.[62] Even when I discuss Scanlon's ethical contractarianism at the end of Chapter 2, expressing considerable sympathy with it, I shall still ask whether the bare procedural idea of rational acceptability can do all the work he has in mind for it, in the absence of an antecedent and independent account of the human good. Surely in political theory, at any rate, some such account is necessary.

This reply to the contractarian, however, reveals a feature of the capabilities approach that may seem troubling. That is, this approach seems to rely on intuition to a greater degree than procedural approaches. We just taste the pasta and see how we like it. Is that really enough, without a powerful mechanism on which we can rely, especially given the fact that intuitions are formed in nonideal background conditions and may contain serious distortions? We can agree that the capabilities approach does indeed rely on intuition—although not on uncriticized preferences, as its critique of Utilitarianism makes plain. That is, some deep moral intuitions and considered judgments about human dignity do play a fundamental role in the theory, although they are never immune from criticism in the light of other elements of the theory.[63] But it is plain that contractarians, too, rely on intuitions and considered judgments, in the design of the procedure itself. So it is not terribly clear that the difference is significant. (We should remember that Rawls uses a highly intuitive method, though not one relying on unsorted preferences, when he discusses the way in which each of us assesses any theory whatever against our own considered judgments.)

Rawls expresses opposition to intuitionism because of its reliance on intuition *in balancing competing ends.* Political principles will never be final, but will always admit of trade-offs in the light of intuitionistic balancing. Rawls believes that a theory that entails such a large role for balancing cannot offer principles that are sufficiently stable, precise, or final. (This is one reason why he is determined to measure relative social positions in a precise way, by appeal to income and wealth alone—a part of his theory that causes large difficulties.) We can certainly admit that the capabilities approach contains, indeed stresses, a plurality of ends, all qualitatively distinct, and that social planning must promote all of them. But does this make the theory intuitionistic in a way that is murky and indefinite? There is an issue of principle here. The capabilities approach insists from the start that the elements of a life with human dignity are plural and not single, and thus that the core social entitlements are also plural. It would be a grave error to single out any one of the ten to bear the weight of indexing relative social positions: all are minimum requirements of a life with dignity, and all are distinct in quality. Indeed, recognizing their qualitative distinctness is a way of being more, not less, precise and more, not less, definite about what a decent society must deliver to its citizens. A conception of the social goal that is complex will be more indefinite than a simple one only if its goals are themselves indefinitely specified or are the wrong goals. If life actually contains a plurality of things that have a necessary relation to a life worthy of human dignity, it is precision, and not its opposite, to point that out.

Does the approach therefore prevent political principles from being sufficiently stable, definite, and final? We must return to that question. But an initial response is suggested by the interpretation of the capabilities list itself, which insists that *all* the entitlements should be secured to people as central requirements of justice. It is the whole set of such entitlements, suitably defined, that is held to be required by justice, and no entitlement can substitute for any other. The approach does not invite, and positively forbids, trade-offs and balancing when we are dealing with the threshold level of each of these requirements. (For example, it would be a disastrous misinterpretation of the approach to try to purchase more free speech by curtailing employment opportunities or freedom of association. All are required by justice.)

Now that we see the capabilities approach in its general outlines, we can make some preliminary observations about its relationship to the main features of contractarian approaches as we have outlined them in section iv.

1. *The Circumstances of Justice.* Social contract theories typically stipulate that justice makes sense only when people are so placed that it pays for them to exit from the state of nature and make a compact for mutual advantage. The various specific conditions outlined by Rawls (using Hume) and the classical theorists—moderate scarcity, rough equality, and so on—all emerge from that general idea. By contrast, the capabilities approach takes its start from the Aristotelian/Marxian conception of the human being as a social and political being, who finds fulfillment in relations with others. Whereas contractarians typically think of the family as "natural," and the political as in some significant sense artificial,[64] the capabilities approach makes no such distinc-

tion. Although, as a type of political liberalism, it eschews reliance on any deep metaphysics of human nature, it does operate with a conception of the person that it develops for political purposes, a conception that can, it is hoped, be the object of an overlapping consensus. The political conception of the person that it uses includes the idea of the human being as "by nature" political, that is, as finding deep fulfillment in political relations, including, centrally, relations characterized by the virtue of justice. As Aristotle says in the passage that stands as an epigraph to this book, it would be odd to imagine the human being flourishing outside a network of such relations; such a notion may even be a contradiction in terms, since these relations seem a part of human flourishing. Thus, while contractarians typically imagine a being whose good is in effect apolitical, although this being will respect the constraints of law, the Aristotelian account insists that the good of a human being is both social and political. This idea is present in Rawls's doctrine of reciprocity, although, on account of the social contract framework, he does not extend it to the difficult cases that are my focus.

But if this is so, justice makes sense wherever human beings are around. Human beings want to live together, and they want to live together well, which they understand to include living in accordance with justice. They do not have to be similarly situated in order for such issues to arise, and they do not have to have conditions of moderate scarcity. It may be true that in desperate conditions justice cannot be achieved; that does not mean, however, that it cannot be contemplated, and questions asked about how conditions arose that prevent justice from being realized. Similarly, in a situation of great opulence, such as the classical Golden Age, justice will perhaps seem less urgent. Still, it needs to be contemplated, since the nature of these central goods is such that their distribution matters: food, property, and political rights, for example, are never simply common possessions as water and air may in some circumstances be. (Even the Greek gods have need of justice, since they fight over marriage rights, possessions, and various prerogatives and power.) In short, questions of justice are always on the table. A large asymmetry of power, such as exists, for example, between humans and other animals, might make questions of justice more urgent rather than, as in contractarianism, taking them off the agenda.

Notice that this more flexible relation to questions of justice is available to the capabilities approach in part because it is an outcome-oriented theory and not a procedural theory. Procedural theorists need to structure the contract situation in a tight and relatively determinate manner, so that it will generate a determinate set of outcomes—hence the need to specify the situation of the parties in a rather determinate way. The capabilities approach goes straight to the content of the outcome, looks at it, and asks whether it seems compatible with a life in accordance with human (or, later, animal) dignity. This structure permits us to look at a wide range of problems and situations in which issues of justice may be lurking.

2. *"Free, equal, and independent."* Because the capabilities approach does not use a Humean account of the Circumstances of Justice, it is under no pressure to hypothesize that the parties to the social compact are "free, equal, and independent." This means that it is able to use a political conception of the person that more closely reflects real life—a capacity that may be an advantage in dealing with our three unsolved problems. The Aristotelian conception sees the human being as a "political animal," that is, not just a moral and political being, but one who has an animal body, and whose human dignity, rather than being opposed to this animal nature, inheres in it, and in its temporal trajectory. Humans begin as needy babies, grow up slowly, and require lots of care as they grow. In the prime of life they have

the "normal" needs that the social contract model typically incorporates, but they may also have other needs, stemming from accidents or illnesses that put them in a position of asymmetrical dependency for a shorter or longer time. If they live to old age, they typically need a great deal of care again and are likely to encounter disabilities, either physical or mental or both. Moreover, many human beings are atypically disabled all through their lives. Although in some species impairments such as blindness, deafness, paralysis, and severe cognitive impairment will probably doom the creature to a short and miserable life, with the human species this is not so, or at least need not be so. One dividend of our species' considerable control over its environment is the ability to structure environments that enable such species members to participate in social life.

The conception of the person as a political animal includes an idea related to the contractarian idea of "freedom": the person is imagined as having a deep interest in choice, including the choice of a way of life and of political principles that govern it. This is one of the ways in which the capabilities approach is part of the liberal tradition. Nonetheless, it offers a conception of freedom that is subtly different from that of the contract tradition: it stresses the animal and material underpinnings of human freedom, and it also recognizes a wider range of types of beings who can be free.

Because of its variegated and temporally complex conception of the person, the capabilities approach does not include any analogue of the contractarian conception of the person as "equal" in power and ability. People vary greatly in their needs for resources and care, and the same person may have widely varying needs depending on her time of life. The ability of the capabilities approach to recognize this diversity was one of the strengths that initially commended it over other approaches. Nor are people imagined as "independent." Because they are *political* animals, their interests are thoroughly bound up with the interests of others throughout their lives, and their goals are shared goals. Because they are political *animals,* they depend on others asymmetrically during certain phases of their lives, and some remain in a situation of asymmetrical dependency throughout their lives.

3. *The purpose of social cooperation.* As we have observed, social contract theories insist that the whole point of getting together to form political principles is mutual advantage, where that good is understood in a way that separates it analytically from the constraints of justice and reciprocity the parties agree to respect. Even for Rawls, whose citizens in the Well-Ordered Society have a sense of justice, and who see justice as a part of their good, that sense of justice is still understood as rather sharply separate from each person's pursuit of a personal good and from the means to secure that. Indeed, the list of primary goods is understood as a list of such means to personal projects. Although that list is heterogeneous, Rawls's decision to index relative social positions on the basis of income and wealth alone is not surprising.

This is an area in which the capabilities approach will have particularly insistent criticisms to make of classical social contract views, and will press Rawls's theory in the direction of rejecting some key aspects of those views. The capabilities approach denies that principles of justice have to secure mutual advantage. Even where noncooperation is possible and even habitual (because domination is so easy), justice is good for everyone. Justice is about justice, and justice is one thing that human beings love and pursue. It is always very nice if one can show that justice is compatible with mutual advantage, but the argument for principles of justice should not rest on this hope. Very likely the arrangements we need to make to give justice to developing nations, and to people with severe impairments within our own nation, will be very expensive and will not be justifiable as mutually advantageous in the narrow economic sense of advantage. That is too bad. Justice is also one of our ends, and we limit our pursuit of it too much when we think of it as the outcome of a contract for mutual advantage, however morally constructed and constrained. We also limit ourselves when we imagine reciprocity as obtaining only between rough equals, able to offer one another a benefit.

Rawls's theory looks as though it does not have this problem, because of the way in which moral features are built into the account of the starting point. But really, it does have this problem, in its very account of who is in and who is out, who can be party to the contract and whose interests must be addressed subsequently, if at all. Rawls is well aware of this limitation. I shall argue that the problems can be addressed, but not without altering the description of the initial choice situation.

4. *The motivations of the parties.* Classical theorists of the social contract have widely varying accounts of the moral sentiments underlying political society. Locke, in particular, as we have seen, gives a very important role to benevolence. On the other hand, all rely to some extent on the idea of mutual advantage to generate political principles, and all appear to hold that benevolent sentiments by themselves are insufficient to render political society stable. Hume develops this idea much more fully and explicitly than any of the contractarians. Rawls's position on this issue is complex, and here the differences between Rawls's contractarianism and the capabilities approach are narrow and subtle. Making a contract, as we have said, is typically imagined as a process of pursuing one's own interests, and the sentiments of the contracting parties as related sentiments. Rawls's parties themselves lack benevolence and an intrinsic love of justice; these sentiments, however, are represented by the Veil

of Ignorance. In the Well-Ordered Society, by contrast, people learn principle-dependent sentiments and motives.

The capabilities approach is able to include benevolent sentiments from the start in its account of people's relation to their good. This is so because its political conception of the person includes the ideas of a fundamental sociability and of people's ends as including shared ends.[65] (This idea of ends is of a piece with the rejection of "independence" as a quality of the parties to the formation of social principles.) Prominent among the moral sentiments of people so placed will be compassion, which I conceive as including the judgment that the good of others is an important part of one's own scheme of goals and ends.[66] Thus, when other people suffer capability failure, the citizen I imagine will not simply feel the sentiments required by moral impartiality, viewed as a constraint on her own pursuit of self-interest. Instead, she will feel compassion for them *as a part of her own good*. This is a very subtle difference from the way in which Rawls models benevolence, but I believe that there is a difference. Such benevolent sentiments are ubiquitous in the lives of real people; the problem is that we simply do not extend them consistently or wisely. But an appropriate scheme of public moral education could support their appropriate extension.[67]

Now of course this move does raise the problem Rawls mentioned: benevolence can give indeterminate results. That is why the political principles of the capabilities approach are supported by independent arguments about human dignity. We do not try to generate principles out of compassion alone, but, instead, we seek to support them and render them stable through the development of a compassion that is attuned to the political principles for which we have argued. Nonetheless, it seems to be a merit of the approach that it can tap into what is fine in actual human beings—just in the way that Rawls's approach taps into their capacity for reciprocity and their desire for fair terms of co-operation.

ix. In Search of Global Justice

The three unsolved problems of justice that are the primary topics of this book are all, in different ways, problems of globalizing the theory of justice, that is, extending justice to all those in the world who ought to be treated justly. Social contract theories of justice do superb work for traditional issues of discrimination and exclusion. They are well suited to address inequalities of wealth, class, and status, and can be rather easily extended to address inequalities of race and, in some ways, sex—although our historical sketch has shown how difficult it is to arrive at sex equality from a starting point that insists on equality in power.[68]

Our three unsolved problems, however, prove resistant, because all involve, in different ways, great asymmetries of power and capacity and, in some cases, of moral rationality itself. A satisfactory account of human justice must extend reciprocity and respect to people with impairments, including severe mental impairments. A good analysis requires recognizing the many varieties of impairment, need, and dependency that "normal" human beings experience, and thus the real continuity between "normal" lives and those of people with lifelong mental disabilities. Starting from a conception of the person as a social animal, whose dignity does not derive entirely from an idealized rationality, the capabilities approach can help us to design an adequate conception of the full and equal citizenship of people with mental disabilities.

Social contract theories take the nation-state as their basic unit. For reasons internal to the structure of such theories, they are bound to do so. Such theories cannot provide adequate approaches to problems of global justice, that is, justice that addresses inequalities between richer and poorer nations, and between human beings whatever their nation. To solve these problems we must appreciate the complex interdependencies of citizens in different nations, the moral obligations of both individuals and nations to other nations, and the role of transnational entities (corporations, markets, nongovernmental organizations, international agreements) in securing to people the most basic opportunities for a fully human life. A version of the capabilities approach helps us to think well about what the goal of an international politics should be.

Because social contract theories start from the allegedly crucial importance of human rationality, defining both reciprocity and dignity in terms of it, they deny that we have obligations of justice to nonhuman animals, and view such obligations as we might have as derivative and posterior. We should correct such views in two ways: by recognizing the extent of intelligence in nonhuman animals, and by rejecting the idea that only those who can join in the formation of the social contract are full-fledged subjects of a theory of justice. The capabilities approach, with its emphasis on a continuum of types of capability and functioning, provides guidance that is superior both to that of contract theories and that of Utilitarianism as we seek to do better with these urgent issues of justice.

Up until this point we have been applying the capabilities approach, not greatly modifying it. Only subtle modifications of the theory already developed are required in order for it to deal well with the first two issues on our agenda. Doing justice to the claims of nonhuman animals requires major further development of the approach. But I shall argue that an approach basically Aristotelian in spirit is well placed to give good guidance in this area, and guidance better than that supplied by either Kantian or Utilitarian approaches. The approach is animated by the Aristotelian sense that there is something wonderful and worthy of awe in any complex natural organism—and so it is all ready, in that spirit, to accord respect to animals and recognize their dignity.

With this general idea in view, the capabilities approach can argue that the notion of the characteristic flourishing of a creature of a certain kind should illuminate debates about public policy in this difficult area. Mere sentience is too simple a focus: it neglects the variety of animal capacities and activities, and thus certain areas of damage to flourishing that do not register as pain. Many difficult questions will have to be faced; in particular, since the use of a species norm in the human case is moralized from the ground up, evaluating capacities rather than validating all that exist, it is very difficult to know how a corresponding valuational exercise should be performed in the case of nonhuman species. The capabilities approach does not urge uncritical nature-worship: instead, it urges evaluation of the basic powers of a creature, asking which ones are of central importance for its good. This is a difficult job. Moreover, in this area we inevitably face conflicts and trade-offs that we appear to be able to avoid in the human case, with our emphasis on the coordinated set of all the central capabilities as a minimal social goal. Nonetheless, we can advance the debate by pursuing this new theoretical approach and seeing what fruits it can deliver.

It must be emphasized once again that this project does not aim to dismiss the theory of the social contract from the scene, and least of all Rawls's great theory, which in many ways it follows and extends. Its aim is to see what it would take to extend principles of justice otherwise attractive, and intuitive ideas otherwise attractive, to problems that Rawls believed his arguments could address. It seems to me that this extension requires a new sort of starting point and the rejection of some characteristic elements of the social contract tradition. But contractarian theories, especially in their moralized Kantian form, are close allies of the capabilities approach. And they are important theories to ponder in reflecting about social justice, whatever we end up thinking their shortcomings may be. Proponents of the theories themselves, however, state or imply that there are some problems that they cannot solve, or that are unusually difficult to solve. In this era of human history, these unsolved problems loom large. It seems to be time to see what an examination of these problems will show us about social justice, and what an alternative theory can offer.

2

DISABILITIES AND THE SOCIAL CONTRACT

The problem here is not care of the aged, who have paid for their benefits by earlier productive activity. Life-extending therapies do, however, have an ominous redistributive potential. The primary problem is care for the handicapped. Speaking euphemistically of enabling them to live productive lives, when the services required exceed any possible products, conceals an issue which, understandably, no one wants to face.

—David Gauthier, *Morals by Agreement*

i. Needs for Care, Problems of Justice

Sesha, daughter of philosopher Eva Kittay and her husband Jeffrey, is a young woman in her late twenties. Attractive and affectionate, she loves music and pretty dresses. She responds with joy to the affection and admiration of others. Sesha sways to music and hugs her parents. But she will never walk, talk, or read. Because of congenital cerebral palsy and severe mental retardation, she will always be profoundly dependent on others. She needs to be dressed, washed, fed, wheeled out into Central Park. Beyond such minimal custodial care, if she is to flourish in her own way she needs companionship and love, a visible return of the capacities for affection and delight that are her strongest ways of connecting with others. Her parents, busy professionals, both care for Sesha for long hours themselves and pay a full-time caregiver. Still other helpers are needed on the many occasions when Sesha is ill or has seizures, and cannot help by telling where she hurts.[1]

My nephew Arthur is a big good-looking ten-year-old. He loves machines of all sorts, and by now he has impressive knowledge of their workings. I could talk with Arthur all day about the theory of relativity, if I understood it as well as he does. On the phone with Art, it's always "Hi, Aunt Martha," and then right into the latest mechanical or scientific or historical issue that fascinates him. But Art has been unable to learn in a public school classroom, and he cannot be left alone for a minute when he and his mother are out shopping. He has few social skills, and he seems unable to learn them. Affectionate at home, he becomes terrified if a stranger touches him. Unusually large for his age, he is also very clumsy, unable to play games at which most younger children are adept. He also has distracting bodily tics and makes weird noises.

Arthur has both Asperger's syndrome, which is probably a type of high-functioning autism, and Tourette's syndrome.[2] Both of his parents have full-time jobs, and they cannot afford much help. Fortunately his mother's job, as a church organist, allows her to practice at home, and church people don't mind if she brings Arthur to work. More important still, the state in which they live has agreed, after a struggle, to pay for Arthur's education at a private school equipped to handle his combination of gifts and disabilities. None of us knows whether Arthur will be able to live on his own.[3]

Jamie Bérubé loves B. B. King, Bob Marley, and the Beatles. He can imitate a waiter bringing all his favorite foods, and he has a sly sense of verbal humor. Born with Down syndrome, Jamie has been cared for, since his birth, by a wide range of doctors and therapists, not to mention the nonstop care of his parents, literary critics Michael Bérubé and Janet Lyon. In the early days of his life, Jamie had to be fed through a tube inserted into his nose; his oxygen levels were monitored by a blood-gas machine. At the time his father describes him,[4] Jamie is three. A speech therapist works to develop the muscles of his tongue; another teaches him American Sign Language. A massage therapist elongates the shortened muscles of his neck so that his head can sit straighter. Movement therapists work on the low muscle tone that is the main obstacle to both movement and speech in children with Down syndrome. Equally important, a good local preschool in Champaign, Illinois, includes him in a regular classroom, stimulating his curiosity and giving him precious confidence in relationships with other children, who react well to his sweet personality. Above all, his brother, parents, and friends make a world in which he is not seen as "a child with Down syndrome," far less as "a mongoloid idiot." He is Jamie, a particular child. Jamie will probably be able to live on his own to some extent, and to hold a job. But his parents know that he will, more than many children, need them all his life.

Children and adults with mental impairments are citizens.[5] Any decent society must address their needs for care, education, self-respect, activity, and friendship. Social contract theories, however, imagine the contracting agents who design the basic structure of society as "free, equal, and independent," the citizens whose interests they represent as "fully cooperating members of society over a complete life."[6] They also often imagine them as characterized by a rather idealized rationality. Such approaches do not do well, even with severe cases of physical impairment and disability. It is clear, however, that such theories must handle severe mental impairments and related disabilities as an afterthought, after the basic institutions of society are already designed. Thus, in effect, people with mental impairments are not among those for whom and in reciprocity with whom society's basic institutions are structured.

The failure to deal adequately with the needs of citizens with impairments and disabilities is a serious flaw in modern theories that conceive of basic political principles as the result of a contract for mutual advantage. This flaw goes deep, affecting their adequacy as accounts of human justice more generally.[7] A satisfactory account of human justice requires recognizing the equal citizenship of people with impairments, including mental impairments, and appropriately supporting the labor of caring for and educating them, in such a way as to address the associated disabilities. It also requires recognizing the many varieties of impairment, disability, need, and dependency that "normal" human beings experience, and thus the very great continuity between "normal" lives and those of people with lifelong impairments. I shall argue in Chapter 3 that the capabilities approach can do better. Because it begins from a conception of the person as a social animal, whose dignity does not derive from an idealized rationality, it offers a more adequate conception of the full and equal citizenship of people with physical and mental impairments, and of those who care for them.

Throughout I shall discuss both physical and mental impairments, but I shall focus particularly on the latter, which challenge the theories in question in more fundamental ways. For this reason I focus here on three examples of mental impairment; but later I shall show the implications of my argument for physical impairment and disability as well. Because the practical focus of my argument will be on education, I focus on children; but of course the argument is fully general, and has related practical implications for the treatment of adults.

Impairment and disability raise two distinct problems of social justice here, both of them urgent. First, there is the issue of the fair treatment of people with impairments, many of whom need atypical social arrangements, including varieties of care, if they are to live fully integrated and productive lives. In another era, Sesha and Jamie probably would have died in infancy; if they had lived they would have been institutionalized with minimal custodial care, never getting a chance to develop their capacities for love, joy, and, in Jamie's case, substantial cognitive achievement and, probably, active citizenship.[8] Fifteen years ago, before Asperger's syndrome was recognized as a disease, Arthur would have been treated as a smart kid whose parents had messed him up emotionally. He would probably have been institutionalized, with no opportunity to learn, and they would have lived with crushing guilt. A just society, by contrast, would not stigmatize these children and stunt their development; it would support their health, education, and full participation in social and even, when possible, political life.[9]

A just society, we might think, would also look at the other side of the problem, the burdens on people who provide care for dependents. These people need many things: recognition that what they are doing is work; assistance, both human and financial; opportunities for rewarding employment and for participation in social and political life. This issue is closely connected with issues of gender justice, since most care for dependents is provided by women. Moreover, much of the work of caring for a dependent is unpaid and is not recognized by the market as work. And yet it has a large effect on the rest of such a worker's life. My sister could not hold any job that did not allow her long hours at home. That both the Bérubés and Kittays share their child-care responsibilities more equally than is typical among ambitious professionals is made possible only by the extremely flexible schedule of university teaching and writing. They also can afford a lot of help—most of it, as Kittay notes with unease, provided by women who are themselves not paid very highly and not respected by society, as they should be for performing an expert and vital social service.[10]

These problems cannot be ignored or postponed on the grounds that they affect only a small number of people. That would be a bad reason to postpone them anyway, given that they raise pressing issues of equality, just as it would be bad to postpone issues of racial or religious subordination on the ground that they affect only a small minority. But we should acknowledge, as well, that disability and dependency come in many forms. It is not only the wide range of children and adults with lifelong impairments who need extensive and even hourly care from others. The mental, physical, and social impairments that I have just described all have rough parallels in the conditions of the elderly, who are generally even more difficult to care for than children and young adults with disabilities, more angry, defensive, and embittered, less physically pleasant to be with. Washing the body of a child with Down syndrome seems vastly easier to contemplate than washing the incapacitated and incontinent body of a parent who hates being in such a condition, especially when both the washer and the washed remember the parent's prime. So the way we think about the needs of children and adults with impairments and disabilities is not a special department of life, easily cordoned off from the "average case." It also has implications for the way "normals" (people with average flaws and limitations)[11] think about their parents as they age— and about the needs they themselves are likely to have if they live long enough.[12] As the life span increases, the relative independence that many people sometimes enjoy looks more and more like a temporary condition, a phase of life that we move into gradually and all too quickly begin to leave. Even in our prime, many of us encounter shorter or longer periods of extreme dependency on others—after surgery or a severe injury, or during a period of depression or acute mental stress.[13] Although a theoretical analysis may attempt to distinguish phases of a "normal" life from lifelong impairment, the distinction in real life is hard to draw, and is becoming harder all the time.[14]

But if we recognize the continuity between the situation of people with lifelong impairments and phases of "normal" lives, we must also recognize that the problem of respecting and including people with impairments, and the correlative problem of providing care for people with impairments and disabilities, are vast, affecting virtually every family in every society. There are a lot of people whose health, participation, and self-respect are at stake in the choices we make in this area. Meeting these needs in a way that protects the dignity of the recipients would seem to be one of the important jobs of a just society.

At the same time, there is also a vast amount of care work being done, usually without pay and without public recognition that it is work. Arranging for such care in a way that does not exploit the caregiver would also seem to be a central job of a just society.[15] At one time it used to be assumed that all this work would be done by people (specifically, women) who were not full citizens anyway and did not need to work outside the home. Women were not asked whether they would do this work: it was just theirs to do, and it was assumed that they did it by choice, out of love, even though they usually had few choices in the matter. Now we think that women are equal citizens and are entitled to pursue the full range of occupations. We also generally think that they are entitled to a real choice about whether they will do a disproportionate amount of child care or assume the burden of caring for an elderly parent. Nor would most people say, if asked, that the accident of giving birth to a child with severe impairments should blight all prospects, for the parents or one parent, of living a productive personal and social life. But the realities of life in nations that still assume (as to some extent all modern nations do) that this work will be done for free, "out of love," still put enormous burdens on women across the entire economic spectrum, diminishing their productivity and their contribution to civic and political life.[16] Ordinary child care is still disproportionately done by women, since women are far more likely than men to accept part-time work and the career detours it requires. Fathers who agree to help care for a child who will soon go off to school, moreover, are much less likely to shoulder the taxing long-term burden of care for an extremely impaired child or parent. In some nations, a woman who does such work usually can count on some support from an extended family or community network; in others, she cannot.

ii. Prudential and Moral Versions of the Contract; Public and Private

What have theories of justice in the social contract tradition said about these problems? Virtually nothing. Nor can the omission be easily corrected, for it is built into the structure of our strongest theories.

Some versions of the social contract (Hobbes, Gauthier) begin from egoistic rationality alone; morality emerges (to the extent that it does) from the constraints of having to bargain with others who are similarly situated. Rawls's version, by contrast, adds a representation of moral impartiality in the form of the Veil of Ignorance, which restricts the parties' information about their place in the future society. Thus, although Rawls's parties themselves pursue their own well-being, with no interest in the interests of others,[17] the parties are explicitly not intended as models of whole people, but only as models of parts of people. The other part, the moral part, is supplied by the informational constraints of the Veil. In both the egoistic and the moralized versions of the social contract, though, the idea that the parties are roughly equal in power and capacity plays a very important structural role in setting up the bargaining situation.[18] As we saw, Rawls called Hume's account of the Circumstances of Justice "the normal conditions under which human cooperation is possible and necessary" (*TJ* 126). He never ceases to endorse Hume's constraint, despite his Kantian focus on fair conditions. His theory is to this extent a hybrid,[19] Kantian in its emphasis on fair conditions and classically contractarian in its emphasis on a "state of nature" and on the goal of mutual advantage.

A rough equality of power and capacity might be modeled in

many ways. For example, we could imagine the parties to the social contract as all needy and dependent beings with strong and inelimitable ties to others. But all the major social contract thinkers choose to imagine their parties as rationally competent adults who, as Locke says, are, in the state of nature, "free, equal, and independent."[20] Contemporary contractarians explicitly adopt a related hypothesis. For David Gauthier, people of unusual need or impairment are "not party to the moral relationships grounded by a contractarian theory."[21] Similarly, the parties in Rawls's Original Position know that their abilities, physical and mental, lie within a "normal" range. And citizens in Rawls's Well-Ordered Society, for whom the parties in the Original Position are trustees, are "fully cooperating members of society over a complete life."

This emphasis is built deeply into the logic of the contract situation: the idea is that people will get together with others and contract for basic political principles only in certain circumstances, circumstances in which they can expect mutual benefit and in which all stand to gain from the cooperation. To include in the initial situation people who are unusually expensive or who can be expected to contribute far less than most to the well-being of the group (less than the amount defined by the idea of the "normal," whose use in Rawls we shall study shortly) would run contrary to the logic of the whole exercise. If people are making a cooperative arrangement for mutual advantage, they will want to get together with those from cooperation with whom they may expect to gain, not those who will demand unusual and expensive attention without contributing anything much to the social product, thus depressing the level of society's well-being. As Gauthier frankly acknowledges, this is an unpleasant feature of contract theories that people do not like to mention.[22] Thus the very idea of such a contract leads strongly in the direction of distinguishing between "normal" variations among "normally productive" citizens and the sort of variation that puts some people into a special category of impairment,[23] a move that Rawls explicitly endorses.

Now of course we immediately want to say that people with impairments and related disabilities are not unproductive. They contribute to society in many ways, when society creates conditions in which they may do so. So social contract theorists are just wrong about the facts; if they correct their false factual assumption, they can fully include people with impairments and their unusual needs, mitigating the disabilities associated with these impairments. A defense of social contract theory along these lines is, however, doomed to failure.

Before I turn to a closer consideration of Rawls's theory, let me raise one issue that I shall not treat in full. The very idea of contracting for principles that will govern a public culture is likely to be associated with a neglect of some pressing issues of justice involved in care for dependents, for the following reason. Traditionally, in the history of Western political thought,[24] the realm of contract is taken to be a public realm, characterized by reciprocity among rough equals. This realm is standardly contrasted with another realm, the so-called private realm, or the home, in which people do things out of love and affection rather than mutual respect, contractual relations are not in place, and equality is not a central value. The bonds of family love and the activities that flow from them are imagined as somehow precontractual or natural, not part of what the parties themselves are designing. Even Rawls uses the standard expression "natural affections" to characterize the sentiments that obtain in the family.

By now, however, it is widely acknowledged that the family is itself a political institution that is defined and shaped in fundamental ways by laws and social institutions.[25] Indeed, it should also be clear (and it was already clear to the great John Stuart Mill) that the sentiments it contains are themselves far from natural: they are shaped in many ways by social background conditions and by the expectations and necessities that these impose. None of the thinkers in the social contract tradition gets far in the direction of this insight, however (though in different ways both Hobbes and Rawls have pieces of it). One reason for this failure, I suggest, is the fact that their guiding metaphor for the formation of political principles is the idea of contract, traditionally associated with the ancient distinction between the public and the private realms. There is nothing in the very *idea* of a social contract that would prevent us from using it to think about the design of the family and the work done in the family. Approaches to the family using the ideas of contract and bargain have proven useful in helping us to think about issues of fairness in the relations among family members.[26] One might have thought that Rawls would move in this direction, for he acknowledges that the family is one of the institutions that form part of society's "basic structure," in that it governs people's life chances pervasively, and from the very start of life, and he repudiates the public/private distinction, at least officially. So one might think that he would consider the internal workings of the family as part of what the social compact ought to regulate, although for complex reasons he does not.[27] But, given the history of valuing the family as a realm of private love and affection to be contrasted with the realm of contract, the insight that the family is a political institution is difficult to carry through consistently. None of the theories under consideration treats the family as political in this way. All, in consequence, give very defective guidance concerning problems of justice internal to family life.[28]

iii. Rawls's Kantian Contractarianism: Primary Goods, Kantian Personhood, Rough Equality, Mutual Advantage

Let us now turn to a closer examination of Rawls's Kantian social contract theory, which I believe to be the strongest such theory we have. Rawls's theory is unusually compelling because it does not try to squeeze morality out of nonmorality, but starts from a very attractive model of the moral point of view. The combination of the prudential rationality of the parties in the Original Position with the informational restrictions imposed by the Veil of Ignorance is intended to give us a schematic representation of a moral position that real people can occupy at any time, if they can sufficiently ignore the pressing claims of their own interests. As Rawls says in the stirring final sentence of *A Theory of Justice,* "Purity of heart, if one could attain it, would be to see clearly and to act with grace and self-command from this point of view" (587).[29] Rawls's conception is surely more promising than Gauthier's if we are looking for good answers to our questions about justice for the mentally disabled.

Rawls's theory, however, is also a hybrid theory. Its Kantian elements are sometimes in tension with its classical social-contract elements. We should be prepared to locate these tensions, and to ask, in the case of each problem we find, what element in the theory is its source and what elements, by contrast, we might draw on to mitigate the problem. The four problematic areas that we must probe are the theory's use of income and wealth to index relative social positions, its use of a Kantian conception of the person and of reciprocity, and its commitments to the Circumstances of Justice and to the idea of mutual advantage as what makes cooperation superior to noncooperation.

We should mention a fifth issue as well: Rawls's deep commitment to methodological simplicity and economy. This commitment shapes the treatment of primary goods. But it also affects the shape of his contractarianism in more general ways, for example by leading him to exclude benevolent motivations from the Original Position. The reason he gives for refusing to go along with Locke at this point, including benevolence, is that we want to "insure that the principles of justice do not depend on strong assumptions . . . At the basis of the theory, one tries to assume as little as possible" (*TJ* 129). I shall return to this point later, in discussing the need for benevolence.

Now let us turn to Rawls's explicit treatment of disability, asking how each of these aspects of the theory figures in his arguments for postponing the issue to the "legislative stage," after society's basic principles are already designed.

iv. Postponing the Question of Disability

Rawls's contracting parties are imagined throughout as rational adults, roughly similar in need, and capable of a "normal" level of social cooperation and productivity. In *Political Liberalism* as in *A Theory of Justice*, Rawls stipulates that the parties in the Original Position know that their "various native endowments such as strength and intelligence" lie "all within the normal range" (25). In *PL*, moreover, they represent citizens who are described as "fully cooperating members of society over a complete life" or "normal and fully cooperating members of society over a complete life" (20, 21, 183, and elsewhere). Again, he insists: "I have assumed throughout and shall continue to assume, that while citizens do not have equal capacities, they do have, at least to the essential minimum degree, the moral, intellectual, and physical capacities that enable them to be fully cooperating members of society over a complete life" (183). The "fundamental question of political philosophy," in his theory, is "how to specify the fair terms of cooperation among persons so conceived" (ibid.). The assumption of normal capacities thus enables us "to achieve a clear and uncluttered view of what, for us, is the fundamental question of political justice: namely, what is the most appropriate conception of justice for specifying the terms of social cooperation between citizens regarded as free and equal, and as normal and fully cooperating members of society over a complete life?" (20).[30]

In so conceiving of persons, Rawls omits from the situation of basic political choice the more extreme forms of need and dependency that human beings may experience, both physical and mental, and both permanent and temporary. This is no oversight: it is deliberate design. As we shall see, Rawls recognizes the problem posed by the inclusion of citizens with unusual impairments, but he argues that this problem should be solved at a later stage, after basic political principles are already chosen.

This postponement makes a large difference to his theory of political distribution. For his account of the primary goods, introduced, as it is, as an account of the needs of citizens who are characterized by the two moral powers and by the capacity to be "fully cooperating," has no place for the unusual social arrangements that will need to be made in order to include as fully as possible people with physical and mental impairments. Prominent among these social arrangements is the kind of care we give to people in times of unusual dependency.[31] But other central matters are also affected: for the theory's understandings of liberty, opportunity, and the social bases of self-respect are all keyed to the needs of the "fully cooperating" citizen. Thus the unusual needs of citizens with impairments and associated disabilities—needs for special educational treatment, for the redesign of public space (wheelchair ramps, wheelchair access on buses, tactile signage, and so on)—do not seem to be included at this initial stage, when basic political principles are chosen. Rawls makes it clear that he understands the concept of the "fully cooperating" in a way that excludes people with severe physical and mental impairments. All the unusual needs of people with disabilities, then, will be considered only after society's basic structure has already been designed.

Now of course Rawls is perfectly aware that his theory focuses on some cases and leaves others to one side. He insists that, although the need for care for people who are not "fully cooperating" in his sense is "a pressing practical question," it may reasonably be postponed to the legislative stage, after basic political institutions are designed:

> So let's add that all citizens are fully cooperating members of society over the course of a complete life. This means that everyone has sufficient intellectual powers to play a normal part in society, and no one suffers from unusual needs that are especially difficult to fulfill, for example, unusual and costly medical requirements. Of course, care for those with such requirements is a pressing practical question. But at this initial stage, the fundamental problem of social justice arises between those who are full and active and morally conscientious participants in society, and directly or indirectly associated together throughout a complete life. Therefore, it is sensible to lay aside certain difficult complications. If we can work out a theory that covers the fundamental case, we can try to extend it to other cases later. Plainly a theory that fails for the fundamental case is of no use at all.   (DL 546)

Similarly, in *PL* he states:

> Since we begin from the idea of society as a fair system of cooperation, we assume that persons as citizens have all the capacities that enable them to be cooperating members of society. This is done to achieve a clear and uncluttered view of what, for us, is the fundamental question of political justice: namely, what is the most appropriate conception of justice for specifying the terms of

social cooperation between citizens regarded as free and equal, and as normal and fully cooperating members of society over a complete life?

By taking this as the fundamental question we do not mean to say, of course, that no one ever suffers from illness and accident; such misfortunes are to be expected in the ordinary course of life, and provision for these contingencies must be made. But given our aim, I put aside for the time being these temporary disabilities and also permanent disabilities or mental disorders so severe as to prevent people from being cooperating members of society in the usual sense.   (20)

Shortly after this passage, he again speaks of persons as "normal and fully cooperating," and then mentions, as a problem not dealt with in his conception of justice as so far developed, "the question of what is owed to those who fail to meet this condition, either temporarily (from illness and accident) or permanently, all of which covers a variety of cases" (21). Later, similarly, he draws a sharp distinction between variations in capacity that place people "above" or "below" a "line," drawn between those who have "more" and those who have "less than the minimum essential capacities required to be a normal cooperating member of society" (183). The sort of variation that puts people above this "line" is, he now says, accommodated in the theory as described, especially by its ideas of fair equality of opportunity and free competition; the sort that puts some people below the "line" will be dealt with only later, at the legislative stage, "when the prevalence and kinds of these misfortunes are known and the costs of treating them can be ascertained and balanced along with total government expenditure" (184).

So: it is clear enough that Rawls believes that we can adequately design basic political principles without taking "abnormal" impairments, either physical or mental and either temporary or permanent, into account, and, therefore, without taking them into account when asking what primary goods should be on the list of things that any citizen possessed of the two moral powers could be presumed to want. It also seems clear that he equates the distinction between the "normal" and the atypically impaired with that between the fully cooperating and those who cannot be fully cooperating—even though one might argue that many impairments will not yield functional disabilities if the social context can be sufficiently altered. The conceptual terrain is thus blurry, but it seems reasonable to conclude that the people whose unusual needs Rawls wants to postpone include people who are blind, deaf, wheelchair users, people who have severe mental illnesses (including severe depression), and people with severe cognitive and other developmental impairments, such as those of Arthur, Jamie, and Sesha. Moreover, the exclusion extends to those who have such conditions temporarily.

We must now pose two questions. First, *why* does Rawls think that we need to defer these cases, and what part in his decision is played by each of the four problematic aspects of his theory? Second, is he correct to think that a Kantian social contract theory like his must defer these cases?

Although ultimately we shall focus on people with mental impairments, who pose the most daunting challenge to Rawls's theory, we do well to begin with the apparently simpler case of physical impairment: lifelong impairment first, then temporary impairment. It might seem that Rawls has just made a mistake when he says that his theory cannot handle such cases. An advocate for people with such impairments might reply: People who are blind, deaf, and in wheelchairs have the mental and moral powers described in your theory. Anyone might be such a person, so it seems arbitrary for the parties in the Original Position to deny themselves knowledge of their race, class, and sex, but to permit themselves knowledge that their physical abilities fall within the so-called normal range. Moreover, the case of citizens who are deaf, blind, and wheelchair-users is much closer to the cases of race and sex than people usually think. For people with impairments of this sort can usually be highly productive members of society in the usual economic sense, performing a variety of jobs at a sufficiently high level, if only society adjusts its background conditions to include them. Their relative lack of productivity under current conditions is not "natural"; it is the product of discriminatory social arrangements. People in wheelchairs can get around just fine, and do their work, so long as buildings have ramps, buses have wheelchair access, and so on. People who are blind can work more or less anywhere in these days of varied audio technology and tactile signage, if the workplace includes these technologies. People who are deaf can take advantage of e-mail in place of the telephone, and of the many other visual technologies—again, so long as workplaces structure themselves so as to include such persons. Just as it is sex discrimination not to provide women with pregnancy leave, even though it is a biological fact that only women get pregnant, so, too, it is discrimination against people with impairments not to provide such supports for their productivity, even though it is a biological fact that only they will need them. So: let the parties in the Original Position not know what physical impairment they may or may not have; then, and only then, will the resulting principles be truly fair to people with such impairments.

Why is Rawls unable to accept this apparently reasonable suggestion? I see three reasons, all woven deeply into his theory. The first reason derives from his doctrine of primary goods. By admitting people with physical impairments and related disabilities into the calculation of needs for primary goods, Rawls would lose a simple and straightforward way of measuring who is the least well-off in society, a determination that he needs to make for purposes of thinking about material distribution and redistribution, and which he now makes with reference to income and wealth alone (after guaranteeing the priority of liberty). If the state of one's body in relation to one's social environment is now seen to be a highly variable primary good, then it will be possible for A to be less well-off than B in the sense that matters for well-being, even though A and B have exactly the same income and wealth. This, indeed, is the point that Sen has repeatedly made in recommending a focus on capabilities as a substitute for a list of primary goods: a person who uses a wheelchair may have the same income and wealth as a person with "normal" mobility, and yet be much less well-off in terms of ability to get around. I shall discuss Sen's proposed solution later as well, since it implicates more than one aspect of Rawls's theory. Here I focus only on the relation of Sen's proposal to the doctrine of primary goods.[32]

Rawls clearly sees the attraction in conceiving of primary goods as a multivalued list of capabilities; he treats Sen's proposal with sympathy. And yet he ultimately rejects it. One reason for the rejection clearly derives from his commitment to measuring relative social positions in a single and linear way, with reference to income and wealth alone. In arguing for the Difference Principle he attaches considerable importance to the ability to rank in a definite and unilinear way who is well-off and not well-off. If the measures were plural and heterogeneous, then it would be unclear who is least well-off, and the whole argument for the Difference Principle would be thrown into jeopardy.

This particular problem, then, what we might call the "disability/primary-goods problem," is closely connected to Rawls's specific use of primary goods to index relative social positions in arguing for the Difference Principle. I believe that Rawls already runs into considerable difficulty when he opts for a single linear measure for relative social positions. For he insists that self-respect (or rather its social basis) is "the most important" of the primary goods.[33] And yet, when it comes to measuring who is least well-off in a society, Rawls ignores self-respect, measuring social positions in terms of income and wealth alone. Certain basic liberties and opportunities have been taken care of already; but self-respect has not. It seems perfectly possible, however, for a society to contain a group of persons who are the least well-off in terms of this primary good, and yet not so badly off in terms of wealth and income. One could argue, for example, that gays and lesbians in the United States were in this position in the era before *Lawrence v. Texas* (2003), when their private sex acts could be criminalized; perhaps, given the opposition to gay marriage, they are still in that position. So Rawls has already suggested that we have reason to prefer an analysis of relative social positions that is complex and multivalued, although he himself ultimately refuses such an analysis. If he had moved in this direction, he would have had to face two further problems: first, how to balance one such good against another without giving way to the sort of "intuitionistic" balancing to which he is resolutely opposed; second, how to think about social productivity in new multivalued terms, something that might have consequences for the whole design of the initial choice situation.

The use of primary goods for purposes of indexing relative social positions, while important to Rawls, does not seem to be a necessary part of a contractarian doctrine of his sort. For one might have argued that the parties in the Original Position would favor an ample social minimum rather than the Difference Principle.[34] In this case they would not need to appeal to primary goods for purposes of comparison, least of all a single-valued comparison. Although they would still need some analogue of primary goods in order to know what the social principles are distributing, they might employ a multivalued list of entitlements, and they would not even need to conceive of the primary goods as items easily quantifiable, such as income and wealth. (The list of capabilities that I shall be defending could figure as an account of primary goods in such a theory, as Sen long ago proposed.) So far, then, we have not seen any reason why a theory both contractarian and Kantian in nature could not acknowledge the fact that income and wealth are not good proxies for important social goods such as mobility and social inclusion. To the extent that Rawls's postponement of the issue of disability grows out of the disability/primary-goods worry, such a contractarian could easily reject the postponement.

The second reason why Rawls cannot accept the apparently reasonable proposal that the parties in the Original Position should be ignorant of their physical and mental abilities and disabilities, however, grows directly out of his adherence to the social contract tradition. The parties in the Original Position (as Rawls actually designs it) know general facts about the world, and they know, therefore, that some impairments, for example back trouble, are very common and that others, for example blindness and deafness, are much less common. The very idea of the "normal," employed in the definition of them and their abilities, insofar as they know them, is just this idea of statistical frequency. And of course in all societies these facts of statistical frequency determine the shape of public and private space and the general nature of daily life. It is not that "normals" do not have bodily impairments, such as mortality for one, and limits of height and arm span, and weak backs, and hearing that catches only some of the frequencies that exist.[35] But we do not find our workplaces relying on equipment that produces sounds inaudible to human ears and audible only to dog ears; nor do we find in them staircases with steps so high that only the giants of Brobdingnag could climb them. Public space is arranged to cater to the impairments of the "normal" case. What is different about people who are blind and deaf and wheelchair-users is that their abilities are typically not catered for, because they are impaired in an unusual way. When they are allowed to compete on a playing field that is not thus slanted against them, things are indeed different: thus, wheelchair times in marathons are always much shorter than times for people using their legs. If someone objects that a wheelchair is a prosthesis, we can then observe that "normals" routinely use prostheses, such as cars and buses, and that public space is also arranged to cater to these prostheses. It is not arranged to cater to those used by the atypically disabled. We pave roads, we create bus routes, often failing at the same time to create wheelchair ramps and wheelchair access on buses. Certainly we do not require that "normals" demonstrate an ability to perform all work-related activities without mechanical assistance in order to regard them as "productive." Public space is an artifact of ideas about inclusion. By maintaining the streets in one way and not in another, we exclude a person who is highly competent and "productive" but who happens to be blind, as eminent legal scholar Jacobus tenBroek observed in his famous article "The Right to Be in the World: The Disabled and the Law of Torts."[36]

The real issue for the contractarian, however, is the relative rarity of the non-"normal" impairments (defined *as* not "normal" just by reference to their relative rarity); this rarity entails that expensive and difficult arrangements will have to be made to make work and public space fully accessible to people who have them, enabling them to be "normally" productive. Such expenditures, in general, greatly outweigh the return in economic productivity made possible by the full inclusion of people with "abnormal" impairments, because they involve redesigning facilities for all, for the sake of the needs of a very small number of people. Thus, as Gauthier makes explicit, such arrangements are not mutually advantageous in the economic sense. Such is not the case with arrangements ending discrimination on grounds of race and sex, which can at least be argued to be economically efficient, because they include in the workforce, without expensive redesigning,[37] a large group of productive workers who might otherwise not be included.[38] So even if we concede to the disability advocate that workers with impairments outside the "normal" range can be highly productive, it is unlikely that anyone could show that in general their economic productivity offsets the costs of fully including them. Here we really do have a choice: cooperation and full inclusion, or noncooperation (with extensive charity at a later stage). Rawls's original account of why cooperation is preferable to noncooperation relies on an idea of mutual advantage that is associated with his account of "normal" social cooperation. I believe that Rawls cannot explain why the ones below the "line" are owed justice rather than charity, without fundamentally modifying this aspect of his theory.

The social contract thinker will now add a third point. Although people who are blind, deaf, and wheelchair-users can be highly productive workers if their circumstances are right, it is implausible to think that this is generally true of all persons with physical impairments. Some impairments greatly interfere with life functioning, and thus seem to be disabilities in many if not most social environments. (Indeed, that criterion, interference with a "major life function," is used in the Americans with Disabilities Act in order to define disability.) Among those that so interfere, at least some will be difficult to accommodate in such a way as to make the worker fully productive in the usual sense. So even if the case for full inclusion of some workers with impairments could be made by appeal to expected economic productivity, such an argument would surely not cover all cases of physical impairments.

Here we see the naked face of the contract idea. Moralize the starting point as we may, the bottom line is that the whole point of departing from the state of nature is to reap benefits from mutual cooperation, and the benefits are defined by all such theorists in a quite familiar economic way. Such a picture of cooperation is intimately linked to the idea that we must restrict the initial group of bargainers to those who have "normal" productive capacities. It is no trivial matter for the contractarian who is "in" and who is "out" at this initial stage, for, as David Gauthier says, our society now has medical technologies "that make possible an ever-increasing transfer of benefits to persons who decrease [the average level of well-being]." And so he insists, plausibly enough, that the atypically disabled must be excluded from the start: "Speaking euphemistically of enabling them to live productive lives, when the services required exceed any possible products, conceals an issue which, understandably, no one wants to face . . . Such persons are not party to the moral relationships grounded by a contractarian theory."[39]

Rawls's theory displays a deep tension at this point. On the one hand, one of its central purposes is to give questions of justice priority over questions of efficiency. The idea that each person is an end lies at the core of the theory. And of course this Kantian core is thoroughly embedded in the Original Position, in the sense that once the deliberation is under way, it is structured in such a way that the parties may not pursue overall well-being in a way that is unfair to any individual. On the other hand, the account of why the parties prefer cooperation to non-cooperation, and what they are pursuing, is still a classical social contract account, with Hume's account of the Circumstances of Justice taking the place of the state of nature. The structural feature of rough equality and the goal of mutual advantage still shape the account of who is initially included and what each party is trying to get out of cooperating. We cannot extend the core idea of inviolability and the related idea of reciprocity to people with severe physical and mental impairments without calling these features into question, and thus, in effect, severing ties with the classical social contract tradition.

Rawls is well aware of this point. That is why he mentions, as one of the questions that is difficult for his theory to answer, "what is owed to" people who fail to meet the condition of being "normal and fully cooperating members of society over a complete life . . . either temporarily (from illness and accident) or permanently, all of which covers a variety of cases." Recall that he says of this and the other three problems under discussion, "While we would like eventually to answer all these questions, I very much doubt whether that is possible within the scope of justice as fairness as a political conception" (*PL* 21). Moreover, although he expresses optimism with respect to two of the problems (justice between nations and the problem of future generations), he is pessimistic with regard to the other two (the disability question and "what is owed to animals and the rest of nature"); he calls these "problems on which justice as fairness may fail." With regard to these cases, he sees two possibilities. One is "that the idea of political justice does not cover everything, nor should we expect it to." The other possibility is that the problems are indeed problems of justice "but justice as fairness is not correct in this case, however well it may do for other cases. How deep a fault this is must wait until the case itself can be examined" (ibid.). In other words, although he does propose a way of dealing with the problem—postponing these questions to the legislative stage—he is not confident that it is a good solution to the problem. Certainly it does not treat the problem as one of basic justice, one that needs to be solved when society's basic principles are designed. I am agreeing with Rawls's second suggestion—impairment and disability do indeed raise problems of justice—and it is my hope that the analysis here will provide at least a part of the examination that will show how a theory that starts from Rawls's intuitive ideas might solve the problem.

Two questions become pressing at this point. First, why could

Rawls not simply adopt a more moralized conception of the benefits of social cooperation, one that includes the goods of inclusion, respect for human dignity, and justice itself as among the benefits the parties are seeking out of their social cooperation? Second, why could he not use the idea of insurance against accident, given that every human being, as we have insisted, faces the possibility of extreme physical impairment and disability?

The first line of reply looks very promising. In some form, it looks like just what a Kantian like Rawls ought to say. We choose to respect and include people with impairments because it is good in itself to do so, whether it is economically efficient or not. Benefit should not be understood in purely economic terms, for there is the great good of justice itself to be considered. This reply is clearly in tune with one deep strand in Rawls's thinking, and it is the sort of reply he makes often (e.g., *PL* 208), when he is talking about the idea of overlapping consensus and why the agreement of citizens in a Well-Ordered Society is no mere *modus vivendi*. But it is very unclear indeed whether Rawls could introduce this consideration into the design of the Original Position itself, giving the parties, defined as people who want to advance their own goals as far as possible, a wider set of moralized ends to consider. It was always wrong to say that Rawls's view of human nature is that people are self-interested maximizers: for, as I have insisted, the parties in the Original Position are only one part of people, the other (moral) part being supplied by the Veil of Ignorance. But the Original Position does not allow the parties to know whether they care about others or not. Some conceptions of the good include concern for others, and other conceptions do not; they do not know what conception they have. They are presumed to be capable of a sense of justice, but they do not even apply any particular conception of justice; all they can presume is that they will all understand and conform to whatever principles they finally agree to (*TJ* 145). Far less do they know anything about their love of others and their desire to include those others. Their interests and aims are not presumed to be egoistic, but they are not presumed to be benevolent either. These dispositions are aspects of their conception of the good that they simply do not know (129). It is very important to Rawls that this is so: he argues that "[a] conception of justice should not assume . . . extensive ties of natural sentiment" (ibid.). Assumptions should be as few and as weak as possible at the basis of a theory.

Rawls's stated objection to the inclusion of broad-based benevolence in the Original Position is a theoretical one, having to do with his desire to base the theory on a small number of assumptions. A different sort of contractarian could include benevolence; Locke does so. But how wide a benevolence would ultimately be compatible with the contractarian emphasis on society as a scheme for mutual advantage? (As I suggested in Chapter 1, section v, there is a tension in Locke's theory at this point.) The benevolence that that full inclusion of people with impairments requires is extensive and deep, requiring the willingness to sacrifice not only one's own advantage, but also the advantage of the group. It means cooperating with people with whom it is both possible and advantageous not to cooperate at all. Many have even questioned whether Rawls's Difference Principle, which requires that the parties be willing to sacrifice group advantage in order to raise the position of the least well-off, is actually justified by the argument he offers, without presupposing an unrealistic degree of risk-aversion on the part of the parties. But the parties, in that argument, at least know that their productive capacities all lie within the normal range, so they can expect a return from their willingness to forgo a group advantage. The benevolence required fully to include people with impairments is different in kind, not only in degree. So even if Rawls were to waive his theoretical objection to benevo-lence, it seems unlikely that he could include the right sort of benevolence without ceasing to hold that mutual advantage is the goal of cooperation (as opposed to non-cooperation) in the Original Position.

In short: Rawls takes over from the contractarian tradition its idea of a cooperation for mutual advantage and its idea of the circumstances within which such cooperation makes sense. The inclusion of a broader list of moralized social goals would require a redesign of the rationality of the parties, since they would now have to know that they care about other people's in-terests, not only their own. This change, Rawls objects, would greatly complicate and perhaps render indeterminate the whole question of what principles would be chosen. But if the benevo-lence added were sufficiently deep and inclusive, the change would also require the approach to depart so far from the idea of a contract for mutual advantage that there would be no point to using the metaphor of the social contract at all. If the tie to the social contract tradition is not abandoned, then, given that peo-ple with severe impairments happen to be in society, their inter-ests can be considered at the later, legislative, stage. But the par-ties have to be aware, as Rawls in fact makes them aware, that they themselves are not such people. It is in effect out of charity that these interests will be considered later on, not out of basic justice.

What about the insurance idea? Even Richard Epstein, who does not favor laws protecting the rights of the disabled, notes that they are in one way very plausible. For we all recognize that we ourselves may through accident suffer an impairment, and we therefore have motivations to choose a political regime that protects us from the worst consequences of that contingency.[40] In addressing this point we must at the same time confront a related question: why does Rawls exclude from the scope of justice as fairness not only lifelong impairments but also temporary ones, which, once again, he explicitly insists on handling at the legislative stage, after basic principles have already been designed? Surely such temporary impairments, and the associated disabilities, are a paradigm of what insurance can cover.

There are two answers to this question, closely related to our analysis above. The first reply is given by Rawls in replying to Amartya Sen. He argues that taking on the question of compensation for temporary impairments that put people "below the line" complicates (as Sen explicitly says) the use of primary goods, in particular income and wealth, to rank social positions. We saw this problem earlier when we considered lifelong impairment; but it arises for the case of temporary impairment as well.[41] Rawls appears to grant to Sen that once we consider such cases, it makes sense to measure relative well-being by capabilities, not just by income and wealth. So even if an insurance scheme does seem a natural thing for the parties in the Original Position to want to design for themselves, given the general facts of human life, the theoretical costs of including this part of human life in the design of basic political principles are very great. We lose the clarity afforded by the use of income and wealth to index social positions, and we are required to shift to a much more cumbersome list of capabilities, which will inevitably generate a plurality of rankings of the well- and not-so-well-off. Social choice appears to be forced into the area of intuitionistic balancing that Rawls wants so much to avoid. Although he acknowledges the importance of the problem Sen has raised, he believes that he can postpone it to the legislative stage and that, if he can, he must, in order to have a theory with the kind of clarity and finality that he is seeking and in order to keep the argument for the Difference Principle that he has so carefully worked out.[42]

Nor is it plausible to treat temporary impairment as an isolated case in which income and wealth are bad proxies for well-being. As Sen has also insisted, variations and asymmetries in physical need are simply not isolated or easily isolable cases: they are a pervasive fact of human life: pregnant or lactating women need more nutrients than nonpregnant persons, children need more protein than adults, and the very young and very old need more care than others in most areas of their lives. Even within the clearly recognized terrain of the "fully cooperating," then, the theory of primary goods seems flawed if it does not take such variations into account in measuring who is and is not the least well-off, rather than, as the theory recommends, determining that status by income and wealth alone. The problem of variation in need is pervasive. So even in order to take account of the physical needs of those (fictional) citizens who never have the type of impairment that puts them below the "line," even temporarily, Rawls will need a way of measuring well-being that does not rely on income and wealth alone, but looks at the abilities of citizens to engage in a wide range of human activities.

As we have said, this particular reason for postponing the question of disability derives from an aspect of Rawls's theory that is important to him, but not necessary to a contractarianism of his type.

The second issue raised by the insurance-against-accident idea is one that Rawls does not mention explicitly; but it is implicit in his cautious and repeated statements that we are dealing, always, with people whose abilities fall within the "normal" range. The issue is that there really is a continuum between the cases of lifelong impairment that Rawls has already postponed on contractarian grounds and the periods of impairment imposed by illness, accident, and old age. As Gauthier says, we are living in an age in which medicine makes it more and more possible to maintain people who are not "productive." And although Rawls uses the term "normal" and speaks of a "line," of course he is aware that the "line" is arbitrary, and that there is more similarity between the lifelong-impaired person and a person who becomes paralyzed at age twenty and remains so, than there is between this latter person and a person who has a severe illness for a week and then returns to "normal" functioning. Some people may live longer with a "temporary" impairment than the person with a lifelong impairment lives at all. So it seems arbitrary to include the temporarily impaired and not to include the whole class of people with lifelong impairments. Especially as more people live longer into old age, with its myriad and long-lasting impairments and disabilities, the continuity between one group and the other becomes very great. But this continuity means that thinking about social productivity even with regard to temporary impairment requires complicated individualized calculations. As Epstein says, thinking about insurance well requires considering factors such as the probability that any person will become impaired, the alternative uses of the same resources, the level of support required, and, of course, the productivity of each type of impaired person under varying levels of support. Whether insurance of various types is efficient will depend on these empirical issues, which vary over time. This looks like a good reason for Rawls to leave them to the legislative stage.

This reason for postponement, unlike the previous one, derives directly from the logic of Rawls's social contract theory. The reason why individualized calculations would have to be made is that we would need to figure out whether insurance is efficient in economic terms, and to what extent it is efficient. But we need to think about efficiency at the point of framing basic principles of justice and inclusion only because we are envisaging society as a scheme of cooperation for mutual advantage. To include an ample commitment to insurance among the principles chosen in the Original Position would compromise that goal, and it would be impossible to tell *ex ante* whether a society including ample insurance would be able to deliver that goal at all.

But the postponement is not innocent, clearly. The parties are being asked to imagine themselves as if they represent citizens who really are "fully cooperating . . . over a complete life," and thus as if citizens have no needs for care in times of extreme dependency. This fiction obliterates much that characterizes human life, and obliterates, as well, the continuity between the so-called normal and people with lifelong impairments. It skews the choice of primary goods, concealing the fact that health care and other forms of care are, for real people, central goods making well-being possible; for the reasons given by Sen, income and wealth are not good proxies for these goods. More generally, care for children, elderly people, and people with mental and physical disabilities is a major part of the work that needs to be done in any society, and in most societies it is a source of great injustice. Any theory of justice needs to think about the problem from the beginning, in the design of the basic institutional structure, and particularly in its theory of the primary goods.[43]

v. Kantian Personhood and Mental Impairment

So far, then, the problems facing Rawls's theory derive from his particular use of the notion of primary goods and also from his social contract commitments to the twin ideas of "rough equality" and mutual advantage, not from his Kantianism. Indeed, as I have suggested, in this area the Kantian emphasis of the theory is in tension with the contract doctrine. Kantianism requires treating every person as an end, and does not allow the subordination of any individual to the cause of general social well-being. Furthermore, Kantian citizens, in the Well-Ordered

Society, clearly do think of justice and respect as intrinsic goods, and their concept of the benefits of social cooperation is a rich, multivalued one. Kantian citizens could see, *ex post,* good reasons for having accorded people with impairments full respect and inclusion; the problem is that *ex ante,* in the Original Position, the social contract framework prevents this route from being chosen.

Now, however, we must consider the issue of severe mental impairment. All the problems that Rawls's theory has with physical impairment it has with mental impairment. But it has other problems in addition, problems that flow directly from the Kantian aspects of his theory, which in other areas seem to support respect and inclusion.

First, then, people with severe mental impairments pose acute problems for the social contract/mutual-advantage aspects of the theory. If the idea of the citizen as a productive augmenter of social well-being is strained by the inclusion of people with physical impairments, it positively breaks down when we confront it with the lives of Jamie, Sesha, and Arthur. None of the three is likely to be economically productive in a way that even begins to compensate society for the expense it incurs in educating them. Jamie will probably be able to hold some kind of job, and perhaps to play a role in political life; but one can be sure that he will not "repay" in the economic sense the vast medical and educational expenses he has incurred.[44] If the course of his education goes well, Arthur might hold a job that is commensurate with his high intelligence, and thus be "productive" in the economic sense, but the likelihood of this happy outcome is uncertain. Meanwhile he is costing the state in which he lives a good deal for private education, and his medical expenses are also a large social cost. For Sesha, not even this limited chance of a "return" for the expense of caring for her will ever be possible.

Such cases strip contractarianism bare, so to speak, and reveal a face often concealed by the moralized elements present in the strongest such doctrines. Now obviously there are limits to any program of social benefit. At the margins, there are indeed questions to be asked about how much the state should invest in Arthur's special education, for example. But the point of a cooperation that includes Arthur, Jamie, and Sesha, and seeks both to educate them and to support their development with appropriate care, should not be seen in terms of mutual advantage alone as that idea is traditionally understood. That question seems to be the wrong one to start from, and the wrong account of the primary basis for social cooperation. The benefit to society of interacting with Jamie, Arthur, and Sesha and fully supporting them is multifaceted and diffuse. It includes, in the first instance, what John Stuart Mill called "the advantage of having one of the most universal and pervading of all human relations regulated by justice instead of injustice"[45]—only here we are talking not about marriage and the family, as Mill was, but about the relations of care in which all human beings in some ways, at some times, and to some degree stand. It includes, that is, the advantage of respecting the dignity of people with mental disabilities and developing their human potential, whether or not this potential is socially "useful" in the narrower sense. It includes, as well, the advantage of understanding humanity and its diversity that comes from associating with mentally disabled people on terms of mutual respect and reciprocity. (Bérubé argues cogently that the other children who go to school with Jamie get at least as much out of his presence in a "normal" classroom as he derives from being there.) It includes new insight about the dignity of the aging and of ourselves as we age. And of course it includes the value of all the aforementioned interactions and relationships for people with mental disabilities themselves, who without special social support would live, as they once did, isolated and stigmatized lives. Even though the advocate for the physically disabled pressed for an understanding of these citizens as "productive," that did not seem to be a fully adequate reply even for these cases. When we reach the case of mental disability, we see with utter clarity the extent to which the idea of mutual advantage distorts our understanding of the benefits of social cooperation.

In the case of physical disability there is, we have said, a pull in the other direction in Rawls's theory, in the form of his Kantian doctrine of reciprocity. Where people with mental disabilities are concerned, however, this very doctrine is the source of yet further difficulties. As we have seen, this doctrine is articulated in terms of a Kantian conception of the person, which makes possession of the mental and moral powers central both to equality and to the key idea of reciprocity. Given its Kantian flavor, the conception at least suggests the idea of a split between moral personality and animality. We should therefore begin our critical examination of Rawls's theory by setting out clearly some problematic aspects of the Kantian split, so that we can see to what extent Rawls's theory suffers from those problems.

Kant's conception of the person lies in a long tradition that goes straight back to the Greek and Roman Stoics, in which personhood is identified with reason (including, prominently, the capacity for moral judgment), and in which reason, so construed, is taken to be a feature of human beings that sets them sharply apart from nonhuman animals and from their own animality. For the Stoics, there is a sharp split, not only between humans and other animals, but also between human life when moral rationality gets going and human life at other times (including, in their view, childhood up to adolescence).[46] Although the Stoics were aware of theories (Platonist, Aristotelian, Epicurean) that saw considerable continuity between human capacity and the capacities of other animals, they themselves insisted on a very sharp division. Indeed, their most common way of articulating the idea of the characteristically human is to suggest that it is what raises us above "the beasts." Pejorative remarks about animals frequently substitute for argument in their accounts of human nature and human dignity.

Kant's theory takes the split even further. Stoics were compatibilists, who saw the realm of human freedom as also, at the very same time, a realm of nature that follows deterministic laws. Whether rightly or not, they believed that we do not need to exempt human freedom from natural laws in order to value it as we ought. Kant, of course, does not agree, and thus is led to think of the human being as a fundamentally split being who dwells in two realms: the realm of natural necessity and the realm of rational/moral freedom. He thinks of all nonhuman animals, and the animal side of human life, as belonging to the deterministic realm of nature. It is in virtue of our capacity for moral rationality, and that alone, that we rise above that realm and exist, as well, in a realm of ends. Therefore, for Kant, human dignity and our moral capacity, dignity's source, are radically separate from the natural world. Insofar as we exist merely in the realm of nature, we are not ends in ourselves and do not have a dignity; things in that realm simply have a price (as Kant puts it, *pretium usus*). Insofar as we enter the realm of ends, thus far, and thus far alone, we have dignity and transcend price. Morality certainly has the task of providing for human neediness, but the person, seen as the rational/moral aspects of the human being, is the goal of these ministrations. Animality itself is not an end. In keeping with this view, Kant denies that we have any moral duties to animals; they have no independent value, only a "relative value" in relation to human ends.[47] What is true of animals is bound to be true of all beings who lack the rather complex capacity for moral and prudential reasoning that in Kant's view is characteristic of mature human beings.

The Kantian split between personhood and animality is deeply problematic. First, it denies a fact that ought to be evident to one who thinks clearly about this issue: namely, the fact that our dignity just is the dignity of a certain sort of animal. It is the animal sort of dignity, and that very sort of dignity could not be possessed by a being who was not mortal and vulnerable, just as the beauty of a cherry tree in bloom could not be possessed by a diamond. If it makes sense to think of God or angels (Kant's other rational beings) as having dignity (magnificence and awe-inspiringness seem more appropriate attributes), it is emphatically not dignity of that type.[48] To put things more mundanely, if we imagine a being who is purely rational and moral, but without animal neediness and animal capacities (and science fiction provides us with some good examples of such beings), we see, I believe, that the dignity of such a being, whatever it is, is not the same sort of dignity as the dignity of a human being, who is characterized throughout life, as Marx put it, by "rich human need," prominently including needs for other people.

Second, the split wrongly denies that animality can itself have a dignity. Thus it leads us to slight aspects of our own lives that have worth, and to distort our relation to the other animals.

Third, the Kantian split at least suggests the idea that the core of our personality is self-sufficient rather than needy, and purely active rather than also passive. In so thinking we greatly distort the nature of our own morality and rationality, which are themselves thoroughly material and animal; we learn to ignore the fact that disease, old age, and accident can impede the moral and rational functions, just as much as the other animal functions.

Fourth, the split makes us think of the core of ourselves as atemporal, since moral agency (in the Kantian view) looks like something that does not grow, mature, and decline, but rather like something that is utterly removed, in its dignity, from these natural events. Thinking in this way, we may forget that the usual human life cycle brings with it periods of extreme dependency, in which our functioning is very similar to that experienced by people with mental or physical disabilities throughout their lives.

It is important to notice that the split goes wrong in both directions: it suggests, as I have said, that our rationality is independent of our vulnerable animality; and it also suggests that animality and nonhuman animals lack intelligence, are just brutish and "dumb." Both implications of the split should be called into question: in nature we find a rich continuum of types of intelligence, and practical capacities of many types; we cannot understand ourselves well without situating ourselves within that continuum.

Rawls does not endorse the metaphysical elements of Kant's position, although he does elsewhere show a deep interest in them.[49] He does not subscribe to a two-world view, and he understands his Kantianism as empirical. Nonetheless, by retaining a concept of the person based on Kant's, and by defining the basis of political equality in terms of the possession of moral capacity, he runs into some of the same difficulties with mental disability that Kant's theory plainly encounters. Indeed, people with severe mental impairments appear to be those "scattered individuals" (*TJ* 506) who, lacking the moral capacities to some essential minimum degree, fail to qualify for equality. Moreover, just as Kant and Rawls explicitly deny that reciprocity and relations of justice, hold between humans and nonhuman animals, so, too, they are required to hold that there is no reciprocity, in the requisite sense, between "normal" human beings and people with severe mental impairments. Rawls defines reciprocity as a relation between citizens understood in terms of the Kantian conception of the person (*PL* 16).

But if we consider the lives of people with mental impairments and those who live with them, it seems obvious that their lives involve complex forms of reciprocity. Jamie interacts in a loving, playful, and generous way both with his family and with other children. Sesha hugs those who care for her, dances with joy when they play music that she loves, and shows appreciation for the care she is given.

The area of reciprocity is precisely where Arthur's disability is located, and yet Arthur, in the context of his immediate family, is an extremely affectionate child, exchanging love and humor with his parents, his much-loved dog, his newly adopted brother, and relatives who come to visit the home. Whenever he is not frightened, and is able to trust, his capacity for affectionate exchange flourishes. Even outside the narrow circle of trust, education makes a huge difference in expanding his capacity for reciprocity. At the beginning of this chapter I described a typical telephone conversation with Arthur when he was ten. After two years of state-supported private education, things are very different. One day when he was just twelve I was talking with him and, quite of his own accord, he said, "And how are you, Aunt Martha? What are you doing?" This simple question brought tears to my eyes, such was the progress that it marked. He recently had a very successful twelfth birthday party with a group of seven other Asperger's children from his school, at a video-games arcade. These peer relationships contain genuine reciprocity, even if not of the most familiar sort.

But probably none of this would count as reciprocity in Rawls's Kantian sense. And no other type of reciprocity is recognized or given political salience. That is a large defect, it seems to me. Moreover, it is likely that neither Rawls nor Kant has devoted much thought to the question. Jamie may lack the capacity for forming a life plan and an overall conception of the good. When he was asked what he wants to be when he grows up, his father reports that, while other children gave accounts of their careers, Jamie simply said, "Big." There was insight in that answer, and the other children learned from it; but it was not an answer of the sort that would demonstrate Jamie's membership in the Kantian moral community. Arthur may or may not have the capacity for a sense of justice in Kant's sense. Sesha clearly does not have the two moral powers. Moreover, because these three citizens lack or partly lack the two moral powers, they also fail to fit in with Rawls's conception of social cooperation, which is also defined in terms of the Kantian conception of the person. Finally, they also fail to qualify for freedom in Rawls's sense, because freedom, in his theory, also has a Kantian flavor, and involves being a "self-authenticating source of valid claims" (*PL* 32).[50]

Thus people with mental impairments and disabilities pose a double challenge to Rawls's theory. The contract doctrine seems unable to accommodate their needs for special social attention, for the reasons of social productivity and cost that pertain to all people with impairments. But they are disqualified from citizenship in a deeper way as well, because they do not conform to the rather idealized picture of moral rationality that is used to define the citizen in the Well-Ordered Society. Like nonhuman animals, they are not regarded as capable of reciprocity of the requisite sort. And like animals again, they will have "some protection certainly" but not the status of full-fledged citizens.[51] Again, Rawls's own conclusion seems appropriate: either we should say that these are not issues of justice, or we should say that justice as fairness does not offer a complete account of social justice, and we should figure out what we would need to alter in order to make the theory capable of going further.

Thomas Scanlon confronts these problems facing a Kantian contract doctrine more explicitly than does Rawls. He offers two proposals that ought to be considered. Taking cognizance of the problem posed for such a theory by people with various impairments, and by nonhuman animals, Scanlon concludes that we may recognize facts of extreme dependency in such a doctrine in one of two ways. Either we may persist in our pursuit of the contract doctrine, and say that the contracting parties are also trustees for those who are incapable of participating in that process; or we may say that the contract doctrine offers an account of only one part of morality: we will need a different account to cope with the facts of extreme dependency.[52]

Scanlon's own hypothetical contract situation does not employ the Humean idea of the Circumstances of Justice, and it does not envisage the contract as one that must explain the good of social cooperation by pointing to a mutual advantage to be derived by the parties from their agreement. He is not exploring the choice of basic political principles, and his contract situation is thus not an initial situation out of which such principles may be chosen. In many ways, then, his proposal is unlike the form of social contract doctrine that I have been criticizing. Nonetheless, it seems reasonable to ask whether his proposed solution to the problem of mental impairment can be used by Rawls to avoid a postponement of all such issues to the legislative stage.

Applied to the Rawlsian project of selecting principles of justice that will form the basic structure of society,[53] then, Scanlon's disjunctive proposal is that we either take the parties in the Original Position to be (knowingly) trustees for the interests of all dependent members of society (as they currently are trustees for "normal" citizens and for future generations); or else we should grant that the Original Position, as designed, is not a complete device for generating political justice, and that other approaches are also required.

The first (trusteeship) solution is unavailable to Rawls because of his commitment to parsimony of assumptions and thus to excluding benevolence from the Original Position. While it complicates the model only a little to make the parties trustees for future generations (as well as for "normal" citizens), since trusteeship in that case does not require them to know anything about their own conceptions of the good, the present-time sort of trusteeship would require them to know that they do have benevolence and how strong it is. The trusteeship solution is probably unavailable on contract-doctrine grounds as well, since it would require them to forgo, to a rather serious extent, the expectation that the contract will generate a mutual advantage, by contrast to a perfectly possible noncooperation (later to be combined with charity). Finally, that solution seems unavailable on Kantian grounds as well, since Rawls understands justice itself in terms of Kantian reciprocity, and thus apparently denies that there are any issues of justice between people who have the Kantian moral capacities and people (or animals) who do not.

Is the trusteeship solution even satisfactory? Obviously enough, forms of guardianship and mentorship must be designed, if we are adequately to protect the legal rights of people with severe mental disabilities. But the question here is not whether we need to use guardianship to solve practical political problems. It is whether guardianship is an adequate way to imagine the citizenship of people with impairments and disabilities in the context of designing fundamental political principles, *when we have already assumed that those who design such principles are also the primary subjects of justice.*[54] Guardianship is not intrinsically incompatible with treating these people as full-fledged citizens and equal subjects of justice. In a social contract doctrine, however, it is not obvious that this equality could be adequately modeled. It is bad enough that people with mental disabilities are altogether excluded from the framing of principles, since many may be capable of active citizenship. More serious still is the fact that the group of people for whom principles are chosen is the same group as the people who choose the principles. The whole idea is to choose a way in which "we" will live together in political society. The proposal we are considering would add, "we live together and take care of our dependents." But that makes the dependents not full parts of the "we" and the "our," not fully equal subjects of political justice. They are taken into account because some member of the "we" happens to care about their interests, not because they are citizens with rights, equal ends in themselves.

Moreover, the "trustee" solution retains, and even reinforces, the troublesome features in Rawls's notions of reciprocity and social cooperation. Rather than recognizing that reciprocity has many forms in this world, the trustee solution retains the Kantian split between the rational/reasonable person and everything else in nature; only people with Kantian powers in their full-fledged "normal" form can be fully included, and party to the social contract, even though people with Down syndrome, for example, might actually be perfectly capable of performing many functions of citizenship on their own. They, like many people with mental disabilities, are worthy of concern only derivatively, in relation to those parties' interests. In addition to being an unfortunate way to think about children and adults with mental impairments and disabilities, this conception may well prejudice "normals" when thinking about the dignity of a wide range of capabilities in themselves. Are we not in effect saying that the full range of human and animal powers will get support only insofar as it is an object of interest and concern for Kantian rational beings? And doesn't this slight the dignity and worth that needy human animals surely possess even when they are not "fully cooperating"? Surely, if it is not necessary to require such split thinking, we should avoid it.

Thus even if Rawls were able to admit the trusteeship solution, as I argue he is not, I prefer (where political principles are concerned) Scanlon's second solution, which is similar to Rawls's own second proposal in the important passage at *PL* 21: namely, to grant that the contract doctrine does not provide a complete theory. But this reply, which seems fine for Scanlon, because he is doing ethical theory, employs no hypothetical initial contract situation, and makes no claims to completeness, creates large problems for the contract doctrine in the area of political theory. Any approach to the design of basic political institutions must aim at a certain degree of comprehensiveness, attempting to cover the major entitlements of citizens. Rawls's doctrine explicitly aims at completeness and finality.[55] Even if a view (such as my capabilities view) does not aim at completeness, it ought to show that no major and fundamental entitlement of citizens has been ignored. We are designing the basic structure of society, which Rawls defines as those institutions that influence all citizens' life chances pervasively and from the start. The principles we choose will affect the entire shape of the society, including its constitutional entitlements and the understanding of how those entitlements are grounded. It is very important for Rawls (as for Gauthier) that the principles emerge from a situation that is set up on the basis of the Circumstances of Justice, in the light of the proposed advantages of social cooperation. It seems that Rawls is right in judging that there is no plausible solution to the problem of mental impairment that we can extract from his initial contract situation. And yet it seems inadequate to defer this problem, in the context of basic political theory. For it is not open to us to say: we have done one part of that task, but of course other parts, equally basic, based on completely different principles, will come along later. Such postponement will leave large areas of political justice up for grabs and will entail the recognition of much indeterminacy in the account of basic justice as so far worked out.

The problem, furthermore, is not one of incompleteness; it is one of misdirection. The list of primary goods selected by Rawls's parties omits items (above all, care, but more generally, a wide range of human capabilities) that appear absolutely central for real dependent humans of "normal" capacity, as well as for the mentally and physically disabled. The account of social cooperation and its benefits is restricted in ways that seem unfortunate, both by the contract doctrine and by the Kantian account of persons.

vi. Care and Disability: Kittay and Sen

Eva Kittay and Amartya Sen have proposed ways of reformulating Rawls's theory in order to address issues of impairment and disability. I have already suggested, discussing both Kittay and Sen, that Rawls has deep reasons for resisting proposed solutions of this type, and I have examined the exchange between Rawls and Sen on the question of primary goods. But we must now look at their proposals again, since they implicate more than one area of Rawls's theory.

Kittay's central suggestion is that we ought to add the need for care during periods of extreme and asymmetrical dependency to the Rawlsian list of primary goods, thinking of care as among the basic needs of citizens.[56] This proposal seems reasonable enough, if we are thinking of the project as simply that of making a list of the most important social benefits that any real society must distribute. Surely Kittay is right that a viable account of political justice ought to make the appropriate distribution of care one of its central goals.

But, as should by now be evident, it is no simple matter simply to add this to Rawls's list. One problem is the familiar one of heterogeneity versus linear ranking: for two people may be equally well-off with respect to income and wealth and yet one less well-off with regard to care (either because they have daunting caregiving duties or because their own needs for care are not recognized). Rawls's doctrine of primary goods gets in the way of accepting Kittay's proposal for the same reason that it prevents him from accepting Sen's.

But the reasons for rejection of the Kittay proposal do not derive from this source alone (in which case they might be addressed by a different type of Kantian contractarianism, one less committed to a single linear ranking of relative social positions). For the list of primary goods is a list of needs of citizens as characterized by the two moral powers; this already leaves out people with severe mental impairments and any people who are like them for long stretches of their life. This omission, as we said, stems from Rawls's Kantian model of the person. Without extensive modification of the political conception of the person, Rawls cannot imagine primary goods as including the needs for care that characterize citizens with severe mental impairments, whether lifelong or temporary.

Finally, the omission of care from the list of primary goods derives, as well, from Rawls's contractarian commitment to mutual advantage/rough equality. The parties are imagined as rough equals seeking mutual advantage. I have argued that these commitments preclude even a limited recognition of needs for care during periods of nonproductivity, at least when we are thinking about what parties in the Original Position would consider as they design society's basic principles. Rawls's idealizing fiction of people who are "fully cooperating . . . over a complete life" is no mere mistake that might be corrected by a longer list of primary goods.

Sen's more radical proposal, which we have briefly examined, is that the entire list of primary goods should be seen as a list of capabilities rather than a list of things.[57] His analysis starts from the fact that Rawls's list of primary goods is already quite heterogeneous in its structure. Some of its components are thing-like items such as income and wealth; but some are already more like human capabilities to function in various ways: the liberties, opportunities, and powers, and also the social basis of self-respect. This change would not only enable us to deal better with people's needs for various types of love and care as elements of the list, but would also answer the point that Sen has repeatedly made all along about the unreliability of income and wealth as indices of well-being. The relative social positions will now be measured not by the sheer amount of income and wealth they have, but by the degree to which they have the various capabilities on the list. One may be well off in terms of income and wealth, and yet unable to function well in the workplace, because of burdens of caregiving at home.

Sen's proposal offers a productive approach to the needs of citizens with impairments, as we shall see. Like Kittay's, it is no minor modification, but a change that goes to the very heart of the theory, with its commitment to an economic understanding of the benefits of cooperation and its consequent reliance on income and wealth as indicators of relative social position.[58] Rawls is wiser than Sen, not more stubborn and shortsighted, when he says that he cannot accept this suggestion, meritorious though it obviously is. Much the same should be said about my own earlier suggestion that Rawls could add other capability-like items to the list of basic goods, such as the social bases of health, imagination, and emotional well-being.[59] For Rawls is already in difficulty enough through his addition of the social bases of self-respect, which greatly strains the contract doctrine in one way, although in another way it seems to fulfill some of its deeper moral aspirations. He will be in very great difficulty, in the terms he has set for himself, if he admits this highly heterogeneous list of "primary goods," all of which seem highly relevant to the determination of relevant social positions. A desired simplicity, both in indexing relative social positions and in describing the point of social cooperation, will be jeopardized.

In what was perhaps Rawls's last writing on this question, in *Justice as Fairness: A Restatement,* he faces some of these difficulties more squarely than in any other discussion.[60] He makes a major concession to the sort of criticism that Sen has raised and that I have developed: he accepts the idea of insurance against accident for *temporary* impairments, and he grants that the right way for the parties to think of human life is as having a succession of temporal stages, including childhood and old age. He admits that he has assumed that "with respect to the kinds of needs and requirements that political justice should take into account, citizens' needs and requirements are sufficiently similar for an index of primary goods to serve as a suitable and fair basis for interpersonal comparison" (170). He focuses, as before, on the role of income and wealth in indexing relative social positions. Once more, he puts to one side "the more extreme cases of persons with such grave disabilities that they can never be normal contributing members of social cooperation"—apparently continuing to understand that notion in terms of economic contribution, and as entailing the exclusion of all severe lifelong impairments, mental and physical. Finally, he simply takes over from *PL* its conception of a "line" that separates those whose abilities lie within a "normal" range from others. All these parts of his theory are unchanged.

With regard to temporary impairments befalling those whose abilities lie within the "normal" range, however, Rawls now argues that the index of primary goods (focusing on income and wealth) is best understood as an index of *expectations* of primary goods over the "normal course of a complete life."[61] Thus individuals may have equal expectations of primary goods *ex ante,* even though the goods they actually receive *ex post* are different, because some have had accidents and others have not. In other words, we are to view primary goods as like an insurance policy: citizens may all have the same insurance policy, even though they will get different benefits on account of the different accidents of life. Rawls now explicitly adds to the index of primary goods an account of an "expectation of an assured provision of health care at a certain level (calculated by estimated cost)," insisting, still, that income and wealth are in this sense good proxies for citizens' capabilities. In designing health insurance, the parties are explicitly directed to consider all the phases of a normal life, asking how people who view themselves as living through all these phases would balance the claims that we make in these different phases.

In some ways, this frank admission that life has distinct temporal phases is a significant improvement; and the idea of insurance that Rawls introduces with it surely covers some of the problems I have raised. It is not at all clear, however, that Rawls has squarely faced all aspects of Sen's challenge. The question whether a single monetary metric is really a good proxy for all of citizens' diverse physical and mental capabilities in the areas of health, mobility, and mental health has not been given sustained attention. Nor has attention been paid to Sen's claim that the diversity in needs for primary goods is not just a matter of this or that accident, but a pervasive feature of daily life, affecting society every day. It is one thing to use insurance to handle discrete accidents generating medical claims, quite another to use it to handle the daily nutritional needs of children and adults, or of pregnant and nonpregnant women. Finally, Rawls has not addressed the continuity between the "normal" case, with its periods of disability, and the situation of people with lifelong impairments. An elderly "normal" person may be disabled for thirty or forty years, perhaps longer (as we have noted) than the total life span of some people with a lifelong disability. So the continued use of the "line" seems highly problematic, even from the point of view of thinking about the needs of "normal" persons.

Moreover, the reaffirmation of the "line" continues to bring with it all the difficulties it has had all along, as a way of thinking about the citizenship of people with impairments and disabilities. Indeed, the unpleasant sense that these people are being shunted to the side is actually increased by Rawls's new willingness to think about the temporary health needs of "normal" citizens. And when he describes the way in which the parties will think about balancing health claims over the phases of life, we see the extent to which the goal of mutual advantage, understood in economic terms, still plays a guiding role in Rawls's theory, complicating its commitment to fairness and equal respect. For those who will get first attention, whose claims are treated as having "great urgency" (*JF* 174), are those who have the capacity to return to the workforce and resume their productivity. This way of thinking about the phases of a "normal" life in relation to medical claims has clear implications for the way the parties will eventually view the claims of those who fall beneath the "line" of normalcy.

Thus although Rawls has courageously faced these difficult questions, they remain difficult (as he is the first to say). It seems to me that all the major problems with his treatment remain unsolved.

vii. Reconstructing Contractarianism?

Issues of impairment and disability prove very revealing for the entire structure of Rawls's contract doctrine and, more generally, for the project of basing principles of justice on reciprocity between rough equals (in capacity) who are imagined as joining together to reap a mutual benefit. Despite the moral elements that go very deep in Rawls's theory—and in a sense, also, because of them, or the particular Kantian shape they take—Rawls does not altogether outstrip the particular limitations of the social contract doctrine, which derive from its basic picture of why people live together and what they hope to gain therefrom.

Let us recapitulate. Many of the problems Rawls's theory faces in the area of disability derive from his interest in theoretical simplicity as it shapes his account of the role of primary goods in indexing relative social positions. A contractarian might, I have argued, reformulate the theory of primary goods, accepting Kittay's and Sen's proposals. But for Rawls to become such a contractarian would require a major overhaul of the theory, particularly as a theory of economic justice. This overhaul might lead to some other distributional principle rather than the Difference Principle. At the very least, new arguments for this principle would be required.

Other limitations derive from the theory's Kantianism, which poses problems for the full and equal inclusion of people with severe mental impairments. These limitations are not problems for a contractarian like Scanlon, since he is not choosing basic political principles and does not envisage his contract as one in which "we" decide on principles by which "we" will live together in a political community. In the context of his ethical contractarianism, the two solutions he proposes (guardianship or a mixed ethical theory) both seem adequate. In the context of political theory, these solutions are more problematic. The Kantian account of the basis of political equality excludes people with severe mental impairments from the start. The Kantian doctrine of the person, when put into a traditional social contract frame, colors the key ideas of reciprocity, of freedom, and of the reasons for social cooperation. If the theory had a wholly different structure—for example, one that began from human rights and their realization and then worked out an account of social duties—the Kantian elements in the theory would do less damage, although it would be important that the key notion of the "human" in "human rights" was not exhaustively cashed out in terms of Kantian moral powers.[62] Certainly the Kantian ideas that each human being is an end, and that one may not violate any human being on the way to a greater social benefit, are deeply valuable ideas that any theory of justice for people with disabilities should use, in a suitably extended form.

So the disability/primary-goods problem can be fixed, albeit with some theoretical cost. The Kantianism needs modification, but some aspects of it guide political thinking on these issues well. The largest and most insoluble problems for issues of impairment and disability derive from Rawls's attachment—increasingly strained, but real enough—to the twin ideas of "rough equality" (Humean Circumstances of Justice) and the advantage of social cooperation. These ideas really do seem to lie at the heart of all the political contract doctrines in the classical social contract tradition, although they are absent in Scanlon's purely ethical contract doctrine. (These ideas are closely linked to a further methodological commitment to simplicity: the rejection of benevolent motivations derives from a commitment to simplicity and finality, the avoidance of intuitionistic balancing.)

Could we have a political social contract doctrine that did away with the Humean/contractarian starting point and with the idealized Kantian notion of rationality, focusing only on the core ideas of impartiality, inviolability, and reciprocity (suitably modified to include people with severe mental disabilities), allowing the parties to vary more widely in power and ability and to pursue a richer set of goals for social cooperation? Perhaps, indeed, we could, if we also, like Locke, endowed the parties with a rich and comprehensive benevolence. But we would then need to abandon the classical idea that people choose to depart from the state of nature because cooperation is more advantageous than noncooperation. The idea of the state of nature might still be used to model moral equality, but it would play a diminished role, and we would have to advance new reasons for the choice to cooperate with people who, because of their asymmetrical weakness, pose no threat and can be either dominated or treated with charity.

Why, then, given that these people are not rough equals, should we see our relations with them as involving issues of basic justice rather than as questions that we can settle later by other moral principles, such as principles of charity? The social contract doctrine has no insight to offer us at this point. Kant's ideas of inviolability and reciprocity do offer guidance, as do Locke's ideas of human dignity, natural rights, and the duties of benevolence. But these ideas are conceptually separate from the social contract tradition's depiction of the choice situation.

One type of contractarianism that could meet these criticisms would be a modified Lockean conception, working with the twin ideas of agreement and benevolence, and with a Lockean account of natural rights or basic entitlements. Such a view would develop the strand in Locke that focuses on the idea of a life worthy of human dignity. It is clear that such a contractarianism would be rather far from current political contractarianisms, both because it would have an independent account of the good, or entitlements, and because it would have a moral psychology based on compassion or benevolence. In many respects it would look like the good-based account of capabilities that I shall be developing, which still, as we shall see, preserves some role for the idea of reasonable agreement. And it would very probably lack the methodological simplicity, the economy of principles, that Rawls, at any rate, wants from his alliance with the social contract tradition. If we eschew the ideas of the state of nature, mutual advantage, and the status of the parties as "free, equal, and independent," it seems fair to say that such an account would no longer fall within the classical theory of the social contract.

On the other hand, we might also see whether we could mine the Kantian ideas of respect and reasonable agreement for a political contractarianism that is Kantian in spirit without involving the problematic aspects of the classical theory of the social contract. We could then begin, as does Scanlon's ethical contractarianism, with parties who are not situated in anything like a state of nature and whose deliberations focus on the related ideas of impartiality, equal respect, and agreement. Rawls could retain the intuitive underpinnings of his theory if he took this route, and he could thus extend his principles of justice to people for whom, as things now stand, he offers no principles of justice at all. But he would need to modify his account of equality, making it less Kantian in flavor; and he would need to admit benevolence to a role in the theory that he now denies it. The view that I shall develop makes many of these moves, though from a somewhat different perspective. Finally, he would need to modify his theory of the good to accommodate Sen's criticisms and the importance of care as a primary good.

At this point Rawls's theory offers better guidance than that offered by Scanlon's ethical contractarianism, because it does contain a theory of primary goods, albeit incomplete. Indeed, even in Scanlon's ethical contractarianism we may feel the need for an independent account of the good. Since Scanlon (plausibly) rejects desire as a source of the goods that the parties are pursuing, where does the account of the good come from, and why does the good matter? Scanlon sees clearly that the bare idea of agreement by itself is insufficient to generate an account of the good, and yet he is hopeful that he can make his ethical theory work without offering any independent account of the good, simply by applying the ideas of contractarianism as a test to any good that the parties may pursue. And yet, at this point he faces an objection: If the good matters, can't we look to its value directly? Why do we need to get there via the idea of agreement? Or, as Scanlon puts the objection: "Still, someone might agree that what happens to these people matters morally, yet question whether our concern about them is at bottom concern about the justifiability of our actions to them. Why isn't it more plausible to say simply that their lives have value and that what a moral person is moved by is the recognition of that value?"[63]

Scanlon's reply to this challenge is, to some extent, a powerful one: he convincingly establishes that one cannot value persons as persons, see their *distinctive* value, without appeal to ideas of justifiability, which (to put it in my own words, not his) give us a good way of capturing all-important ideas of respect and of the person as an end. My difficulty with the response is that, while he establishes that contractarianism is a good way of capturing *part* of what is valuable about human beings and their lives, he does not seem to me to respond to a more moderate and plausible challenge, which would say, yes, these values are indeed *part* of what is valuable, but they are not the whole. Freedom from pain and illness, bodily integrity, love and comfort—these would appear to have a value that does not derive entirely from the idea of justifiability. (This point is closely linked to my critique of Kant's account of the person above.) I can grant to Scanlon that "the idea of justifiability to others can be seen to play an important role in shaping our thinking about right and wrong"[64] without ceasing to feel that these and other goods have an independent value. Perhaps Scanlon does not intend to deny this.

When we move from the domain of ethics to the domain of political justice, however, the need for an independent theory of the good becomes obvious. As Rawls says, we have to know what we are distributing, and we have to know that these things are good.[65] A theory of the good may be closely linked to ideas of agreement and justifiability, but it seems unlikely that the bare idea of reasonable agreement will by itself generate such an account. So at this point we seem likely to have at most a partial contractarianism, with the need for some independent account of political goods or entitlements. Scanlon agrees with this point.[66]

Moreover, when we remove the machinery of the state of nature, the equality (in capacity) of the parties, the goal of mutual advantage, and the indexing of social positions by wealth and income—as I have argued we must if questions of disability are to be adequately addressed—the bare idea of agreement seems exceedingly bare: there is just much less machinery left than there is in Rawls, and the likelihood increases that an independent and multivalued account of the good will end up doing a lot of the important work.[67]

The most promising attempt to date to create a political contractarianism using the core ideas of Scanlon's theory is Brian Barry's *Justice as Impartiality*. Barry makes effective objections to the classical social contract idea of mutual advantage.[68] While his objections to Rawls are not precisely the same ones that I have raised, they are complementary, and Barry understands why the difficulty posed for Rawls by problems of disability is nothing superficial or easily removed.[69] Like my argument, Barry's sees Rawls as too attached to the classical social contract idea of reciprocity—although he does not mention what seems to me fundamental, Rawls's acceptance of Humean Circumstances of Justice as his analogue for the state of nature. And, like my argument, Barry's sees a profound tension between the Kantian elements of Rawls's view and the classical social contract elements. Barry's own aim is to produce a view that follows the Kantian idea only, in the form given it by Scanlon, but in the realm of political theory.

This significant attempt shows, I believe, when combined with Scanlon's more detailed ethical proposal, that the contractarian ideas of reasonable refusal and reasonable agreement are still powerful ideas in political theory, ideas that can illuminate the structure of political principles. The device of the Original Position is one expression of those ideas; when pried loose from its Humean/social contract moorings, it, too, can greatly illuminate core political ideas. Nonetheless, the sketchy nature of Barry's theory shows us very clearly the importance of having a worked-out theory of the good, if such an account is to provide even a partial political conception. Nor does his account respond to the worries I have raised about the difficulties, for the inclusion of citizens with mental impairments, inherent in the idea of reasonable agreement and the closely associated Kantian conception of the person. It remains unclear to me exactly how Barry's notion of hypothetical agreement will include people with severe mental disabilities. Barry gives no detailed account of the psychological abilities of his contracting parties, nor does he give any account of how his own theory deals with this problem, after saying, correctly, that Rawls's theory does not adequately do so. There is reason to think that there will be a strain at this point in any theory built on the idea of mutual respect *among the parties to a hypothetical agreement;* the conflation of the "by whom" and the "for whom" is built into the argument's structure in such a way that the respect in question is extended to citizens with severe mental impairments only derivatively.

Attempts in this vein must surely be pursued further. What we see, however, is that such theories are likely to succeed in addressing problems of disability as problems of justice only to the extent that they jettison some characteristic features of social contract theories and, at the same time, adopt an independent theory of the good (as Rawls has already in effect[70] done). In so doing they will converge greatly with the theory that I shall recommend. For the reasons given by Sen, and mostly conceded by Rawls, a theory of the good in terms of a list of things will not do, and a list of human capabilities looks like the right sort of list to aim at. Moreover, such a theory will succeed only if it contains a more complex political psychology that makes it clear how a cooperation that is not understood in terms of mutual advantage alone will be sustained, and a political conception of the person that contains a more inclusive account of what is wonderful and dignified about persons than Kantian rationality alone.

Rawls and I are thus in full agreement about what parts a theory has to have: it needs a political psychology, a political account of the person, a political theory of the good, and an account of justification. I have expressed some doubts about his particular solutions to some of these problems, and I have suggested that he could answer the doubts only by developing a theory that severs its tie to the classical social contract doctrine. But at the same time I believe that the *kind* of multipart structure he is seeking is crucial, and that Barry's theory, while in some ways an improvement, leaves these other parts out; at least they are not yet very much developed.

At this point, it might prove illuminating to try approaching the question from a different vantage point, starting from the account of the key political entitlements or goods and from a different, non-Kantian political account of the person. As we shall soon see, my own theory does not depart altogether from contractarianism. By adopting the Rawlsian ideas of political liberalism and overlapping consensus, it builds in a role for reasonable agreement. But in other respects it orders the parts of the theory differently and conceives of some of the parts rather differently. In particular, it takes the value of people's opportunities to live good lives to be primary, and the account of political justification to be posterior to an account of what makes lives in accordance with human dignity possible (an account itself closely linked to a non-Kantian political conception of the person and of human dignity). It is my hope that this attempt will complement and inform future attempts to work out a political contractarianism, and that the conversation between the two will enrich the structure of political principles.

3

CAPABILITIES AND DISABILITIES

For Jamie came into the world asking us a question more basic than
any I've yet dealt with, in this book or in my life: Assuming that we
can even imagine a form of social organization in which citizens like
James are nourished, supported, and encouraged to reach their full
human potential, why might we seek to create it at all?

—Michael Bérubé, *Life as We Know It*

i. The Capabilities Approach:
A Noncontractarian Account of Care

The capabilities approach is a political doctrine about basic
entitlements, not a comprehensive moral doctrine. It does not
even claim to be a complete political doctrine, since it simply
specifies some necessary conditions for a decently just society, in
the form of a set of fundamental entitlements of all citizens. Failure to secure these to citizens is a particularly grave violation of
basic justice, since these entitlements are held to be implicit in
the very notions of human dignity and a life that is worthy of
human dignity. One way of thinking about the capabilities list is
to think of it as embodied in a list of constitutional guarantees,
in something analogous to the Fundamental Rights section of
the Indian Constitution or the (shorter) Bill of Rights of the
U.S. Constitution. Such entitlements would subsequently be
implemented by both legislative and judicial action. Indeed it is
by design that the capabilities list starts from an intuitive idea,
that of human dignity, that is already basic to constitutional
framing in many nations of the world (prominently including
India, Germany, and South Africa). Because this notion has, by
now, a long record of judicial interpretation behind it, we may

assess its practical potential by seeing what creative jurisprudence has been able to make of it in various areas of human life.[1]

I have said that my approach contains some convergences with contractarianism of Scanlon's ethical type, but also some very striking departures, and even more striking departures from the Rawlsian form of political contractarianism. Let us now proceed to a closer examination of those differences.

ii. The Bases of Social Cooperation

For the social contract tradition, the idea of mutual advantage is central: parties depart from the state of nature in order to gain a mutual benefit. Rawls accepts this idea and, with it, the account of the parties' relative equality in power that goes closely with it. Although some contractarians—Locke, for example—understand advantage in a way that includes benevolent interest in the interests of others, Rawls does not; the parties pursue the realization of their own conceptions of the good within the constraints of impartiality imposed by the Original Position. Thus, although citizens in the Well-Ordered Society have, as I have argued, a wider set of moralized ends, and could see *ex post* good reasons for the full inclusion of people with impairments, the contract situation prevents, *ex ante,* an adequate resolution of this issue.

In the capabilities approach, the account of the benefits and aims of social cooperation is moralized, and socialized, from the very start. Although the approach does not employ a hypothetical initial situation (being an outcome-oriented rather than a procedural approach), it envisages human beings as cooperating out of a wide range of motives, including the love of justice itself, and prominently including a moralized compassion for those who have less than they need to lead decent and dignified lives. There is no reason to think that such a society would be unstable; indeed, I have argued that it can meet acceptable conditions of political stability over time.[2]

Crucially, there is no assumption, either overt or tacit, that justice is relevant only where the Humean Circumstances of Justice obtain. In other words, I do not assume that only a situation of rough equality, in which people are motivated to make a deal for mutual advantage, can get justice off the ground. Rawls's endorsement of Hume's account of the Circumstances of Justice is in serious tension with other elements of his view. Nonetheless, he never abandons it; he evidently believes that it offers a good account of the circumstances in which justice between persons makes sense.

Hume's assessment of human beings is too bleak. (And it is a little odd that it is Hume who makes it, since Hume displays an outstanding awareness of human capacities for sympathy and benevolence.) Human beings are held together by many ties: by ties of love and compassion as well as ties of advantage, by the love of justice as well as the need for justice.[3] Real people often attend to the needs of others in a way that is narrow or arbitrarily uneven. But education can do a great deal to make these ties deeper, more pervasive, and more evenhanded. Rawls agrees; but then it is perhaps unfortunate that he endorses Hume's account of the Circumstances of Justice and related aspects of the classical social contract tradition. I would argue, indeed, that the changes we have seen in recent years toward the greater social inclusion of people with impairments give us strong evidence that the decency of human beings does aim at justice for its own sake, frequently enough to make a large political difference. If this is so even in Western societies, dominated as they typically are by economic motives and considerations of efficiency, how much more might we expect of human beings in a society that truly supported the human capabilities of all citizens, and devised a system of education to reproduce these values over time.

Rawls's refusal to include benevolent motivations in the Original Position is motivated not by a view that these motivations do not exist or are not powerful. It is motivated instead by the idea (similar to Hume's) that these motivations are uneven and partial, and thus would not support determinate political principles. To some extent I concede that charge, by defending only a partial conception based on the idea of a social minimum, rather than Rawls's more ambitious and complete conception. To some extent, though, I believe that the charge of excessive reliance on intuition can be answered (see section v).

Thus the capabilities approach feels free to use an account of cooperation that treats justice and inclusiveness as ends of intrinsic value from the beginning, and that views human beings as held together by many altruistic ties as well as by ties of mutual advantage. Together with this, it uses a political conception of the person that views the person, with Aristotle, as a political and social animal, who seeks a good that is social through and through, and who shares complex ends with others at many levels. The good of others is not just a constraint on this person's pursuit of her own good; it is a part of her good. Thus, instead of being a matter left to individual conceptions of the good, as in Rawls's theory, a strong commitment to the good of others is a part of the shared *public* conception of the person from the start. The person leaves the state of nature (if, indeed, there remains any use for this fiction) not because it is more mutually advantageous to make a deal with others, but because she cannot imagine living well without shared ends and a shared life. Living with and toward others, with both benevolence and justice, is part of the shared public conception of the person that all affirm for political purposes.

Clearly it is more demanding to build strong benevolence and a commitment to justice into the foundations of a theory than to remain agnostic about these matters. Rawls is correct on this point. But if the weaker assumptions do not handle the problem, we need stronger assumptions. Moreover, it is not altogether clear to me that parsimony in these matters is always a good thing. Rawls did well to reject the Gauthier-style demand for the sort of parsimony that leaves moral commitments out of the starting point. My approach simply goes a little further in the same direction.

iii. Dignity: Aristotelian, not Kantian

A second fundamental departure from contractarianism pertains to the notion of dignity, and thus to Rawls's Kantian conception of the person, which makes a notion of dignity basic. Kant contrasts the humanity of human beings with their animality. Although Rawls does not do so explicitly, he does make personhood reside in (moral and prudential) rationality, not in the needs that human beings share with other animals. The capabilities approach, by contrast, sees rationality and animality as thoroughly unified. Taking its cue from Aristotle's notion of the human being as a political animal, and from Marx's idea that the human being is a creature "in need of a plurality of life-activities," it sees the rational as simply one aspect of the animal, and, at that, not the only one that is pertinent to a notion of truly human functioning. More generally, the capabilities approach sees the world as containing many different types of animal dignity, all of which deserve respect and even awe. The specifically human kind is indeed characterized, usually, by a kind of rationality, but rationality is not idealized and set in opposition to animality; it is just garden-variety practical reasoning, which is one way animals have of functioning. Sociability, moreover, is equally fundamental and equally pervasive. And bodily need, including the need for care, is a feature of our rationality and our sociability; it is one aspect of our dignity, then, rather than something to be contrasted with it.

Thus, in the design of the political conception of the person out of which basic political principles grow, we build in an acknowledgment that we are needy temporal animal beings who begin as babies and end, often, in other forms of dependency. We draw attention to these areas of vulnerability, insisting that rationality and sociability are themselves temporal, having growth, maturity, and (if time permits) decline. We acknowledge, as well, that the kind of sociability that is fully human includes symmetrical relations, such as those that are central for Rawls, but also relations of more or less extreme asymmetry; we insist that the nonsymmetrical relations can still contain reciprocity and truly human functioning.

We can now connect the two fundamental departures from contractarianism, by saying that this new conception of what is dignified and worthy in the human being supports the departure from Humean/Rawlsian Circumstances of Justice. We do not have to win the respect of others by being productive. We have a claim to support in the dignity of our human need itself. Society is held together by a wide range of attachments and concerns, only some of which concern productivity. Productivity is necessary, and even good; but it is not the main end of social life.

iv. The Priority of the Good, the Role of Agreement

Discussing the thin type of ethical contractarianism developed by Thomas Scanlon in ethics, I have argued that it could not be the basis for political principles without a theory of the good that cannot be derived from the thin idea of mutual respect and reciprocity. (As I mentioned, Scanlon agrees with this.) For

Rawls, the theory of primary goods is closely linked to a Kantian conception of the person: primary goods are introduced as goods that people characterized by the two moral powers would want in order to pursue their life plans. How, then, is my own theory of the good related to my (non-Kantian) account of human dignity? If the capabilities are viewed as simply means to a life with human dignity, not valuable in their own right, then my theory is not after all very different from a contractarian theory: the Aristotelian account of dignity takes the place of Rawls's account of the moral powers (or Scanlon's account of reciprocity), but the account of the good is still envisaged as (instrumentally) dependent on that account of moral rationality and, in effect, generated by it. Thus the theory of the good would play a role very similar to the role it could play in a contractarian theory, and the difference between the two theories would be at least reduced. One might then wonder whether the capabilities approach does not suffer from the problem I imputed to the thinner type of contractarianism, namely, of trying to derive too much from one thin moral notion.

It is of course not surprising to find convergence between contractarianism and the capabilities approach at this point, since both are fundamentally shaped by some similar intuitions about human beings as moral equals and since both hold that political equality requires support for a wide range of life activities and life choices. Such convergence is welcome to me, since the contractarian type of theory is, in my view, the strongest theory of basic social justice we have so far. But I believe that there remain important and subtle differences between the two approaches. The capabilities are not understood as instrumental to a life with human dignity: they are understood, instead, as ways of realizing a life with human dignity, in the different areas of life with which human beings typically engage. The guiding idea behind the list is to move through these different areas (life, health, and so on) and to ask, in each of these areas in which we live and act, what would be a way of being able to live and act that is minimally compatible with human dignity? Dignity is not defined prior to and independently of the capabilities, but in a way intertwined with them and their definition. (Of course the architectonic capabilities of sociability and practical reason play a guiding role throughout, as they do for the young Marx, as indices of when a way of eating, or moving, or interacting is compatible with human dignity.) The guiding notion therefore is not that of dignity itself, as if that could be separated from capabilities to live a life, but, rather, that of a life with, or worthy of, human dignity, where that life is constituted, at least in part, by having the capabilities on the list. In this way, the right and the good seem thoroughly intertwined.

For Scanlon's ethical contractarianism, as we have seen, that is not the case: the idea of reciprocity takes precedence, and Scanlon hopes that he can derive a relatively complete account of ethics from that idea alone, without an independently articulated idea of the good (although he never rejects the modest contention that such an account of the good might offer one part of an account of what is valuable about human beings and their lives). As for Rawls, although he abandons the early conception of primary goods as all-purpose means to whatever conception of the good the parties are pursuing, he continues to envisage the primary goods as instrumental to Kantian life planning, goods that parties conceived of in terms of the Kantian moral powers would want. There remains, then, a subtle difference between my account of the capabilities list and both forms of contractarianism. If the idea that the good is prior is in some sense misleading, given the role played by an idea of dignity in the account of the good itself, that idea is correct if we recognize that the capabilities approach does not separate the right and the good in the Kantian way but, rather, operates with a richer and moralized account of the good.

There is another place, however, where the capabilities approach converges with contractarianism. The capabilities approach is articulated in terms of a Rawlsian idea of *political liberalism:* that is, the account of entitlements is envisaged as a partial account of the good, for political purposes, which citizens may attach to different comprehensive conceptions of the good. It is articulated, or at least we hope so, in terms of freestanding ethical ideas only, without reliance on metaphysical and epistemological doctrines (such as those of the soul, or revelation, or the denial of either of these) that would divide citizens along lines of religion or comprehensive ethical doctrine. It is therefore hoped that this conception can be the object of an *overlapping consensus* among citizens who otherwise have different comprehensive views.

Unlike Rawls, and like the framers of the Universal Declaration of Human Rights, I view such a consensus as fully available internationally across lines of tradition and religion. Our hope for an overlapping consensus does not require an additional premise that all the materials in our argument are drawn from the traditions of Western democracies (see Chapter 5, section vi). But I still retain a role for the notion of overlapping consensus and the related notion of agreement. Thus it is part of what justifies the conception: that it can over time be justified to people who hold different comprehensive conceptions of the good life. Justification thus involves an idea of acceptability to all, or at least to the major conceptions of value. Acceptability is relevant to justification both for reasons of stability—a conception that is acceptable to all can be stable over time—and for reasons of respect.

This being the case, there is once again a measure of convergence with contractarianism, at least of Scanlon's ethical type. Requiring acceptability as a condition of justification builds in the idea that the theory of the good is not independent of human agreement, but can be justified as the right political conception of the good only in relation to the possibility of such an agreement (for good reasons, not just as a mere *modus vivendi*). Thus it would seem that my conception has the same moving parts as Scanlon's conception (as it would be translated to politics through the addition of a theory of the good), although it arranges them in a subtly different way and uses a different political conception of the person.

v. Why Capabilities?

Sen proposed that Rawls should replace the heterogeneous list of primary goods, with its prominent use of resources (income and wealth) as indices of well-being, with a list of capabilities, all of which would then be used in measuring quality of life. One of his primary arguments for this shift was the inadequacy of wealth and income as indices of the well-being of people with disabilities: the person in a wheelchair may have the same income and wealth as a person of "normal" mobility and yet be unequal in capability to move from place to place.[4] Rawls was unable to accept this proposal because of his commitment to the use of income and wealth as indices of relative social positions, for the purposes of argument for the Difference Principle,[5] and also, probably, because of the structure of his social contract doctrine. In addition, his opposition to the intuitionistic balancing of plural ends suggests that he would be unable to accept any plural-valued index of relative positions.

My capabilities approach supports Sen's proposal, using Sen's arguments and some additional arguments. Sen bases the case for capabilities on individuals' varying needs for resources, and also on their varying abilities to convert resources into functionings. Variations in need, he insists, are pervasive features of human life: children need more protein (an expensive nutrient) than adults, for example, and pregnant or lactating women need more nutrition than nonpregnant women. So the question of variation cannot be postponed; it is omnipresent.

Sen also insists, however, that the need to focus on capability becomes especially clear when we consider cases in which individuals are hampered in various atypical ways by the very structure of their society. A culture that traditionally discourages women from becoming educated will need to devote more resources to female literacy than to male literacy. Although Sen does not say so, and although he tends to treat the case of disability as involving a natural asymmetry, his famous example of the person in a wheelchair has a similar structure. The reason why this person has less capability than the "normal" person to get around in public space is thoroughly social: society has not provided wheelchair access in public spaces.

This argument, however, can be taken much further. For Sen's critique of Rawls suggests that income and wealth *would* be good proxies for what is truly relevant, if we were able to fill in the amounts in ways that take these asymmetries into account: thus, if we were to give a child appropriately more money for food than an adult, and a person in a wheelchair an appropriately larger amount in connection with mobility, then in principle income and wealth might still be appropriate measures of relative social position. Of course we could get the amounts right only by looking at the capabilities, so capabilities would still be primary; but we could still regard them as fungible in terms of income and wealth, at least for the purposes of social calculation. At least that is how Sen's critique might be read.

The capabilities approach, however, can make a much more radical critique of the focus on income and wealth. It is of the essence of the focus on capabilities to insist that the primary goods to be distributed by society are plural and not single, and that they are not commensurable in terms of any single quantitative standard.

Before we can develop such a critique cogently, however, we need to adopt some list, however tentative and open-ended, of which capabilities are going to be regarded as central human entitlements in terms of which basic social justice is defined. I have suggested elsewhere that Sen's reluctance to make such a list makes it difficult for him to use capabilities to define a theory of social justice. Some capabilities (the ability to vote) are important, and some (the ability to drive a motorcycle without a helmet) are relatively trivial; a just constitution will protect the important ones and not the trivial ones. Some capabilities are actually bad, and should be inhibited by law (the ability to discriminate on grounds of race or sex or disability, the ability to pollute the environment).[6] No constitution protects capabilities *qua* capabilities. There must be a prior evaluation, deciding which are good, and, among the good, which are most central, most clearly involved in defining the minimum conditions for a life with human dignity.

Once we have committed ourselves to some working list of the central capabilities, at least for purposes of constitution-making and institutional design, we then pose the question whether income and wealth can be good proxies for capabilities, provided that we factor in the unusual needs of people who start from positions of social disadvantage. Here we run into a very serious obstacle. As I have defended the capabilities, they are all, each and every one, fundamental entitlements of citizens, all necessary for a decent and dignified human life. That is part of the account of what justifies the placement of a capability on the list. This account entails that the capabilities are radically nonfungible: lacks in one area cannot be made up simply by giving people a larger amount of another capability. This limits the kind of trade-offs that it will be reasonable to make, and thus limits the applicability of quantitative cost-benefit analysis. All citizens have entitlements based on justice to all the capabilities, up to an appropriate threshold level. If people are below the threshold on any one of the capabilities, that is a failure of basic justice, no matter how high up they are on all the others.[7] So what is wrong with the use of income and wealth as measures of social position cannot be fully captured by insisting on the variability of need for resources: there is a problem already in treating capabilities as fungible according to a single measure. Human beings are characterized by what Marx called "rich human need," that is to say, need for an irreducible plurality of opportunities for life activity.

Moreover, the Rawlsian emphasis on income and wealth suggests that the relevant resources are items that we can distribute to individuals. Sen's critique does not explicitly dispute this. Give the person in the wheelchair enough money, he seems to say, and he will be able to move from here to there; the only problem is to determine the amount of money. This reply is insufficient. No matter how much money we give the person in the wheelchair, he will still not have adequate access to public space unless public space itself is redesigned. Maybe a very rich person could afford a full-time chauffeur and a set of bearers who could carry him up the stairs of rampless buildings. But even if making people with impairments that rich were a sensible goal of public policy, as it is not, we would still have not gotten to the root of the matter, which is that this person should not *have* to rely on a chauffeur or on bearers. There should be wheelchair access on buses and sidewalks, and all buildings should have ramps and wheelchair-accessible elevators. That redesign of public space is essential to the dignity and self-respect of people with impairments. In short, the task of integrating people with impairments into public space is a public task, which requires public planning and a public use of resources. The relevant question to ask is not how much money do individuals with impairments have, but what are they actually able to do and to be? And then, once we have ascertained that, what are the obstacles in the way of their ability to function up to the appropriate threshold level?

vi. Care and the Capabilities List

It is now quite easy to make the role of care in a conception of justice as fundamental as it ought to be. First, we understand the need for care in times of acute or asymmetrical dependency as among the primary needs of citizens, the fulfillment of which, up to a suitable level, will be one of the hallmarks of a decently just society. How should this insight be incorporated into the capabilities list? I shall address this question in a general way before moving to the special case of the mentally disabled. I would argue that care is not a single thing, and therefore that it should not be, or at least need not be,[8] introduced as a single separate extra capability in addition to the others. Thinking well about care means thinking about a wide range of capabilities on the side of both the cared-for and the caregiver. Good care for dependents, whether children, elderly, ill, or disabled, focuses on support for capabilities of life, health, and bodily integrity. It also provides stimulation for senses, imagination, and thought. It supports emotional attachments and removes "overwhelming fear and anxiety"; indeed, good care constitutes a valuable form of attachment. Good care also supports the capacity of the cared-for for practical reason and choice; it encourages affiliations of many other sorts, including social and political affiliations where appropriate. It protects the crucial good of self-respect. It supports the capacity to play and enjoy life. It supports control over one's material and political environment: rather than being regarded as mere property themselves, people with impairments and disabilities need to be regarded as dignified citizens who have the claim to property, employment, and so forth. Citizens with impairments often have diminished opportunities to enjoy nature; good care supports this capability as well.[9] In short, given the intimate and foundational role that care plays in the lives of the cared-for, we have to say that it addresses, or should address, the entire range of the central human capabilities.

People with severe mental impairments, like other human beings, have needs in the areas covered by all the capabilities. Good care will address all of these needs. Beyond this, little can be said in a general way. Good care for a person with a mental impairment—and good public policies supporting care—must be knowledgeable about and attentive to the particular nature of the person's impairment. Good care for Sesha will focus on attachment, emotional equanimity, and health. Her large capacity for affection and joy must always be central to any relationship with her. Good care will also nourish her need for cognitive stimulation—her love of music and movement, for example, her strong interest in not being confined to a single physical environment.[10] But the cognitive engagement must be at a level that is appropriate to her capacities. Employment, political participation, and the choice of a way of life seem less pertinent to her situation.

Arthur is altogether different: his large cognitive abilities need to be nurtured in an atmosphere that does not cause him emotional trauma through bullying or his general fear of groups. He needs constant and concerted support for his relational capacities; care that would be fine for most children will be inadequate for him in this area. Relationships with animals and nature play a very valuable role in this development. With good support and luck, he will be capable of holding a job and participating in the larger social world. Indeed, at the age of twelve he already has a highly sophisticated understanding of politics, which combines oddly with his affective rigidity. For example, he decided that a good way to express his disgust about the disputed election of 2000 was to refer to Bush as "The Resident" rather than "The President." Having made this quite sophisticated joke, he then became extremely upset if anyone else, including teachers at his school, referred to Bush in any other way. Good care for Arthur must be well suited to these jolting disparities in development.

In short, then, good care for a person with a mental impairment (including elderly people with dementia or Alzheimer's) is individualized care. I shall return to this question in section x, asking how public policy and constitutional provisions can capture that individuality. But let me now turn to the general capability-needs of the caregiver.

On the side of the caregiver, we have, once again, a wide range of concerns. Caregivers frequently lose out in all sorts of ways through bad arrangements. Their health suffers; their emotional equanimity is sorely compromised; they lose many other capabilities they otherwise would have had. A decent society cannot ensure that all caregivers actually have happy lives: but it can provide them with a threshold level of capability in each of the key areas. For example, in the area of emotional equanimity, which seems particularly intangible, good public arrangements and a decent public culture can make it possible that the care of an elderly or disabled dependent would not involve constant anxiety about how the job will get done, and with what resources; such arrangements would also lift the crushing burden of guilt on family members who are simply unable to provide the needed care. Again, good support for practical reason in this area would be public policies that make the choice to care for a dependent a real choice, not an imposition born of social indifference. Women would actually have the opportunity to make a plan of life for themselves and decide what role care for dependents would play in it. And they, too, would get a little time to play. Once again, then: we have not a single thing, but a way of thinking about all the items on the list. I shall later return to the public policy implications of this analysis.

vii. Capability or Functioning?

In thinking about impairment and disability, as in other political contexts, the question naturally arises: Is it just capability that should be promoted in each of these areas, or actual functioning? In *Women and Human Development* I argue that in certain areas of human life this question rightly becomes controversial. With items such as political participation, religious functioning, and play, it seems obvious that it is the capability or opportunity to engage in such activities that is the appropriate social goal. To dragoon all citizens into functioning in these ways would be dictatorial and illiberal. But in other areas things become more difficult. Richard Arneson holds, for example, that it is appropriate for political planning to promote actual health as a social goal rather than merely to promote the capability to choose a healthy life.[11] I myself take a more libertarian line here: that is, I do not favor policies that would make unhealthy activities such as boxing, unsafe sex, football, and smoking illegal, although education about risk seems to be highly appropriate, and the infliction of harm on others (for example, by not disclosing positive HIV status to a sex partner) could rightly be penalized. Similarly, I think that patients have a wide range of rights concerning medical treatment, and those rights should be expanded (with more access to information and choices of care) rather than contracted. With emotional equanimity and practical reason, there are surely large conceptual difficulties involved in distinguishing capability from functioning; but again, I believe that in principle it is right to promote the opportunity to plan a life for oneself, and to achieve emotional health, but not to preclude choices citizens may make to lead lives that inspire fear or involve deference to authority. (For example, the choice of a career in the military might seem to preclude some uses of practical reason, and to put emotional health at risk; and yet I do not think there is any reason to preclude it, and indeed strong reasons to make it available, quite apart from the obvious social need for a strong military.)

Only in the area of self-respect and dignity itself do I think that actual functioning is the appropriate aim of public policy. Suppose a state were to say, "We give you the option of being treated with dignity. Here is a penny. If you give it back to us, we will treat you respectfully, but if you prefer, you may keep the penny, and we will humiliate you." This would be a bizarre and unfortunate nation, hardly compatible, it seems, with basic justice.[12] We want political principles that offer respect to all citizens, and, in this one instance, the principles should give them no choice in the matter.

For children, however, functioning may be made the goal in many areas. Thus I have defended compulsory education, compulsory health care, and other aspects of compulsory functioning. (For example, I support an age of consent for sexual intercourse, so that children's bodily integrity is protected whether they like it or not.) Compulsory functioning is justified both by the child's cognitive immaturity and by the importance of such functioning in enabling adult capabilities.

These ideas have obvious implications for the treatment of people with severe mental impairments. It seems clear that in many instances many of these people cannot make choices about their health care, or consent to sexual relations, or make an assessment of the riskiness of a job or occupation. So there will be many areas, for many of these people, in which functioning, rather than capability, will be an appropriate goal. In section ix I shall go into this question in greater detail, asking in a general way how the list, the idea of the threshold, and the idea of the social goal must all be adjusted to meet the needs of people with cognitive impairments.

viii. The Charge of Intuitionism

Rawls's commitment to a single linear measure of quality of life involves a methodological aspect: he rejects the balancing of plural and diverse principles as objectionably intuitionistic (*TJ* 34–40). It is easy to imagine him leveling this charge against the capabilities approach: because of its commitment to a plurality of heterogeneous entitlements, all fundamental for social justice, it rests social justice on an objectionably intuitionistic foundation, one that requires balancing and that does not yield a definite ordering. Let us now investigate the hypothetical charge. I think we shall find that it is in all important respects mistaken.

The charge as I imagine it has two parts: first, that there is an unacceptable reliance on intuition in the generation of basic political principles; second, that the multivalued nature of the capabilities list makes inevitable a reliance on intuitionistic balancing that would make political principles indeterminate and never final. To the first charge, we should reply (as I already have in Chapter 1) that there is no more and no less reliance on intuition in the capabilities approach than in justice as fairness—the reliance just comes in a slightly different place. In justice as fairness, intuitions and considered judgments are consulted in the design of the Original Position; in the capabilities approach, they are consulted in the making of the capabilities list. This difference is not surprising, since justice as fairness is a procedural approach and the capabilities approach is an outcome-oriented approach. But both approaches follow Rawls's general method of assessing a theoretical structure against the background of "considered judgments," holding no point immune from revision, but seeking consistency and fit in theory and judgments taken as a group.[13] Indeed, it is not surprising that this methodological similarity obtains, since Rawls explicitly traces his method to Aristotle, who is also the ancestor of the method used in my capabilities approach.

The appearance of a difference in the role of intuitions stems, I believe, from the more general difference between procedural and outcome-oriented approaches, which I discussed in Chapter 1. Devotees of procedural approaches typically feel squeamish about the naked appeal to the idea of human dignity in the capabilities approach, in a way that they do not feel squeamish about the similar role of an idea of human inviolability and a related intuitive idea of respect for persons in Rawls's theory—simply because there are so many moving parts in between that intuitive idea and the final output that one can fail to notice how much work these intuitive ideas are doing. I do not think that Rawls argues in this way. He does insist, plausibly, that political principles are needed to give determinate content to the ideas of respect and human dignity (*TJ* 586), but I believe that the capabilities approach avoids this problem insofar as it considers the account of entitlements not as derived from the ideas of dignity and respect but rather as ways of fleshing out those ideas. Surely ideas of dignity and respect are very basic in Rawls's theory, as Charles Larmore has rightly insisted.[14] Therefore, I believe that Rawls's more significant objection to the use of intuition lies in the area of the second charge.

What, then, about the idea that the capabilities approach, with its ten ends, is doomed to intuitionistic balancing of particulars in a way that makes its political principles hopelessly indeterminate? This charge, which might be accurate when applied to some theories one might imagine, is altogether inaccurate when applied to the capabilities approach. What the theory says is: *all ten of these plural and diverse ends are minimum requirements of justice,* at least up to the threshold level. In other words, the theory does *not* countenance intuitionistic balancing or trade-offs among them. The constitutional structure (once they are put into a constitution or some other similar set of basic understandings) demands that they *all* be secured to each and every citizen, up to some appropriate threshold level. In desperate circumstances, it may not be possible for a nation to secure them all up to the threshold level, but then it becomes a purely practical question what to do next, not a question of justice. The question of justice is already answered: justice has not been fully done here.[15]

Now of course intuition may frequently be involved when we consider where to set the threshold for a given capability, and in *Women and Human Development* I imagine that the judicial process is one place where this sort of incremental work will be done. But Rawls thinks no differently: indeed his own discussion of free speech in *Political Liberalism* is a perfectly mainstream discussion of judicial reasoning, one that does not purport to deduce the appropriate threshold from unerring first principles. It is true that I emphasize that one way of setting the threshold right will be to look at the other capabilities that are affected: thus, a court deciding the limits of religious free exercise might legitimately consider the fundamental right of all children to education, and so forth. But this is hardly to make trade-offs in an unacceptable sense: it is just what follows from the fact that the capabilities are understood as a coherent overall set, not as conflicting among themselves.[16] In other words, it is to *avoid* the need to make trade-offs that we might look across to the other capabilities, making sure that the whole set is coherent and can be delivered as a whole.

The one place where Rawls's theory looks less intuitionistic than the capabilities approach is in its measurement of relative social positions, where only wealth and income are used. Of course this measure is precise, and much more straightforward than measuring by self-respect, political inclusion, education, wealth, and so forth. But it is precision purchased at a cost: for, as Sen has argued and as I have argued here, Rawls has simply left out lots of things that are highly pertinent to any real construal of well-being and relative social position, things for which wealth and income are not good proxies. In real life, people may be well placed with regard to some of the capabilities, and very badly placed with regard to others.

ix. The Capabilities Approach and Rawls's Principles of Justice

Rawls, as we have seen, emphasizes that his theory has two independent parts: the principles of justice (together with the intuitive ideas of dignity, inviolability, and reciprocity that they express and render precise) and the initial choice situation. We may, he says, accept one part and reject the other. I have urged that in order to deal with problems of disability as problems of justice, Rawls would need to make major modifications in his description of the initial choice situation, rejecting certain features on which the classical social contract tradition relied. (At that point, depending on the nature of the modifications introduced, there is likely to be considerable convergence between his theory and the capabilities approach, although other issues I have raised—the absence of benevolent motivations in the initial choice situation, the limitations of a theory of the good described in terms of the needs of rational persons, the more general difficulty of equating the choosing parties with the primary subjects of justice—might still lead us to prefer the latter. We must wait to see these modifications before the case can be fully examined.) I have also said that the intuitive ideas of dignity and reciprocity provide excellent guidance, particularly in thinking of the way in which *each person* is an end and cannot be sacrificed to a large social good. We need to recast those ideas in order to extricate them from the Kantian rationalism that makes it difficult to extend them to people with severe mental impairments; but we may do that without, I believe, losing the intuitive core.

What, then, of the principles of justice themselves? Rawls himself advances no principles at all for the case of people with severe physical and mental impairments, and he does not even commit himself to treating these issues as issues of justice. Certainly he denies that they are issues of *basic* justice, affecting society's most fundamental political principles. So the question must be not, what do we think of the principles that Rawls proposes for this case, but rather, how would it be to extend the principles he proposes for the "normal" case to this case, which he does not treat? Would the famous two principles, guaranteeing a strong priority for a set of basic liberties and opportunities, and then proposing to deal with economic inequalities by the Difference Principle (inequalities are permitted only so long as they raise the level of wealth and income of the least well-off) provide good guidance for this further case?

Starting from a different vantage point, the capabilities approach has come up with principles that converge strikingly, in many ways, with Rawls's two principles. The philosophical motivation is profoundly similar, since in both cases the principles are attempts to capture and render politically concrete the idea of a life in accordance with human dignity. Beyond this point the comparison cannot be precise, because my theory speaks only of a social minimum and does not address inequalities above that (very ample) social floor. But that move is one that Rawls himself would probably need to make, had he accepted Sen's suggestion that a list of heterogeneous capabilities replace the list of primary goods, with its focus on indexing relative positions with reference to income and wealth. The idea that each and every citizen is entitled to an ample amount of each of these diverse goods, seen as capabilities, and that society may not pursue overall advantage in a way that slights any citizen's claim to them, is an idea that has a close relationship, at least, to the two principles.

Consideration of the case of disability leads us to focus on the importance of care as a primary social entitlement. This substantive difference from Rawls's view is highly significant, since his assumption that citizens are "fully cooperating" prevents him from giving care a sufficiently central role. But this is the major difference in content between Rawls's principles (extended to this new case) and my own for this case; otherwise there is considerable overlap.

Perhaps we could go on to argue for something like the Difference Principle—certainly a most appealing principle—reconceiving of economic inequality in terms of capability. But how to argue for such a principle, once we admit plural heterogeneous goods, defined as capabilities, presents many problems. Should we have a Difference Principle for each and every single capability? That suggestion seems baroque in the extreme, and hard to conceptualize. But any other approach requires aggregating the capabilities, where the appeal of the idea of capabilities is its ability to capture the heterogeneity and noncommensurability of goods. I conclude that we capture the moral core of Rawls's principles in this new framework, at least up to a point, by insisting on an ample minimum for all the capabilities. Perhaps later we can develop further principles to deal with the as yet unheard-of case in which a society has fulfilled such entitlements.

Although Rawls argues for a lexical ordering of the two principles, he also stipulates that some basic economic needs must be satisfied before the first principle kicks in. I have expressed dissatisfaction with some of his formulations, but it would surely be wrong to say that Rawls does not see the interpenetration of issues of liberty with issues of economic entitlement. His discussion of campaign finance reform in *PL* shows clearly how important he thinks economic issues are to the fair value of the political liberties. So my capabilities approach, which insists that all capabilities have a material aspect and require material conditions, simply takes the argument one step further, rejecting the lexical ordering on the ground that the issues are too interdependent for it to be anything but misleading to suggest that liberties and opportunities can be settled prior to economic matters. Nonetheless, my view does make something of the separation Rawls suggests, by insisting that some entitlements must be distributed on a basis of strict equality, whereas for others (more narrowly economic in nature) adequacy is what we are after. My reasons for insisting on strict equality for religious liberty, liberty of speech, and political liberty are Rawlsian in nature, having to do with considerations of respect and reciprocity.

All in all, then, the spirit of the principles survives, despite the great changes in starting point and in details of formulation.

x. Types and Levels of Dignity: The Species Norm

The capabilities approach operates with a list that is the same for all citizens, and it uses the notion of a threshold level of each of the capabilities, which is taken to be a minimum beneath which a decently dignified life for citizens is not available. The approach as set forth in my philosophical account specifies this threshold only in a general and approximate way, both because I hold that the threshold level may shift in subtle ways over time, and because I hold that the appropriate threshold level of a capability may, at the margins, be differently set by different societies in accordance with their histories and circumstances. Thus a free-speech right that seems appropriate for Germany (allowing the prohibition of antisemitic speech and political organizing) would be too restrictive in the different climate of the United States; both nations seem to have made reasonable choices in this area, in the light of their histories. Similarly, precisely where the line should go as to the level of education that should be provided free of charge by the state may vary somewhat in accordance with the type of economy and employment in a state, although the level should not vary as much as levels do in reality. Thus, whether a school-leaving age of seventeen or nineteen is appropriate, for example, might be debated; whether twelve is appropriate cannot currently be debated, given the structure of employment opportunities and the prerequisites of political activity in the contemporary world. In such cases, the approach urges that the best way of working out an appropriate precise specification is incremental, with legislatures, courts, and administrative agencies playing the roles that seem appropriate in the light of the specific character of each nation's institutions and their institutional competence.

Why does the approach specify a single list of capabilities and a single threshold? This question must now be faced, because it is obviously crucial for approaching issues about the capabilities of people with mental impairments. The capabilities approach begins from a political conception of the human being, and of a life that is worthy of the dignity of the human being. A notion of the species and of the characteristic activities of a species does, then, inform it. But we must be very careful to say what the use of an idea of human nature does and does not provide, because there are other approaches in ethics and political thought that use the idea of human nature very differently.[17]

First of all, the notion of human nature in my theory is explicitly and from the start *evaluative,* and, in particular, *ethically evaluative:* among the many actual features of a characteristic human form of life, we select some that seem so normatively fundamental that a life without any possibility at all of exercising one of them, at any level, is not a fully human life, a life worthy of human dignity, even if the others are present. If enough of them are impossible (as in the case of a person in a persistent vegetative state), we may judge that the life is not a human life at all, any more. Then, having identified that (extreme) threshold, we seek a higher threshold, the level above which not just mere human life, but *good life,* becomes possible.

In other words, we say of some conditions of a being, let us say a permanent vegetative state of a (former) human being, that this just is not a human life at all, in any meaningful way, because possibilities of thought, perception, attachment, and so on are irrevocably cut off. (Notice that we do not say this if just one or more of the perceptual modalities is cut off; we say this only if the entirety of a group of major human capabilities is irrevocably and entirely cut off. Thus there is a close relation between this threshold and the medical definition of death. And we do not say this if any random one of the capabilities is cut off: it would have to be a group of them, sufficiently significant to constitute the death of anything like a characteristic human form of life. The person in a persistent vegetative condition and the anencephalic child would be examples.)[18] We then seek, intuitively and roughly, a higher point above which a good life for a human being is available, focusing on the social conditions of that life. There may also be natural such conditions, but as biology changes medical possibilities, we must be constantly alert to the fact that some possibility that used to belong to the realm of chance or nature now might belong to the social realm, the realm shaped by justice.[19] The job of a decent society is to give all citizens the (social conditions of the) capabilities, up to an appropriate threshold level.

The theory's notions of the human and of central human capabilities are, then, evaluative and ethical. Some things that human beings can be and do (cruelty, for example) do not figure on the list. And because the list is designed to be the basis of an overlapping consensus in a pluralistic society, it is explicitly nonmetaphysical. It is designed to avoid concepts that belong to one major comprehensive metaphysical or epistemological view of the human being rather than another, such as the concept of the soul, or of a natural teleology, or of self-evident truth. Insofar as a highly general idea of human flourishing and its possibilities does figure in the approach, it is not a single idea of flourishing, as in Aristotle's own normative theory, but rather an idea of a space for diverse possibilities of flourishing. The claim that is made by the use of this single list, then, is not that there is a single type of flourishing for the human being, but, rather, that these capabilities can be agreed by reasonable citizens to be important prerequisites of reasonable conceptions of human flourishing, in connection with the political conception of the person as a political animal, both needy and dignified; and thus these are good bases for an idea of basic political entitlements in a just society.

The list is single, then, not because citizens' ideas of flourishing are single, but because it seems reasonable for people to agree on a single set of fundamental constitutional entitlements that provide the underpinning for many different ways of life, entitlements that seem to inhere in the idea of human dignity. But now a difficult question has to be confronted. Let us imagine a citizen who actually will not use one of the capabilities on the list: for example, an Amish citizen, who believes that it is wrong to participate in politics. It is reasonable enough to expect that this person can still support the inclusion of the right to vote as an element on this list, because she has chosen to be in a democratic society, and she can believe that the possibility of voting is in general a valuable thing to have in such a society, even though she herself will not vote. Presumably members of religious groups that prohibit their members from access to the popular press and other media can still support the idea of freedom of the press as an important value for a democratic society to contain, even though it has nothing much to do with their own conception of flourishing.[20] Similarly, presumably atheists, agnostics, and even people who hate and disdain religion can still support the capability of religious free exercise as an important part of what a society will contain, because they can see from a study of history that religious oppression is a very severe danger in all societies, and that this sort of oppression cripples many human possibilities. They will rightly insist on an understanding of religious freedom that includes equal rights for atheists and agnostics; but they are likely to favor that capability, so understood, rather than compulsory atheism, given that they have accepted core ideas of human dignity and mutual respect for practical reason.

Now the question is: Exactly how do notions of the human being, and of human dignity, play a part in what we ask such citizens to affirm? Do we ask the Amish citizen to state that human flourishing and a life compatible with human dignity are not possible without the right to vote? This she may well not believe. Do we ask the ultraorthodox citizen to affirm that human flourishing and a life compatible with human dignity are not possible without a free press? Again, his religion may well deny this. Do we ask the atheist to affirm that human flourishing and a life compatible with human dignity are not possible without the freedom to choose religion? These people are willing to agree that these rights are good things for a society to have, because they recognize that other people use them, and they respect their fellow citizens. But they may not want to be forced by the political conception to say that these rights are implicit in the notion of human dignity and human flourishing. So it would appear that we are asking them to say something more, and more controversial, than we suggested, and that it is the notion of the human that is, after all, creating the problem.

Let me try to reply as follows. These people have chosen to live in a pluralistic democracy and to show respect for its values. Nor, we are supposing, do they think that the values of the public culture are just things that they put up with because they get stability and protection for their way of life out of them; they actually affirm these values. To that extent, they are different from other members of their religious group whom we could imagine.[21] So, they do after all think that these values are very important political values, even though the associated function is one that they will not use. They think, that is, that there is something good about having choice in these matters: the choice to vote or not to vote, the choice to read a free press or not to read it, the choice to pursue religion or nonreligion. Choice is good in part because of the fact of reasonable pluralism: other fellow citizens make different choices, and respecting them includes respecting the space within which those choices are made. The citizens in question may also believe that choice is good *for them:* to be a nonvoter in a nation that has no elections expresses nothing much about human values; to pursue nonreligion in a state that persecutes religion expresses nothing much about the values of the nonreligious person. If we place the accent firmly on capability rather than on functioning, it is a not implausible reconstruction of their thinking to ascribe to them the thought that a dignified life for a human being requires these *capabili-*

ties—which include, of course, the right not to use them. Just as a person who chooses to ruin his health and not to avail himself of any available health care may yet consistently support public health care as an essential minimum condition of a decent human life, so, too, these people may consistently support the space for choice in this area, even though they also believe that they themselves can rightly make only one (negative) choice.[22]

Suppose we now say to such people, "You don't think highly of political participation [or a free press], because the associated functioning is forbidden in your comprehensive conception of value. So why should we give you those capabilities at all, asking you to affirm them as implicit in the idea of a decent human life? Why don't we instead simply have a different list of capabilities for you, including only the ones that really do figure in your comprehensive conception of the flourishing life?" What would be wrong with a solution of plural lists for plural conceptions?

For a start, of course, as a practical matter such a solution would be unworkable. Moreover, one of the reasons it would be practically unworkable is itself normatively deep: namely, it would fail to offer people full exit options from one comprehensive conception to another. Orthodox Jews in Brooklyn have a vastly greater possibility of exit from that community, even if by choice they do not read secular newspapers, than would such Jews in a state that had no free press. But a still more problematic feature of the idea is the very fact that it would create discrete orders of citizens, some with basic rights that others do not have. There would be hierarchy instead of full equality. Presumably the Amish would reject this idea, and they would reject it because they want to have the same rights as their fellow citizens; they regard this as part of the social bases of self-respect for them and their children. They, too, want equality. Therefore, they attach importance to the idea of social unanimity about basic entitlements at the level of capability, just as they also attach importance to the idea of space for pluralism at the level of functioning.

Nor is it enough to say that they value sameness: for I think it is fair to say that they value not just any old sameness, but *this* sameness. That is, these citizens would not consider themselves as well off in a benevolent dictatorship that denied all people the right to vote. They have chosen to affirm the public culture as more than a convenient *modus vivendi:* so it is not after all so implausible to say that they hold that these capabilities are prerequisites of a decent human life in a political community. Similarly, the atheist who hates religion and hopes it will someday disappear from human life will still prefer the free choice of religion to a state, let's say a Marxist state, that left people no choice in these matters, on the grounds that allowing people choice in these matters is an aspect of respect for human dignity. So again: it is not implausible to say of them that, even though they dislike religion, they think that the free exercise of religion is a prerequisite of a decent human life. The distinction between capability and functioning is thus crucial.

There are, then, good reasons why the capabilities list is single, even though the conceptions of flourishing are plural. Nor does it seem that the appeal to a notion of the human causes difficulty for the type of pluralism that the approach is committed to respecting. We can accept without profound metaphysics the idea that human life has a characteristic shape and form, and that certain abilities, meaning certain spaces for choice, are generally agreed to be very important to its success—even if for personal or religious reasons one will in some cases renounce the actual functioning in question.

Now we arrive at the issue toward which this discussion has been heading. Should the political list of capabilities remain the same when we consider the lives of citizens with mental impairments? And should the social threshold also be the same? Our Aristotelian focus on the characteristic functioning of the human being appears to cause a puzzle at this point.[23] Sesha will not vote, not because she holds a comprehensive conception of value that forbids voting, but because her cognitive capacities will never reach a level at which she has a meaningful possibility of voting. Similarly, freedom of the press means nothing to her, not for the reasons of the ultraorthodox, but because her cognitive level makes reading and verbal communication impossible. Try as it will, society cannot bring her up to the level at which she has in any meaningful sense the capabilities in question. It now would appear that the view that emphasizes the species norm must choose: either we say that Sesha has a different form of life altogether, or we say that she will never be able to have a flourishing human life, despite our best efforts.[24]

The first response appears to be correct for some very extreme impairments. Some types of mental deprivation are so acute that it seems sensible to say that the life there is simply not a human life at all, but a different form of life. Only sentiment leads us to call the person in a persistent vegetative condition, or an anencephalic child, human.[25] What makes us wish to call Sesha's life human, and what difference does that make? Of course the fact that she has a human body and is the child of two human parents plays a large role here, and may distort our thinking. We should not summarily dismiss the possibility that the right thing to say is that her life is some other sort of life, but not close enough to a characteristically human form of life for the term "human" to be more than a metaphor. That is the right thing to say in the two cases I mentioned, because all possibility of conscious awareness and communication with others is absent. To the extent that we do think of Sesha's life as a human life, and I think we are not deceived when we do, it is presumably because at least some of the most important human capabilities are manifest in it, and these capabilities link her to the human community rather than to some other: the ability to love and relate to others, perception, delight in movement and play. In this sense the fact that she is the child of human parents matters: her life is bound up in a network of human relations, and she is able to participate actively in many of those relations, albeit not in all.

Still, it seems implausible to say that even the best care will produce all the capabilities on this list, up to the socially appropriate threshold level. Should we then introduce a different list for her, as our social goal? And should we introduce a different threshold for the items on the list, as our political goal for what she should attain?

The cases of Arthur and Jamie show that, from a practical point of view, any such tinkering with the list is very dangerous. The persistent tendency of all modern societies is to denigrate the competence of people with impairments and their potential contribution to society. In part because full support for these abilities is very costly, it is easier to avoid the evidence that people with serious impairments actually can in many cases come up to a high level of functioning. The use of terms suggesting the inevitability and "naturalness" of such impairments masks a refusal to spend enough money to change things on a large scale for people with impairments. Not so long ago it would have been assumed that even a person who was blind or deaf simply couldn't participate in higher education or political life, that a person in a wheelchair could not participate in sports or perform in a wide range of jobs. Impediments that were thoroughly social were seen as natural.[26] Thus it seemed possible to avoid the costly issue of redesigning public facilities to accommodate these people.

Often the expense involved was waved away by characterizing people with impairments as permanently and inevitably dependent on others: thus public space for people with visual impairments was imagined in such a way that they would have to go around with a sighted guide. The law of torts was designed as if people who are blind had no right to occupy public space as independent adults.[27] This situation should make us reflect long and hard when we speak about the need for care: for at times the idea that a person needs (unusual or asymmetrical) care is a ruse, masking the possibility of full adult independence for many people with impairments, if only public space could be adequately designed to support them. Thus making care available when people want and need it should be sharply distinguished from forcing people into a situation in which they have to depend on others, even if that is not what they want. People with physical disabilities want medical care for their needs, the way we all do. But they also want to be respected as equal citizens with options for diverse forms of choice and functioning in life, comparable to those of other citizens. Nor can we avoid the problem of adaptive preferences here; so even if people say that dependency is what they prefer, that fact should not stop us from offering alternatives.

The problem of constructed failure to fulfill human potential is even more acute in the case of people with mental impairments. Michael Bérubé's description of Jamie shows that many problems of children with Down syndrome that had been taken to be unalterable cognitive limitations are actually treatable bodily limitations: the weak muscles of the neck, especially, which prevent exploration of the environment at a crucial time; and the weak muscles of the tongue, which prevent speech from developing. The prejudice that these children were just "dumb" and ineducable prevented an accurate understanding of what they could achieve. It is precisely because parents and other advocates attached importance to cognitive development and kept insisting on it that these discoveries were made and programs designed to implement them. Again, Arthur might have been prematurely judged to be a child who simply could not form good relationships with other children and who would never be able to be a member of society. But because parents, educators, and, ultimately, the law (as I shall discuss later) placed great emphasis on sociability in the public conception of education, Arthur was assigned, at public expense, to a school with other Asperger's children, where he has learned good social skills and has made friends.

In short, then, using a different list of capabilities or even a different threshold of capability as the appropriate social goal for people with impairments is practically dangerous, because it is an easy way of getting off the hook, by assuming from the start that we cannot or should not meet a goal that would be difficult and expensive to meet. Strategically, the right course seems to be to harp on the single list as a set of nonnegotiable social entitlements, and to work tirelessly to bring all children with disabilities up to the same threshold of capability that we set for other citizens. Treatments and programs should indeed be individualized, as indeed they ought to be for all children. But for political purposes it is generally reasonable to insist that the central capabilities are very important for all citizens, and thus worth the expenditures that may have to be made on those with unusual impairments. One good way of insisting is to use the language of human flourishing, saying that Jamie and Arthur deserve all the prerequisites of a good human life, and that they can get these with suitable education and care.

Such an emphasis on singleness is important not just strategically, but also normatively: for it reminds us of the respect we owe to people with mental impairments as fully equal citizens who are members of the human community and who have the ability to lead a good human life. It also reminds us of the continuity between so-called normal people and people with impairments. All have impediments that education must address, in an individualized way where possible; and all, given suitable care, can become capable of the central functions on the list. Instead of segmenting off people with impairments, as if they belonged to a different (and lower) kind, we insist on their equal entitlement to the wherewithal of good lives.

Indeed, insisting on the singleness of the list for political purposes, a strategy that seems at first blush to ignore the individual situations of each person with a mental impairment, seems to be a good way of respecting the individuality of people with mental impairments. For what we are saying (returning to our theoretical concern about equal respect) is that they are just as much individuals as anyone else is, not *types,* not a lower kind that we set off from the human kind. That sort of typing been one of the most pervasive ways in which people with disabilities get stigmatized. Erving Goffman's classic study of social stigma shows again and again that a central feature of the operation of stigma, especially toward people with impairments and disabilities, is the denial of individuality: the entire encounter with such a person is articulated in terms of the stigmatized trait, and we come to believe that the person with the stigma is not fully or really human.[28] When such a person performs the most normal actions of a human life, "normals" often express surprise, as if they were saying, "Fancy that! In some ways you're just like a human being!"[29] If we were to adopt one capabilities list for "normals" and another for "Down syndrome children," as if they were a different species, this baneful tendency would be reinforced: the unfortunate implication would be that "normals" are the individuals (for they know they are, and nobody denies this), and children with Down syndrome are a type without significant individuality and diversity, defined entirely by their type characteristics.

Moreover, an emphasis on the species norm makes sense even

when we are considering a woman like Sesha, who may never be able to attain the whole list of capabilities on her own, and may need to attain some of them (political participation, for example) through the proxy of her guardians. For what the species norm says to us is that Sesha's life is to that extent unfortunate, in a way that the life of a contented chimpanzee is not unfortunate. People with severe mental impairments are all too often compared to higher animals. In some ways this analogy can be revealing, reminding us of the complex cognitive abilities of animals. But in other ways it is quite misleading. For it suggests that Sesha belongs to a species that has a normal form of life that is her own; that she has fellow species members with similar capacities with whom to form sexual and family relationships; that she is surrounded by species members with similar abilities, with whom she can play and live. But this is false: Sesha is surrounded by humans who lack her impairments. She lacks the relative independence that most adult members of her species community have (and that animals of other species typically attain). She lives with a good deal of pain and illness. To the extent that all this is true, she has a diminished prospect of a life that has spontaneous joy in sexuality and childrearing, and perhaps no prospect of a life with significant political activity initiated by herself. In all of these ways she is very unlike an average chimpanzee. Moreover, the life of an animal with typical species abilities has an organic harmony about it, whether the animal is human or nonhuman: the various abilities interlock in a way that is more harmonious than disharmonious. Sesha, by contrast, has abilities for love, play, and delight that are not well related to her cognitive level and her motor skills; moreover, she has large-scale physical disabilities that leave her in a lot of pain. So what we clearly ought to say, it seems to me, is that some of the capabilities on the list will not be attainable for her, but that this is extremely unfortunate, not a sign that she is flourishing in a different form of life.

Society should strive to give her as many of the capabilities as possible directly; and where direct empowerment is not possible, society ought to give her the capabilities through a suitable arrangement of guardianship. But guardianship, however well designed (and we will speak further about this shortly), is not as good for Sesha as it would be to have the capabilities on her own. We have emphasized the capabilities on the list because they have human importance: we have evaluated these options to function, and we say that they are really important and good. When someone does not attain them, this is an unhappy state of affairs, whether or not this is anyone's fault: the only way that Sesha can ever flourish is as a human being.

To say this is not to say that Sesha's life cannot be judged good and successful in many respects. But it is to say that if we could cure her condition and bring her up to the capabilities threshold, that is what we would do, because it is good, indeed important, for a human being to be able to function in these ways. If such a treatment should become available, society would be obliged to pay for it, and would not be able to offer the excuse that she is impaired "by nature." And, further, if we could engineer the genetic aspects of it in the womb, so that she would not be born with impairments so severe, that, again, is what a decent society would do.[30] Notice that we do not say this about Jamie or Arthur, precisely because there is a realistic prospect that they will attain the capabilities that we have evaluated as humanly central. Thus the view does not entail engineering Down syndrome away, or Asperger's, or blindness and deafness, although it does not clearly speak against this either.

The main role of the list in thinking about public policy toward Sesha will be to pose the question: Has the public political arrangement in which she lives extended to her the *social basis of* all the capabilities on the list? If so, then the public conception has done its job, even if her own impairments may prevent a full choice of functioning in one or more areas. Right now, it is obvious that most of the work that has been done to give Sesha many of the capabilities on the list has been done by her parents, in spite of defects in the public political conception (the primary focus of Kittay's book). The public culture has gradually become more responsive to the needs of children like Jamie and Arthur. Sesha still receives care with little help from the state and its public policies. Even so, Sesha's life is in many ways a dignified and fruitful human life: but that is because of the work of her parents and other caregivers. Her success depends to some extent on the fact that her parents are highly educated and relatively well-off. A just society would not permit such crucial matters to depend on chance in this way.

In more concrete terms, thinking about how the list and its threshold might direct public policy toward Sesha, we should attach more importance to the large items on the list than to their more specific subsections. Thus, even if Sesha cannot become a potential voter, we should ask what other ways there might be to give her political membership and the possibility of some political activity (although we also would allow her a vote through a guardian, as a sign of her full political equality). It is clear that citizens with Down syndrome have participated successfully in their political environment.[31] We should ask how we might arrange that Sesha, too, could have some of these functionings available to her. Again, citizens with many mental impairments are capable of employment. If Sesha cannot hold a job, well, what other ways might there be to give her some measure of control over her material environment? Again, if it turns out that Sesha would not be able to raise and care for a child herself, even with assistance (this is not altogether clear), then what alternative relations to children might be devised to increase the richness of her life? Maintaining a single list of capabilities raises all these questions, and they are vital ones, if people with mental impairments and disabilities are to be fully equal as citizens.

xi. Public Policy: The Question of Guardianship

It is impossible for a discussion of this sort to do more than sketch some of the policy implications such an approach to the situation of people with mental impairments might have. In this section I shall focus on guardianship; in the next I shall focus on the education of children with mental impairments; finally I shall sketch a general approach to the general issue of care and its social recognition.

Most states protect (at least some of) the capabilities of people with mental impairments through forms of guardianship. But this whole relation needs to be carefully thought through in the light of the emphasis on practical reason and sociability that is central to the capabilities approach. The U.S. system of guardianship varies from state to state, but the general approach has been rather amorphous, and the issues have rarely been spelled out with the imagination and clarity that other nations have exercised. Protecting the due process rights of people with mental impairments favors limited guardianship, on constitutional grounds.[32] Nonetheless, many people with mental impairments are unable to vote, even when there is no cognitive impairment of a type that would make voting an unrealistic social goal. Even when states offer various forms of partial or temporary guardianship, there is a general lack of clarity "about which options maximize autonomy" that "can lead to the unnecessary disempowerment of some persons with disabilities."[33] Forty-two states and three territories bar at least some individuals with intellectual disabilities from voting.[34]

By contrast, a number of other nations, including various European nations, Israel, and New Zealand, have recently reviewed the relationship and come up with creative alternatives in which the focus on human dignity and choice is typically central.[35] For example, Israel's Equal Rights for Persons with Disabilities Law, passed in 1999, states that people with disabilities have the right to "equal and active participation in all the major spheres of life" and the right to support for human needs in such as way as to "enable her/him to live with maximum independence, in privacy and in dignity, realizing her/his potential to the full." The law states that "a person with a disability has the right to make decisions that pertain to her/his life according to her/his wishes and preferences." The provisions of the law apply to a wide range of people with impairments and disabilities, including those with severe physical, intellectual, and emotional disabilities.[36]

A particularly creative approach to the social-service and legal structure of guardianship can be found in recent Swedish law.[37] Rather than a single relationship, Sweden since 1994 has had a flexible plurality of such relationships. The preferred form of support service for persons with mental disabilities is that of mentorship (the *god man*). The relationship of mentorship does not alter the civil rights of the mentee. The *god man* acts only with the consent of the person and has rights and duties roughly similar to those of someone with a power of attorney. The court that appoints a *god man* may tailor the relationship to the needs of the individual. Application for these services may be made by the person in question, a relative, or the public trustees. These mentors are paid for their services by the state. The largest number of people with mentors are elderly.

Where mentorship seems insufficient because of the nature of a person's disability, somewhat more decisional control is provided by the relationship of administrator or trustee *(forvaltare)*. When other forms of assistance are insufficient and the person with a disability seems to be in severe jeopardy, a trustee may be appointed and, unlike a mentor, may make substitute decisions. One primary use of this category is to protect a person from the economic effects of improvident transactions. But the person still retains civil rights, including the right to vote.

Nor is that the full extent of the varieties of guardianship and assistance: other social services include that of "contact person" *(kontakt)*, paid by public funds, who provides companionship activities for a person who would otherwise be isolated or inactive; the "personal assistant," hired and fired by the person with a disability, but paid by the government, who assists the person in many transactions; and the "escort person," who accompanies the person with a disability to cultural, sporting, and other leisuretime activities, again paid by the national government, in combination with municipalities.[38]

Sweden's approach is complemented by Germany's 1992 reform of its guardianship law *(Betreuungsgesetz)*, which offers a procedural approach to the problem, with an emphasis on general principles to safeguard the liberty of persons with disabilities. The "principle of necessity" bars guardianship if the person can manage with the support of other social services. A "principle of flexibility" limits the scope of the guardian's authority, mandating the least restrictive alternative: the *betreuer* is to "follow the wishes of the supported individual as long as the well-being of the handicapped person is not likely to be impaired," and the law recognizes that well-being includes "the possibility to lead a self-determined life to the highest possible degree." A "principle of self-determination" permits a durable power of attorney as a substitute for a guardian. A "principle of rights preservation" emphasizes financial subsidy of practical support and the "avoidance of formal legal incapacitation," in such a way that the appointment of a guardian does not automatically deprive the person with a mental impairment of the rights to vote, to marry, and to make a will. The law goes on to establish a variety of procedural safeguards, including personal interviews, appeal procedures, and limited duration of guardianship.[39]

If we combine the underlying vision of human dignity and equality in the Israeli law with the general principles asserted in the German law and the flexible structure of legal and social categories embodied in the Swedish law, we have a good example of what the capabilities approach would favor as a template for reform in this area. More practical legal and political work clearly needs to be done to flesh all this out further.

All of these legal reforms, sought by people with mental impairments and disabilities and their advocates in the growing international movement for fully equal rights, underline the importance of an approach that sees people with disabilities as holders of fully equal rights, entitled to a wide range of social services that ensure that they get a chance to exercise their rights. As Mary Robinson writes in her introduction to a new study of these international developments:

> It is intolerable that any man, woman, or child go through life segregated and deprived of their rights for any reason, much less because they were born into a body or mind that our global society may deem too different to accommodate. That their separation is due to a physical or mental disability, as opposed to one of the more "traditional" or visible classifications like race or religion or gender, makes the violation of their rights no less severe. True equality for the disabled means more than access to buildings and methods of transportation. It mandates a change in attitude in the larger social fabric—of which we are all a part—to ensure that they are no longer viewed as problems, but as holders of rights that deserve to be met with the same urgency we afford to our own. Equality puts an end to our tendency to perceive

"flaws" in the individual, and moves our attention to the deficiencies in social and economic mechanisms that do not accommodate differences.[40]

In the approach that I, with Robinson, favor, guardianship becomes not a matter of dealing with the "incompetence" of a person, but a way of facilitating that person's access to all the central capabilities. The norm should always be to put the person herself in a position to choose functioning of the relevant sort. Where that is not possible, temporarily or permanently, the sort of guardianship to strive for will be one that is narrowly tailored to assist the person where assistance is needed, in a way that invites the person to participate as much as possible in decisionmaking and choice.

xii. Public Policy: Education and Inclusion

All modern societies have had gross inequities in their treatment of children with unusual mental impairments. Often such children do not get the medical care and the therapy they need. (Often, indeed, assumptions of cognitive incompetence have prevented people from recognizing that they need forms of physical therapy that can greatly augment their cognitive potential. For example, muscle therapy for children with Down syndrome can make it possible for these children to negotiate their world in a way that promotes active learning.) More, even, than people with many physical impairments, children with mental impairments have been shunned and stigmatized. Many of them have been relegated to institutions that make no effort to develop their potential. And they are persistently treated as if they have no right to occupy public space. In the congressional hearings prior to the Americans with Disabilities Act (ADA), many examples of this shunning were cited. One case concerned children

with Down syndrome who were denied admission to a zoo so as
not to upset the chimpanzee.[41]

An especially egregious gap has been in the area of education.
Stigmatized as either ineducable or not worth the expense, children with mental disabilities have been denied access to suitable
education. Adults of my generation can recall the classrooms for
"special" children that were typically hidden away in basements
of schools, so that "normal" children did not have to look at
these children. And in many cases children with mental impairments were turned away from the public schools altogether.

Early court cases upheld these exclusions. For example, in
1892 the Supreme Judicial Court of Massachusetts upheld the
exclusion of John Watson, born with mental retardation, from
the Cambridge public schools. The opinion cites the disruptive
effect of his appearance and unusual behavior (which, it was
conceded, was not harmful or disobedient) on the experience
of the other children. Similar was the case of Merritt Beattie,
whose paralytic condition produced symptoms that were held to
have a "depressing and nauseating effect upon the teachers and
school children."[42]

The struggle against these problems in the United States
illustrates both the problems with which all modern societies
are contending and some strategies that are likely to prove
more generally fruitful. In the early 1970s, advocates for people
with mental disabilities began a systematic attempt to challenge
the exclusion of these children from education, achieving two
influential victories. In *Pennsylvania Association for Retarded
Children v. Pennsylvania*, a federal district court issued a consent
decree compelling Pennsylvania public schools to provide "free
appropriate education" to children with mental disabilities. The
plaintiffs alleged that the right to education is a fundamental
right, and that the school system therefore needed to show a

"compelling state interest" in order lawfully to exclude children with disabilities.[43]

In the same year, in *Mills v. Board of Education,* the U.S. District Court for the District of Columbia ruled in favor of a group of children with mental disabilities who challenged their exclusions from the District of Columbia public schools. This group was broader than the group of plaintiffs in the Pennsylvania case: it included children with a wide range of learning disabilities, not just mental retardation. In an analysis that self-consciously set out to apply *Brown v. Board of Education,* the landmark case that found racial segregation in public schools to be a violation of the equal protection clause, the court held that the denial of free suitable public education to the mentally disabled is an equal protection violation. Moreover, very important for our purposes, the court held that this equal protection violation could not be reasoned away by saying that the system had insufficient funds and these children were unusually expensive to include. "The inadequacies of the District of Columbia Public School System, whether occasioned by insufficient funding or administrative inefficiency, certainly cannot be permitted to bear more heavily on the 'exceptional' or handicapped child than on the normal child," the opinion argues.[44] Significantly, at this point the opinion cites *Goldberg v. Kelly,* a case that concerned welfare rights, in which the Supreme Court held that the state's interest in the welfare of its citizens "clearly outweighs" its competing concern "to prevent any increase in its fiscal and administrative burdens." Similarly, the district court reasoned, the District of Columbia's interest in the education of these excluded children "clearly must outweigh its interest in preserving its financial resources."[45]

Goldberg v. Kelly and its echo in *Mills* are highly significant cases for the purposes of the approach that I am defending here.

They articulate a conception of social cooperation and the purposes of political principles that go profoundly against those embodied in the mutual-advantage type of contractarianism that I have criticized, supporting those articulated in the capabilities approach. In *Goldberg*, in an opinion written by Justice Brennan, the Court held:

> From its founding the Nation's basic commitment has been to foster the dignity and well-being of all persons within its borders. We have come to recognize that forces not within the control of the poor contribute to their poverty . . . Welfare, by meeting the basic demands of subsistence, can help bring within the reach of the poor the same opportunities that are available to others to participate meaningfully in the life of the community . . . Public assistance, then, is not mere charity, but a means to "promote the general Welfare, and secure the Blessings of Liberty to ourselves and our Posterity."[46]

In other words, the purpose of social cooperation is not to gain an advantage; it is to foster the dignity and well-being of each and every citizen.[47] This goal is interpreted to mean that expenditures on poverty, though they may be costly, are required by the very nature of our social commitment. Now of course Rawls would agree with this in the case of the poor; but what seems halfhearted about his approach to human dignity and social inclusion is that he refuses to commit the state to full support for people with physical and mental impairments in the basic political principles themselves, deferring that issue until a time when basic principles will already have been fixed. *Mills* says that such a distinction is unacceptable: we must support these citizens as equals, in and through our basic political principles, even if it is costly to do so. It is entailed by our basic political principles.

Now of course the Court's ruling in *Goldberg* does not ask that people do the impossible. It does not ask, for example, that the state provide all citizens with a free college education. What it requires is support on a basis of equality, even where that entails changes that may be expensive. Similarly, the court in *Mills* holds that justice requires such support, and that our fundamental principle of equal protection entails it. If justice requires it, we must bend all our efforts to make sure that it is done, even if it proves costly. The court also notes that costs may be inflated by administrative inefficiency, and that this outcome is very likely regarding the education of children with impairments, given widespread public ignorance and lack of teacher training. We may add that in relation to any rare commodity, prices are often artificially inflated in a way that can be changed without grave loss (as prices for pharmaceuticals to treat AIDS in Africa are also artificially inflated). In the case of educating children with mental disabilities, the main changes that will be required are changes in attitude and in teacher training, all of which would not be unduly costly once introduced and entrenched in the curriculum.

With this fundamental insight securely articulated, the two cases touched off a national debate, focused on both equal access and funding. In 1975 Congress passed the Education for All Handicapped Children Act (EAHCA), which turned the *Mills* decision into federal law, giving a wide range of mentally disabled[48] children enforceable rights to free suitable public education, and making funds available to the states to help them meet their constitutional obligation.[49] This law was slightly modified and elaborated in 1997 in the form of the Individuals with Disabilities Education Act (IDEA).

Before we turn to the new education law, however, there is a very important intervening piece of the picture that we need to consider, because it directly confronts the issue of stigma and exclusion. *City of Cleburne v. Cleburne Living Center* concerns a city in Texas that denied a permit for a group home for the mentally retarded, following a city zoning law that requires special permits for such group homes. (Permits were not required for convalescent homes, homes for the elderly, and sanatoriums— only for "homes for the insane of feeble-minded or alcoholics or drug addicts.") The denial of the permit was plainly prompted by fear of people with mental disabilities and other negative attitudes expressed by nearby property owners. The city further alleged that the occupants of the home might be in danger by being located on a "five hundred year flood plain," since in the event of a flood they might be slow to escape from the building.[50]

In a very surprising ruling, the Supreme Court held that the permit denial had no rational basis, resting only on "invidious discrimination," "an irrational prejudice against the mentally retarded," and "vague, undifferentiated fears."[51] This ruling is surprising because until then virtually any law that was passed anywhere was understood to have a rational basis; the rational-basis standard was extremely weak.[52] The Court has thus now endowed the standard with meaningful teeth, at least in this case: mere stigma, and the desire to exclude an unpopular minority, cannot count as a reason. Here the idea of equal respect for dignity that is at the heart of the capabilities approach is articulated, again in a way that seems to constitute a major break with the values implicit in the mutual-advantage model of the social contract. For we should observe that in that model's sense of "reason," the residents of Cleburne had very good reasons to deny the permit: their property values would surely suffer, and no doubt they would suffer emotionally as well. Keeping people with mental impairments on the periphery of political society, or at least relegating them to a position of derivative and second-class citizenship, makes good economic sense in the light of such considerations, which are bound to weigh heavily in any mutual-advantage approach unless independent considerations of justice and respect intervene. The Court ruled that these reasons cannot count as reasons for purposes of public choice.[53]

With this conception of social cooperation established, or at least prominently on the table, the time was ripe for a further development in the area of education. In 1997 Congress passed the Individuals with Disabilities Education Act. IDEA begins from a simple yet profound idea: that of human individuality. I have said that this is one of the core liberal ideas that we should retain while we criticize the bargaining tradition, and now we will be able to see more clearly the work it can do in this area. Rather than regarding the various types of disabled persons as faceless classes of persons, the act assumes that they are in fact individuals, with varying needs, and that therefore all prescription for groups of them would be inappropriate. The guiding idea of the act is that of the Individualized Education Program (IEP), "a written statement for each child with a disability that is developed, reviewed, and revised." IDEA requires that states affirmatively undertake to identify and locate all children with disabilities whose needs have not been addressed. It also requires that districts establish extensive procedural safeguards to give parents input in decisions regarding the evaluation and placement of their children, as well as access to records and rights to participation in due process hearings and judicial review. (Other sections of the act concern early intervention service for toddlers and preschool-age children, and the funding of research and professional training.)

In general IDEA obliges states to educate children with disabilities in the "least restrictive environment" appropriate to meet their needs. It thus urges "mainstreaming" of these children. This practice can be defended on grounds of the benefit to the mentally disabled child, who will be given more incentives to develop cognitively and who may be less likely to be stigmatized as a type apart. It can also be defended because of the benefit it offers to so-called normal children, who learn about humanity and its diversity by being in a classroom with a child who has unusual impairments. They learn to think about themselves, their own weaknesses, and the variety of human capability, in a new way, as Bérubé's account of Jamie's career in public school eloquently shows.

But for purposes of the law, the underlying recognition of individuality is paramount: thus, when a child seems to profit more from special education than from mainstreaming, the state is required to support such a special placement. When might this be? First, there may be cases in which a child's cognitive level is so out of step with those of other children of his or her age that more progress can be made through special education. Second, there are cases in which the child's problems include behavioral difficulties that are likely to lead to stigmatizing and ostracism. Children with Down syndrome are typically sweet and easy to be with. In contrast, Arthur's Asperger's, combined with the tics of Tourette's syndrome, is disturbing to other children, even when the children are encouraged to be understanding.

One reason why integration is so difficult in Arthur's case is that he does not look different: thus, people expect "normal" behavior of him. And his social disabilities often take the form of rudeness and tantrums that seem inappropriate for a boy of his age who looks normal. Indeed, his cognitive gifts make it all the easier for people to think, when he says something that seems rude, that he must be a bad kid. Take the example of Arthur's combination of cognitive advancement with behavioral rigidity. After the election of 2000, Arthur decided that Bush had not been duly elected, and should therefore be called "the Resident" rather than "the President." After thinking up this quite subtle and impressive joke, he simply would not drop it, and every time the teacher referred to Bush as "President Bush," he insisted on correcting her. Such behavior obviously does not go down well in a public school classroom in a rather conservative state. It is difficult for children and even teachers to believe that someone who can think this way has a disability. They find it easier to believe that he has a bad character and/or bad parents.

After some years of failure with the public school system, even with a special monitor, the state agreed to support Arthur's education in a special private school for children with this disability. He is now making rapid cognitive and behavioral/affective progress. He holds parties and has friends. He simply is no longer stigmatized. His cognitive gifts are progressing rapidly as well. He has developed a strong interest in Japanese culture and is beginning to study Japanese. (But he may not encounter such respect and inclusion if he goes there!)

In short, respect for individuality has to be paramount, if the goals inherent in the capabilities approach are to be realized. Moreover, this respect for citizens is *equal respect* in a very strong sense: the law includes a "zero reject" policy. In an important 1989 case, *Timothy W. v. Rochester New Hampshire School District*, the First Circuit Court of Appeals emphasized that IDEA requires inclusion of *all* children with disabilities, not only those who can demonstrate that they will benefit from education. "The language of the Act in its entirety makes clear that a 'zero reject' policy is at the core of the Act."[54] Thus inclusion itself is a type of respect required by IDEA, and understood, ultimately, in terms of the equality of citizens. In practice, children as severely impaired as Timothy W. (who had severe perceptual, motor, and cognitive impairments that seem comparable to those of Sesha Kittay) will not always be sent to school by their parents; Sesha has flourished in a different type of care. But the point is that there is no requirement to show a specific set of skills and abilities in order to be entitled to education like any other citizen. The underlying recognition of human dignity (in my sense, where dignity is not seen as based on a specific set of skills) is the touchstone.

IDEA is far from being perfect, in theory or in practice. In practice it suffers, first of all, from lack of funding: for although the statute refers to federal funding, the amount envisaged has never actually been appropriated.[55] Furthermore, its practical implementation is rarely as individualized as it ought to be: formulas are typically found for common disorders. Arthur has profited from the fact that Asperger's is a recently recognized condition without much of a track record: in such a case, educators are willing to look and see what seems to work for a particular child. Finally, the practical implementation of the law is often unequal, giving better results to parents who are well-read about their child's disorder and energetic in prodding the local school system. Thus it is no accident that the Bérubés, both college professors, and my sister, a professional musician with a graduate degree, have succeeded in using the system to their advantage, while many other parents have not. The Internet is a very valuable source of information and exchange for parents of children with disabilities; thus the "digital divide" also raises legitimate concerns about inequality of outcome.

Theoretically, too, there are serious problems with IDEA. It reaches out to embrace not only the pervasive cognitive disabilities we have been discussing, but also a wide variety of "specific learning disabilities" whose etiology and nature are poorly understood. "Specific learning disabilities" are very different from Down syndrome and autism, in that they are conceptualized as specific impediments that typically conceal the student's true ability: thus a diagnosis of "learning disabled" (LD) is made on the basis of evidence of a discrepancy between "true ability" (often measured on an I.Q. test) and school achievement in one or more subject areas.

In principle, it seems like a very good thing to be attentive to these discrepancies. Such a strategy looks like just what the capabilities approach would recommend. But in practice it is very hard to distinguish a child with a learning disability from a child who is simply slow or less talented than many. Nor is the conceptual framework of learning disabilities secure: the theory suggests an organic cause of a specific impediment, and yet it is not clear that such causes exist for the wide range of impediments recognized. Nonetheless, the financial incentives created by IDEA give school districts reasons to rush toward classifying children as learning disabled, in order to qualify for federal funding. Such classifications may not always help the child: they can be stigmatizing in their own right, and they do not always point to a useful course of treatment. Moreover, they tend to be unfair to children who have problems in school but who cannot be plausibly classified as learning disabled. One feels that all children should be helped to reach their cognitive potential; but the system promotes some children over others in a way that is more than a little arbitrary.[56] In practice, this defect has been somewhat mitigated by the looseness of the classificatory system, as school districts seek to include as many children as possible in the funding-eligible pool.[57]

The largest problem with these laws, conceptually, might seem to be the fact that they still single out children with mental impairments as a class apart, and say that for them education should be individualized and aimed at fostering human capabilities. Obviously this should actually be the goal of any good school system for every child. So one can understand the irritation of parents whose children are not learning well, but who have no classifiable disability, when law protects the education of classifiable children, while their own is left to languish with insufficient attention. Children with mental impairments do need special attention, since all school systems are designed for the

"normal" child. Still, it would be progress if we could acknowledge that there really is no such thing as "the normal child": instead, there are *children*, with varying capabilities and varying
impediments, all of whom need individualized attention as their
capabilities are developed.

We can defend the law, however, by pointing out that "normal" children, who today are usually understood to be individuals, with many differences of personality, have all too often been
understood to be members of a faceless class of subhuman persons, without significant individuality. When people think of
Down syndrome, they tend to think of a set of people with identical facial features and no significant human differences. When
they think of autism, the image of a person banging his head
against a wall comes to the fore, and the idea that such a child
might have a personality of his or her own is not included. As
Goffman says, stigma tends to submerge individuality: one's entire interaction with the person is with the stigmatized trait. In
this situation, it makes sense that law will focus on protecting
what most urgently needs protection: the claim of stigmatized
children to be seen, and educated, as individuals.

Despite all of these difficulties and others, the law has proven
a major achievement. It is now under threat. In the spring of
2004 both the House and the Senate supported reauthorization
of IDEA, but with very different bills, each involving at least
some retreat from the goals of the 1997 law. The Senate bill,
S. 1248, passed by a vote of 95 to 3, is relatively close to the
1997 law. Unfortunately, an amendment providing for mandatory full funding fell 4 votes short of the necessary 60. Some
other provisions of the new version are troubling: for example, an amendment proposed by Pennsylvania's Senator Rick
Santorum allows up to fifteen states to obtain waivers to "reduce
paperwork" connected with the administration of IDEA; this
amendment may seriously erode the oversight required for suc-

cessful administration of the law. Another amendment allows school districts to recover attorneys' fees when parents file "frivolous" lawsuits alleging that their disabled child has received inadequate schooling. Given the lack of clarity about the definition of "frivolous," this amendment, too, may inhibit the act's implementation. Finally, the bill (like its House counterpart) omits the 1997 law's requirement that state standards for "related services personnel" (including school counselors) be based on the "highest requirements in the state applicable to a specific profession or discipline." On the whole, however, the Senate version is reasonably good. The House version, H.R. 1350, passed 251–171, would represent a major setback. (Most national disability organizations opposed the bill as worded, and it drew the most negative votes of any special education bill in recent history.) Whereas the Senate bill requires a behavioral assessment to determine whether a child's violation of school conduct codes is the result of a child's disability or a school's failure to implement the IEP, the House version omits this safeguard. It also omits related safeguards regarding changes of school placement for disciplinary reasons. There are other concerns about omissions of short-term goals in the IEP. In December 2004, the president signed a compromise version of the bill that retains some of the protections for disabled students in the Senate version, especially concerning expulsion for disciplinary violations, and also reasserts the goal of 40 percent federal funding by the year 2011. It is clear, however, that IDEA remains vulnerable to politics, nor is it even close to being adequately funded.

xiii. Public Policy: The Work of Care

Now we must return to the general problem of care, asking what policies are suggested by the capabilities approach. I argued that care has implications for more or less all the central capabilities of both the cared-for and the caregiver, and that the capabilities list provides a highly useful set of social benchmarks as we consider what policies we want to adopt. The policy issue has two faces, then: the cared-for (children and adults with disabilities)[58] and the lives of those who care for them (usually adults and most often women, both related and unrelated, paid and unpaid). And it has three "locations": the public sector, the educational system, and the workplace.

As I have noted, the capabilities approach rejects the familiar liberal distinction between the public and the private spheres, regarding the family as a social and political institution that forms part of the basic structure of society.[59] The distribution of resources and opportunities within the family thus becomes an object of intense concern. Adult freedom of association still supplies substantial limits to state interference with family life. Thus it would not be acceptable for the state simply to mandate that husbands and wives divide care labor equally. But recognition of the political nature of the family institution is the beginning of progress, for it immediately leads us to ask: What laws are implicated in the problems we currently have before us, and how might law do its job better?

One obvious defect of the current legal situation is that women's work within the family is not recognized as work. Eva Kittay has suggested that the best way to remedy this situation would be a direct payment to family members who perform care work. Such a payment, she argues, should not be means-tested, since the whole idea is to treat it like a salary, giving social dignity and recognition to the work in question, and salaries are not means-tested.[60]

Although at first such a strategy might sound unrealistic, similar measures have in fact been adopted in a number of countries. To give just a couple of examples: in Finland and Denmark, municipalities contract with a caregiver to provide certain services, and the (home-based) caregiver is paid by the municipality. France, Austria, Germany, and the Netherlands have programs that provide cash payments for at least some care services.[61] Some U.S. states have adopted demonstration programs along these lines. Other nations provide compensation for loss of income during a period of care for a disabled relative; still others give means-tested support to family members whose income is low because of care work. (Examples of the latter approach are the Invalid Care Allowance and the Carer Premium in the United Kingdom and the Carer's Allowance in Ireland.)

In speaking of cash payments and income support, we have already been speaking about the role of the public sector. But the public sector has a larger set of roles here. Programs supporting parental leave from work with pay are common in Europe, and a very limited such program, the Families and Medical Leave Act of 1993, still exists in the United States, although a related program, Aid to Families with Dependent Children, has been cut. Another area that deserves much more exploration is that of national youth service. In Germany, for example, young people are given the option of military service for two years or alternative service for three. Much of the work that alternative service performs is care work. It seems to me that the United States (and other nations) can reap many benefits from such a program, in addition to the obvious one of getting a lot of this work done by energetic young people at relatively low cost. Young people, both men and women, would learn what this work is like, how important it is, and how difficult; this experience could be expected to shape their attitudes in political debates and in family life. They would also see different parts of the country, different social classes, and one another—something that the abolition of the military draft has made very rare in the experience of most Americans. If national service included a military option, this would also restore civilian control over the military. It is a sad comment on the legacy of the social contract tradition that people are ready enough to trumpet the importance of moral and religious values, but unwilling to support such a policy, which would seem to be the basic minimum that such values would advocate. Instead, young people and their parents seem preoccupied with "getting ahead," and the idea that two or three years of life would actually be given to others is regarded as absurd—despite the fact that this work is being done every day, usually by people who are far less able than the middle-class young to afford the drain on time and energy that it imposes.

At the same time, it is highly desirable that public education should emphasize the importance of care work as a part of life for both men and women, trying to break down the reluctance men feel about doing this sort of work. Obviously this reluctance is not innate. It is taught in social conceptions of manliness and success, and it can be taught differently. If we adopt a capabilities approach, its political conception of the person, in which need for care is a salient aspect, can and should be taught to children at all ages. Such teaching ought to shift in many subtle ways the conception of manliness that so often makes men reluctant to take on the work of care or even to think about it seriously. This shift should lead to more respect for the work involved in care, and thus to more public willingness to spend money on it and deliberate seriously about it as a public issue. It should also lead to less reluctance to take on some of this work in the home.

But another transformation is required, if any of this is to have any serious impact. This is the transformation of the workplace. As Joan Williams emphasizes in her recent study of family leave policies and their relation to norms at work, even good public arrangements will do little good if the structure of careers still sends people the message that they will be regarded as second-class workers if they avail themselves of policies such as family and parental leaves. Through comparative data, Williams shows that in countries with a promising range of state policies (Sweden, for example), women still do most of the work of caring for dependents.[62] The reason, she plausibly argues, is that men do not want to jeopardize their career advancement or to be perceived as marginal part-timers. They are not averse to sharing domestic responsibilities, but they do not want to pay the price in career terms that such a decision would now exact. At present, in many different types of work, the expectation is that workers will either work full-time and have normal opportunities for promotion, or they will work part-time, with greatly diminished opportunities for promotion. In some workplaces (for example, in large U.S. law firms) things are even worse: there is a macho competition for long hours on the job, and anyone who refuses to work overtime is perceived as a marginal player.

This is a ubiquitous problem in both developed and developing countries, and at all levels of prestige and pay. It appears to be getting worse, with the escalating pressure for profit and the growing centralization of work under large corporate conglomerates, many of global reach. Even when a local employer might have had sympathy for employees who care for a parent or child or a disabled relative, many now have no choice in the matter: they are held to the norms of the remote corporate structure.[63] New technologies make possible enhanced flexibility in the time and place of work. But these possibilities are too rarely used in a humane manner. The capabilities approach suggests that a major aim of public policy ought to be the transformation of the workplace, through new flexibility and new ethical norms. These changes and the changes I propose in public education are strongly complementary: as young workers learn to think of care as part of their lives, they become less willing to accept rigid workplaces, and employers who offer flex-time and part-time options will attract the most skilled workers. Williams argues that this is to some extent already happening, even in the very rigid workplace climate of the United States.

xiv. Liberalism and Human Capabilities

I have argued that all the capabilities, including practical reason and control over one's political and material environment, are important human and political goals. Moreover, my version of the capabilities approach has long asserted a basic *principle of each person as end*.[64] in other words, the person, not the group, is the primary subject of political justice, and policies that improve the lot of a group are to be rejected unless they deliver the central capabilities to *each and every person*. In these ways, my approach to the issue of care lies squarely within the liberal tradition.

The capabilities approach criticizes some strands within that tradition for insufficiently attending to the material and institutional prerequisites of genuine freedom. Nor does it fetishize freedom as an all-purpose social good: some freedoms are important, and others are not; some (the freedom of the rich to make large campaign contributions, the freedom of industry to pollute the environment, the freedom of men to harass women in the workplace) are positively harmful, and should be regulated by law.[65] Finally, it uses a flexible and variegated conception of freedom that is capable of appreciating the capacity for freedom in citizens with mental impairments, rejecting political conceptions of the person grounded in an idealized rationality. In these ways, its neo-Aristotelianism departs from some strands within the liberal tradition. Nonetheless, although one could of course develop an illiberal or even antiliberal type of neo-

Aristotelianism, and some philosophers have done so,[66] my own version of a capabilities approach is emphatically liberal. Individuality, freedom, and choice are still goods, and very important goods at that.

Kittay, however, suggests that when we ponder issues of disability and care we should be led to make deeper criticisms of dominant liberal models of justice, ultimately departing from that tradition altogether. She suggests that Western political theory must be radically reconfigured to put the fact of dependency at its heart. The fact, she says, that we are all "some mother's child," existing in intertwined relations of dependency, should be the guiding image for political thought.[67] Such a care-based theory, she thinks, is likely to be very different from any liberal theory, since the liberal tradition is deeply committed to goals of independence and liberty. Although Kittay supplies few details to clarify the practical meaning of the difference, her idea seems to be that the care-based theory would support a type of politics that provides comprehensive support for need throughout all citizens' lives, as in some familiar ideals of the welfare state—but a welfare state in which liberty is far less important than security and well-being.

Kittay is not altogether consistent on this point. At times she herself uses classic liberal arguments, saying that we need to remember that caregivers have their own lives to lead, and to support policies that give them more choices.[68] But on the whole she rejects, in the abstract, solutions that emphasize freedom as a central political goal. The concrete measures she favors, however, do not seem to have such sweeping antiliberal implications. The restoration and expansion of Aid to Families with Dependent Children; expansion of the Family and Medical Leave Act of 1993; various educational measures promoting the dignity of people with impairments and disabilities, through a judicious combination of "mainstreaming" and separate education[69]—all these are familiar liberal policies, which can be combined with an emphasis on choice and liberty as important social goals. Kittay's most controversial proposal, that of the direct non-means-tested payment to those who care for family dependents at home—clearly has, or could have, a liberal rationale: that of ensuring that these people are seen as active, dignified workers rather than passive noncontributors.

Her theoretical proposal, nonetheless, does go in an anti-liberal direction, in ways that have concrete policy implications for the treatment of children such as Jamie and Arthur. Presumably Kittay's state would attach far less importance than a liberal state to fostering independence, political participation, and the ability to make choices with regard to employment and way of life. Insofar as being cared for is the central image of the state's relation to the citizen, then full and equal citizenship does not require independence or a wide range of options for active functioning. By contrast, although my view insists that human beings are inevitably dependent and interdependent, and holds that dignity may be found in relations of dependency, citizens enjoy full equality only when they are capable of exercising the whole range of capabilities. At times this may have to be done through a guardian (see section xi below), but the goal is always to put the person herself in the position of full capability. So society is instructed to make it possible for people to have all the capabilities on this list—not because of social productivity, but because it is humanly good. All citizens should have the chance to develop the full range of human powers, at whatever level their condition allows, and to enjoy the sort of liberty and independence their condition allows.

Would we do better to reject this goal in favor of Kittay's idea, rejecting independence as a major social goal and conceiving of the state as a universal mother? To be sure, nobody is ever self-sufficient; the independence we enjoy is always both temporary and partial, and it is good to be reminded of that fact by a theory that also stresses the importance of care in times of dependency. But is being "some mother's child" a sufficient image for the citizen in a just society? (And is care a sufficient image for motherhood?) I think we need a lot more: liberty and opportunity, the chance to form a plan of life, the chance to learn and imagine on one's own, the chance to form friendships and other political relationships that are chosen and not merely given.

These goals are as important for people with mental impairments as they are for others, though much more difficult to achieve. Although Kittay's daughter Sesha will never live on her own (and although Kittay is right to say that independence should not be seen as a necessary condition of dignity for all people with mental disabilities),[70] even Sesha found joy in a new environment, outside her home, where she was not always directly cared for by her parents.[71] Many other people with mental disabilities do aspire to hold a job, and vote, and tell their own story. Michael Bérubé ends his compelling account of his son's life with the hope that Jamie, too, will write a book about himself, as two adults with Down syndrome recently have.[72] Recall that when Jamie was asked what he wanted to be when he grew up, he did not say the usual things, such as fireman, ballet dancer, basketball star. He just said, "Big." And his literal answer, said the teacher, taught them all something about the question: just getting to be "big," an adult in society, is itself an achievement. Bérubé, too, wants, simply, a society in which his son will be able to be "big": healthy, educated, loving, active, seen as a particular person with something distinctive to contribute, rather than as "a retarded child."

For that to happen, Jamie's dependencies must be understood and supported. But so, too, must his need to be distinct and an individual; and at this point Bérubé refers sympathetically to the liberal tradition. He argues that the idea at the heart of the educational reform that led to the inclusion of Jamie in a regular public school classroom is ultimately a liberal idea, an idea about the importance of individuality and freedom for all citizens. One of the most important kinds of support that children with mental disabilities need is the support required to be freely choosing adults, each in his or her own way. As Bérubé writes: "My job, for now, is to represent my son, to set his place at our collective table. But I know I am merely trying my best to prepare for the day he sets his own place. For I have no sweeter dream than to imagine—aesthetically and ethically and parentally—that Jamie will someday be his own advocate, his own author, his own best representative."[73] For this reason, Bérubé begins his narrative of his son's life with an extended description of activity and individuality: Jamie, imitating a waiter bringing his favorite foods, in a way that is characteristic of him as an individual. Insofar as Kittay suggests that we downplay or marginalize such liberal notions in favor of a conception of the state that makes it the maternal supporter of its "children's" needs, I think she goes too far, misconceiving what justice would be for both people with disabilities and aging people. Even for Sesha, who will never vote or write, doesn't a full human life involve a kind of freedom and individuality, namely, a space in which to exchange love and enjoy light and sound, free from confinement and mockery?

My argument has suggested that liberal theory needs to question some of its most traditional starting points—including the Kantian notion of the person, the Humean account of the Circumstances of Justice, and the contractarian idea of mutual advantage as the purpose of social cooperation. There are some very deep problems for liberalism in its reliance on the idea of a contract for mutual advantage. Kant's own endorsement of such a model seems in some ways deeply at odds with the central insight of his moral theory, namely, that each person is to be treated as an end, and none as a mere means to the ends of others. Rawls builds a lot more of Kantian ethics into his political theory than Kant himself does: the idea of the person as an end is one of the guiding ideas of the whole Rawlsian structure. Nonetheless, in the end his own ability to carry this insight through successfully for the case of disabilities is compromised by his adherence to the Humean account of the Circumstances of Justice and the consequently impoverished picture of the purposes of social cooperation. Moreover, Rawls's use of Kantian ethics is itself not free from difficulty, when we consider the way in which its emphasis on a rather idealized rationality makes more difficult an adequate political treatment of the needs and capacities of people with mental impairments.

If, however, we hold that the most important insights of liberalism concern the equal worth of persons and their liberty, we should conclude that these criticisms do not disable liberalism; instead, they ask us to reject some common liberal strategies in the name of the deepest and most central liberal goals. They challenge us to produce a new form of liberalism, which rejects feudalism and hierarchy in an even more thoroughgoing way than classical liberalism did, rejecting the hierarchy between men and women in the family and the hierarchy, in all of society, between "normal" and atypically disabled citizens. Such an account sees the bases of social cooperation as complex and multiple, including love, respect for humanity, and the passion for justice, as well as the search for advantage. Its political conception of the person holds that human beings are vulnerable temporal creatures, both capable and needy, disabled in many different ways and "in need of a rich plurality of life-activities."

This sort of revised liberalism offers a great deal to people with mental impairments and their advocates. The core liberal goals seem even more urgently important for people with mental impairments than for "normals," because it is their individuality, not that of "normals," that is persistently denied; it is their freedom that has been characteristically abridged through prejudice, lack of education, and lack of social support; and it is their equal entitlement to the prerequisites of flourishing life that has been ignored, as societies pursue impoverished understandings of the benefits and burdens of social cooperation.

The lives of citizens with mental impairments, and of those who care for them, will continue to be unusually difficult lives. For, as I have argued, we ought to acknowledge that such people encounter unusual impediments on the way to flourishing, not all of which can necessarily be removed by wise social action. The lives of those who care for such a child or adult may contain the sadness that such a residual impairment brings, in addition to the daily burdens of caring for someone who is atypically disabled. When we deal with the elderly, sadness is always in the wings in the form of the prospect of death. But the lives of either people with disabilities or their caregivers need not contain the stigma and insult and the inordinate burdens that they used to contain ubiquitously, and now often still contain. A decent society will organize public space, public education, and other relevant areas of public policy to support such lives and fully include them, giving the caregivers all the capabilities on our list, and the disabled as many of them, and as fully, as is possible.

Why would people ever create such a society? Bérubé's question, which I have quoted as my epigraph to this chapter, makes good sense, in a world in which, as he observes, we do not even support the full human development of all "normal" children. I have argued that it cannot be because we think we will gain thereby, in a narrow economic or self-interested sense of "gain." It can only be out of our attachment to justice and our love of others, our sense that our lives are intertwined with theirs and that we share ends with them. But this means that our dominant theories of the social contract give us the wrong message. For centuries they have been giving us a defective story about why people get together to form a society. It is because we have taken on that message and folded it deeply into our own self-understanding that we have such a difficult time with Bérubé's question. Theories of the social contract, which already expressed things that people thought and felt, have, through their success and prestige, profoundly reinforced those views of society, and generated them in people who did not have them before. Theories are only one influence on people's lives, but they *are* one influence. Images of who we are and why we get together do have power in shaping our projects. It is time, then, to see what a new account of social cooperation and its goals can do to advance the search for justice, in one of the most difficult areas of human life.

4

MUTUAL ADVANTAGE AND GLOBAL INEQUALITY

THE TRANSNATIONAL SOCIAL CONTRACT

Global inequalities in income increased in the twentieth century by orders of magnitude out of proportion to anything experienced before. The distance between the incomes of the richest and poorest country was about 3 to 1 in 1820, 35 to 1 in 1950, 44 to 1 in 1973 and 72 to 1 in 1992.

—United Nations Development Programme,
Human Development Report 2000

i. A World of Inequalities

A child born in Sweden today has a life expectancy at birth of 79.9 years. A child born in Sierra Leone has a life expectancy at birth of 34.5 years.[1] In the United States, gross domestic product per capita is $34,320; in Sierra Leone it is $470. Twenty-four nations among the 175 surveyed by the United Nations Development Programme have GDP per capita over $20,000. Sixteen nations have GDP per capita under $1,000. Eighty-three nations are under $5,000, and 126 nations are under $10,000. Adult literacy rates in the top 20 nations are around 99 percent. In Sierra Leone the literacy rate is 36 percent. In 24 nations the adult literacy rate is under 50 percent.

The world contains inequalities that are morally alarming, and the gap between richer and poorer nations is widening. The chance event of being born in one nation rather than another pervasively determines the life chances of every child who is born. Any theory of justice that proposes political principles defining basic human entitlements ought to be able to confront these inequalities and the challenge they pose, in a world in which the power of the global market and of multinational corporations has considerably eroded the power and autonomy of nations.

Nor do these data, being aggregates, tell us all we need to know about how the most deprived people in the world are doing. Women, for example, notoriously lag behind men in education, employment opportunities, and even in basic life chances.[2] Other inequalities influence basic opportunities: inequalities of class, caste, race, religion, ethnicity, and between rural and urban populations. Deprivations imposed by these inequalities are to some extent independent of general poverty, although general prosperity does typically raise the floor of entitlement to education, health care, and other basic opportunities. Any theory of justice that aims to provide a basis for decent life chances and opportunities for all human beings must take cognizance both of inequalities internal to each nation and of inequalities between nations, and must be prepared to address the complex intersections of these inequalities in a world of increased and increasing global interconnection.

In our world the global market, multinational corporations, and the nature of the global economic system pervasively influence the life chances of children in every nation. Other new global actors are also prominent: nongovernmental organizations and social movements, many of these multinational; international treaties and other documents; international or multinational agencies and institutions. Again, a viable theory of justice for the contemporary world ought to have some way of coming to grips with the changing centers of influence and advantage that make our world very different from the world of free republican states envisaged in Kant's *Perpetual Peace*.

The dominant theory of justice currently used to think about

global matters—when a sheer amoralist realism does not predominate—is the social contract theory in some form, a theory
that sees global agreements as the outcome of a contract that
people make, for mutual advantage, to leave the state of nature
and govern themselves by law. Such theories have been influential in thinking about global justice from the time of Kant, and
they have recently received a good deal of attention thanks to
the influential work of John Rawls. Despite their great strengths
in thinking about justice, social contract theories have some
structural defects that make them yield very imperfect results
when we apply them to the world as a whole. I shall first describe
the two different strategies used by contractarians to address the
problems of justice between nations: the strategy of what I shall
call the *two-stage contract* and the strategy of what I shall call the
global contract. Taking John Rawls's *The Law of Peoples* as a best
case of the former strategy, I shall argue that this approach cannot provide an adequate account of global justice. The strategy
of the *global contract* looks more promising; but it cannot defend redistribution from richer to poorer nations without departing in major ways from the contractarian approach.

Although my arguments are directed against social contract
approaches to global justice, I choose these approaches because
they are stronger than some others we have—stronger, in particular, than models of global development based on contemporary economic Utilitarianism. The "human development approach" that I favor can make alliance with contractarians, up
to a point, against that crude approach. It is this subtle debate
between two worthy opponents that concerns me here. And
my main contention will be that we cannot arrive at an adequate
account of global justice by envisaging international cooperation as a contract for mutual advantage among parties similarly
placed in a state of nature. We can produce such an account only
by thinking of what all human beings require to live a richly hu-

man life—a set of basic entitlements for all people—and by developing a conception of the purpose of social cooperation that focuses on fellowship as well as on mutual advantage. Contractarian ways of thinking, especially the idea that we ought to expect advantage from cooperation with others, have untold influence on public debate. My aim is to supply something both new and old, resurrecting the richer ideas of human fellowship across national boundaries that we find in Grotius and other exponents of the natural law tradition.

Before we begin, we need to have before us very clearly three features of social contract conceptions that are salient in their analysis of global issues. (Although this involves some recapitulation from Chapters 1 and 2, these issues need to be mentioned again in the context of a new set of problems.) These are all features on which Rawls continues to rely throughout his work—despite the fact that his hybrid theory, as we have seen, mixes Kantian moral elements with the idea of a social contract.[3] First, we must continue to focus critical attention on Rawls's endorsement of the idea that the social contract is made between parties who are roughly equal in power and resources, so that no one can dominate the others—the idea that he associates both with Hume's account of the Circumstances of Justice and with classical social contract doctrine. We must bear in mind, as we turn to the global plane, that this rough equality of the parties is Rawls's analogue to the idea of the state of nature in classical social contract doctrine (see *TJ* 12).

Second, a closely connected point, the social contract is imagined as one made for mutual advantage, where advantage is typically defined in familiar economic terms. Although the Veil of Ignorance introduces moral constraints on the ways in which the parties achieve their own interest, the parties are still imagined as exiting from the state of nature in the first place because it is in their interest to do so, as they attempt to further their plans of life. Thus, while the Veil sharply limits the role played by interest once they enter the Original Position, interests in promoting one's own conception of the good continue to play a large part in determining who is in and who is out at the initial stage. Rawls believes that a contract for mutual advantage makes sense only between rough equals. Despite his Kantianism, Rawls remains a contractarian in these two crucial respects.

Finally, social contract theories take the nation-state as their basic unit, conceiving of their contracting parties as choosing principles for such a state. This focus is dictated by their starting point: they imagine people choosing to depart from the state of nature only when they have found principles by which to live a cooperative life together under law. This starting point is a grave limitation when we consider transnational agreements, as we shall see.

Two other features of Rawls's theory on which I have focused attention in Chapter 2 will not concern me here. First, his use of wealth and income as a way of indexing relative social positions, though central to his own account of mutual advantage, is less important in discussing his treatment of global issues than the more general idea of a contract for mutual advantage. Second, Rawls's use of a reason-based Kantian conception of the person for political purposes plays no role in his analysis of international relations.

Before we begin, there is a question we must face. Both Kant and Rawls stress the symmetry between first-stage and second-stage contracts, and both clearly think that the contract between nations establishes essential moral foundations for international relations. One might, however, try to argue that Rawls's project never was to think about global justice in general; instead, his aim is only to describe the correct foreign policy for decent liberal societies. He certainly describes his aim in this way, both in *TJ* and in *LP*. Thus, the interlocutor might say, it is not surprising that domestic arrangements are treated as fixed and that the inquiry focuses only on matters of war and peace: for Rawls is not trying to talk about global justice at all.

We might have some doubts about whether these two aspects of the theory really do follow from the idea of articulating the foreign policy of a liberal society: for perhaps a decent foreign policy for such a society ought to think about the well-being of others in a comprehensive and robust way. More generally, we might doubt whether these two projects can be separated in the way the interlocutor suggests. Once one grants, as modern contractarians do, that foreign policy is correctly founded on moral principles and not only on (Hobbesian) considerations of national security and power, one might then doubt that domestic arrangements can be insulated from scrutiny, if they are such as to make it impossible for people in other nations to live decent lives. The whole idea that our transnational duties involve matters of war and peace only, and not matters of economic justice, may be questioned as both inadequate and, possibly, incoherent (in the sense that the adequate pursuit of global peace almost certainly involves economic redistribution). Certainly we cannot assume that a just foreign policy for a decent liberal society is indeed one that adopts such a thin account of the terrain of foreign policy, shielding domestic arrangements from scrutiny.

Is Rawls's project, however, the thin project of talking about liberal foreign policy alone, under a very narrow definition of what foreign policy involves? The discussion of the topic in *TJ* may suggest this reading; but a closer scrutiny shows that the project is clearly to extend Rawls's own normative conception, justice as fairness, to the international plane, not simply to describe a nation's foreign policy (see the summary at *PL* 21). Rawls makes it clear that the Veil of Ignorance imposes moral constraints on international relations that are analogous to the demands of fairness in the domestic case: the second-stage contract is designed to "nullif[y] the contingencies and biases of historical fate" (*TJ* 378). Certainly, by the time we arrive at the fuller discussion of the second-stage contract in *LP*, it is abundantly clear that international justice is Rawls's theme: "a particular political conception of right and justice that applies to the principles and norms of international law and practice" is Rawls's own definition of "Law of Peoples" in the book's first sentence, and the project is that of describing a "realistic utopia," a world fulfilling certain moral conditions. The focus on human rights in *LP* shows, as well, that Rawls is concerned with the idea of a world that is in some crucial ways fair to all. Thus even if Rawls continues to characterize his project as that of thinking about the foreign policy of a liberal society, it is clear that he understands that project in a broad sense, as involving a set of understandings that are fair to all, and even utopian.

ii. *A Theory of Justice:* The Two-Stage Contract Introduced

The precontractarian natural law tradition, represented by the ancient Greek and Roman Stoics and early modern successors such as Hugo Grotius and Samuel Pufendorf, holds that relations between states, like the rest of the world of human affairs, are regulated by "natural law," that is, binding moral laws that supply normative constraints on states, whether or not these dictates are incorporated into any system of positive law. Grotius' version of this approach has had enormous influence on the history of thought about global principles. For Grotius, all entitlements in the international community, including national sovereignty itself, derive ultimately from the dignity and the sociability of the human being. That is the approach that I shall ultimately be favoring.

The social contract tradition, by contrast, understands the situation that exists between states as a state of nature, and imagined principles of justice being contracted as if between virtual persons. The major social contract thinkers all understand the state of nature as involving some natural rights and duties; it is the insecurity of those entitlements that makes a contract necessary. Thus their thought is in many ways continuous with that of Grotius and Pufendorf. Modern contractarians, however, forgo any account of natural (prepolitical) entitlements, viewing entitlements as generated by the procedures of the contract themselves. Thus their thought departs far more radically from that of Grotius and Pufendorf than did that of their early modern forebears. As we study the idea of the second-stage contract, we should keep this difference firmly in mind.

The clearest example of this two-stage approach, and the most significant for Rawls, is Kant, who writes in *The Metaphysical Elements of Justice* (part I of *Metaphysics of Morals*) that a state is like a household situated alongside others. Under the Law of Nations, he continues, a state is "a moral Person living with and in opposition to another state in a condition of natural freedom, which itself is a condition of continual war." This situation gives states the right "to compel each other to abandon the state of war and to establish a constitution that will guarantee an enduring peace." The Postulate of Public Law in the state of nature says, "If you are so situated as to be unavoidably side by side with others, you ought to abandon the state of nature and enter, with all others, a juridical state of affairs, that is, a state of distributive legal justice."[4] This postulate is applied in the first instance to persons, enjoining that they leave the state of nature and enter a politically constituted state. It is then applied a second time over to states themselves,[5] enjoining that they enter some kind of juridical state of affairs.[6]

Kant's views about this state of affairs change over time. In

"Idea for a Universal History" and "Theory and Practice," he favors a system of coercive laws binding the federated states of the world. In *Perpetual Peace,* while he still mentions this idea as a rational one, he does not press the analogy between persons and states this far. States, he holds, "already have a lawful internal constitution, and have thus outgrown the coercive right of others to subject them to a wider legal constitution in accordance with their conception of right." He favors a voluntary agreement to enter a *foedus pacificum,* a peace-committed federation, which would not, however, have the force of public law or coercive power.[7] Nonetheless, international principles of right, whether conceived as binding law or only as the moral rules of a federation, are still held to apply in the first instance to states, not directly to their inhabitants, and are understood to be the ways in which states depart from the state of nature that exists between them, insofar as they do.

In *A Theory of Justice,* Rawls continues this Kantian approach. He assumes that the principles of justice applying to each society have already been fixed: each has a "basic structure" whose form is determined by those principles (377). The "basic structure" of a society is defined as "the way in which the major social institutions distribute fundamental rights and duties and determine the division of advantages from social cooperation" (7). It is said to be equivalent to those structures that have effects that are "profound and present from the start," affecting "men's initial chances in life" (ibid.).

We now imagine a second-stage Original Position, whose parties are "representatives of different nations who must choose together the fundamental principles to adjudicate conflicting claims among states" (*TJ* 378). (The parties are also called "representatives of states.") They know that they represent nations "each living under the normal circumstances of human life," but they know nothing about the particular circumstances of their own nation, its "power and strength in comparison with other nations." They are allowed "only enough knowledge to make a rational choice to protect their interests but not so much that the more fortunate among them can take advantage of their special situation." This second-stage contract is designed to "nullif[y] the contingencies and biases of historical fate" (ibid.).

Rawls says little about the principles that would be chosen in this situation, but he indicates that they would include most of the familiar principles of the current law of nations: treaties must be kept; each nation has a right of self-determination and nonintervention; nations have a right to self-defense and to defensive alliances; just war is limited to war in self-defense; conduct in war is governed by the traditional norms of the law of war; the aim of war must always be a just and lasting peace (*TJ* 378–379).

Let us now consider the analogy between states and "moral persons" (Kant's term), which Rawls recreates by treating representatives of states as analogous to the parties in the Original Position. One of the problems of the analogy is that many nations of the world do not have governments that represent the interests of the people taken as a whole. Even when a nation has a government that is not a mere tyranny, large segments of the population (women, racial minorities) may be completely excluded from governance. Thus Rawls's device of representation is indeterminate. In such cases, if the representative represents the state and its basic structure, as Rawls strongly implies, he is likely by this very fact *not* to represent the interests of most of the people. If, instead, he is imagined as somehow representing the real interests of the people, this is idealism carried to a point at which it loses useful contact with reality: for we are asked to imagine that, holding firm the unjust basic structure of the state, a representative somehow emerges who can truly represent the people's real interests.

A second problem concerns the fixity of the domestic basic structure. Rawls seems to accord legitimacy to the status quo, even when it is not fully accountable to people. One of the things people themselves might actually want out of international relations is help in overthrowing an unjust regime, or winning full inclusion in one that excludes them. (Thus women, for example, often turn to international agencies and agreements in search of domestic reform.) There is no place for this in Rawls's early scheme.

But the gravest problem with the analogy is its assumption of the self-sufficiency of states. In designing principles at the first stage, the society is assumed to be "a closed system isolated from other societies" (*TJ* 8). (Thus it is no surprise that the relations between states are envisaged as occupying a very thin terrain, that of the traditional law of war and peace.)

This isolation and self-sufficiency is so far from being true of the world in which we live that it seems most unhelpful. Rawls's structure has no room even for a supranational political/economic structure such as that of the European Union, far less for the complex interdependencies that characterize the contemporary world as a whole. Some states are more influenced by "external" matters than others, and the most powerful sometimes do act as if they were lone cowboys on the frontier. All, nonetheless, are far from being self-sufficient. For poorer states, the economic policies of the International Monetary Fund and the World Bank, international trade agreements, in general the global economic order, are all decisive influences on well-being. For almost every nation, the presence of multinational corporations influences both economic and political life. Political yet nongovernmental entities such as the International Labour Organization, the diverse organizations that make up the international women's movement, and many others are prominent ways in which citizens within each state fight for their rights. International tribunals deal with offenders in certain types of domestic conflicts. Environmental issues of necessity cross national borders. For such reasons, it is not helpful to regard the basic structures of states as fixed and closed to external influence. Even as an idealizing device, it takes us so far from the real world that the key problems of that world cannot be well framed.

The assumption of the fixity and finality of states makes the second-stage contract assume a very thin and restricted form, precluding any serious consideration of economic redistribution, or even substantial aid, from richer to poorer nations.[8] Indeed, Rawls waves that problem away from the start by his contractarian assumption of a rough equality between the parties: no one is supposed to be able to dominate the others. Of course, in our world these conditions are not fulfilled: one probably can dominate all the others. At any rate, the G8 do effectively dominate all the others. To assume a rough equality between parties is to assume something so grossly false of the world as to make the resulting theory unable to address the world's most urgent problems.

Even had Rawls not assumed a rough equality among the parties, the very assumption of fixity and finality would itself preclude any serious consideration of the distribution of primary goods among states. Within a state, parties are assumed to want and need a whole range of primary goods, including liberties, opportunities, income, wealth, and the social bases of self-respect. The contract concerns the distribution of this wide range of goods. It seems plausible to think that a contract among nations would talk about these resources also: for surely representatives of nations, not knowing which their nation is, would want to ensure that the distribution of primary goods among nations is a fair one, and that no nation is crippled by poverty or humiliated before others. Initially it looks as if Rawls has just made an error in limiting the topics of the contract to the traditional issues of war and peace. Why shouldn't the contract concern, as in the first stage, the entire range of primary goods? Once we face this question, however, we see its answer: because, in that case, the state could not be taken as a fixed and closed system. Redistributing income and wealth to other states would necessitate a rethinking of domestic priorities. And this Rawls has already ruled out.

By assuming the fixity of states as his starting point, then, Rawls has effectively prevented any serious consideration of economic inequalities and inequalities of power among states. He has ratified philosophically what the powerful nations of the world, especially the United States, like to do anyway: they pretend that their system is fixed and final, and resist with might and main any demand that they change internally, whether in matters of human rights or in environmental matters or in matters of economic policy, either in response to the situation of the rest of the world or in response to international treaties and agreements. The demand for change in domestic priorities is typically met as an illicit imposition: Who are you to ask us to change our own internal affairs? These are our business, and we have fixed them already, prior to entering into any relations or discussions with you. In the real world, however, we see this tactic for what it is: an arrogant mentality that is culpably unresponsive to grave problems. One should not grant it philosophical respectability.

Notice, too, that starting from the assumption of the existence and finality of states, we do not get any interesting answer to the question why states might be thought to matter, why it might be important to make sure that national sovereignty does not get fatally eroded by the power of economic globalization. Here again, the problem lies with the analogy between states and persons. There is a good reason to begin with persons and to give them salience in a theory of justice. We are each born and live our lives as persons, each body separate in its birth, death, nutrition, pain, and pleasure from every other body. Utilitarianism ignores this separateness at its peril, pretending that lives are just locations of satisfactions and that the salient fact for ethics is the totality of satisfactions in the system as a whole. Thus one person's great pain and misery can be compensated for by a plurality of people's exceeding good fortune. Here a moral fact of paramount importance—that each person has only one life to live—has been effaced.

We cannot say, in a similar way, that the state is a necessary moral starting point. While it is true that each person lives, at any given moment, within the borders of some state, people can move from state to state as they do not and cannot migrate from body to body. Moreover, as I have argued, structures other than the state influence their lives in fundamental ways. We may add that the modern nation-state is a historically bounded phenomenon: thus it is not even clear, in terms of Rawls's own argument, that the parties in the Original Position, who lack knowledge of their time in history, ought to be thinking from the start in terms of the nation-state. In any case, we need an account of why states matter to persons and what their appropriate role is. Why might people want the state, rather than corporations or international agencies, to supply much of the basic structure for their lives? By simply taking the state as a fixed starting point, Rawls precludes any illuminating answer to this question.

According to Rawls, "Political philosophy is realistically utopian when it extends what are ordinarily thought of as the limits of practical political possibility" (*LP* 6). The defects I have described suggest that the two-stage contractarian approach is not a helpful extension of ordinary practical thought for the contemporary world. Confirmation of this suspicion must, however, await examination of Rawls's detailed confrontation with international issues in *The Law of Peoples*. I believe that the book makes a little progress on some of the problems, but none on others; and it introduces new problems of its own.

iii. *The Law of Peoples:* The Two-Stage Contract Reaffirmed and Modified

The Law of Peoples "is an extension of a liberal conception of justice for a domestic regime to a Society of Peoples" (9). Its intention is to work out "the ideals and principles of the *foreign policy* of a reasonably just *liberal* people" (10).[9] It is also abundantly clear that this aim does not preclude, for Rawls, another, wider aim: to describe a "realistic utopia," a world in which, through the extension of justice as fairness, a decently just international structure obtains. The book thus attempts to answer the question posed in *Political Liberalism* (21), concerning whether Rawls's political conception can be extended to give good answers to questions of justice in the realm of international relations. Even to the extent that his project is one of asking about foreign policy, there is no reason to think that foreign policy must deal with matters of war and peace only; in *LP* it is clear that Rawls himself does not hold such a narrow definition of its concerns.

As in *A Theory of Justice,* Rawls takes the domestic principles and policies of liberal societies as fixed, including their economic policies, and simply inquires into their foreign policies. The fixity and basic importance of the domestic "basic structure" are the starting point—although, as we shall see, Rawls's distinction between states and peoples introduces some ambiguity on this point. The traditional concerns of international law are the book's center; it contains no discussion of the shifting configurations of the global economic order, the role of multinational and international agreements, institutions, and agencies, or the role of nongovernmental organizations, political movements, and other bodies that influence policy, frequently in ways that cross national boundaries.

At the same time, however, Rawls is more than usually concerned to reassure his reader that his analysis is realistic. Uncharacteristically, he devotes a substantial portion of the book to questions of nonideal theory. Moreover, he argues that utopian or ideal theory can be a valuable guide to practice in the contemporary world, provided that it is "realistically utopian." Whenever the two-stage structure shows signs of strain, Rawls is at pains to maintain that the problem in question really can be solved through a procedure that fixes the domestic basic structure first and then addresses, at a second stage, problems between nations.

Thus he mentions immigration, only to reassure us that the need for immigration would "disappear" (*LP* 9) if all nations had an internally decent political structure. Among the causes of immigration he mentions religious and ethnic persecution, political oppression, famine (which he holds to be preventable by domestic policies alone),[10] and population pressure (which, again, he holds to be controllable by changes in domestic policy). In "the Society of liberal and decent Peoples" these causes would not exist. Absent from his list, however, is one of the greatest causes of emigration, economic inequality—along with malnutrition, ill health, and lack of education, which so often accompany poverty.

Similarly, discussing the "burdened peoples," who on account of their poverty will not be part of the Society of Peoples, he justifies not discussing economic inequality between nations by insisting that extreme poverty can be eradicated by reasonable domestic policies:

> I believe that the causes of the wealth of a people and the forms it
> takes lie in their political culture and in the religious, philosophi-

cal, and moral traditions that support the basic structure of their political and social institutions, as well as in the industriousness and cooperative talents of its members, all supported by their political virtues. I would further conjecture that there is no society anywhere in the world—except for marginal cases [the footnote mentions "Arctic Eskimos"]—with resources so scarce that it could not, were it reasonably and rationally organized and governed, become well-ordered. Historical examples seem to indicate that resource-poor countries may do very well (e.g., Japan), while resource-rich countries may have serious difficulties (e.g., Argentina). The crucial elements that make the difference are the political culture, the political virtues and civic society of the country, its members' probity and industriousness, their capacity for innovation, and much else. [He mentions population control.]   (*LP* 108)

This analysis states a partial truth. But it ignores many salient issues. Even if we ignore the damage done by colonialism both to resources and to the economic and political culture of many contemporary nations, we should acknowledge the fact that the international economic system, and the activities of multinational corporations, create severe, disproportionate burdens for poorer nations, which cannot solve their problems by wise internal policies alone. Clearly, in the domestic case Rawls would not consider it sufficient, if the basic structure imposes unfair disadvantages on the poor, to point out that poor families can get by on thrift and virtue. Even to the extent that it may be true that thrift and virtue can overcome such obstacles, that fact does not dispose of the question of justice.

Let us now investigate Rawls's central argument. As in *TJ*, the device of the Original Position is applied in two stages: first domestically within each liberal society, and then between those societies. However, a major new feature of the book is that

Rawls also holds that a decent Society of Peoples includes as members in good standing certain nonliberal peoples who have "decent hierarchical societies." But these societies, being nonliberal, do not apply the Original Position domestically. They have other ways of establishing their political principles (*LP*70). So, there are three applications of the Original Position device: domestically by liberal peoples, then internationally by liberal peoples, then, in a further step, internationally by the nonliberal peoples who decide to sign on to the Society of Peoples.

Why are there two separate applications of the second-stage Original Position? Why not simply put all the decent societies together in a single second-stage contract? The reason seems to be that the principles are *derived* as an *extension of* the liberal first-stage contract, and then ratified, though not similarly derived, by the decent hierarchical societies. Thus liberal societies know that they are liberal societies, and the decent hierarchical societies, similarly, know that they are nonliberal and yet decent societies, although in other respects their ignorance of their situation is extensive. Rawls clearly thinks it unreasonable to expect them to derive the principles that they ratify from domestic liberal procedures: for, after all, they are not liberal societies. Rawls seems to think that they are more respected if they are asked to contract first with other similar societies, using whatever principles they favor among themselves, rather than being thrown directly into a structure that in essence derives from liberalism. But then it is a little unclear why he thinks that these societies will indeed agree on the same Law of Peoples that is chosen by the liberal societies. This whole part of the argument needs further work. Rawls seems to acknowledge as much, concluding that we could also "think of liberal and decent peoples together in an original position when joining together into regional associations or federations of some kind" (*LP*70).

As in *TJ,* the traditional concerns of foreign policy are the focus of both second-stage contracts, and a stable peace is at the core of their aspiration. Thus, among the eight principles of the Law of Peoples (*LP* 37), six deal with familiar topics of international law, such as independence and self-determination, nonaggression, the binding force of treaties, nonintervention, the right of self-defense, and restrictions on the conduct of war. But Rawls expands his account to include agreement on some essential human rights and a duty to assist other peoples living under unfavorable conditions "that prevent their having a just or decent political and social regime" (ibid.). The long-term goal of their cooperation is a "democratic peace" of the sort envisaged by Kant, in which decent democratic regimes increasingly come to power in all societies, thus eliminating religious persecution, war (Rawls insists that democracies never make war on one another), and the other greatest evils of the modern era. Here Rawls follows Kant: a perpetual peace may be envisaged as a result of the establishment of a federation of free republican states.

The goal thus described seems somewhat richer than the understanding of mutual advantage sketched in *TJ*, although, as we shall see, Rawls's interpretation of it is constrained by his refusal to consider substantial material redistribution across national boundaries. But how far does it really go beyond the contractarian idea of a fair contract for mutual advantage? Clearly, democratic peace would confer a great advantage on every society. It is thus rather difficult to know to what extent Rawls understands the goal as embodying a good that transcends the advantages of the parties (on fair terms), linking them all into a new global society. To understand this further, we need to examine *LP*'s treatment of the state/person analogy, asking to what extent Rawls diverges from his previous treatment of the basic structure.

As in *TJ*, Rawls treats the domestic principles of justice, in both liberal and nonliberal peoples, as fixed and not up for grabs in the second-stage contract. For none of these states, then, will the second-stage contract call into question anything about their assignment of liberties and opportunities or, importantly, about their domestic economic arrangements. Thus no international treaty that bears on these nations' domestic arrangements, in areas going beyond the thin menu of human rights that nations are assumed to respect, will be permitted to alter any nation's basic structure. Many international treaties in today's world, however, do have implications for nations' domestic arrangements, in matters concerning the basic structure of societies. (For example, the provisions of the Convention on the Elimination of All Forms of Discrimination against Women—CEDAW—concerning marital rape, the determination of nationality, and marriage and divorce require modification of domestic law in many nations, and these changes touch on the basic structure, since they concern the family.) So Rawls's position would appear to be that nations should not and do not ratify such treaties. He conspicuously refrains from stipulating that they have already met, domestically, the human rights norms spelled out in them. Only in the few areas covered by the small number of human rights norms he does recognize (to be discussed shortly) do transnational norms have the power to affect domestic structures; but it has already been assumed that all the nations involved already incorporate these human rights norms. Any extension of human rights thinking, by which nations decide to change their structures in response to international debate, is precluded by Rawls's assumptions.

In *TJ*, I have argued, the assumption of fixity and finality means that we get no interesting account of why states and their basic structure matter. This problem, which persists in *LP*, is made more acute by a distinction between states and peoples that Rawls now makes central to his argument. It is worth spending some time on this distinction, since it surfaces often in thinking about the international realm. Although Rawls at first appears to treat states, and their basic structures, as his starting point, further examination shows that he does not in fact do so. Instead, he insists that the principles of international relations apply in the first instance among "peoples" and not among states. What is a "people," and why does Rawls make this distinction? If a "people" is a group of human beings who share a comprehensive conception of the good,[11] or at least a set of traditions that come close to that, then it is a recognizable concept, but we should not imagine that we shall often find any coincidence between a people and national boundaries. Even in a nation with a strongly dominant religious tradition, such as Italy, there are religious minorities and nonreligious citizens. Religions themselves contain serious internal differences.[12] Moreover, in any group the women of that group may well not share in all respects the comprehensive doctrine of the men. What parades as the tradition or doctrine of a group is all too often a male construct, from the making of which women have been excluded.

If we now turn away from small and relatively homogeneous states to larger nations such as India, Peru, Turkey, and the United States, we find very pronounced divisions of comprehensive doctrine within the nation, just as we do in the domestic society envisaged by Rawls in *PL*. According to Rawls's own views, this heterogeneity is no accident, since he agrees with Charles Larmore that reasonable disagreement about comprehensive doctrines is a characteristic feature of modernity under conditions of freedom of thought (see *PL* 54–58). *LP* has assumed that at least some degree of freedom of thought is observed in all the participating societies, so on that account *LP* should anticipate a reasonable pluralism of comprehensive doctrines in all the societies in question. Thus we should not expect to find any of these societies meeting the conditions for being a people, if such conditions are taken to include a shared comprehensive doctrine.

Rawls suggests, however, that the requirements for being a people are somewhat weaker than that of sharing a comprehensive doctrine: only "common sympathies" are required; and "common sympathies," in turn, do not require a common culture with common language and history, though these, he says, are certainly helpful in constituting a people (*LP* 24). Do the societies he is considering constitute peoples so defined? At this point the concept may have become too vague to offer any guidance. It seems likely that women around the world have "common sympathies" with women in other nations to a greater degree than women do with men in nations characterized by sex hierarchy. Indeed, when people live close together in conditions of inequality, resentment and lack of mutual sympathy are especially likely to be found, more likely than when people live at a distance and see one another rarely. To the extent that we are inclined to say that the people in a nation have "common sympathies," it is usually because we manage to overlook such facts of subordination and to take the dominant group's word for how things are. Such facts are quite well known to Rawls elsewhere: in *PL*, his very concept of the state, and of community within it, is built upon such facts about pluralism and disagreement. It is for such reasons that Rawls repeatedly insists that the individual person is the only appropriate subject of a theory of justice.[13]

If we leave "common sympathies" to one side, we are left with Rawls's other necessary condition for being a people, a willingness to live together under the same set of democratic institutions. But this brings us back to the state, and alludes to what Grotius and other writers in the tradition would characterize as the fundamental bond between citizens and the basic structure within which they live. We do not need an extra concept to talk well about this bond, and the concept of "people," with its vague suggestion of social homogeneity, offers no useful clarification. Why, then, does Rawls express skepticism about the concept of the state, and hold that international relations must be seen primarily as relations between peoples and not relations between states?

At this stage, his argument takes a strange turn: for he speaks not of the state *simpliciter*, but of "states as traditionally conceived" (*LP* 25), and characterizes the state in a way that builds into it certain powers that states are traditionally believed to have, such as warmaking powers. Because he wants to deny that states rightly have such powers in a well-functioning international society, he concludes that the state cannot be the subject of a theory of international justice. Why not conclude, instead, that the traditional conception of the state is, in part, mistaken, ascribing to the state certain powers that states, rightly understood, do not really have? Such a line of argument would serve Rawls's overall purpose better.

Again, Rawls argues that states are rational actors pursuing self-interest alone (*LP* 28); here he refers to traditional realist conceptions of foreign policy. But once again, why not simply say that these conceptions of the state, like narrow economic conceptions of the person, are mistaken: states are both self-interested and moral? Such a line of argument would have served Rawls's overall purpose well. If Rawls had criticized the traditional conception of the state and advanced a more moralized conception, similar to that of Grotius, he would then have had no need to build his argument on the idea of respect for putatively homogeneous peoples, an idea that seems confused and confusing.

In certain ways, then, the formulations in *LP* are more confusing and less adequate than those in *TJ*.

On some vexing issues left over from *TJ*, however, *LP* makes progress. Recall that the analogy between states and persons suggests that states somehow represent the interests of the people within them; this, however, we have noted, is not true of many nations in the world. Rawls now explicitly acknowledges this fact and gives it structural importance. The second-stage Original Position includes only states that respect human rights and have either a liberal-democratic constitution or a "decent hierarchical" arrangement that includes a "common good conception of justice" and a "decent consultation hierarchy." On the outside of the Society of Peoples are "outlaw states," which do not respect human rights, and "burdened societies," which are defined as not only poor but also politically badly organized. Rawls holds that one important task of the Society of Peoples is to restrain the outlaw states. In this way, the argument has at least some bearing on the opportunities of people who are oppressed by these societies. All members, moreover, have duties to assist the burdened societies. For Rawls, such assistance chiefly entails helping them to develop stable democratic institutions, which he takes to be the main ingredient of their eventual prosperity. This is a limited understanding of what we owe other nations, but at least it is something.[14]

The most important development beyond the approach of *TJ* lies in Rawls's recognition of the transnational force of human rights. Membership in the Society of Peoples requires respect for a list of such rights, which constrain national sovereignty. Respect for these rights is sufficient to exclude forcible intervention by other nations (*LP* 80). The list is understood to be only a subgroup of those rights that liberal societies typically protect internally, "a special class of urgent rights, such as freedom from slavery and serfdom, liberty (but not equal liberty) of conscience, and security of ethnic groups from mass murder and genocide" (79). Although this commitment to human rights marks clear progress beyond *TJ*, it is important to notice how thin the list of rights is: it explicitly omits more than half the rights enumerated in the Universal Declaration, including full equality under law (since unequal liberty is permitted), the freedom of speech and opinion, the freedom of assembly, the free choice of employment, the right to equal pay for equal work, and the right to education.[15] Moreover, the fixity of the basic structure entails that no international agreement in the area of human rights going beyond this thin menu will have the power to alter domestic institutions.

So: Rawls makes only a little progress toward a richer conception of international society. Insofar as he does make progress, we can now observe, this progress is made possible not by the contractual approach itself, but by some very dramatic departures from it, in the direction of an approach more like the one I shall favor, which defines a minimal conception of social justice in terms of the realization of certain positive outcomes, what people are actually able to do and to be. The criteria used to judge who is part of the Society of Peoples and who is not include ethical outcome-oriented criteria: respect for human rights.[16] The fulfillment of these human rights sets the stage for the limited use of a contractual approach. In that sense *LP* ceases in some crucial ways to be a contractarian approach at all: some especially important matters are settled in another way, before the contract even gets off the ground.

Moreover, it appears that Rawls may have jettisoned the traditional Humean criterion of rough equality, understood in terms of similar economic circumstances. For clearly enough, nations that uphold human rights and are either liberal or "decent" are not rough equals at all. Rawls seems to imagine the contract as taking place between the United States and Canada and the nations of Europe and Australasia (adding in Japan and South Korea?), nations that might at least be claimed to be rough equals. But where do we place nations such as India, Bangladesh, Turkey, and South Africa, liberal rights-respecting democracies that are grossly unequal to Australia and the others in basic economic advantage? The GDP per capita of the United States, we recall, is $34,320, that of Bangladesh $1,610, that of India $2,840, that of Turkey $5,890, that of South Africa $11,290. (Real differences are probably greater than these figures suggest.) So these nations are extremely far from being rough equals of the nations of North America, Europe, Australasia, and (parts of) East Asia, and also far from being rough equals of one another.

The upshot is as follows. Either Rawls will have to admit that the principles and circumstances that bring societies together to form the second-stage contract are very different from the Humean Circumstances of Justice, with their focus on rough equality and mutual advantage, or he will stand firm on those conditions. If he departs from Hume, relaxing the condition of rough equality and the associated understanding of the motivation of the parties (they can all expect to gain from cooperation), then he can include all the nations I have mentioned, with their staggering inequalities. But then he will have to offer a new account of why they cooperate together, since the contract can no longer be seen as one for mutual advantage. Peace, of course, is in the interests of all human beings, but, as in the cases of "outlaw states," peace can be promoted externally, so to speak, and need not be promoted by including the poor democracies in the contract itself. So we must have a richer account of the purposes these very different nations pursue together. If, on the other hand, Rawls stands firm with Hume and with classical social contract doctrine, then he ought to say that India, Bangladesh, Turkey, and South Africa do not belong in the second-stage contract, much though his other criteria tell in favor of their inclusion. They are just too poor for the richer nations to gain anything from treating them as rough equals. They will have to be grouped with the "burdened societies"—although this grouping itself would show a problem with that category, since it cannot plausibly be claimed that what these societies need is help in developing democratic institutions.

If Rawls takes this course, excluding the poorer nations from the second-stage contract, he will be right in line with the current world order, in which most decisions about important economic matters are made with little input from the poorer nations, which are certainly not heard as equals, even when they are heard.[17] Rawls has not thought this through; his lack of clarity at this point makes *LP* an unsatisfactory work.

There is a striking parallel between the situation of poorer nations and the situation of people with disabilities. In both cases, the human dignity of people who are fully human is omitted from the crucial stage of the political contract in which basic principles are chosen, because they are not "rough equals" of the contracting parties in power and capacity. For that reason a contract for mutual advantage cannot include them as equal participants. They are a drag on the whole system, and different principles will have to be chosen to deal with them. Furthermore, because the contractarian approach conflates the contract's framers with the primary subjects of justice, the people who are not "rough equals" cannot count as primary subjects of justice.

Such a strategy is as objectionable for nations as it is for persons: they (or their citizens) are bearers of equal human dignity, and if they have special problems, those problems need to be addressed from the start, in the design of the entire system of global justice, not as an afterthought and a matter of charity. But including them fully from the start requires a different account of the purposes of social cooperation. Rawls veers in the direction of a new account with his inclusion of human rights requirements; but his shift is timid, and does not amount to the wholesale rethinking of the contract framework that seems to be required.

One more aspect of *LP*'s inadequacy remains to be noted. As we have said, Rawls's Society of Peoples admits "decent hierarchical societies."[18] Rawls justifies this move by appeal to a principle of toleration that makes a highly questionable use of the state-person analogy. Rawls argues as follows:

> Surely tyrannical and dictatorial regimes cannot be accepted as members in good standing of a reasonable society of peoples. But equally not all regimes can reasonably be required to be liberal, otherwise the law of peoples itself would not express liberalism's own principle of toleration for other reasonable ways of ordering society nor further its attempt to find a shared basis of agreement among reasonable peoples. Just as a citizen in a liberal society must respect other persons' comprehensive religious, philosophical, and moral doctrines provided they are pursued in accordance with a reasonable political conception of justice, so a liberal society must respect other societies organized by comprehensive doctrines, provided their political and social institutions meet certain conditions that lead the society to adhere to a reasonable law of peoples.   ("LP" 42–43)

In other words: just as Americans are required to respect the comprehensive doctrines of believing Roman Catholics, and Buddhists, and Muslims, provided that they respect the reasonable political conception of justice defended in *PL*, so, too, a liberal society is required to show respect both for other liberal societies and for decent hierarchical societies, provided that these societies adhere to the constraints and standards spelled out in the Law of Peoples. Toleration is said to require not only refraining from exercising military, economic, or diplomatic sanctions against a people, but also recognizing the nonliberal societies as equal members of the Society of Peoples.

Let us now examine this analogy. In fact there are both analogy and disanalogy. Inside a liberal society, there are many hierarchical conceptions of the good. These conceptions will be respected as reasonable, provided that their adherents accept, as a constituent part or "module" within their comprehensive doctrine, the principles of justice that shape the basic structure of their society.[19] In other words, the religious conceptions must include Rawls's principles of justice, even if originally they did not do so. Comprehensive doctrines that promulgate teachings conflicting with those will not find their members' speech suppressed, except in the exceptional conditions Rawls specifies in his doctrine of free political speech (a grave constitutional crisis). Nonetheless, such unreasonable comprehensive doctrines will not be respected in society's constitutional structure, in the sense that principles that conflict with these doctrines will be entrenched in the nation's constitution; for this reason their proposals will not be allowed to come forward for straightforward majority vote.

In the transnational case, things are very different. The religious or traditional doctrine is tolerated, in the sense that it will be recognized as a member of the community of peoples in good and equal standing, whenever certain far weaker conditions obtain. There must still be respect for a small list of human rights. But it is clear that a people may win equal respect in the community of peoples even if property rights,[20] voting rights, and religious freedom are unequally assigned to different actors within the society—men and women, for instance.[21] The requirements of political democracy, equal liberty, and universal suffrage[22] are replaced by the weaker requirement of a "reasonable consultation hierarchy."[23] Even free political speech need not be accorded to all persons, so long as certain "associations and corporate bodies" ("LP" 62) allow them to express dissent in some way, and take their views seriously. A decent society may also give different groups unequal situations with respect to discrimination in the workplace.[24]

In the domestic case, Rawls's principle of toleration is a person-centered principle: it involves respecting persons and their conceptions of the good. In the transnational case, although Rawls depicts himself as applying the same principle, the principle is fundamentally different: it respects groups rather than persons, and shows deficient respect for persons, allowing their entitlements to be dictated by the dominant group in their vicinity, whether they like that group or not. Rawls still focuses on persons to the extent of insisting on a small list of urgent human rights. But he allows groups to have a power in the national case that they do not have in the domestic theory.[25]

This asymmetry is especially peculiar in light of the fact that Rawls's central objection to Utilitarianism, in *TJ*, is that it is not sufficiently person-centered: by treating the community as a superperson and treating all satisfactions as fungible within this single structure, it neglects the fundamental distinctness of persons and their lives, treating them as "so many different lines along which rights and duties are to be assigned (*PL* 27).[26] Rawls's theory of international justice neglects the inviolability of each person that is a key to Rawls's domestic theory. But persons are persons, and violation is violation, wherever it occurs.

Furthermore, in the domestic case, any concessions that are made to the group are made against the background of exit options: persons are free to depart from one religion and to join another or to have no religion at all. Rawls knows well that the basic structure of a nation offers no, or few, exit options;[27] this is why he thinks it is so important that the institutions that form part of the basic structure should be just. The basic structure shapes people's life chances pervasively and from the start. And yet in the transnational case, Rawls has lost sight of this insight, allowing a local tradition to shape people's life chances pervasively, in ways that depart from principles of justice, even though there are no exit options for those who do not endorse that doctrine. Indeed, by assuming that there will be no immigration, Rawls has removed from his ideal theory even those exit options that reality sometimes offers. (We are now reminded of yet one more reason for immigration that is not adequately covered in Rawls's discussion of that topic.)

Rawls might reply that this argument against his analogy presupposes a peculiarly Western concern with the individual. In "LP," for example, he writes: "Many societies have political traditions that are different from Western individualism in its many forms" (69).[28] Now I have already argued that there is nothing particularly Western about the idea that each and every person has certain basic rights, just as there is nothing particularly Western about corporatist or associationist views of rights—a point that Rawls seems to grant in *LP* by citing Hegel as an example of the latter view. In India, for example, the shoe is often on the other foot: Western colonial traditions that included a strong corporatist element (giving political power to established churches, for example) are increasingly inhibited by ideas of human dignity that derive from a long Indian tradition of thought about persons and their dignity. These ideas may have some resemblance to some Western ideas, but judicial opinions often cite indigenous sources in order to make the multiple origins of these ideas clear. What happens in Rawls's argument, then, is that the very same traditions, whether Western or nonwestern, are treated differently because of the accident of setting up as a separate state, not because of any deeper phenomenon of organic unity or universal consent. If the corporatist tradition happens to dominate in a separate state, it gets to prevail; if it is but one element in a liberal state, it does not prevail.

But we can go further than this: it seems extremely likely that there is no tradition anywhere, nor ever has been, in which its subordinated or minority members simply endorse the lower lot in life they are offered. Women, for example, are often cowed, isolated, unable to resist effectively. But their "everyday resistance" has been amply documented all over the world.[29] So the very idea that women (or other minorities) do *not* see themselves as distinct persons who have lives to plan, separate from those of the males (or the dominant group) with whom they live, is an idea that would be extremely difficult to establish, and one that probably cannot be established.

I conclude that Rawls's analogy is deeply flawed. So far as his argument goes, at least, there seems to be no moral obstacle to justifying a single, far more expansive set of human rights or human capabilities as fundamental norms for all persons.

iv. Justification and Implementation

There is another issue that troubles Rawls, however, and it ought to trouble us. Rawls clearly thinks that if we conclude that another nation has defective norms we will intervene in some way, whether militarily or through economic and political sanctions. Usually he treats the question "Is this nation worthy of respect as a member of the Society of Peoples?" as if it is equivalent to the question "Should we refrain from intervening in that nation to seek the implementation of our own moral standards?" Indeed, it is in large part because, for Kantian reasons, he believes that intervention in the sovereign affairs of another republic is morally problematic that he is eager to conclude that we may respect hierarchical nations as members in good standing of the Society of Peoples.

But of course the two questions need not be linked in this way. We may think that the standards of a given nation are defective, and that we can justify as applicable to that nation a more extensive menu of basic rights and liberties than it now recognizes, thus making justified criticisms of that nation, without thinking that we have the right to intervene in its affairs, either militarily or through economic or political sanctions. We may take this line if we believe that there are independent grounds for refraining from interference with other nations under certain conditions, grounds that do not depend on our believing that we ought to express respect for the hierarchies around which this society has organized itself.

What might those independent grounds be? I believe that they are the very grounds suggested by Kant in *Perpetual Peace:* a moral loathing of colonial domination and a related moral belief that one should respect the sovereignty of any nation that is organized in a sufficiently accountable way, whether or not its institutions are fully just. Recognition of the moral importance of the state as an expression of human autonomy is already a prominent feature of Grotius' discussion of humanitarian intervention in *De Iure Belli ac Pacis (On the Law of War and Peace):* by forming sovereign states and giving themselves laws, human beings assert their moral autonomy.[30] Because one respects the citizens of a nation, and because one believes that the nation is, if in many respects imperfect, still above a certain threshold of inclusiveness and accountability, therefore one will refrain from military intervention into the affairs of that nation, and one will negotiate with its duly elected government as a legitimate government.

This recognition of a salient distinction between justification and implementation is typical of the modern human rights movement, which uses persuasion in most cases and urges forcible intervention in a very small number of cases. The United States receives heavy international criticism for its recognition of the death penalty, but there is no mainstream campaign for military or economic intervention against the United States on this account. Cases of genocide, torture, and other very severe human rights violations do give rise to discussion of forcible intervention or economic sanctions (for example, in the case of apartheid in South Africa).

What is the rationale for this deference to the state, if one believes that one can justify certain moral principles as binding on all? There may, of course, be strong prudential arguments against countenancing widespread humanitarian intervention. Such interventions may destabilize the world; moreover, the more powerful states are likely to view any robust practice of moralistic intervention as an excuse to tyrannize over the weaker. Kant already pointed out that colonial domination, in his time, proceeded behind a mask of moral improvement.

But Grotius' reflections on national sovereignty suggest a deeper argument against widespread intervention, one that derives from the dignity of the individual human being. The ability to join with others to give one another laws is a fundamental aspect of human freedom. Being autonomous in this sense is no trivial matter: it is part of having the chance to live a fully human life. In our day, as in Grotius' time, the fundamental unit through which people exercise this fundamental aspect of human freedom is the nation-state: it is the largest and most foundational unit that still has any chance of being decently accountable to the people who live there. International agencies and bodies like the United Nations are simply not (or not yet) accountable in this way; even the European Union as currently constituted raises serious issues of accountability. Nor do local exercises of autonomy at the city or village or even state level suffice, for the reason given by Rawls: the "basic structure" of the nation-state influences people's life chances pervasively and from the start. Thus the nation-state and its basic structure are, as Grotius has already argued, a key locus for persons' exercise of their freedom.

This argument concerns the state and the institutions that

form its basic structure. It is an argument about laws and institutions. It has nothing at all to do with the murky question of "peoples" with "common sympathies," a notion that I have already criticized as not very helpful in the context of our questions. This argument is just as applicable to India, heterogeneous and polyglot as it is, as to Bangladesh, far smaller and at least a little more homogeneous.

Following Grotius and Kant, we are working our way toward what the contractarian approach was unable to supply: a *moral/political* argument for the salience of national sovereignty. Rawls simply begins from the state (setting aside, for a moment, his detour through the concept of a "people"). In today's world, however, one cannot simply take the state as given (if one ever could), since national sovereignty is under threat from a variety of directions, above all from the influence of multinational corporations and the global economic structure. Rawls can give us no insight into why we might care about state sovereignty or try to prop it up against its competitors; our Grotian argument gives us at least the germ of such an insight.

Consider in the light of this argument the case of a nation that fails, for example, to offer women equal property rights. (India is an example of such a nation.)[31] So long as this nation is above a certain threshold in terms of democratic legitimacy, much though one might deplore the inequalities of women under that state's constitution, it would not be right to intervene in coercive ways. These threshold conditions would be weaker than those required for being respected as a fully and equally just society in the Society of Peoples. Most nations in the world today are unjust in one or more respects, and it is right for discussions in international society to argue that they are unjust and to hold up to them standards of full equality and dignity that one can recommend as applicable to them. But it would not be right to impose economic sanctions on them, far less military force, so long as they pass a much weaker test of accountability, a test that today's United States and today's India, for example, will pass, even though both fall well below the standards of full human rights protection that we can justify and rightly recommend. The case of South Africa under apartheid was different: a large majority of the population was completely excluded from governance. India acquired problematic status after the genocide and mass rapes in Gujarat in March 2002, and before the electoral defeat of the Hindu right in May 2004.[32] By even the narrowest and most traditional accounts of humanitarian intervention, Gujarat was a case for it. The argument against intervention in that case is in part prudential: intervention would surely have created far more problems than it solved, and we can now see in retrospect that internal electoral processes worked very well. But there is a further argument to be made on the basis of an idea of citizen autonomy: so long as democratic processes in India are robust, as they were and are, we should prefer to allow them to take their course, out of respect for these processes themselves and the citizens involved in them, in the hope that over time duly elected officials and duly appointed courts will bring the offenders to book and prevent further abuses, as seems to be happening in the aftermath of the elections of May 2004. In such a case, intervention can appropriately be confined to diplomatic efforts and public persuasion— although there might have been more of that than there was.

What is the threshold of legitimacy? A reasonable accountability of government to people: and here Rawls's conception of a "reasonable consultation hierarchy" may offer good guidance. We should note, however, that the case of women is extremely difficult in this regard. If South African apartheid met the criteria for intervention, there are many such cases in the world regarding women. Often they are not given equal voting rights, sometimes no voting rights; their property rights are unequal.

Would such human rights violations be sufficient to warrant economic sanctions? In moral terms there is a strong case to be
made, and it is shocking that one hears so little about this in international debate.[33] Brutal and oppressive discrimination on
grounds of race is taken to be unacceptable in the global community; but brutal and oppressive discrimination on grounds of
sex is often taken to be a legitimate expression of cultural difference. Clearly, we can justify the same norms for all nations. But
any complete or virtually complete exclusion of women from
the political process gives rise, as well, to a moral case for economic sanctions or some other form of coercion. The arguments
against such policies will be primarily prudential.

Someone might ask whether we do really show respect for a
state and its people if we criticize it and suggest that it has violated important moral norms that can be justified for all. It is important to approach this question by insisting at the start that no
existing state is fully just. All contain violations of important
moral principles. It is surely not respectful of another nation
when state actors or concerned citizens criticize only other nations and fail to criticize their own. For example, if the United
States keeps on harping on human rights violations abroad and
fails to take cognizance of the fact that its own stance on capital punishment is unacceptable to the international community,
and that its situation with regard to social and economic rights
lags well behind that of most developed nations, this conduct
seems disrespectful. On the other hand, it is perfectly possible to
express criticism in the context of an acknowledgment of one's
own failure fully to live up to principles of justice.

Where there is a gap between what we can justify morally
for all and what we are morally entitled to implement, what
should we do? One obvious thing we may and should do is
to work out international treaties protecting the human rights
that we believe we can justify and then work to get the nations

of the world to adopt and implement them. Beyond this, it seems to me that nations are often entitled to offer aid in ways that reinforce causes they believe important. Thus it would be legitimate for the United States, in giving aid to India, to target education, health care, and, as Clinton did, the empowerment of poor women, and to try to make sure that the aid gets used on these things rather than on building more nuclear bombs or "Hinduizing" textbooks.[34] It would also be legitimate to use diplomatic exchange as a way of drawing attention to those issues, as when Clinton used the occasion of his visit to India to draw attention to the situation of poor rural women struggling for credit and property rights. In the case of India, the legitimacy of this way of proceeding is uncontroversial, given that the cause of female empowerment and equality is a deep part of the Indian constitutional tradition itself. To the extent that a nation fails to endorse such goals publicly and constitutionally, we would be right to proceed in a more cautious way, but we would probably still be entitled to focus aid on projects that seem to us morally good. And of course individuals are always free to focus their aid on projects they favor.[35]

At this point Rawls might say that I have conceded his basic point: that we should treat nations as decent members in good standing of the Society of Peoples on a much weaker showing of liberal freedom and equality than we would demand within a liberal society. And indeed Rawls and I have converged in some respects on a set of practical principles. Am I not in effect conceding that we refrain from these impositions out of respect for a people and its traditions?

No, I am not. First of all, my argument has had no use for the concept of a people. I am arguing that we ought to respect the state, that is, the institutions of the basic structure of society that a given group of people have accepted and that are accountable to them. The state is seen as morally important because it is an expression of human choice and autonomy; and of course it is the state, not the "people," that expresses the desire of human beings to live under laws they give to themselves. It makes no difference to my argument whether the inhabitants of the state can be said to constitute a people in Rawls's sense, that is, sharing traditions and a relatively extensive conception of the good. Nor does my argument require us to relax in any way the moral judgments we make about the wrongness of actions in another nation, as Rawls's argument clearly does. It does not rely on any recognition of group rights, as Rawls's appears to, and it continues to maintain that the person is the basic subject of the theory of justice. It simply recognizes the fundamental bond between citizens and the basic structure of the state that is theirs, and it shows respect for that bond, as a way of respecting persons. More simply put, it is an argument about implementation, not justification, and it insists that there is a basic distinction between those two issues.

v. Assessing the Two-Stage Contract

Our close examination of Rawls's two-stage contract has put us in a position to assess, more generally, the prospects and defects of the two-stage social contract structure. The approach has grave difficulties as an approach to problems of global justice. Starting from the nation-state as its basic unit, it fails to take cognizance of the global economic order and the disadvantages it imposes on poorer nations. Nations are supposed to solve their problems by thrift and good character, as if there were no transnational structural obstacles to their doing well. The assumption of the fixity and finality of the domestic basic structure prevents serious consideration of economic redistribution across national boundaries, and it also precludes a role for treaties and international agreements in prompting domestic political change. Nor can the two-stage contract even offer an attractive account of why national sovereignty should be thought morally salient, because it is simply taken for granted as the starting point.

Rawls's analogy between persons and states, buttressed by his second-stage principle of toleration, is, moreover, insufficiently respectful of disadvantaged groups within each nation. His toleration argument justifies as fully and equally just systems that violate many of the human rights that the international order currently recognizes. No convincing argument is given as to why a much richer and deeper set of norms could not be justified for all the world's people, taking the person as the basic subject of justice.[36] To the extent that human rights do enter the picture, their role in the theory represents a departure from the contractarian approach, in the direction of an outcomes-oriented approach.

Even more fundamentally: the contractarian approach, based as it is on the idea of mutual advantage, requires that all parties believe they have something to gain by departing from the state of nature and entering into a contract. They must be rough equals, in Humean Circumstances of Justice (if we assume that Rawls still accepts that requirement): no one can dominate all the others, and none is so disabled as to be a drag on the cooperative enterprise. This is not the situation of the world. Rawls's attempt to address this problem by separating "burdened societies" from the ones that make the contract represents, once again, a departure from the contractarian approach, in that he allows the parties to use empirical information about global inequalities to structure the contract. Moreover, even this departure is insufficient: for the inequalities that obtain *among* liberal democratic states are extremely severe, with some having GDP per capita approximately thirty-four times as great as others. So the problem is not removed—unless we simply rule by fiat that

South Africa, Bangladesh, India, and so forth are not members in good standing of the Society of Peoples, and thus not participants in the contract. But why should we say this? No good reason has been offered to exclude them. Even the admission that there is a problem about including them betrays the contractarian's reliance on mutual advantage as the cement of the contracting group.

vi. The Global Contract: Beitz and Pogge

A far more appealing use of a contractarian approach is made by Charles Beitz and Thomas Pogge.[37] For both of these theorists, the right way to use Rawlsian insights in crafting a theory of global justice is to think of the Original Position as applied directly to the world as a whole. The insight guiding this strategy is that national origin is rather like class background, parental wealth, race, and sex: namely, a contingent fact about a person that should not be permitted to deform a person's life.[38] People's basic opportunities in life should not be violated by unfair hierarchy, whether the hierarchy is based on race or sex or class, or on birth within a particular nation.

Pogge and Beitz argue convincingly that the only way to be sufficiently respectful of the individual as the subject of justice, within a Rawlsian framework, is to imagine that the whole global system is up for grabs, and that the parties are contracting as individuals for a just global structure. Both argue, in different ways, that the resulting structure will be one that optimizes the position of the least well-off. For Beitz, natural resources will no longer be viewed as the property of the nation within whose territory they lie. Instead, a global redistribution principle will be created to govern rights over these assets. For Beitz, natural resources are like natural talents, and he interprets Rawls as holding that individuals do not have ownership rights in their natural talents (136–142). Pogge points out, correctly, that Rawls's view is subtly different: individuals may keep and use their natural talents, but they do not have an unqualified right to the profit derived from those talents. The overall system will ensure that advantages derived from these talents are used in a way that optimizes the position of the least well-off.

Beyond this, Pogge's view (which he calls "only illustrative speculation"; 273) envisages an initial global agreement on a list of human rights, which, over time, becomes more robust, including a system of global economic constraints. The list of human rights is considerably thicker than that defended by Rawls: it includes the entirety of the Universal Declaration, plus an effective right to emigrate (272). Natural resources are also subject to redistribution. Pogge does not insist that all nations satisfy Rawls's Difference Principle internally, so long as they bring it about that the position of the least advantaged people in the world is optimized.

The Pogge-Beitz proposal is a big improvement over the two-stage contract. The global Veil of Ignorance is an insightful way of capturing the idea that a just global order will not be based on existing hierarchies of power, but will be fair to all human beings, all of whom count as moral equals. The proposal also embodies an attractive idea of human freedom, in that it depicts all parties as equal choosers of the global order that will ensure.

One significant difficulty with these proposals is their vague and speculative nature. We are not told in detail how the design of the global Original Position will work. For example: What kinds of general information will the parties have and not have? Obviously they are not supposed to know what their own nation is; but if Rawls's idea is really being followed through with literal accuracy, they should not know their century either, and this means that they should not know whether their world has technology or not, whether it contains nation-states or not, whether it contains multinational corporations and global trade agreements or not. But that is far too much vagueness. If you do not know that a multinational corporation exists, you will probably not imagine one as a part of an ideal structure of global justice; but then you will not have anything useful to say about how to control such entities, how to relate them to nation-states, and how to make sure that they take on some important moral commitments in their dealings with others. If you do not know about the Internet, it will not be easy to imagine it; but then you will not be able to address the inequalities created by differential access to it. And so on.

In short, the world we live in exhibits changing configurations of power at the level of basic structure itself; even one hundred years ago it would have been difficult to predict what those structures would be. The new structures govern people's life chances pervasively and from the start. To require so much ignorance is to make the project utopian in a bad and unrealistic sense; it ensures that pressing problems of justice will be ignored. But if general social facts like these are to be known to the parties, then we need an account of what they know and what they don't know.

A related area of unfortunate vagueness concerns the role of the nation-state. Pogge and Beitz set out to question the finality and closed character of domestic state structures. But they do not tell us how far they really want to go. Are we standing back so far from current events that the very concept of the state will have to be reinvented, and considered against other options for arranging people's lives? But it is hard to arrange human lives in a complete vacuum. How can we say whether the state is or is not a good structure, without first assessing its relation to other aspects of life, such as trade, the flow of information, the presence of international agencies and agreements? The moral arguments that commend the state as an important expression of human autonomy did not arise in a vacuum, and it is not clear that they can be successfully made in a vacuum. Moreover, it seems an empty exercise to justify the state unless and until we have a sense of what the real forces are that might undermine it or provide alternatives to it. Without this knowledge we cannot choose well. If the parties do have such historical knowledge at their disposal, Pogge needs to be explicit about this departure from Rawls.

Finally, we need to know more about what primary goods the parties are imagined as pursuing. Pogge depicts himself as following Rawls closely, and yet he also thinks that his parties will agree on a long list of human rights, going well beyond the Rawlsian list of primary goods and also beyond the thin list of rights recognized in *LP.* Following the Universal Declaration, against both the Rawls of *TJ* and the Rawls of *LP,* Pogge links the sphere of liberty and the economic sphere very closely together, arguing that the major liberties have a material aspect. And like the Universal Declaration, Pogge seems to measure relative social positions by the fulfillment of rights, rather than by income and wealth. Once again, Pogge needs to tell us how far he really intends to depart from Rawls's idea. If his primary goods are human rights, understood in a way that links liberty with its material underpinnings, then his view will converge substantially with the capabilities approach, in ways that seem to take it away from Rawls's own view.

These are all questions that might be answered, although an adequate response will probably require departures from the Rawlsian framework in the area of information and in the conception of primary goods. At this point, however, we arrive at the most serious difficulty with the Pogge-Beitz proposal: What is the contract all about? The Rawlsian social contract takes place in Humean Circumstances of Justice, and it is a contract for mutual advantage. Pogge focuses on the requirement of fairness that is built into Rawls's Veil of Ignorance and simply omits mention of Rawls's endorsement of Humean Circumstances of Justice as the starting point for the contract. As Rawls insists, the requirement of equality among the parties is his analogue to the state of nature in classical social contract doctrine, so Pogge would also appear to have omitted the state of nature. At least he does not mention it. But if that is omitted, we have a major departure from the social contract tradition. Pogge certainly does not tell us that he is departing from that tradition: for example, he does not endorse Scanlon's pure Kantian contractarianism or Barry's political version of it. He focuses on Rawls, and apparently refuses to modify Rawls's theory in the direction of a pure Kantian contractarianism of the Barry/Scanlon type.[39] He clearly keeps Rawls's Veil of Ignorance and the moral equality it imposes. But it looks as if he simply has not taken a stand on the issue of rough equality and Humean Circumstances of Justice, crucial though that issue is for the interpretation of his theory.

We have already seen that when the contract is envisaged as taking place among nations, it cannot be cast in standard social contract form unless we omit not only nonliberal states, but also pretty much everyone except the G8. If we imagine the contract as taking place among individual persons, things are indeed different: for the individual persons of the world are at least morally equal, and in some ways they—at least, all those who are not disabled—might be argued to be roughly equal in basic economic productivity and life chances before the contingencies of life begin to affect them. But when is that? Surely not at any time after birth, for every child is born into a world that begins to affect its life chances directly and dramatically, through differential nutrition, differential cognitive stimulation, differential exposure to kindness or violence, and so on. As we have seen, life expectancy at birth in the poorest nations is less than half of what it is in the richest nations; these aggregate figures derive from all kinds of differences at the level of individual lives.

Are individuals equal in life chances before birth? Surely not. Whatever account we give of the fetus, we must say that by the time a human being is born, differences in maternal nutrition, health care, bodily integrity, and emotional well-being, not to mention HIV status, have already affected its life chances. The prenatal transmission of HIV affects staggering numbers of people in Africa today. For that matter, even getting the chance to be born is not a matter with respect to which there is rough equality: the alarming rise in sex-selective abortion in many developing (and some developed) countries means that females conceived in some parts of the world are grossly unequal in life chances both to boys in that same part of the world and to girls and boys in other parts of the world.[40]

Unfortunately, then, the inequalities between nations that make the two-stage contract exclude some nations in order to conform to the Humean Circumstances of Justice are translated into inequalities between persons in basic life chances. There is no time when a human or even a potential human is alive that such inequalities do not obtain.

Pogge and Beitz abhor such inequalities in basic life chances. To cope with them, providing a philosophical rationale for an ambitious commitment to global redistribution, is the whole point of their project. But this commitment is not so easily reconciled with the Rawlsian framework, even in the improved non-Rawlsian way in which they use it. It is all very well to say that the Original Position should be applied at the global level; that idea does dramatize some important issues of fairness. But once we go into things in more detail, we find that the global contract they propose requires a departure of major proportions from the Rawlsian framework. For it requires abandoning the

Humean Circumstances of Justice as setting the stage for the contract, and including from the start all who are currently unequal in power. Above all, it requires admitting from the start that the point of the contract is not, and cannot be, mutual advantage among "rough equals." It must be human fellowship, and human respect, in a more expansive sense.

Perhaps it is not surprising that in the light of these problems Pogge has turned, in recent work, toward a full-fledged human-rights approach, very close to the capabilities approach that I shall favor, and away from Rawlsian proceduralism.[41]

vii. Prospects for an International Contractrarianism

In the international domain, contractarianism of a Kantian type has strong attractions. To begin with, it is a normative ethical approach to international relations. As such, it is superior to Hobbesian/realist approaches that see the space between nations as a space devoid of binding moral requirement, a space where nations may unrestrainedly pursue power and security interests.[42] Such approaches have dominated in the international sphere in recent years, as they apparently did in the time before Grotius, and they have led to a debasement of international relations. Among the ethical approaches we might use, contractarianism seems greatly superior to economic Utilitarianism. It takes seriously the equal dignity of each and every human life, as Utilitarianism, committed as it is to aggregation, cannot fully do. And it takes seriously as well the idea that preference and desire can be deformed by unjust background conditions; so it does not attempt to build up the political account of basic justice simply from a reliance on people's preferences. In all these ways, contractarianism agrees with the approach that I shall ultimately favor.

Moreover, the central idea of contractarianism, that of fair terms of cooperation, is a powerful and necessary idea, which is captured elegantly in the procedural device of the Original Position. In the world arena even more than in the domestic sphere, it is immensely valuable and clarifying to insist that we want the basic principles that govern people's life chances to be fair to all of them, and chosen in such a way that nobody could reasonably reject them. These ideas, as well, will play a role in my own normative approach.

The most severe difficulties with Rawlsian contractarianism come, once again, from the elements in contractarianism that I have singled out as problematic from the start: the commitment to a rough equality of power in framing the initial contract situation and the associated commitment to mutual advantage as the goal of the contract. Can a contractarian give up the commitment to mutual advantage, along with the whole idea of the state of nature? Not unless there is another account of the purposes of social cooperation, and another story about what goods the parties are imagined as pursuing. Once again, a contractarianism along Scanlonian lines, equipped with a suitable political theory of primary goods, can still perform an important philosophical task, and such a theory will remain one of the important alternatives to an entitlement-based theory of the sort that I shall offer. There will be great convergence between such an approach and mine, because that approach will need an account of the good, and mine needs a role for rational acceptability in its account of a potential overlapping consensus in the international domain.

Can a contractarian approach also do away with the new difficulty that Rawls's theory has in the global domain, namely its commitment to the fixity and finality of the domestic basic structure? Again, I see no reason why not, once it is prepared to jettison the classical idea of choosing principles in a state of nature, which does strongly suggest the classical doctrine that the parties are choosing principles for a state of some sort. There are strong reasons why no contractarian approach currently on offer is responsive to the changing configurations and loci of power in today's world, including multinational corporations and international agencies alongside states, in its thought about basic justice. But a Scanlonian type of contractarianism can probably include those entities and can also treat domestic basic structures as modifiable by international agreements.

Expressed in Scanlon's way, then, the idea of fair terms of cooperation (terms that cannot be reasonably refused) is a powerful intuitive way of capturing the idea that human beings are moral equals despite their widely differing circumstances in an unequal world. This idea is important in the discussion of global justice. But it can do little work in political thought without a political account of the good, particularly an account that specifies the basic entitlements of all human beings. The capabilities approach begins from such an account.

5

CAPABILITIES ACROSS NATIONAL BOUNDARIES

> But among the traits characteristic of the human being is an im-
> pelling desire for fellowship, that is for common life, not of just
> any kind, but a peaceful life, and organized according to the mea-
> sure of his intelligence, with those who are of his kind . . . Stated
> as a universal truth, therefore, the assertion that every animal is
> impelled by nature to seek only its own good cannot be conceded.
>
> —Hugo Grotius, *On the Law of War and Peace*

i. Social Cooperation: The Priority of Entitlements

We live in a world in which it is simply not true that cooperating
with others on fair terms will be advantageous to all. Giving all
human beings the basic opportunities on which we have focused
will surely require sacrifice from richer individuals and nations.
Thus the classic theory of the social contract, even its moralized
Kantian form, does not suffice to ground an inclusive form of
social cooperation that treats all human beings with equal respect. But the shortcomings of this view of cooperation should
not dismay us. Before the doctrine of the social contract was in-
vented we had, and used, richer and more inclusive ideas of human cooperation. Beginning at least from Aristotle, and developed in the international context by Cicero and the Roman
Stoics, we have available to us a political conception of the human being as a being capable of ethical reasoning, and also a being who wants and needs to live with others. These two features,
ethical reason and sociability, combine in the Grotian idea that
we are beings who have a common good and who seek a "com-

mon life . . . organized according to the measure of [our] intelligence."

This intelligence is a moral intelligence. The three central facts about human beings that this moral intelligence apprehends are the dignity of the human being as an ethical being, a dignity that is fully equal no matter where humans are placed; human sociability, which means that part of a life with human dignity is a common life with others organized so as to respect that equal dignity; and the multiple facts of human need, which suggest that this common life must do something for us all, fulfilling needs up to a point at which human dignity is not undermined by hunger, or violent assault, or unequal treatment in the political realm. Combining the fact of sociability with the other two facts, we arrive at the idea that a central part of our own good, each and every one of us—insofar as we agree that we want to live on decent and respectful terms with others—is to produce, and live in, a world that is morally decent, a world in which all human beings have what they need to live a life worthy of human dignity.

The capabilities approach is an outcome-oriented approach that supplies a partial account of basic social justice. In other words, it says that a world in which people have all the capabilities on the list is a minimally just and decent world. Domestically, it holds that one central purpose of social cooperation is to establish principles and institutions that guarantee that all human beings have the capabilities on the list or can effectively claim them if they do not. It thus has a close relationship to institutional and constitutional design.

In the international case, how should the approach proceed? Once again, we have options. We may begin with the design of a fair procedure, as in the thin Scanlonian contractarianism we imagined at the end of Chapter 4; or we may begin with outcomes, with the basic goods to be realized. I suggested that

Scanlon's theory ultimately needs a political theory of the good. On the other side, the idea of equal dignity already builds a quasi-contractarian component into my good-based theory, stipulating from the start that any distribution of basic goods must be one that shows equal respect to all. We shall see in section iv that another contractarian notion, the idea of reasonable agreement, will play a role in our theory as well, in articulating the idea of an international overlapping consensus. With these important qualifications, the capabilities approach begins from a theory of the good in terms of an account of basic human entitlements.

Before we can move further in articulating that approach, there is another challenge that we need to face: Is it, after all, coherent to begin from entitlements, or must we not, instead, begin from the idea of duties? One influential approach to global justice, represented most prominently by Onora O'Neill (following Kant), argues that we must begin with duties.[1] We think about what we have a duty to do and not to do to and for human beings, and this reflection informs us about what the recipient is entitled to receive. The other side in this debate, represented by Seneca and Cicero, by Grotius, by the modern human rights movement, and by human-rights-oriented thinkers such as Henry Shue and Charles Jones,[2] argues that we should begin with entitlements. We consider what people are entitled to receive, and, even before we can say who may have the duties, we conclude that there are such duties, and that we have some sort of collective obligation to make sure that people get what they are due. The capabilities approach begins with entitlements, both in the domestic and in the international case. We need, then, to confront the arguments of the other side.

No real approach is a pure duties-based approach. For we cannot possibly say to whom we owe something without thinking about people's needs, as Kant's example of the maxim of

nonbeneficence famously shows.[3] The world without beneficence is not a world that the agent can will—because, on reflection, he sees that in that world he would lack things that he
needs, and to which he feels entitled.[4] Similarly, Rawls's Kantian
proceduralism begins from Circumstances of Justice that include the needs of human beings for basic goods of life, and his
account of just distribution relies heavily on an account of the
"primary goods" that all human beings need to pursue their
projects. We have said that the Scanlonian contractarianism that
seems preferable to Rawls's as a basis for global justice will need,
similarly, a robust theory of the good. Duties, in short, are never
generated in a vacuum: the idea of needs, and of entitlements
based upon needs, always enters in to inform us why the duty is
a duty, and why it matters.

Nor is the duty-based tradition successful when it tries to argue that a duty-based account supplies political thought with a
clarity and definiteness that entitlement-based accounts must
lack. O'Neill claims that if we begin with people's needs for food
and shelter, we have no clear way of assigning transnational duties. If, however, we begin with Kantian duties not to assault,
not to lie, not to use another as a means, we have (she claims) no
problem assigning those duties to everyone, and everyone can
fulfill them. This distinction, however, is less clear than it at first
appears.[5] First of all, the entire Western tradition of reflection
about global justice, beginning at least from Cicero, has understood the duty not to assault, and so on, to include, as well, a
duty to protect people who are unjustly assaulted. This arm of
the nonassault duty imposes taxing requirements, and is as difficult to assign to individuals and institutions as the duty to feed.
Indeed, as Shue has argued, the military expenditures required
to protect people from assault, torture, and so on are greater
than the expense required to give all the world's people enough
food.

Second, the duty not to use people as a means cannot be plausibly separated from critical scrutiny of the global economy and its workings, and thus from a consideration of possible global redistribution and other associated social and economic entitlements. People can be treated as means by being enslaved, raped, or tortured. But they are also surely treated as means when corporations put them to work in substandard conditions in order to maximize profit. The idea of treating human beings as ends has been a prominent part of critical reflection about working conditions, since Marx at least if not before. The related idea of protecting human dignity, as it is used in modern constitutional and legal thought, is understood to have clear implications for economic conditions and conditions of work. These concerns are at the heart of the account of entitlement in the capabilities approach, which traces its origins to the early Marx's conception of truly human functioning. And they are intensified by the current globalization of capitalism and profit-taking. It is clear that many people are being used as means, although it is not fully clear who has the duty to prevent this.

Furthermore, the notion of using a human being as a means, which lies at the heart of O'Neill's Kantian account of duty, can hardly be made clear without a related concept of human dignity, and of treatment worthy of it. But that is a concept that belongs to the side of entitlement: we need to have some sense of what it is to respect human dignity, of what treatment human dignity requires from the world, if we are to be clear about what treatment violates it.

I would argue, indeed, that so far as definiteness goes, the shoe is squarely on the other foot: we can give a pretty clear and definite account of what all world citizens should have, what their human dignity entitles them to, prior to and to some extent independently of solving the difficult problem of assigning the duties—although obviously there must be a level of generality in our account of entitlements until we get a sense of how and what we might be able to deliver. The list of capabilities, deriving from the concept of a life worthy of human dignity, is much easier to draw up and justify than any particular assignment of the correlative duties, given the multiplicity of institutional and individual actors with which our account must deal. Furthermore, human need is a relatively stable matter, and thus there is some hope that we can give an account of basic human needs that will remain a reasonably constant one over time, whereas the shifting configurations of power in the global economy entail that any account of duties (unless it ignores institutions) will have to remain flexible and time-sensitive.

We think about human dignity and what it requires. My approach does this in an Aristotelian/Marxian way, thinking about the prerequisites for living a life that is fully human rather than subhuman, a life worthy of the dignity of the human being. We include in this idea the idea of sociability and, further, the idea of the human being as a being with, in Marx's phrase, "rich human need." We insist that need and capacity, rationality and animality, are thoroughly interwoven, and that the dignity of the human being is the dignity of a needy enmattered being. Moreover, the "basic capabilities" of human beings are sources of moral claims wherever we find them: they exert a moral claim that they should be developed and given a life that is flourishing rather than stunted.

We now argue, moving through the various areas of human life in which political planning makes choices that influence people's lives at a basic level, that this fully human life requires many things from the world: adequate nutrition, education of the faculties, protection of bodily integrity, liberty for speech and religious self-expression—and so forth. In each case, an intuitive argument must be made that a life without a sufficient level of each of these entitlements is a life so reduced that it is not compatible with human dignity.

These arguments are based in a kind of freestanding reflective intuition, not on existing preferences. For example, the argument that equal access to primary and secondary education is a fundamental human entitlement is based on the intuitive idea that human beings are stunted and "mutilated" (to use Adam Smith's word as he developed just such an argument) by not having the chance to develop their faculties through education. It is not by polling people and asking what they currently prefer that we reach this conclusion, for existing preferences about matters of education (especially, perhaps, women's preferences) are frequently deformed by lack of information, by intimidation, and by adaptation to a view of life according to which boys are entitled to education and girls are not. Nonetheless, as I have argued in criticizing informed-desire approaches in *Women and Human Development*,[6] it is a good sign if these arguments converge with the deliverances of the best informed-desire approaches, those that build in informational and ethical constraints. Thus, for example, it is a good sign if women's groups, organized in accordance with procedures of adequate information, nondomination, and nonintimidation, are pressing for such entitlements; or if the best constitutional courts (such as those of India and South Africa), interpreting ideas of human dignity that increasingly figure in the world's constitutions, find such entitlements implicit in this idea of human dignity.

If this is so, then we all have entitlements based in justice to a minimum of each of the central goods on the capabilities list. So far, things are very definite, albeit at a high level of abstraction and generality: the idea of what human beings need for fully human living is among the most vivid intuitive ideas we share.

But if human beings have such entitlements, then we are all

under a collective obligation to provide the people of the world with what they need. Thus the first answer to the question "Who has the duties?" is that we all do. We may later find some good reason for delegating this obligation to a subgroup of human beings, but so far no such reason has been given, and we are imagining that we are all trying to find a decent way to live together. So far, then, humanity is under a collective obligation to find ways of living and cooperating together so that all human beings have decent lives. Now, after getting clear on that, we begin to think about how to bring that about.

Thus we begin with an intuitive conception that has great power and reach, including cross-cultural power. (This means that the freestanding argument can be made anywhere; it doesn't mean that preferences are the same everywhere, although, as I have said, the freestanding argument does derive confirmation from the convergence of constitutional courts, international human rights movements, and so forth.) Although no idea commands universal consensus in this sphere, the capabilities idea can command quite a broad consensus, just as modern human rights conceptions do. It seems likely that we are better thinkers about human functioning, and which lives are so reduced as to be violations of human dignity, than we are about the assignment of moral duties. To put the problem in terms of duty first, asking what duties we have to people in other nations, is likely to make our ethical thinking stop short when we reach a problem that seems difficult to solve.

For example, we think of the huge problem of global hunger and we say, of course we really can't have a duty to feed all the poor in India. Or, how on earth can we bring it about that all children in Africa learn to read? So we can't possibly have any duties related to education in Africa. Or, we say that we in the United States could not possibly have a duty to solve the enormous problem of HIV/AIDS in Africa, since the problem looks so distant from our sphere of control. Duties and entitlements are ultimately correlative; but starting from duties is likely to make us throw up our hands when we reach a problem that looks unwieldy. Starting from entitlements prods us to think further and more radically, rather than pulling up short, as does O'Neill (like Cicero and Kant before her). We see that the problem has to be solved, if human dignity is to be respected. So there is a collective duty there, which we might have missed if we began simply from asking: "What ought I to do here?" We see duties we might have missed, and we give ourselves a strong incentive to solve the problem of their allocation. Quite simply, our world is not a decent and minimally just world, unless we have secured the ten capabilities, up to an appropriate threshold level, to all the world's people.

ii. Why Capabilities?

The capabilities approach is an outcome-oriented approach. It measures justice (or partial, minimal social justice) in terms of a nation's ability to secure to citizens a list of central capabilities, under some appropriate specification and up to a suitable threshold level. At this point, then, it seems important to ask why capabilities should be the measure chosen, rather than opulence, or utility, or the distribution of resources to individuals. These are familiar issues: indeed it was in connection with these criticisms of previously dominant approaches that the capabilities approach was originally introduced, and the arguments that commend it over standard Utilitarian approaches have been laid out in Chapter 1, section vi. Nonetheless, the current international debate still ubiquitously uses other ideas, even though the idea of capability is making inroads. So the arguments need a brief recapitulation, to which we shall now be able to add a critique of resource-based conceptions.[7]

Before the capabilities approach was introduced, the dominant way of measuring well-being or quality of life in a nation (an issue relevant to the question of justice, though not always explicitly connected to it) was simply to ask about GNP per capita. That crude measure, of course, did not even take distribution into account, and thus rewarded nations for growth even if they contained great poverty and high rates of inequality. As Sissy Jupe says of her economics lesson in Charles Dickens' novel *Hard Times*, the dominant approach did not tell one "who had got the money and whether any of it was mine." The GNP approach also failed to take cognizance of other aspects of the quality of life that are not well correlated with economic advantage, even when distribution is factored in: aspects such as health, education, political and religious liberty, gender, and racial justice.

Slightly less inadequate was the common device of measuring well-being in terms of total or average utility, construed as the satisfaction of preferences. This account of social outcomes is in many ways very powerful, and it has certainly generated important work that promotes transnational redistribution.[8] But it has a number of problems, on which the defenders of capabilities have long focused.[9] First, it treats the individual as an input into a social calculus, and thus is insufficiently sensitive to the distinctness of each individual life. The misery of a few at the bottom can in principle be bought off by the exceeding well-being of many at the top. In general, thinking about total or average utility does not seem to be a good way of thinking about social justice, which ought to treat each and every person as an end, none as a means to the ends of others. Capabilities theorists and contractarians are utterly in agreement about that criticism.

Second, Utilitarianism in most of its forms treats all the important goods in a human life as commensurable with one another and fungible in terms of one another.[10] But, once again, that approach does not seem to be a very adequate way of thinking about social justice. One cannot atone for denials of the freedoms of speech and press by simply giving people a large amount of leisure time or some other social good. Each important entitlement is a distinctive thing in its own right.

Third, human preferences are highly malleable; they are particularly likely to adapt to expectations and possibilities. People often learn not to want things that convention and political reality have placed out of their reach. Economists call this the phenomenon of "adaptive preferences"; we observe it particularly often in women's aspirations, which adjust to time-sanctioned depictions of a woman's proper role, a woman's bodily weakness, and so forth. Even at the level of basic health and strength, women may come to be content with a bad state of affairs, if no better one is available. In this way, preference-based approaches frequently end up supporting an unjust status quo and opposing real change.[11]

Finally, by focusing on the state of satisfaction, Utilitarianism shows a deficient regard for agency. Contentment is not the only thing that matters in a human life; active striving matters, too.

Far more adequate than the GNP and Utilitarian approaches is an approach to justice in distribution that measures social positions in terms of resources, adopting some account of the distribution that is required by justice. This approach, of which the economic part of Rawls's theory of justice is an instance, comes much closer to adequacy, when combined with a plausible account of distribution. There are problems, however, with Rawls's reliance on income and wealth as indices of relative social positions: social position is also affected by a variety of goods that are noncommensurable with wealth and income, and for which wealth and income are not good proxies. Furthermore, people vary in their need for resources of different sorts, and also in their ability to convert resources into actual functioning.

People who use wheelchairs need more resources than "normal" people if they are to become fully mobile, and some of the relevant resources will have to involve redesigning society, not just doling out money to individuals. In general, promoting the human development of traditionally deprived groups requires more money than promoting the development of the advantaged, and often it requires expensive structural changes as well. The resource-based approach thus can also reinforce the status quo.

iii. Capabilities and Rights

The capabilities approach, as should by now be evident, is closely allied to the human rights approach. Indeed, I regard it as a species of the human rights approach. The capabilities that I include in my capabilities list, like those that Amartya Sen mentions in illustration of his approach, include many of the entitlements that are also stressed in the human rights movement: political liberties, freedom of association, the free choice of occupation, and a variety of economic and social rights. And capabilities, like human rights, supply a moral and humanly rich set of goals for development, in place of "the wealth and poverty of the economists," as Marx so nicely put it. In effect, capabilities cover the terrain occupied by both the so-called first-generation rights (political and civil liberties) and the so-called second-generation rights (economic and social rights). And they play a similar role, providing an account of extremely important fundamental entitlements that can be used as a basis both for constitutional thought within a nation and for thinking about international justice.

I would argue, however, that the language of capabilities, as both Sen and I have developed it, gives important precision and supplementation to the language of rights. The idea of human rights is by no means a crystal-clear idea. Rights have been understood in many different ways, and difficult theoretical questions are frequently obscured by the use of rights language, which can give the illusion of agreement where there is deep philosophical disagreement. People differ about what the *basis* of a rights claim is: rationality, sentience, and mere life have all had their defenders. They differ, too, about whether rights are prepolitical or artifacts of laws and institutions. The capabilities approach has the advantage of taking clear positions on these disputed issues, while stating clearly what the motivating concerns are and what the goal is. As one can see from the analysis already provided in Chapter 3, the capabilities approach holds that the basis of a claim is a person's existence as a human being—not just the actual possession of a set of rudimentary "basic capabilities," pertinent though these are to the more precise delineation of social obligation, but the very birth of a person into the human community. Thus Sesha's entitlements are not based solely upon the actual "basic capabilities" that she has, but on the basic capacities characteristic of the human species. Even if Sesha herself does not have the capacity for language, then, the political conception is required to arrange vehicles of expression for her, through adequate forms of guardianship. Such entitlements would not exist were capabilities based only on individual endowment, rather than on the species norm. Most human rights approaches fail to give definite answers to such questions.

Moreover, the capabilities approach, again as both Sen and I have developed it, holds very clearly that the relevant entitlements are prepolitical, not merely artifacts of laws and institutions. Thus a nation that has not recognized these entitlements is to that extent unjust. Most human rights approaches in today's world also hold this, but one significant tradition in thought about rights disagrees, holding that rights are political artifacts. Once again, the capabilities approach is a species of rights approach that provides clear answers to some urgent questions.

There are two ambiguities in rights talk that seem more important than others, in thinking about why we need capabilities language as well. One involves the issue of "negative liberty," the other the relationship between first-generation and second-generation rights. Some thinkers about rights hold that securing a right to a person requires only the inhibition of interfering state action. Fundamental entitlements have often been understood as prohibitions against such state action. If the state keeps its hands off, those rights are taken to have been secured; the state has no further affirmative task. Indeed, if one reads the U.S. Constitution, one sees this conception directly. Negative phrasing concerning state action predominates, as in the First Amendment: "Congress shall make no law respecting an establishment of religion, or prohibiting the free exercise thereof; or abridging the freedom of speech, or of the press; or the right of the people peaceably to assemble, and petition the Government for a redress of grievances." Similarly, the Fourteenth Amendment's all-important guarantees are stated in terms of what the state may not do: "No State shall make or enforce any law which shall abridge the privileges or immunities of citizens of the United States; nor shall any State deprive any person of life, liberty, or property, without due process of law; nor deny to any person within its jurisdiction the equal protection of the laws." This phraseology, deriving from the Enlightenment tradition of negative liberty, leaves things notoriously indeterminate as to whether impediments supplied by the market or by private actors are to be considered violations of fundamental rights of citizens. Although the United States has to some extent moved beyond this thin conception of entitlements, through its tradition of constitutional interpretation, the thin approach is still evident in some areas.

The capabilities approach, by contrast, understands the securing of a right as an affirmative task. This understanding has been central to both Sen's and my version of the approach. The right to political participation, the right to the free exercise of religion, the right of free speech—these and others are all best thought of as secured to people only when the relevant capabilities to function are present. In other words, to secure a right to citizens in these areas is to put them in a position of capability to function in that area. To the extent that rights are used in defining social justice, we should not grant that the society is just unless the capabilities have been effectively achieved. Of course, people may have a prepolitical right to good treatment in this area that has not yet been recognized or implemented; or it may be recognized formally and yet not implemented. But by defining the securing of rights in terms of capabilities, we make it clear that a people in country C don't really have an effective right to political participation, for example, a right in the sense that matters for judging that the society is a just one, simply because this language exists on paper; they really have been given the right only if there are effective measures to make people truly capable of political exercise. Women in many nations have a nominal right of political participation without having this right in the sense of capability: for example, they may be threatened with violence should they leave the home. In short, thinking in terms of capability gives us a benchmark as we think about what it really is to secure a right to someone. It makes clear that to do this involves affirmative material and institutional support, not simply a failure to impede.

The Indian Constitution, unlike the U.S. Constitution, typically specifies rights affirmatively. Thus, for example: "All citizens shall have the right to freedom of speech and expression; to assemble peaceably and without arms; to form associations or unions" (art. 19). These locutions have usually been understood to imply that impediments supplied by nonstate actors may also be deemed violations of constitutional rights. Moreover, the Constitution is quite explicit that affirmative action programs to aid the lower castes and women not only are not incompatible with constitutional guarantees, but are actually in their spirit. Such an approach seems very important for full justice: the state needs to take action if traditionally marginalized groups are to be treated fairly. Whether a nation has a written constitution or not, it should understand fundamental entitlements in this way. The capabilities approach, we may now say, sides with the Indian Constitution, and against the neoliberal interpretation of the U.S. Constitution. It makes it clear that securing a right to someone requires more than the absence of negative state action. Measures such as the recent constitutional amendments in India that guarantee women one-third representation in the local *panchayats,* or village councils, are strongly suggested by the capabilities approach, which directs government to think from the start about what obstacles there are to full and effective empowerment for all citizens, and to devise measures that address these obstacles.

A related ambiguity in the tradition of rights talk concerns the relationship between the first-generation and second-generation rights. Can political and civil liberties be secured prior to, and independently of, the securing of social and economic rights? So one very influential strand in the tradition of liberal political philosophy suggests, and so the very use of these terms in international human rights talk also suggests. Rawls's theory of justice is part of that tradition: his conception of justice gives liberty lexical priority over economic principles, although he also holds that at a lower stage of economic development the denial of equal liberty can be accepted "to enhance the quality of civilization so that in due course the equal freedoms can be enjoyed by all" (*TJ* 542). Both assertions strongly suggest the conceptual independence of the two spheres, and the lexical ordering suggests that after a certain stage of development, liberty is causally independent of economic redistribution. One might, however, think differently: one might believe that an adequate account of freedom of speech involves discussion of economic distribution (for example, the distribution of education); even if one did not believe the two spheres to be conceptually interdependent, one might hold that freedom of speech and political freedom have material prerequisites, even in a developed society. One might argue, for example, that people who have inadequate or unequal access to education have not been fully given freedom of speech, since illiterate people are unlikely to be able to exercise political speech on a basis of equality with others. As Justice Marshall wrote in his dissenting opinion in a case concerning unequal educational funding, "Education directly affects the ability of a child to exercise his First amendment rights, both as a source and as a receiver of information and ideas."[12] Influential human rights thinkers have frequently stressed this interdependency, but it has not altogether been incorporated into documents and the discourse around them, which often rely on the (to my mind misleading) first-generation/second-generation distinction. In *Political Liberalism,* Rawls appears to grant this point, though with a tantalizing brevity: he suggests that the first principle covering equal basic liberties might be preceded by a lexically prior principle requiring that citizens' basic needs be met, "at least insofar as their being met is necessary for citizens to understand and to be able fruitfully to exercise those rights and liberties" (7). Rawls does not elaborate on the requirements imposed by this principle, but at least here he acknowledges the interdependence of liberty with economic factors.

The capabilities approach insists throughout on the material aspects of all the human goods, by directing our attention to what people are actually able to do and to be. All the basic liberties are defined as abilities to do something. They have not been secured to people if, because of economic or educational deprivation, people are unable actually to function in accordance with the liberties that are guaranteed to them on paper. Thus the approach stresses the interdependency of liberties and economic arrangements.

A further advantage of the capabilities approach is that, by focusing from the start on what people are actually able to do and to be, it is well placed to foreground and address inequalities that women suffer inside the family: inequalities in resources and opportunities, educational deprivations, the failure of work to be recognized as work, insults to bodily integrity. Traditional rights talk has neglected these issues, and this neglect is no accident, I would argue: for rights language is strongly linked with the traditional distinction between a public sphere, which the state regulates, and a private sphere, which it must leave alone. More recently, feminists have won international recognition of many important human rights of women. But to do so they have had to challenge the public/private distinction, which is deeply bound up with traditional liberal rights thinking.[13]

The language of rights still plays an important role in public discourse, despite its unsatisfactory features. It emphasizes the idea of an urgent claim based upon justice. To say that people have a right to something is to say that they have an urgent entitlement to it. The idea of capability all on its own does not yet express the idea of an urgent entitlement based on justice. However, the capabilities approach makes this idea of a fundamental entitlement clear, by arguing that the central human capabilities are not simply desirable social goals, but urgent entitlements grounded in justice.

Like the human rights approach, the capabilities approach is a partial account of social justice. In my version of the approach, it specifies not only a list of the ten central capabilities, but also (in a general way) a minimum threshold level to be met by the world community. Like the human rights approach, it insists that each and every human being in the world has entitlements to these important goods, and it assigns to humanity generally the duty of realizing these entitlements. Like the human rights approach, it is in one way nation-centered, recommending that the capabilities list be used as a criterion of social justice internally to each society, as in an account of basic constitutional entitlements.[14] But it also supplies, as do human rights documents, goals for the international community as a whole, and for humanity as a whole. As we shall see, these two aspects are simultaneous and complementary: the world community and nation-states should be working toward these goals together.

Thus the capabilities approach should not be seen as a rival of the human rights approach. Especially as that approach is used in international discourse, for example in the *Human Development Reports* of the United Nations Development Programme, the approach dovetails well with the emphases of the capabilities approach, so that it seems best to regard the capabilities approach as one species of a human rights approach. But important work is still done by the emphasis on capabilities, which emphasizes the affirmative tasks of the public sphere and the interdependence of liberty with economic adequacy. Such an emphasis is particularly important in the United States and nations influenced by U.S. traditions of thinking about "negative liberty."

iv. Equality and Adequacy

The capabilities approach uses the idea of a threshold: for each important entitlement, there is some appropriate level beneath which it seems right to say that the relevant entitlement has not been secured. The intuitive idea of a life with human dignity already suggests this: people are entitled not only to mere life, but to a life compatible with human dignity, and this entitlement means that the relevant goods must be available at a sufficiently high level. Up until now, however, the approach has insisted only on the idea of adequacy or sufficiency, and has stated that the question of what to do with inequalities above this minimum threshold is a further question that the approach has not yet answered. It is in that way as yet incomplete.

It seems crucial, however, to say more about the threshold: for we must indicate where, and to what extent, equality is part of the very idea of the threshold itself. The list itself suggests that there are some instances in which we will not tolerate inequality. Capability 7B, for example, speaks of "having the social bases of self-respect and nonhumiliation; being able to be treated as a dignified being whose worth is equal to that of others." And it connects this idea to the idea of nondiscrimination. It seems crucial to go further at this point, spelling out the role of an idea of *equal* entitlement in the approach.[15] Addressing the problem seems especially urgent in the international context, given the staggering inequalities we have mentioned.

The touchstones should be, I believe, the idea of human dignity and the closely related idea of the social bases of self-respect and nonhumiliation. Equality of capability is an essential social goal where its absence would be connected with a deficit in dignity and self-respect. We have seen that the idea of dignity is spelled out from the beginning in terms of equality: it is the *equal dignity* of human beings that demands recognition. Here the idea of equality is essential: we must add it to the bare idea of dignity in order to articulate the goal in an adequate way. But this idea has implications for many of the capabilities on our list as well. It appears that all the political, religious, and civil liberties can be *adequately* secured only if they are *equally* secured. To give some groups of people unequal voting rights, or unequal religious liberty, is to set them up in a position of subordination and indignity vis-à-vis others. It is to fail to recognize their equal human dignity.

On the other side, there are other capabilities, closely connected with the idea of property or instrumental goods, where what seems appropriate is *enough*. For example, an *adequate* house or other shelter seems to be inherent in the idea of human dignity, and it seems right that constitutions all over the world are beginning to recognize the right to housing as a constitutional entitlement, following the creative lead of South African jurisprudence. It is not at all clear that an *equal* house is required by the very idea of human dignity or even of equal human dignity; for indeed a mansion may not be better than a modest house. House size, above a certain threshold, does not seem intrinsically related to equal dignity. Insofar as envy and competition make people *feel* that an unequal house is a sign of unequal dignity, we might wonder whether these judgments are not based on an excessive valuation of material goods, which a just society might decide not to honor. The case is not clear. As Adam Smith observed, what is compatible with human dignity may itself vary from society to society. In England, the ability to appear in public without shame requires a shirt; in some other nations it does not. We might add that the ability to sit in the front of the bus is connected to human dignity not timelessly, but through a set of social norms and practices. Thus the fact that house size is connected to dignity through social norms does not suffice to undermine the connection. It does, however, prompt a further inquiry. At least sometimes we may find that excessive valuation of competitive goods lies behind a social norm; a just society could decide not to honor that valuation.

This is surely one area where different nations with their different traditions will need to work out the problem for themselves through ample public deliberation.

In some areas that seem to fall on the material side, however, it does seem clear that grossly unequal shares fail to meet the adequacy condition. If education, for example, is arranged as it currently is in the United States, in such a way that students in a rich school district may have as much as 75 or 100 times as much spent on them as is spent on students in a poor district, such an allocation does seem to be an intrinsic violation of a norm of equal dignity and equal political liberty.[16] At least where primary and secondary education are concerned, adequacy does appear to require something close to equality, or at least a very high minimum (perhaps allowing for divergences in aspects of education that are not firmly linked to basic opportunity and political participation). The same is true of basic essential health care. Whether higher education and nonessential health care are matters in which we may accept unequal shares as compatible with the threshold of adequacy, remains a question that societies will have to hammer out. In the international case we should aggressively pursue equality between nations in capabilities that are especially closely linked to the idea of equal human dignity, including primary and secondary education and access to basic health care. Whether inequalities elsewhere in the systems of education and health, and other material inequalities, are compatible with the recognition of equal human dignity will properly be a topic of ongoing cross-national debate.

Harry Frankfurt influentially argues that equality all on its own is not a distinct political value; it becomes important when it affects some other capacity, such as the capacity for speech, or self-respect, or a life with dignity, or for relationships not predicated on hierarchy.[17] Apart from its connection to the content of these values, it remains a bare formal notion. The matter is very difficult to think about, and all statements ought to be tentative. For the capabilities approach, at any rate, equality is important at the very base of the theory; for it is not just human dignity that must be respected, it is equal human dignity. This role for equality, however, does not entail that equality is a reasonable goal with regard to all the central capabilities, a position that has been the target of reasonable criticism by Ronald Dworkin and others.[18] Some capabilities must be secured to citizens on a basis of equality, or equal dignity has not been respected. Others, however, do not seem to have this intrinsic relationship to dignity; with these, the capabilities approach supplies a threshold of adequacy. Some nations and individuals may prefer a more egalitarian solution with these capabilities as well. But it seems likely that if we want a political conception that can achieve an overlapping consensus among people who differ in their comprehensive ethical and religious doctrines, especially when we are considering transnational transfers of wealth, this conception is more likely to prove broadly acceptable than one that insists on equality in all the central capabilities. Individuals whose comprehensive doctrine is more exigent can at least recognize the political conception as compatible with their own doctrine, though it does not deliver everything that they would favor.[19]

v. Pluralism and Toleration

As we have seen, Rawls adopts a highly problematic principle of toleration in order to accommodate a wider range of traditional views and practices, in the international realm, than he was willing to accommodate in the domestic case. The capabilities approach remains focused on the person as the ultimate subject of justice, and thus refuses to compromise on the justification of the capabilities list itself. Nonetheless, a concern for cultural variety (both within a nation and across nations) has been a prominent part of my version of the approach. This concern is internal to the capabilities list itself, with its robust protections for religious freedom, freedom of association, and so forth.

The rationale for this concern is, once again, the all-important idea of dignity and the associated idea of respect. All modern nations contain, internally, a wide range of religious and other views about human life. And the international community contains an even greater variety than does any single nation. So it is important to be respectful of the many ways citizens choose to live, provided that those do not cause harm to others in areas touched upon by the central capabilities. Such respect is what human dignity requires. Pluralism is therefore protected in six different ways in the content and use of the list. We may summarize them briefly here, showing how they affect the extension of the approach to the space between nations.

First, the list is understood as open-ended and subject to ongoing revision and rethinking. This open-endedness is even more important when we extend the approach to the international community, because we are more likely to hear in such debates good ideas that we did not hear before, or criticisms of our own ways of life that we had previously not taken seriously.

Second, the items on the list are specified in a somewhat abstract and general way, precisely in order to leave room for the activities of specifying and deliberating by citizens and their legislatures and courts in each nation. Once again, leaving space here is particularly important in the international arena. Respecting differences in the way nations specify a given capability, with attention to their histories, is part of the respect for human autonomy that is involved in allowing the nation to play a large role on the world stage. Because respect for nations derives from respect for persons, it has limited latitude. Thus I have not endorsed Rawls's far broader principle of toleration, which allows nations to restrict religious liberty unequally or to deny certain groups voting rights. On the other hand, in the gray area where there appear to be several different permissible ways of specifying the capability in question, respect for persons does seem to require respect for national differences.

Third, the list represents a freestanding "partial moral conception," introduced for political purposes only, and without any grounding in metaphysical ideas of the sort that divide people along lines of culture and religion, such as the idea of the immortal soul, or the idea of god or gods. It provides the basis for an overlapping consensus. With regard to overlapping consensus, the very definiteness of the list is actually an asset, not a liability. We show respect for others when we make explicit and public the items concerning which we want their agreement. Moreover, the fact that it is a relatively short list is itself respectful: we ask you to agree on these ten basic entitlements, but as for the rest, we leave you to your own devices. Thus I prefer my own definite list, for such reasons, to Sen's general defense of a "perspective of freedom," which might suggest the kind of comprehensive preference for free or autonomous lives that we find in liberal thinkers such as Joseph Raz and John Stuart Mill, a preference that usually ends up not showing equal respect for people who adhere to authoritarian religions. My approach, by contrast, says, "We ask you to sign on to this short list, but we say nothing about what makes lives go well in general." In this way, we allow the Amish, the Roman Catholic, and other believing citizens to join the international consensus without feeling derogated.[20]

Fourth, if we insist that the appropriate political target is capability and not functioning, we protect pluralism here again.[21] Many people who are willing to support a given capability as a fundamental entitlement would feel violated were the associated functioning made basic. Once again, this sensitivity seems particularly important when confronting the variety of cultures in today's world. A Muslim woman may prefer to remain veiled, and the approach says nothing against this, provided that there are sufficient political, educational, and other capabilities present to ensure that the choice is a choice.

Fifth, the major liberties that protect pluralism are central items on the list: freedom of speech, freedom of association, freedom of conscience. A nation that does not protect these is halfhearted about pluralism, or worse.

Sixth and finally, the approach, as we have already said, makes a strong distinction between issues of justification and issues of implementation. I believe that we can justify this list as a good basis for political principles all around the world. But this does not mean that we thereby license intervention with the affairs of a state that does not recognize them. It is a basis for persuasion.

In all these ways, the approach can claim to be respectful of pluralism and difference, without compromising on the basic entitlements of each person.

vi. An International "Overlapping Consensus"?

One of the features of Rawls's *Political Liberalism* that troubles many of his readers is his apparent shift in the direction of something like cultural relativism: the political conception is to be justified in terms of certain ideas understood to be implicit in the traditions of a liberal constitutional democracy. Rawls's frequent discussions of the history of Europe and North America indicate that he thinks of these Western traditions as in certain ways *sui generis,* and of the aftermath of the Reformation and the Wars of Religion as a distinctive cultural formation (see *PL* xxiii–xxviii). So it may be that Rawls believes his political conception justified only for democracies that are the heirs of that tradition, or even defined in terms of ideas that belong to that tradition.

This result would be disappointing to people who believe that something like his political liberalism can be justified as a good one for nations all around the world and even as a basis for transnational agreements.[22] The ideas of Rawlsian political liberalism are ubiquitous in international discussions of peace and reconciliation among nations. I have heard them defended as bases for a stable peace between Israel and Palestine; for a stable evolution toward democracy in the Arab world; for the ongoing pursuit of pluralism in the Indian constitutional tradition. One may, of course, appropriate Rawls's ideas for these purposes no matter what he says, if they seem good ones for the job. But it seems important to ask whether he has any good arguments for his restriction, arguments that ought to make us think that nations outside Europe and North America cannot reasonably pursue a political liberalism along Rawlsian lines.

We must begin by distinguishing several distinct questions:

1. Does Rawls really relativize the justification of political liberalism (insofar as it goes beyond the human rights norms defended for all decent nations in *LP*) to the Western tradition, or does he admit all liberal constitutional democracies? And, if the former, does he give a good analysis of what he takes to be the distinctive history of these Western democracies?

2. Can a Rawlsian who accepts his political conception detach it from these limits and commend it as a good norm for societies worldwide, and how would such a Rawlsian answer Rawls's legitimate concerns about justification and stability?

3. Can a Rawlsian reasonably commend something like his norms as good norms for transnational society?

Rawls's idea of political justification is always holistic and "internal." In *A Theory of Justice,* the search for reflective equilibrium begins with "considered judgments" and systematically considers the alternative conceptions with those convictions in play, striving for the best overall coherence and fit in the set of judgments and theories taken as a whole. What is new in *PL* is, first, a shift from a one-to-one "Socratic" conception of justification to a public political conception, in which "all citizens can examine before one another whether their political and social institutions are just" (9); and, second, the insistence that the conception to be justified must be built from, and expressed in terms of, "certain fundamental ideas seen as implicit in the public political culture of a democratic society" (13); elsewhere, and most often, Rawls adds that the democracy is "constitutional." The "tradition of democratic thought," whose content is "familiar and intelligible to the educated common sense of citizens generally," serves as "a fund of implicitly shared ideas and principles" (14). In that sense, the conception "starts from within a certain political tradition."

These two shifts are clearly connected with the central issue of stability. Rawls plainly believes that a conception cannot be justified unless we can show that it can be stable over time for the right reasons; and he also seems to think that we cannot show that it can be stable unless the conception uses materials that are already implicit in the political tradition. Of course he knows that these ideas (of "free and equal citizens," "fair terms of cooperation," and so forth) are far from the only ideas embedded in the tradition; many ideas that are in tension with these ideas are present also in the nations he is considering. But he does rely on the salience and longevity of the ideas on which he builds.

In his "Reply to Habermas," published along with *PL* in the expanded edition, Rawls distinguishes three types or levels of justification. *Pro tanto* justification takes place when the political conception is duly laid out and it is shown how it answers a wide range of political questions, so that it seems to be complete (*PL* 386). Second, full justification is carried out "by an individual citizen as a member of civil society," by "embedding [the political conception] in some way into the citizen's comprehensive doctrine as either true or reasonable" (ibid.). This part of the justification process corresponds most closely to the Socratic account of justification in *TJ*. At this stage, the person does not yet ask whether other people accept the political conception. Finally, the doctrine must be justified publicly by political society. That final justification happens only "when all the reasonable members of political society carry out a justification of the shared political conception by embedding it in their several reasonable comprehensive views," in the process taking one another into account (*PL* 387). For this stage to occur, the society must be one that is already well ordered by the political conception. Justification requires the existence of an overlapping consensus and records the fact of that consensus.

In Rawls's view, then, none of the existing nations, Western or nonwestern, can as yet carry out the third stage of justification, because none is well ordered in accordance with his political conception. So the fact that there is not currently an overlapping consensus about Rawls's ideas in a given society does not disqualify that society from being the sort of society for which such a conception may over time be fully justified. As Rawls explicitly says, "political liberalism looks for a political conception of justice that we hope can gain the support of an overlapping consensus of reasonable religious, philosophical, and moral doctrines in a society regulated by it" (*PL* 10). That is of course very different from claiming that the society must already have such a consensus. All that seems to be required is that the requisite ideas be embedded there in some form.

At times, however, Rawls suggests a further narrowing: the core ideas of the conception are to be drawn from the political tradition of a constitutional democracy. In other words, only a nation that is already a constitutional democracy can use these ideas, not one in which such ideas are present without as yet having brought about the transition to constitutional democracy. At times, in talking about the Reformation and its aftermath, he indicates yet a further restriction: "the historical origin of political liberalism (and of liberalism more generally) is the Reformation and its aftermath, with the long controversies over religious toleration in the sixteenth and seventeenth centuries" (*PL* xxvi). He argues that the Reformation introduced something "new," namely, the idea of "a transcendent element not admitting of compromise." He argues that neither the Greco-Roman world nor the medieval world contained this idea (xxiii–xxviii). So these historical ruminations, if we connect them closely to the definition of political liberalism, suggest that political liberalism must be made up from the traditions of nations that experienced the particular sort of clash that the Reformation inaugurated. This limitation might mean not only that the account is justifiable only within Western constitutional democracies, but also that it is justifiable only within democracies that were seriously marked by the experience of the Reformation and the Wars of Religion: thus, perhaps not the Nordic countries, or Italy, or Russia, or the nations of Eastern Europe, or Greece, all of whose histories are significantly different from those of Germany, France, the Netherlands, Great Britain, Ireland, Canada, and the United States, which are the central cases for Rawls's historical idea.

There are many difficulties with Rawls's reading of European and U.S. history. For one thing, it underestimates the amount of conflict over comprehensive doctrines within the Greco-Roman world. But let us leave this issue to one side, since it is not relevant to our question about the extension of political liberalism. What is more serious is that Rawls seems totally to neglect the existence of nonwestern constitutional democracies with their own traditions of toleration and accommodation: India, Bangladesh, South Africa, Turkey, Japan, and by now many others. In the cases of Turkey and India, the history of clashes and accommodations is long and complex. For India one may plausibly argue that ideas of religious respect and toleration are far older than they are in the so-called Western tradition: the edicts of Ashoka, himself a convert from Hinduism to Buddhism in the third century B.C.E., promulgate a norm of mutual respect and toleration. So, too, did the official policies, much later, of several leading emperors of the Moghul Empire. In the case of Turkey, the Ottoman Empire had well-known policies of religious accommodation. None of these is identical with the norms favored by Rawls, but then no norm that old is identical with Rawls's norms. Even the Peace of Westphalia established religious pluralism *among* nations, allowing repression within each nation. So, too, with the founding of the United States, which permitted individual states to continue establishing a particular religion and disfavoring others. Even the free exercise clause was not applied to the states until after the Civil War, although all state constitutions favored the idea.

In short, if we hold that a political tradition of relevant ideas is a necessary basis for political liberalism, we ought to hold that this condition is fulfilled by India and Turkey and, I would say, many if not most of the existing constitutional democracies of the world, all of which have traditions, longer or shorter, of committing themselves to similar ideas—not only the idea of toleration itself, but also ideas of equality, respect, and human dignity. Indeed, one might argue that equality of capability is a far more prominent feature of the Indian and South African constitutional orders than of the U.S. constitutional order.

What about nations that are not currently liberal constitutional democracies? Can't one argue that Rawls's ideas are good ones for them, too? After all, there is nowhere in today's world where ideas of human rights, human dignity, human equality, and fair terms of cooperation are not widespread. Even in China, where there is not yet a liberal constitutional democracy and where tradition is in some ways at odds with the key ideas in Rawls's conception, there are also long-standing seeds of such ideas, and the modern debate has drawn on them, moving liberal ideas into the forefront of political thinking.[23] It seems not implausible to think that we may build on these ideas, offering public arguments in the international arena that these ideas are the ones that ought to prevail within nations where they do not yet prevail.

At this point, we run into the key issue of stability: the more radical a conception is, within a given society, the more difficult it will be to maintain that Rawls's conception can over time become the object of an overlapping consensus. But it seems to me that in the modern world the ideas of human rights are by now so deeply rooted and so widespread that it is not possible to say of any nation that it cannot achieve such a consensus over time. (Nor it seems to me, is it possible to affirm with confidence that a nation such as our own cannot move in the opposite direction. Indeed, on many of the issues of concern to Rawls, the United States has been moving further and further away from anything like consensus.) So I am inclined to say that the elastic requirement of hope-for-consensus that Rawls introduces is good enough for any nation living under modern conditions in a world characterized by a world culture of human rights. People need only draw on the ideas inherent in that world culture, whether or not their own nation currently exhibits the structure of a constitutional liberal democracy.

What of transnational agreements? May we hope that a conception of international society based on the central human capabilities could over time achieve a consensus of the Rawlsian type? In fact the ideas of political liberalism are even better established in the international realm than they are in the domestic setting. The Universal Declaration of Human Rights was framed with reference to just such ideas. Well before the Rawlsian idea of "political liberalism" had currency, Jacques Maritain, one of the architects of the Universal Declaration, maintained that people who differed about metaphysical matters could agree for practical political purposes on a list of human rights.[24] And in the actual framing of the declaration this distinction between a practical agreement and the metaphysical realm proved extremely important as participants from different religious traditions tried to show respect for one another's differences.[25]

The Universal Declaration offered only a thin basis for international society, in that it still envisaged the securing of human rights as a matter for individual state action, not for the international community as a whole. But the trend toward cooperation and mutuality in enforcement suggests that these ideas have gradually taken center stage as bases for international agreements, institutions, and organizations.

I conclude that there is no barrier of principle or argument against pursuing the central human capabilities as goals for every nation, and also for international society. Indeed, what makes Rawls's conception particularly attractive in this context is its deep respect for religious traditions and its careful distinction between comprehensive doctrines and the domain of the shared political conception. Many people who would not sign on to a comprehensive liberalism of the traditional Western sort can, let us hope, support a consensus that allows metaphysical matters to remain on the outside of the political, a part of each person's comprehensive doctrine. The chance for such a consensus is increased by the content of the capabilities approach itself, which includes many items that have been central to discussion in the international community, such as education, health care, housing, and labor conditions, all items that are not discussed in Rawls's conception.

vii. Globalizing the Capabilities Approach: The Role of Institutions

So far the capabilities approach has announced some ambitious goals for the world, and some general principles regarding pluralism and national sovereignty. Obviously, however, a great deal more remains to be said about precisely how the approach can be used to generate political principles for today's world. To some extent, this job is a practical job, a job for economists, political scientists, diplomats, and policymakers. Philosophy is good at normative reasoning and at laying out general structures of thought. In a rapidly changing world, however, any very concrete prescriptions for implementation need to be made in partnership with other disciplines.

To say this is not to say that philosophy is not urgently practical. Ideas shape the way policymakers do their work. That is why, from its very inception, the capabilities approach has contested the idea of development as economic growth, insisting on the idea of "human development." Reconceiving development as "human development" does influence the goals that policymakers pursue and the strategies they choose. Similarly, it is of urgent practical importance to challenge the idea that mutual advantage is the goal of social cooperation. The capabilities approach is not remote and impractical, but urgently practical, when it urges us to rethink our ideas of social cooperation. For we can see that many short-sighted policies in the development area and even in the area of international financial policy flow from such ideas.[26] There is perhaps nothing more urgent, in a world increasingly driven by multinational corporations and the power motive that is built into their operations, than to articulate a set of humanly rich goals for development, and a set of more general attitudes about the purposes of cooperation that will be needed to sustain people in the pursuit of these goals.

There remains, however, a legitimate question about where the sphere of philosophical normative thinking leaves off and the sphere of the more empirical disciplines begins. Philosophy seems best at articulating basic political principles at a rather high level of abstraction, leaving it to other disciplines to think how, as institutions and their configurations change, those principles can be made reality.

Nonetheless, we can certainly go somewhat further than we have in speaking about the realization of the capabilities in the modern world. One question that must certainly be confronted is the question of how to allocate the duties of promoting the capabilities in a world that contains nations, transnational economic agreements and agencies, other international agreements and agencies, corporations, NGOs, political movements, and individual people. To say that "we all" have the duties is all very well, and true. But it would be good if we could go further, saying at least something about the proper allocation of duties between individuals and institutions, and among institutions of various kinds.

Institutions are made by people, and it is ultimately people who should be seen as having moral duties to promote human capabilities. Nonetheless, there are four reasons why we should think of the duties as assigned, derivatively, to institutional structures. First of all, there are *collective action problems*. Think of a nation. If we say that its citizens have duties to maintain the system of property rights, the tax structure, the system of criminal justice, and so forth, we are in one sense saying something true and important. There are no living beings in the state other than its people; there is no magical superperson who will shoulder the work. Nonetheless, if each person tries to think individually what is to be done, this would be a recipe for massive confusion and failure. It is far better to create a decent institutional structure and then to regard individuals as having delegated their personal ethical responsibility to that structure. Much the same would seem to be true of the international sphere, although the analogy is not precise, as we shall see.

Second, there are issues of *fairness*. If I care a lot about the poor in my country, and give a lot of my personal money to support their needs, I am thus impoverishing myself and my family in comparison to those who begin in the same place but who do nothing for the poor. Any system of voluntary philanthropy has this problem. As long as others are not made to pay their fair share, whatever that is, the ones who do pay both have to do more (if the problem is to be solved) and have to incur a relative disadvantage that they would not incur if the system imposed a proportional burden on everyone.[27]

Third, there is a point about *capacity:* it is possible to argue cogently that institutions have both cognitive and causal powers that individuals do not have, powers that are pertinent to the allocation of responsibility. If we think about a harm such as global warming, the share contributed by each individual may be so small as to be causally insignificant, whereas a nation or a corporation will have a recognizable causal role. Moreover, nations and corporations have powers of prediction and foresight that individuals in isolation do not have. It seems plausible that such facts give us a further reason to think of responsibilities for promoting human capabilities as institutional rather than personal.[28]

Finally, there is a more subtle issue, or set of issues, about the personal life. In classical Utilitarianism, with all moral responsibility being understood as personal responsibility to maximize total or average welfare, there is a large question about what becomes of the person and the sense that a person has a life. People are just engines of maximization. More or less all of their energy has to be devoted to calculating the right thing to do, and then doing it. They will have to choose careers, friendships, and political commitments that maximize total or average well-being. The sense that there is anything that is really them or their own is difficult to maintain.[29] This worry is really a set of closely related worries, for the unlimited sense of responsibility in Utilitarianism raises questions about personal integrity, about agency, about friendship and family, about the sources of the meaning of life, and about the nature of political agency.

We do not need to elaborate all of these concerns further here in order to see that there is a great deal in them. Moreover, there is a great deal in them from the perspective of the capabilities approach itself. The capabilities approach aims at giving people the necessary conditions of a truly human life. It would be a self-defeating theory indeed if it were understood in such a way that the injunction to promote human capabilities devoured the life of each person, removing personal projects, concerns, and space to such an extent that nobody at all had the chance to lead a truly human life (assuming such concerns are part of a truly human life, as the capabilities list suggests).

We can see that these worries are closely related to the collective action problem and the fairness problem. One reason why Utilitarian calculation looks so costly and time-consuming is that it involves calculations in which the likely behavior of others is highly uncertain; one reason why its removal of personal liberty seems unusually extreme is that we typically imagine the Utilitarian agent as shouldering the burden of maximizing good in a world in which most people are going their own selfish ways.

It seems plausible that a good solution to this problem, as to its relatives, is to assign the responsibility for promoting others' well-being (capabilities) to institutions, giving individuals broad discretion about how to use their lives apart from the sphere in which institutions exact duties.[30] Institutions impose on all, in a suitable fair way, the responsibility to support the capabilities of all, up to a minimum threshold. Beyond that (so far as fundamental entitlements go), people are free to use their money, time, and other resources as their own comprehensive conception of the good dictates. (The full requirements of justice, once spelled out, may alter the picture, but on those the jury is still out.) There will be ethical norms internal to each religious or ethical comprehensive doctrine that determine how far each person is ethically responsible for doing more than what is institutionally required. But the political task of supporting the capabilities threshold itself is assigned in the first instance to institutions.

We can see that this division between the institutional and the ethical corresponds to a familiar distinction, in liberal (and especially political-liberal) theory, between the political sphere and the spheres of people's own personal (or shared) comprehensive conceptions of value.[31] Indeed, liberalism, understood as a political liberalism committed to respect for a wide diversity of religious and other comprehensive conceptions of value, requires such a division. The principles that citizens endorse for the political sphere are but a subset of the ethical principles that they endorse in their lives as a whole. Were that not the case, there would not be enough room in the system for plurality and diversity, and that system would be dictatorial, rather than respectful of the diversity of people's comprehensive value-commitments. So the general structure of political liberalism requires a sphere of ethical choice outside that which is politically compulsory. Such a bifurcation between political values and broader social values is also required by some more specific precepts that lie at the heart of the capabilities approach, such as freedom of association, the free choice of occupation, freedom of religion, and freedom of travel.

viii. Globalizing the Capabilities Approach:
What Institutions?

Institutions, then, must play a large role in promoting human capabilities. But here the analogy between the domestic situation and the global situation begins to break down. In the domestic case, we can easily say quite a lot about the set of institutions that have the responsibility of supporting the human capabilities of the nation's citizens. The responsibility-bearing structure is what John Rawls has called a nation's "basic structure," that set of institutions that determines people's life chances pervasively and from the start of a human life. This structure will include legislature, courts, administration and at least some administrative agencies, laws defining the institution of the family and allocating privileges to its members, the system of taxation and welfare, the overall structure of the economic system of the nation, the general outlines of the criminal justice system, and probably other structures as well. Although what belongs in the "basic structure" changes over time, in the sense that a given part of the administration (for example, the Environmental Protection Agency or the Department of Education) might come to seem a more fundamental and basic part of the structure of promoting human capabilities at one time than at another time, there is general clarity about what the institutional structure involves, and even some clarity about what duties belong to each of its parts.

We can go somewhat further. Some general principles concerning institutions and their relationships can be defended as crucial to the promotion of human capabilities.[32] *Separation of powers,* along with *judicial review,* has emerged over time as a structure that is essential to the protection of citizen capabilities. (Nowhere is this clearer than in India's Emergency—1975–1977—in which Indira Gandhi's assault on judicial review led to a suspension of many Fundamental Rights. The current system, highly protective of the judiciary's role, is a response to that grave failure.) An appropriate degree of *federalism* or *decentralization* also seems an important aspect of making the governmental structure responsive to people's voices and protective of their capabilities. The very arguments that lead us to support the nation as a structure expressive of people's autonomy also lead us, especially in very large nations such as India and the United States, to favor a certain measure of federalism or local autonomy, which, however, should not have the power to compromise the equality of citizens or to abrogate fundamental entitlements.[33] Another important feature of a modern nation protective of human capabilities will be *independent administrative agencies,* whose expertise is essential to protecting capabilities in health, environment, and other areas, and whose independence from partisan control is therefore an important structural feature of a nation adequately designed to protect capabilities. Since corruption is one of the problems, in modern nations, that most severely threaten human capabilities, *mechanisms to detect and prevent corruption,* both in government and in business, are absolutely essential to the stability of the capabilities and the conception based on them. We can also insist that *legal education* and the *training of law enforcement officers* should be done with the protection of citizen capabilities in mind. Thus, where discrimination on the basis of race, religion, or sex is a pressing social problem, education should incorporate a focus on race and gender issues.

Finally, and most generally, we should insist that the whole public order be designed so as to prevent gross inequalities of access and power. A nation may have an admirable constitution but be, in daily life, a plutocracy, if the media and political campaigns are unduly controlled by wealthy individuals and groups.

Such is the case in today's United States; for that reason, human capabilities are gravely at risk.

Thus the capabilities approach is rights-centered, in the sense that the entitlements of persons based on human dignity lie at the core of the conception, and structural features are judged good or bad in relation to these. But this does not mean that the capabilities approach can have nothing to say about structure: indeed, the very fact that the promotion of human capabilities is the central goal gives the debate about structure a point and a focus, and gives us clear reasons for preferring some structures to others.

When we move to the global plane, however, nothing is clear. If a world state were desirable, we could at least describe what its structure might be like. But it seems that such a state is far from desirable. Unlike domestic basic structures, a world state would be very unlikely to have a decent level of accountability to its citizens. It is just too vast an undertaking, and differences of culture and language make the requisite communication too difficult, at least at present. Nor does it seem clear that we ought to promote the sort of cultural and linguistic homogeneity that would make such a state more workable. Diversity is a valuable part of our world, and is already under threat. We should not further undermine it without very strong reasons.

A world state would also be dangerous. If a nation becomes unjust, pressure from other nations may prevent it from committing heinous crimes (whether against its citizens or against other nations). If the world state should become unjust, there would be no corresponding recourse; the only hope would be for rebellion from within. In history that hope has not always proven reliable: the worst tyrannies in modern times have not fallen without external pressure.

Moreover, even if those problems could be overcome, there

is a deep moral problem with the idea of a world state, uniform in its institutions and requirements. National sovereignty, I have argued, has moral importance, as a way people have of asserting their autonomy, their right to give themselves laws of their own making. If we think about this moral importance historically, we can see that one very important part of this autonomy was the right to do things differently from one's neighbors. To be sure, this freedom assumed a particular salience because each nation was internally not respectful of different religions and ways of life. Thus the only way for a Protestant to enjoy religious liberty was to live in a Protestant nation, and so on. To the extent that respect for pluralism is a part of each domestic structure, the case for national variety grows somewhat weaker. And yet it does not disappear: for there are differences of language, culture, and history that still may legitimately be defended as salient. The capabilities approach insists that certain core entitlements should be part of domestic constitutions the world over. But it leaves a great deal of room for diversity of interpretation and institutional structure, and for diversity in areas outside the core. To protect national sovereignty in a world of pluralism is an important part of protecting human freedom. In that sense, any world state is *ipso facto* tyrannical.

If these arguments are good ones, the institutional structure at the global level ought to remain thin and decentralized. Part of it will consist, quite simply, of the domestic basic structures, to which we shall assign responsibilities for redistributing some of their wealth to other nations. Part of it will consist of multinational corporations, to which we shall assign certain responsibilities for promoting human capabilities in the nations in which they do business. Part of it will consist of global economic policies, agencies, and agreements, including the World Bank, the International Monetary Fund, and various trade agreements. Part will consist of other international bodies, such as the United Nations, the International Labour Organization, the World Court and the new world criminal court, and of international agreements in many areas, such as human rights, labor, and environment. Part of it will consist of nongovernmental organizations of many kinds, ranging from the large and multinational (such as OXFAM) to the small and local.

The form this structure has assumed up until now is the result of a combination of historical factors, rather than of deliberate normative reflection. There is thus an odd fit between normative political philosophy and the details of a set of institutions as oddly assorted as this. It is also clear that the allocation of responsibility among these different parts of the global structure must remain provisional and informal, and subject to change and rethinking. Notice, as well, that the allocation is an ethical allocation, and political only in the sense that it is aspirational and we should try to bring it about, since there is no coercive structure over the whole that would enforce on any given part a definite set of tasks. In that sense, my approach is a version of the old natural law approach: the requirements at the world level are moral requirements, not captured fully in any set of coercive political structures.

Nonetheless, we can articulate at least some principles for a world order of this kind, which can at least help us think about how human capabilities can be promoted in a world of inequalities.

ix. Ten Principles for the Global Structure

1. *Overdetermination of responsibility: the domestic never escapes it.* Most nations, well and honestly run, can promote many or even most of the human capabilities up to some reasonable threshold level. As Amartya Sen has stressed, famine can be avoided by a decent system of entitlements, together with a free

press and political democracy. I have argued against the use John Rawls makes of Sen's theory, for he uses it to deny that richer nations need to give economic aid to poorer nations. If justice requires the mitigation of global inequality, justice is not satisfied even if poor nations can promote the capabilities internally —any more than domestic justice is satisfied without redistribution just because thrifty poor families may eke out a minimally acceptable existence. Without endorsing any specific principle of redistribution, such as the Rawlsian Difference Principle, and operating only with our idea of the social minimum as expressed in the capability threshold, we can say that it is unjust if poorer nations have to struggle against greater obstacles than rich nations in order to meet their fundamental commitments. Nonetheless, we can begin by insisting that they do all that is in their power. Assigning responsibility to the world economic structure does not mean that we excuse the domestic structure from responsibility. If the fulfillment of capabilities is overdetermined, so much the better.

2. *National sovereignty should be respected, within the constraints of promoting human capabilities.* In my section on justification and implementation (Chapter 4, section iv) I have already outlined the ideas behind this principle. In general, coercive intervention is justified only in a limited range of circumstances; international treaties and agreements can also play a coercive role, as discussed in Principle 6 below. But persuasion and persuasive use of funding are always a good thing. This brings us to the next principle.

3. *Prosperous nations have a responsibility to give a substantial portion of their GDP to poorer nations.* The prosperous nations of the world have the responsibility of supporting the human capabilities of their own citizens, as Principle 1 asserts. But they also have additional responsibilities. In a world in which so many human beings have luxuries that do not meet any central human

need and so many more are deprived of what they need, it seems unconscionable that a world based on the ideas of mutual cooperation and respect for human dignity should not commit itself to very significant redistribution. Richer nations can reasonably be expected to give a great deal more than they currently give to assist poorer nations: the figure of 2 percent of GDP, though arbitrary, is a good sign of what might begin to be morally adequate. (The United States currently devotes .01 percent of GDP to foreign aid; the European nations devote something less than 1 percent, though some, such as Denmark and Norway, come close.) The precise figure is debatable; the general principle is not.

Less clear is the form such aid ought to take: Should it be given in the first instance to governments, or also to NGOs? Again, this decision should be left for contextual determination: the general principle would be not to undermine national sovereignty if the recipient nation is democratic, but at the same time to give aid in an efficient way, and a way that shows respect for the capabilities on the list. If the democratic nation has serious problems of governmental corruption, there may be good reason to give aid through NGOs rather than through the government. Another reason for bypassing the government might be that it deals unfairly with deprived minorities. Thus nations seeking to fund education in India in 2003 might have been better advised to give to NGOs rather than to the national government, if an education ministry was focusing on Hinduizing the curriculum, for example, rather than on extending basic opportunities to all.[34] Efficiency, concern for the capabilities on the list, and concern with the disadvantaged and excluded all suggest a focus on groups that provide education for women and other neglected groups.[35]

4. *Multinational corporations have responsibilities for promoting human capabilities in the regions in which they operate.* The

understanding of what a corporation is for, up until now, has been dominated by the profit motive. This understanding has not prevented corporations from devoting quite a lot of money to charity domestically, but there is no generally accepted standard of moral responsibility. The new global order must have a clear public understanding that part of doing business decently is to devote a substantial amount of one's profits to the promotion of education and good environmental conditions in the regions in which the corporation does business. There are good efficiency arguments for this: for example, corporations do better with a stable, well-educated workforce. Education also promotes political engagement, crucial for the health of a democracy; and corporations do well under conditions of political stability. Nonetheless, those arguments should be subsidiary to a general public understanding that such support is what decency requires. At the same time, corporations should undertake to promote good labor conditions, going beyond what local laws may require of them.

To some extent corporations can be controlled by domestic laws in each country. But the difficulty is that all countries want to attract them, and there is sometimes a race to the bottom as each one seeks to offer cheaper labor and less burdensome environmental regulations than its competitors. So the main responsibility must rest on the members of the corporation themselves, their lawyers, and, very importantly, their consumers, who may bring pressure to bear on a corporation to perform better than it has been performing.

In some instances a corporation, or type of corporation, may face special responsibilities inherent in its subject matter. Thus today pharmaceutical companies face special responsibilities to address the global AIDS crisis, by marketing their products at affordable prices in the countries most affected, and by contributing to the development of a health infrastructure sufficient to enable delivery of them. Again, the consumer is a crucial agent in enforcing this responsibility: so at this point we do come back to the question of individual responsibility, as the source of the pressure to assume a corporate responsibility already allocated (in our ethical argument).

5. *The main structures of the global economic order must be designed to be fair to poor and developing countries.* The fact that many nations can feed all their people does not mean that it is fair for some countries to have additional obstacles placed in their way. Exactly what this principle involves is a matter that economists debate, and will long continue debating.[36] But there is pretty general agreement that the ways in which the IMF and various global trade agreements have been operating are insufficiently informed by careful ethical reflection about these issues. The World Bank has recently been somewhat more attentive to ethical issues and issues of poverty, and its development in this direction continues. In part, the problem is that of any bureaucratic structure: the norms of the most thoughtful people typically seem too complicated to give a clear and immediate policy prescription that the bureaucrat can go out and implement.[37] In part, too, there is the persistent sense that ethical norms are "soft" and not what the hardheaded policymaker should be thinking about. The world community must continue to apply pressure to these agencies, since voices of protest have been quite important in getting the voices of deprived people to be heard. In the area of trade, particularly, protests and public pressure are likely to be the only mechanisms that will successfully promote attention to urgent moral norms.

6. *We should cultivate a thin, decentralized, and yet forceful global public sphere.* A world state is not an appropriate aspiration. But there is no reason why a thin system of global governance, with at least some coercive powers, should not be compatible with the sovereignty and freedom of individual nations.

This system should include a world criminal court of the sort currently being initiated, to deal with grave human rights violations; a set of world environmental regulations with enforcement mechanisms, plus a tax on the industrial nations of the North to support the development of pollution controls in the South; a set of global trade regulations that would try to harness the juggernaut of globalization to a set of moral goals for human development, as set forth in the capabilities list; a set of global labor standards for both the formal and the informal sector, together with sanctions for companies that do not obey them; some limited forms of global taxation that would effect transfers of wealth from richer to poorer nations (such as the global resource tax suggested by Thomas Pogge);[38] and, finally, a wide range of international accords and treaties that, once ratified by the nations, can be incorporated into the nations' domestic systems of law through judicial and legislative action.[39] Existing global institutions such as the World Health Organization, the ILO, and the UN Development Programme, UNICEF, and UNESCO can all play a valuable role, but it seems a bad idea to assume that the current structure of such institutions will remain fixed, since we can see how new institutions have in many cases emerged to deal with new problems.

7. *All institutions and (most) individuals should focus on the problems of the disadvantaged in each nation and region.* We have observed that national sovereignty, though morally important, risks insulating from criticism and change the situation of women and other disadvantaged groups within each nation. The situation of people (whoever they are, at any given time) whose quality of life is especially low, as measured by the capabilities list, should therefore be a persistent focus of attention for the world community as a whole: not just for institutions but for all individuals who are not themselves unusually burdened. (Members of disadvantaged groups frequently play a very creative role

in mobilizing world action, as has happened in the international women's movement. Nonetheless, it seems that the duty to solve grave problems should rest primarily with those whose lives are not lived in desperate circumstances.) Although coercive sanctions will be appropriate in only some cases, our ability to justify a richer set of norms should lead to tireless efforts of persuasion and political mobilization, as with the work that led to the Convention on the Elimination of All Forms of Discrimination against Women (CEDAW). Selective use of funding can greatly assist the process of raising the living standard of these people and groups.

8. *Care for the ill, the elderly, children, and the disabled should be a prominent focus of the world community.* A growing problem in today's world, as the population ages and as more and more people are living with HIV/AIDS, is the need to care for people in a condition of dependency. Chapter 3 has already discussed the problems of sex equality posed by currently inadequate arrangements for care. The state, the workplace, and the family must all change so that needs for care are met without crippling the well-being and the aspirations of women. Again, this is a task that requires both domestic and international work, and it is one in which richer countries have a duty to assist poorer ones, for example by developing the nursing and health infrastructure requisite to cope with the HIV crisis.

9. *The family should be treated as a sphere that is precious but not "private."* Social contract theories have long segmented the world into a "public sphere" and a "private sphere," and such theorists have typically treated the family as a domain off-limits to political justice. Rawls's complex and tortuous engagement with this question shows how difficult it is for even the most concerned such theorist to solve the problems posed by inequalities of resources and opportunity within the family.[40] The world community should protect the individual liberties of people, in-

cluding their right to choose to marry and form a family,[41] and various further associated rights, including some parental rights over choices regarding their children. But the protection of the human capabilities of family members is always paramount. The millions of female children who die of neglect and lack of essential food and care are not dying because the state has persecuted them; they are dying because their parents do not want another female mouth to feed (and another dowry to pay), and because the state has not done enough to protect female lives. The world community has been very slow to respond to the problem of differential care for girls and boys, precisely because both Western and nonwestern traditions have constructed the home as an inviolable domain of personal prerogative.[42] Finding a new approach to the family that is both respectful of associational liberty and protective toward the capabilities of children should be a priority of the global public sphere, as of domestic political debate in each nation.

10. *All institutions and individuals have a responsibility to support education, as key to the empowerment of currently disadvantaged people.* Education is a key to all the human capabilities.[43] And, as we have seen, it is among the resources most unequally distributed around the world. Domestic governments can do much more in more or less all cases to promote education in each nation; but corporations, nongovernmental organizations (funded by individual contributions, foreign aid from governments, and so on), and the global public sphere (in international documents and fora) can do a great deal more to promote universal primary and secondary education. Nothing is more important for democracy, for the enjoyment of life, for equality and mobility within one's nation, for effective political action across national boundaries. Education should be construed not merely as a provider of useful technical skills, but

also, and more centrally, as a general empowerment of the person through information, critical thinking, and imagination.

Taken as a group, these principles (and the capabilities approach that lies behind them) seem to fulfill very well the criteria we set out at the end of our critique of Rawls. *Equal respect for persons* is shown by the commitments to promote the human capabilities of each and every person and to remove those structural features of the world system that stand between people and decent life opportunities; also by the commitment to promote each and every one of the capabilities, rather than treating some important human matters as merely instrumental to the pursuit of wealth. The *moral importance of state sovereignty* is recognized clearly in the theory. *Justice* is realized *in multiple relations,* in that responsibilities for promoting human capabilities are assigned to a wide range of distinct global and domestic structures. *Flexibility in domestic institutions* is insisted on by the requirement that all nations do a great deal more to promote the well-being of people in the poorest nations: they will need to alter their domestic structures in order to do this, and thus they cannot and should not insist that their domestic structure is fixed and final. Finally, as we have seen, a *new account of the purposes of international cooperation* animates the spirit of the entire enterprise, with ideas of human development and human global fellowship taking the place of the thinner idea of mutual advantage.

There is no natural place to stop this list of principles. One might have had a list of twenty principles, rather than ten. Moreover, the principles are extremely general, and many hard questions wait in the wings as soon as we begin to implement them. At this point philosophy must turn the job over to other disciplines. But the philosophical part of the inquiry is not useless. Ideas shape public policy at a deep level, influencing what alternatives get onto the table and are taken seriously.[44] These principles, together with the theoretical analysis that supports them, are at least a sign of what the capabilities approach can offer as we move from goals and entitlements to the construction of a decent global society. If our world is to be a decent world in the future, we must acknowledge right now that we are citizens of one interdependent world, held together by mutual fellowship as well as the pursuit of mutual advantage, by compassion as well as by self-interest, by a love of human dignity in all people, even when there is nothing we have to gain from cooperating with them. Or rather, even when what we have to gain is the biggest thing of all: participation in a just and morally decent world.

6

BEYOND "COMPASSION AND HUMANITY"

JUSTICE FOR NONHUMAN ANIMALS

In conclusion, we hold that circus animals . . . are housed in cramped cages, subjected to fear, hunger, pain, not to mention the undignified way of life they have to live, with no respite and the impugned notification has been issued in conformity with the . . . values of human life, philosophy of the Constitution . . . Though not homosapiens, they are also beings entitled to dignified existence and humane treatment sans cruelty and torture . . . Therefore, it is not only our fundamental duty to show compassion to our animal friends, but also to recognise and protect their rights . . . If humans are entitled to fundamental rights, why not animals?

—*Nair v. Union of India*, Kerala High Court, no. 155/ 1999, June 2000

i. "Beings Entitled to Dignified Existence"

In 55 B.C.E. the Roman leader Pompey staged a combat between humans and elephants. Surrounded in the arena, the animals perceived that they had no hope of escape. According to Pliny, they then "entreated the crowd, trying to win their compassion with indescribable gestures, bewailing their plight with a sort of lamentation." The audience, moved to pity and anger by their plight, rose to curse Pompey—feeling, writes Cicero, that the elephants had a relation of commonality *(societas)* with the human race.[1]

We humans share a world and its scarce resources with other intelligent creatures. We have much in common with these creatures, although we also differ in many ways. These commonalities sometimes inspire sympathy and moral concern, although they are more often treated obtusely. We also have many types of relationships with members of other species, relationships involving responsiveness, sympathy, joy in excellence, and concerned interaction, as well as manipulativeness, indifference, and cruelty. It seems plausible to think that these relationships ought to be regulated by justice, instead of the war for survival and power that now, for the most part, obtains.

Nonhuman animals[2] are capable of dignified existence, as the Kerala High Court says. It is difficult to know precisely what that phrase means, but it is rather clear what it does not mean: the conditions of the circus animals in the case, squeezed into cramped and filthy cages, starved, terrorized, and beaten, given only the minimal care that would make them presentable in the ring the following day. Dignified existence would seem at least to include the following: adequate opportunities for nutrition and physical activity; freedom from pain, squalor, and cruelty; freedom to act in ways that are characteristic of the species (rather than to be confined and, as here, made to perform silly and degrading stunts); freedom from fear and opportunities for rewarding interactions with other creatures of the same species, and of different species; a chance to enjoy the light and air in tranquility. The fact that humans act in ways that deny animals a dignified existence appears to be an issue of justice, and an urgent one, although we shall have to say more to those who would deny this. Moreover, although the questions thus raised are in many ways different from the questions we have confronted so far, there seems to be no good reason why existing mechanisms of basic justice, entitlement, and law cannot be extended across the species barrier, as the Indian court boldly does.

Before we can perform this extension with any hope of success, however, we need to articulate an adequate theoretical approach. In this area our conceptual materials are in their infancy. It seems premature to head directly to conclusions, urgent though these conclusions are, and obvious though many of them are, if we do not at the same time seek to refine our philosophical categories.

The capabilities approach provides better theoretical guidance than do other approaches to the question of animal entitlements. Because it is capable of recognizing a wide range of types of animal dignity, and of corresponding needs for flourishing, and because it is attentive to the variety of activities and goals that creatures of many types pursue, the approach is capable of yielding norms of interspecies justice that are subtle and yet demanding, involving fundamental entitlements for creatures of different types. The approach will have to be transformed and extended in order to meet the challenge. But its Aristotelian ingredients enable it to meet the challenge well.

As I have repeatedly emphasized, Kantian social contract theories have great strengths. In this area, however, they fall more clearly short than in any other. Both because of their commitment to rationality as the ground of dignity and because of their conception of political principles as deriving from a contract among rough equals, they deny that we have obligations of justice to nonhuman animals. They view such obligations as we might have either as derivative from obligations to humans or as simply different in kind, as duties of charity and not of justice. I shall argue that we should criticize such views in two ways: by recognizing the extent of intelligence in many nonhuman animals, and by rejecting the idea that only those who can join a contract as rough equals can be primary, nonderivative subjects of a theory of justice.

ii. Kantian Social Contract Views:
Indirect Duties, Duties of Compassion

It is not surprising that one of our most far-reaching legal judgments in favor of animals comes from an Indian court; the
Hindu traditions of India teach reverence for at least many animals, and vegetarianism is an important moral ideal. By contrast, all philosophers writing in the modern Western tradition,
whatever their religious beliefs, have been deeply influenced by
the Judeo-Christian tradition, which teaches that human beings
were given dominion over animals and plants. Even though
Jewish and Christian writers studied the Greeks and Romans
and incorporated many of their ideas, it is not very surprising
that the school of ancient ethical thought that had the greatest
influence on their thinking, with respect to the animal question,
was Stoicism, of all ancient Greco-Roman views the least sympathetic to the idea that animals might have ethical standing.[3] Late
Platonist writers defended an elaborate ethic of vegetarianism
and respect for animal life; but they grounded it in metaphysical doctrines (including the transmigration of souls into animal
bodies) that Jews and Christians repudiated. Aristotelians
argued that all of nature is a continuum, and that all living
creatures are worthy of respect and even wonder. But to make
Aristotelianism compatible with Christianity it was necessary to
revise those particular elements, creating a sharp divide between
humans and other species, as Aquinas and other Christian Aristotelians do. Epicureans argued that humans, like all animals, are
composed of mortal bodies and corporeal souls that disintegrate
upon death. But such doctrines, which at least break down the
sense of unique sanctity surrounding human life, were rejected
by Jews and Christians as paradigmatic of atheism and godless
materialism.

In Stoicism, however, Jews and Christians found a natural

ally: for Stoic views, like Judeo-Christian views, taught that the capacity for reason and moral choice is the unique source of dignity in any natural being. Beings who lack that source of dignity are in an important sense outside the ethical community. Christians, Jews, and Stoics can still hold that we have duties not to abuse animals; indeed, they can also hold that we have duties toward inanimate objects. But animals are not regarded as participants in the ethical community, creatures in partnership with whom we ought to work out our ways of living.

Thus we should begin our scrutiny of social contract theories by recognizing that these theories arose within a more general Stoic/Judeo-Christian culture, and that the treatment of animals, once a prominent ethical issue in the ancient Greco-Roman world, did not become so again until at least the eighteenth century. We must ask which shortcomings in such theories are due to their social contract form, and which to the more general background from which they spring.[4]

Kant does not talk about animals in his major works on moral and political philosophy; he says nothing to connect them to his theory of the social contract. In the earlier *Lectures on Ethics*,[5] however, he does address the topic of duties toward nonhuman animate beings, "animals and spirits."[6] Baumgarten, whose text he uses as the basis for his lecture course, speaks of "duties toward beings which are beneath us and beings which are above us." But Kant denies that we have any duties directly toward animals. Moral duties have to be toward self-conscious beings. Animals have no self-consciousness. Therefore they "are there merely as a means to an end. That end is man. . . . Our duties towards animals are merely indirect duties towards humanity."

Kant's argument for indirect duties begins from an idea of analogical similarity. Animals, he argues, behave in ways that are analogous to the ways human beings behave: for example, they display an analogue of loyalty. If we habituate ourselves to treat animals kindly when they behave this way, we strengthen the disposition to behave kindly to humans when they behave in similar ways. More generally (and here Kant appears to have dropped the point about analogical similarity), when we are kind to animals we strengthen our tendencies of kindness; when we are cruel to animals, we nourish tendencies to be cruel to humans. Kant here alludes to Hogarth's famous and influential engravings, *The Stages of Cruelty,* which depict a young boy torturing animals, and then going on to commit a variety of cruel and wanton acts toward human beings, culminating in murder. Kant thinks that Hogarth's ideas offer important lessons for children. He also expresses approval of the British custom by which butchers and doctors do not sit on juries because they are accustomed to the sight of death and "hardened."[7]

Thus it would appear that Kant rests the whole case for kindness to animals on fragile empirical claims about psychology. He cannot conceive that creatures who (in his view) lack self-consciousness and the capacity for moral reciprocity could possibly be objects of moral duty. ("He does not fail in his duty to the dog," he writes, "for the dog cannot judge.") More generally, he does not believe that such a being can have a dignity, an intrinsic worth. Its value must be derivative and instrumental.

Kant's views about animals are not entailed even by the Judeo-Christian culture of his time. For one might hold that humans rightly have dominion over animals while also holding, as Baumgarten apparently does, that humans have obligations of good stewardship that require them to treat animals decently. Kant's views express his own particular conceptions of moral obligation and of humanity, according to which the capacity for moral rationality is essential for ethical status.

One may, however, be a contractarian—and indeed, in some sense a Kantian—without espousing these narrow views. For Rawls, justice, while "the first virtue of social institutions," is not the only virtue even in the political sphere, and certainly not the entirety of moral virtue. Although his remarks on animals are not lengthy, he does not hesitate to say that there are moral duties to animals, which he calls "duties of compassion and humanity" (*TJ* 512). The fact that animals feel pleasure and pain imposes such duties.

But for Rawls these are not issues of justice, and he is explicit that the contract doctrine cannot be extended to deal with them "in a natural way": "Certainly it is wrong to be cruel to animals . . . The capacity for feelings of pleasure and pain and for the forms of life of which animals are capable clearly impose duties of compassion and humanity in their case. I shall not attempt to explain these considered beliefs. They are outside the scope of the theory of justice, and it does not seem possible to extend the contract doctrine so as to include them in a natural way" (*TJ* 512).

Similarly, in an important earlier section titled "The Basis of Equality," Rawls argues that animals lack those properties of human beings "in virtue of which they are to be treated in accordance with the principles of justice" (504). Being a moral person is a sufficient condition for being entitled to be treated with justice on a basis of equality with others. Rawls defines moral persons with reference to the two features that he later (in *Political Liberalism*) calls the two moral powers: a capacity for a conception of the good and a capacity for a sense of justice, at least "to a certain minimum degree" (505). Similarly, in *PL*, referring back to this discussion, he says "Their having these powers to the requisite minimum degree to be fully cooperating members of society makes persons equal" (19). Although he never insists that the capacity for moral personality is a necessary condition for being owed strict and equal justice, Rawls does indicate his sympathy for that conclusion in the case of animals: "While I have not maintained that the capacity for a sense of justice is necessary in order to be owed the duties of justice, it does seem that we are not required to give strict justice anyway to creatures lacking this capacity . . . Our conduct toward animals is not regulated by these principles, or so it is generally believed" (*TJ* 512, 504).

Once again, we must ask how much of Rawls's position is explained by his contractarianism, and how much by his Kantian political conception of the person. Clearly, the Kantian conception of the person suffices, in Rawls's view, to rule nonhuman animals out as members of the community who work out and are bound by principles of justice. The two moral powers belong, in his view, to humans only, and not to all of these. Animals, like mentally disabled humans, fail to be persons in the requisite sense. Similarly, the political freedom of persons is conceived, as we have seen, in terms of an idealized rationality, including the capacity to be "self-authenticating sources of valid claims." And the dignity and inviolability of persons is also understood in terms of their membership in the moral community. If animals can be said to possess any sort of dignity or inviolability for Rawls, it will not be the sort that persons possess, an "inviolability founded on justice that even the welfare of society as a whole cannot override" (*TJ* 3).[8]

One might try to reply that Rawls's error is empirical rather than philosophical. He has not understood how intelligent animals are, how capable they are of relationships (with both humans and one another) involving complex forms of reciprocity. If we see animals with sufficient richness and complexity, we may after all find the idea of a social compact involving them perfectly plausible, at least as an illuminating hypothesis. But this reply proves inadequate. Rawls's theory is indeed incomplete empirically. He makes no effort to study the intelligence of animals, and he offers no argument that they are incapable of reciprocity. It seems likely that many of them are indeed capable of at least some forms of reciprocity. It seems doubtful, however, that we can include animals sufficiently in a Rawlsian theory simply by acknowledging these facts. First, the capacity for reciprocity is present in only some animals; and yet issues of unfair and cruel treatment extend very broadly. If there is reciprocity between humans and dogs or apes, it is not clear that there is reciprocity between humans and birds or lions. And yet, our treatment of all these animals appears to raise questions of justice. Second, insofar as there is reciprocity between humans and some nonhuman animals, it is not the type of reciprocity described in Rawls's theory, based on the possession of complex reflexive rational and moral capacities.

But we might in principle separate the contractarian doctrine from its Kantian elements, supplying Rawls with a political conception of the person more Aristotelian in spirit, ready to accord dignity to a wide range of creatures in the universe. Let us suppose that we have done so. Would this suffice to make the contract doctrine a suitable way to deal with issues involving animals that appear to be issues of justice, in the sense that animals seem to have a dignity that is being violated, and justifiable moral entitlements that are being denied? I believe not. Here again, as in the case of human beings with mental disabilities, there are problems in the very structure of the contract doctrine.

In a very basic way, the whole idea of a contract involving both humans and nonhuman animals is fantastic, suggesting no clear scenario that would assist our thinking. Although the state of nature is not supposed to be an actual historical condition, it is supposed to be a coherent fiction that can help us think well. This means that it has to have realism, at least, concerning the powers and needs of the parties and their basic circumstances. There is no comparable fiction about our decision to make a deal with other animals that would be similarly coherent and helpful. Even though Hume's Circumstances of Justice are not the only way in which one might understand the need for justice in human affairs, they at least are familiar and plausible circumstances in which a large proportion of human beings actually live. And if we imagine people in such circumstances (or the analogous circumstances posited by Locke and Kant) we can see how they would want to make a contract for mutual advantage, and imagine roughly the kind of contract they might make.

By contrast, although we do share a world of scarce resources with animals, and although there is in a sense a state of rivalry among species that is comparable to the rivalry in the state of nature, the asymmetry of power between humans and nonhuman animals is too great to imagine any contract we might make with them as a real contract. Certainly, we cannot imagine that the contract would actually be for mutual advantage: for if we want to protect ourselves from the incursions of threatening animals we can just kill them, as we do. It has been a long time since human beings were threatened in a general way by the power of "the beasts." Thus, the Rawlsian condition that no one party to the contract is strong enough to dominate or kill all the others is not met. Furthermore, because animals do not make contracts, we are blocked, here again, from imagining plausibly what a social compact would look like. The type of intelligence that animals possess is not the sort that we need to postulate to imagine a contractual process.

So there is no good analogue of the Circumstances of Justice, no good analogue to the contractarian account of the purposes of social cooperation, no good analogue to the account of the abilities of the parties in virtue of which a contract is possible, no good analogue to their situation as "free, equal, and independent" parties. Unlike humans in a state of extreme mental disability, animals may be very independent and in their own way free. Although some depend on humans, many do not. But they certainly are not equals of humans in power and resources, and this asymmetry means that humans seeking to make a contract for mutual advantage will simply omit them, as all existing contract theories imagine the parties as doing. Why make a deal with creatures that are securely controlled and dominated? If the point of social cooperation is seen in social contract terms, no answer is forthcoming.

The omission of animals from the process of making the contract might not matter, if there were some other way of construing them as subjects of justice. For example, humans might represent the interests of animals, assuming that they are among the parties in the society to be designed. Here, however, we run into the conflation we have often had occasion to notice. The parties who frame the social contract are framing principles by which they, those very people, are to live together. The principles are chosen to regulate their dealings with one another. To the extent that the interests of other parties can be included in their deliberations, it will have to be done in a derivative way, and at a later stage. Animals cannot be primary subjects of justice, because they cannot be framers of contracts.

In the case of people with disabilities, moreover, Rawls is prepared to deal with their interests at a later stage; in the case of animals, he denies altogether that the issues before us are issues of justice.

Rawls's omission of animals from the theory of justice is motivated, then, both by his Kantian conception of the person and by the structure of the social contract position. Unlike Kant, he holds that we have some moral duties to animals;[9] justice, however, is confined to the human realm.

I have said that the cruel and oppressive treatment of animals raises issues of justice, but I have not really defended that claim against the Rawlsian alternative. What exactly does it mean to say that these are issues of justice, rather than issues of "compassion and humanity"? The emotion of compassion involves the thought that another creature is suffering significantly, and is not (or not mostly) to blame for that suffering.[10] It does not involve the thought that someone is to blame for that suffering. One may have compassion for the victim of a crime, but one may also have compassion for someone who is dying from disease (in a situation in which that vulnerability to disease is nobody's fault). "Humanity" I take to be a similar idea. So compassion, all by itself, omits the essential element of blame for wrongdoing: that is the first problem. It would seem that analyzing the harms we do to animals in terms of duties of compassion alone entails blurring the important distinction between the compassion we might have for an animal who dies of a disease that is nobody's fault and the response we might have to the sufferings of an animal who is being cruelly treated by humans. But suppose we add that element, saying that duties of compassion involve the thought that it is *wrong* to cause animals suffering. Where that suffering is caused by a wrongful act, a duty of compassion would involve acknowledgment of that wrongfulness. That is, a duty of compassion would not be just a duty to have compassion, but a duty, as a result of one's compassion, to refrain from, inhibit, and punish acts of the sort that cause the suffering occasioning the compassion. I believe that Rawls would probably make this addition, although he certainly does not tell us what he takes duties of compassion to be. What is at stake, further, in the decision to say that the mistreatment of animals is not just morally wrong, but morally wrong in a special way, raising questions of *justice*?

This is a hard question to answer, since justice is a much-disputed notion, and there are many varieties of justice, political, ethical, and so forth. It seems, however, that what we typically mean when we call a bad act unjust is that the creature injured by that act has an entitlement not to be treated in that way, and an entitlement of a particularly urgent or basic type (since we do not believe that all instances of unkindness, thoughtlessness, and so forth are instances of injustice, even if we do believe that people have a right to be treated kindly, and so forth). The sphere of justice is the sphere of basic entitlements. When I say that the mistreatment of animals is unjust, I mean to say not only that it is wrong *of us* to treat them in that way, but also that they have a right, a moral entitlement, not to be treated in that way. It is unfair *to them*.[11]

What other ideas are conceptually linked to seeing animals as having urgent entitlements? I believe that thinking of animals as active beings who have a good naturally leads us to have the further thought that they are entitled to pursue that good. If we have that thought, we are likely to see important damages done to them, blocking them from their pursuit of the good, as unjust. What is lacking in Rawls's account, as in Kant's (though more subtly), is the sense of the animal itself as an agent and a subject, a creature to whom something is due, a creature who is itself an end. As we shall see, the capabilities approach does treat animals as agents seeking a flourishing existence; this basic conception, I believe, is one of its greatest strengths.

We certainly should not deny that compassion is very important in thinking correctly about our duties to animals. Compassion overlaps with the sense of justice, and a full allegiance to justice requires compassion for beings who suffer wrongfully, just as it requires anger at the offenders who inflict wrongful suffering. But compassion by itself is too indeterminate to capture our sense of what is wrong with the treatment of animals. An adequate response involves compassion of a special sort, compassion that focuses on wrongful action and sees the animal as an agent and an end.

iii. Utilitarianism and Animal Flourishing

In general, the capabilities approach is a close ally of contractarian approaches and is more deeply critical of Utilitarianism. And yet in this particular area things look different. Nobody could deny that, historically, Utilitarianism has contributed more than any other ethical theory to the recognition of animal suffering as an evil. Both Bentham and Mill in their time and Peter Singer in our own have courageously taken the lead in freeing ethical thought from the shackles of a narrow species-centered conception of worth and entitlement. No doubt this achievement was connected with the founders' general radicalism and their skepticism about conventional morality, their willingness to follow the ethical argument wherever it leads. These remain very great virtues in the Utilitarian position.

Moreover, Utilitarianism has an outcome-oriented view of justice, which seems required in order to deal well with all three of our problems. Procedural views in the social contract tradition run into difficulty when they ask who is included in the procedures, stipulating conditions, such as the possession of a certain type of rationality, or a rough equality of positions, that restrict entry. Because they conflate the question "Who frames the principles?" with the question "For whom (at least in the first instance) are the principles framed?" they must consider obligations to beings who cannot take part in the contractual process as derivative and posterior. Outcome-oriented views, by contrast, have no difficulty considering, in a primary and nonderivative way, the interests of powerless, disabled, and nonlinguistic beings. Because such views do not conflate the two questions, they may imagine human beings framing principles of justice directly for a much wider group of beings.

Moreover, Utilitarianism's focus on the sentience that links humans with all other animals and on the badness of pain are particularly attractive starting points when we consider issues of justice involving animals: for there is no doubt that a central problem of justice in this area is the problem of pain wrongfully inflicted.

Thus it is in a spirit of alliance that I now address some criticisms to the Utilitarian view. In general, all Utilitarian views have three aspects: *consequentialism, sum-ranking,* and a *substantive view about the good.*[12] *Consequentialism* holds that the right act is the one that promotes the best overall consequences. *Sum-ranking* tells us how to aggregate consequences across lives—namely, by adding together, or aggregating, the goods present in distinct lives. Views about the *good* in Utilitarianism have taken two distinct forms. Bentham's is a pure hedonistic Utilitarianism, asserting the supreme worth of pleasure and the badness of pain.[13] Peter Singer's modern version is somewhat different. He calls it "preference utilitarianism," and it holds that the consequences we should aim to produce are those that on balance "further the interests (i.e. desires or preferences) of those affected."[14] Killing is wrong only when individuals killed have a preference to continue living; the killing is a wrong to that individual.[15]

There are some difficulties with the Utilitarian view, in both of its forms. Having explored some of these in Chapters 1 and 5, we must recapitulate and extend our critique. Consequentialism by itself causes the fewest difficulties, since one may always adjust the account of well-being, or the good, in consequentialism so as to admit many important things that Utilitarians typically do not make salient: plural and heterogeneous goods, the protection of rights, even personal commitments or agent-centered goods. More or less any moral theory can be "consequential-ized," put in a form in which the matters valued by that theory appear in the account of consequences to be produced.[16] There is, however, some question about whether any view that urges us to produce the best[17] overall consequences is the right starting point for political justice.

So far, in framing principles of justice in the capabilities approach, we have focused on a small number of core entitlements. Like Rawls's approach, our approach insists that these entitlements have a special priority or salience for political purposes, constraining the pursuit of other goods. Ever since John Stuart Mill said something like this about justice in chapter 5 of *Utilitarianism,* philosophers have debated whether giving political priority to basic justice, as Mill does, is compatible with consequentialism. Can consequentialism give the requirements of justice sufficient centrality for political purposes? Even if this problem can be solved, there is another and deeper problem to be faced, concerning restraint or parsimony.

Politics is unlike other aspects of life, in that we are choosing principles to govern the lives of people who disagree about the (rest of the) good, who have different religious conceptions and conceptions of value. Respecting them, as I have argued in Chapter 5 (agreeing with the idea of political liberalism developed by Rawls and Larmore),[18] means not imposing on them some other person's comprehensive view of the good. What we want political actors to do, in a liberal state, is *just* to take care of basic justice, and not to be maximizers of overall good. We actively want them *not* to pursue the maximization of overall good, because we don't want them to be in the business of defining what the good is in a comprehensive way. The right division of labor in a liberal society is for political institutions to take care of justice, and for individuals to be left free to pursue on their own other parts of their comprehensive conceptions of the good.

From such a perspective, to ask of political actors that they be consequentialists looks illiberal: for surely people cannot make choices as consequentialists without having some comprehensive conception of the good.[19] But such a conception may be precisely what we do not want political actors to employ, on the grounds that each citizen will have, and pursue, her own, within limits set by justice. Making a short list of the central capabilities, as core entitlements based on justice, is a way of taking a stand on content. But it is also, importantly, a way of announcing our restraint to people with different comprehensive conceptions. We thereby say, "We ask you to endorse, as a linchpin of our society's basic structure, only this partial conception of the good; for the rest, you are free to pursue your religious or secular conception, whatever it is."

Singer's preference Utilitarianism obviously does better with this problem than other types of Utilitarianism; for it is liberal in deferring to what people actually prefer. But it is not clear that this move solves the problem of overambition on the part of the political doctrine. For many comprehensive doctrines that citizens hold do not endorse preference-satisfaction as a correct view of the good; most religious and many moral doctrines disagree with Singer on this point. So even in pursuing satisfaction as a goal, the political actor would be invading territory that the liberal wants to reserve for each person's choices. Preference Utilitarianism has, in addition, some familiar problems, which I have discussed in Chapters 1 and 5:[20] the ambiguity of the very notion of a preference; the existence of preferences shaped by ignorance, greed, and fear; still worse, the existence of "adaptive preferences," preferences that simply adapt to the low level of living one has come to expect.

So I tentatively conclude that, while we do want political principles to focus on consequences, we need to assign them a task more limited than that assigned them by the consequentialist, that of dealing with a limited range of consequences in areas that are matters of basic justice. Outside this sphere society as a whole and its basic structure should not be governed by anyone's single comprehensive conception of the good, even the preference Utilitarian's.

Let us now focus on *sum-ranking*. Outcome-oriented views need not simply add all the relevant goods together. They may weight them in other ways: for example, as in the capabilities approach applied to the human case, they may simply insist that each and every person has an indefeasible entitlement to come up above a threshold on certain key goods. In addition, such a view may focus, as does Rawls's theory, on the situation of the least well-off, refusing to permit inequalities that do not raise that person's position. These ways of considering well-being insist on treating people as ends: they refuse to allow some people's extremely high well-being to be purchased, so to speak, through other people's disadvantage. Even the welfare of society as a whole does not lead us to violate an individual.

Utilitarianism notoriously refuses such insistence on the separateness and inviolability of persons. Because it is committed to sum-ranking of all relevant pleasures and pains (or preference-satisfactions and frustrations), it has no way of ruling out in advance results that are extremely harsh toward a given class or group. Slavery, the lifelong subordination of some to others—none of this is ruled out by the theory's core conception of justice, which treats all satisfactions as fungible in a single system. As we saw in Chapters 1 and 5, such results will be ruled out, if at all, only by empirical considerations regarding total or average well-being. These questions are notoriously indeterminate (especially when the number of individuals involved is also unclear, a point I shall take up later). Even if they were not, it seems that the best reason to be against slavery, torture, and lifelong subordination is a reason of justice, not an empirical calculation of total or average well-being. Even if we could get around that problem, we would then have to confront the problem of adaptive preferences once again, given the fact that unjust treatment often makes allies out of the oppressed.

When we turn to animals, all these problems are acute. Interspecies comparisons of utility are even more difficult and indeterminate than are interpersonal comparisons within a single species. The interpretation of animals' preferences is fraught with obscurity and difficulty. But even if we were able to solve these problems, a more general difficulty awaits us. Utilitarian sum-ranking seems to have no way to rule out, on grounds of basic justice, the great pain and cruel treatment of at least some animals. Suppose the circus animals described in my Indian court case were the only animals who were being treated cruelly: it is not obvious that the pleasure that their performance affords large human audiences could not outweigh the pain suffered by a small number of animals; and yet it seems unfortunate not to be able to say directly, as the Indian court does, "This is intolerable. This is a moral violation." To make basic ethical entitlements contingent on other people's malicious pleasure in this way is to give them far too weak and vulnerable a place, ignoring direct moral reasons for objecting to cruel practices.

Does preference Utilitarianism do better? In the first place, there is conceptual obscurity there, too: it is obviously very difficult to ascribe preferences to animals. I have argued that in the human case the theory has some grave problems, including the problem of misinformed, malicious, fear-induced preferences, and including that of adaptive preferences formed under bad or unjust background conditions. These problems are problems for the preferences of animals, too, though many of the deformed preferences emerge only in diseased relationships between animals and humans. Animals, too, can learn submissive or fear-induced preferences. Martin Seligman's experiments show that dogs who have been conditioned into a mental state of learned helplessness have immense difficulty learning to initiate voluntary movement, if they can ever do so.[21] Creatures accustomed to captivity may never be able to learn to live in the wild. Simply aggregating all these deformed preferences, without winnowing out those that are the product of unjust background conditions, here as in the human case, is a recipe for endorsing an unjust status quo.

Both consequentialism and sum-ranking cause difficulties for the Utilitarian. Let us, finally, consider the views of the good most prevalent within Utilitarianism: hedonism (Bentham) and preference-satisfaction (Singer). Pleasure is a notoriously elusive notion. Is it a single feeling, varying only in intensity and duration, as Bentham thought, or are the different pleasures as qualitatively distinct as the activities with which they are associated? Mill, following Aristotle, believed the latter; but if we once grant that point, we are looking at a view that is very different from standard Utilitarianism, which is firmly wedded to the homogeneity and qualitative singleness of good.

Such a commitment looks like an especially grave error when we consider basic political principles for animal entitlements. For animals as well as humans, each basic entitlement pertains to a separate domain of functioning; it is not bought off, so to speak, by even a very large amount of another entitlement. Animals, like humans, pursue a plurality of distinct goods: friendship and affiliation, freedom from pain, mobility, and many others. Aggregating the pleasures and pains connected to these distinct areas seems premature and misleading: we may want to say that animals have distinct entitlements to all of these things, based on justice.

Once we ask the hedonist to admit plural goods, not commensurable on a single quantitative scale, it is natural to ask, further, whether pleasure and pain are the only things we ought to be looking at when we consider the entitlements of animals. It seems plausible to think that there may be goods they pursue that are not felt as pain and frustration when they are absent: for example, free movement and physical achievement, and also altruistic sacrifice for kin and group. It is also possible that some animal pains may even be valuable: the grief of an animal for a dead child or parent, or for the suffering of a human friend, may be a constituent part of an attachment that is intrinsically good, as may the pain involved in the effort required to master a difficult activity.

Finally, all Utilitarian views are highly vulnerable on the question of numbers. The meat industry brings countless animals into the world who would never have existed but for that. To John Coetzee's fictional character Elizabeth Costello, in *The Lives of Animals,* this is one of the worst aspects of its moral cruelty: it "dwarfs" the Third Reich because "ours is an enterprise without end, self-regenerating, bringing rabbits, rats, poultry, livestock ceaselessly into the world for the purpose of killing them."[22] For the Utilitarian, these births of new animals are not by themselves a bad thing: indeed, we can expect new births to add to the total of social utility. So long as each animal has a life marginally worth living, however close to that margin, the existence of more life experience rather than less is a positive good.

So Utilitarianism has great merits, but also great problems. Consequentialism is in tension with liberal respect for a plurality of comprehensive conceptions of good. Sum-ranking treats some as means to the ends of others. Hedonism and preference Utilitarianism efface the heterogeneity and distinctness of the good, ignore goods that do not reside in sentience, and fail to criticize preferences and pleasures developed under unjust background conditions.

On all of these points, the Utilitarianism of Mill is distinctly preferable to the mainstream Utilitarian views we have just considered. Mill does give justice and rights a central place in thought about social well-being, although there is much dispute as to how consistent this position is with his Utilitarianism. In some works, for example *The Subjection of Women,* Mill refuses to count malicious pleasures for purposes of social choice; he also gives each person's inviolability considerable salience. Finally, Mill insists on the qualitative heterogeneity of pleasures, and even suggests at times that pleasures are best viewed as forms of activity. Indeed, Mill's view strikes an interesting balance between an Aristotelian emphasis on activity and flourishing and a Utilitarian emphasis on pleasure and the absence of pain.[23] This complexity makes his view an important ally of the capabilities approach, as we attempt to extend it into the realm of human-animal relations.

iv. Types of Dignity, Types of Flourishing: Extending the Capabilities Approach

The capabilities approach in its current form does not address the problem of justice for nonhuman animals. It starts from the notion of human dignity and a life worthy of it. And yet I would argue that the capabilities approach lends itself to such an extension far more readily than either of the theories currently under discussion. Its basic moral intuition concerns the dignity of a form of life that possesses both abilities and deep needs. Its basic goal is to address the need for a rich plurality of life activities. With Aristotle and Marx, the approach has insisted that there are waste and tragedy when a living creature with the innate or "ba-

sic" capability for some functions that are evaluated as important
and good never gets the opportunity to perform those functions. Failures to educate women, failures to promote adequate
health care, failures to extend the freedoms of speech and conscience to all citizens—all these are treated as causing a kind of
premature death, the death of a form of flourishing that has
been judged to be worthy of respect and wonder. The idea that
human beings should have a chance to flourish in their own way,
provided they do no harm to others, is thus very deep in the
view's whole approach to the justification of basic political entitlements. (We should bear in mind that any child born into a
species has the dignity relevant to that species, whether or not it
seems to have the "basic capabilities" relevant to that species.
For that reason, it should also have all the capabilities relevant to
the species, either individually or through guardianship.)

The species norm is evaluative, as I have insisted; it does not
simply read off norms from the way nature actually is. But once
we have judged that a capability is essential for a life with human
dignity, we have a very strong moral reason for promoting its
flourishing and removing obstacles to it.

The same attitude to natural powers that guides the approach
in the case of human beings guides it in the case of other animals. For there is a more general attitude behind the respect for
human powers that is basic to the capabilities approach, and it is
different from the type of respect that animates Kantian ethics.
For Kant, only humanity and rationality are worthy of respect
and wonder; the rest of nature is just a set of tools. The capabilities approach judges instead, with the biologist Aristotle, that
there is something wonderful and wonder-inspiring in all the
complex forms of life in nature.[24]

In *The Parts of Animals,* Aristotle gives his students a lecture on why they should not "make a sour face" at the idea of
studying animals, including the ones that seem not very exalted.

(Since Aristotle's main area of research was marine biology, much of the work is focused on marine and shoreline creatures.) He insists that all animals are akin, in being made of organic materials; humans should not plume themselves on being special. "If there is anyone who thinks it is base to study animals, he should have the same thought about himself." All animals are objects of wonder for the person who is interested in understanding:

> We won't leave out any of them if we can help it, whether more exalted or less exalted. For even in the case of those animals that give no delight to our senses, nature the artificer provides countless pleasures to those who can study the causes of things and who have a philosophical spirit . . . So we should not embark on the study of the less exalted animals with a childish disgust: for in everything in nature there is something wonder-inspiring. There is a story that some visitors once wanted to meet Heraclitus, and when they came in they found him warming himself in the kitchen. He told them, "Come in, don't shrink back. There are gods here too." So too, we should approach the study of each type of animal, not making a sour face, knowing that in every one of them is something natural and wonderful.[25]

Heraclitus reminded his visitors that there were gods in the kitchen, too (or in the toilet, since the meaning of the Greek term is disputed). So, too, Aristotle urges his students to look at animals with wonder and curiosity, not disdain.

Aristotle's scientific spirit is not the whole of what the capabilities approach embodies. The approach includes, in addition, an ethical concern that the functions of life not be impeded, that the dignity of living organisms not be violated. Unlike Greek thinkers in the Platonist tradition, Aristotle seems not to have pursued such thoughts. He has nothing to say (or nothing that survives) about the moral case for vegetarianism, or about the humane treatment of animals more generally. And yet, if we feel wonder looking at a complex organism, that wonder at least suggests the idea that it is good for that being to persist and flourish as the kind of thing it is. This idea is at least closely related to an ethical judgment that it is wrong when the flourishing of a creature is blocked by the harmful agency of another. That more complex idea lies at the heart of the capabilities approach.

So I believe that the capabilities approach is well placed, intuitively, to go beyond both contractarian and Utilitarian views. It goes beyond the contractarian view in its starting point, a basic wonder at living beings, and a wish for their flourishing, and for a world in which creatures of many types flourish. It goes beyond the intuitive starting point of Utilitarianism because it takes an interest not just in pleasure and pain, but in complex forms of life and functioning. It wants to see each thing flourish as the sort of thing it is.

Laws and political principles are made by humans. So how can animals be full subjects of justice, when they are not among those who participate in the framing of principles of justice? This way of putting things derives from the contractarian perspective on justice; it is foreign to the capabilities approach. Social contract doctrines, as I have often observed, run together two questions that the capabilities approach keeps carefully distinct. For the contractarian, the question "Who makes the laws and principles?" is treated as having, necessarily, structurally, the same answer as the question "For whom are the laws and principles made?" This is so because of the contractarian's whole picture of social cooperation: people under pressure get together to secure their mutual advantage, by accepting constraints that are dictated by equal respect for the other parties to the bargain. That initial device ensures that they will be considering themselves as the primary if not the only subjects of the principles of justice that they subsequently design. Other beings can enter only derivatively, through relations of concern and trusteeship.

But, once again, there is no reason why these two questions should be put together in this way. Once we understand that the point of justice is to secure a dignified life for many different kinds of beings, why shouldn't the people making the principles include nonhuman beings as full-fledged subjects of the principles they will choose? The capabilities approach, as so far developed for the human case, looks at the world and asks how to arrange that justice be done in it. Justice is among the intrinsic ends that it pursues. People are imagined looking at all the brutality and misery, the goodness and kindness, of the world and trying to think how to make a world in which a core group of very important entitlements, inherent in the notion of human dignity, will be protected. Because they look at the whole of the human world, not just people with resources and powers similar to their own, they are able to be concerned directly and nonderivatively with the good of people with mental disabilities. They want a world in which those lives will not be blighted, or at least blighted as little as possible. The fact that some people with mental disabilities cannot be party to the choice of principles does not suggest to users of this approach any good reasons why the laws should not be *for* and *about* them along with others.

Put another way, the point of social cooperation is not sought in the mutual advantage of "free, equal, and independent" people. Social cooperation (once again, sticking to the human case as so far developed) is seen as having a more capacious and diffuse set of ends, including the pursuit of justice and just interdependency for its own sake, for all sorts of different people, some of them free and some less free or differently free, some of them relatively independent and all in at least some ways dependent, some equal in capacity and others quite unequal in capacity (though this does not mean that they are not morally equal).

Cooperation itself is not seen as a matter of a bunch of similar "normal" people getting together to make a contract; instead, it has many facets, including many different types of dependency and interdependency. Prominent among the purposes of cooperation, and inherent in the approach's account of basic justice, will be prevention of the blighting of valuable natural powers. These features make it easy to extend the approach to include human-animal relations.

Let us now begin the extension. The purpose of social cooperation, by analogy and extension, ought to be to live decently together in a world in which many species try to flourish. (Cooperation itself will now assume multiple and complex forms.) The general aim of the capabilities approach in charting political principles to shape the human-animal relationship, if we follow the intuitive ideas of the theory, would be that no sentient animal should be cut off from the chance for a flourishing life, a life with the type of dignity relevant to that species, and that all sentient animals should enjoy certain positive opportunities to flourish. With due respect for a world that contains many forms of life, we attend with ethical concern to each characteristic type of flourishing, and strive that it not be cut off or fruitless.

Unlike contractarianism, this approach involves direct obligations of justice to animals; it does not make these derivative from or posterior to the duties we have to fellow humans. It treats animals as subjects and agents, not just as objects of compassion. Unlike Utilitarianism, it respects each individual creature, refusing to aggregate the good of different lives and types of lives. No creature is being used as a means to the ends of others, or of society as a whole. The capabilities approach also refuses to aggregate across the diverse constituents of each life and type of life. Thus, unlike Utilitarianism, it can keep in focus the fact that each species has a different form of life and different ends; moreover, within a given species, each life has multiple and heterogeneous ends. (The focus on sentient creatures will be defended below.)

In the human case, the capabilities approach does not operate with a fully comprehensive conception of the good, because of the respect it has for the diverse ways in which people choose to live their lives in a pluralistic society. It aims at securing some core entitlements that are held to be implicit in the idea of a life with dignity, but it aims at capability, not functioning, and it focuses on a small list. In the case of human-animal relations the need for restraint is even more acute, since animals will not in fact be participating directly in the framing of political principles, and thus there is much danger of imposing on them a form of life that is not what they would choose. We would do best, then, to seek a limited set of political principles focused on enabling or protecting, not a comprehensive conception of good animal lives.

v. Methodology: Theory and Imagination

Before we can go further, however, we need to face some difficult questions about proper philosophical method. The capabilities approach follows the method described by John Rawls as the method through which we aim at "reflective equilibrium."[26] Rawls, correctly, traces this method to Aristotle, as well as to Sidgwick. In a process of Socratic self-scrutiny, we scrutinize our moral judgments and intuitions, asking which are the "deepest and most basic," as Aristotle would say, the "considered judgments," as Rawls would say. We then investigate a variety of theories that claim to organize these and other judgments. We hold nothing fixed; we seek consistency and fit among theory and judgments taken as a group. We may revise our considered judgments, if the conclusions of an otherwise powerful theory entail this (although usually we will do so only if other judgments, perhaps more general judgments, support the theory). We may also revise or reject a theory, in the light of our considered judgments. Nothing is held fixed in advance—not even how much weight to attach to formal principles such as simplicity and consistency.[27] The best and only judge is each person, and the community of concerned judges.[28]

One aspect of the Aristotelian type of method that is not emphasized in Rawls's discussion is its use of the imagination. Frequently we inform ourselves about alternative possibilities by imagining the form of life that these possibilities would construct, asking ourselves what suffering or flourishing there would be in lives governed by these political principles.[29] Rawls's Original Position requires such an exercise, since the parties must take the measure of life opportunities in the different social positions they construct for people.[30] Such imaginings will not be used uncritically; always, they are held up against both theories and considered judgments. And yet they can often inform us, as we consider what is at stake in the choice to follow a theory, or to revise one of our considered judgments.

How would such an approach proceed in investigating the ethical claims of nonhuman animals? There is a difficulty about the imagination that looms less large in the human case. As Peter Singer and other Utilitarians have emphasized, the imagination can be a very self-serving instrument. All literary depictions of the lives of animals are made by humans, and it is likely that all our empathic imagining of the experiences of animals is shaped by our human sense of life. For such reasons, Utilitarians tend to prefer a pure reliance on principle: once we lay out the dictates of the correct theory, we simply apply it to the case of animals, and there is no need for slippery exercises of imagining animal suffering.

In practice, of course, no Utilitarian actually argues this way. For it would be difficult to see why Utilitarianism was in fact the correct theory without some reliance on considered judgments and without some imagining of the sufferings of living creatures. If this is true in general, it is doubly true for the case of animals, who cannot offer their own judgments and theories, and whose lives we must somehow assess from our imperfect human point of view. How else, then, could we proceed except by imagining the lives of animals and their suffering? Jeremy Bentham lived at close quarters with animals, interacted with them often, and took delight in these playful interactions, in which such imagination as Bentham possessed was much in evidence.[31] Peter Singer's writing contains some of the most powerful invitations to imagine animal suffering ever written. If even those whose theoretical perspective militates against reliance on imagination do in fact consult it, albeit critically, so much is clearly true of theorists from other starting points. Good imaginative writing has been crucial in motivating opposition to cruelty toward animals.

All human descriptions of animal behavior are in human language, mediated by human experience. As Singer emphasizes, there is a real risk of getting things wrong through anthropomorphic projection. But we should remind ourselves that the same problems vex our human relationships. A real human being, as Proust says, imposes "a dead weight that our sensitivity cannot remove,"[32] an opaque area of mystery that even the most refined other mind can never fully penetrate. Only in our own imaginations can we experience the inner life of anyone else. From this observation Proust derives the startling claim that only literary artistry gives us access to another human mind: what we do when we read a novel is what we have to do always, if we are ever to endow another shape with life.[33] All of our ethical life involves, in this sense, an element of projection, a going beyond the facts as they are given. It does not seem impossible for the sympathetic imagination to cross the species barrier—if we press ourselves, if we require of our imaginations something more than common routine. As J. M. Coetzee's imaginary character Elizabeth Costello, a novelist lecturing on the lives of animals, says, "The heart is the seat of a faculty, *sympathy,* that allows us to share at times the being of another."[34]

So: the capabilities approach uses sympathetic imagining, despite its fallibility, to extend and refine our moral judgments in this area. It also uses theoretical insights about dignity to correct, refine, and extend both judgments and imaginings. There is no surefire recipe for doing this right; but we have to begin somewhere, and it is likely that any thoroughgoing and serious moral exercise will do better in this area than the self-serving and half-baked thinking that most of us typically do on this topic.

Although such a method can be used in conjunction with theories of many different types,[35] I believe that this complex holistic method, with its inclusion of narrative and imagination, does ultimately support the choice of the capabilities approach over other theories in the area of animal entitlements. Imagining and storytelling remind us in no uncertain terms that animal lives are many and diverse, with multiple activities and ends both within each species and across species. It would be odd if a method like this were to yield the conclusion that there is just one big thing that matters in all life, such as sentience or rationality. Imagination also informs us about asymmetries of power that we might miss if we did not closely investigate the texture of lives and relationships. Finally, imagining the lives of animals makes them real to us in a primary way, as potential subjects of justice, whereas a contractarian approach, focused on reciprocity between beings endowed with a specifically human type of rationality, is bound to make them only derivatively important.

In Chapter 3 much was made of the fact that the capabilities approach uses a political concept of the person that is different from that used in Kantian contractarian approaches. This Aristotelian conception situates human morality and rationality firmly within human animality, and insists that human animality itself has dignity. There is dignity in human neediness, in the human temporal history of birth, growth, and decline, and in relations of interdependency and asymmetrical dependency, as well as in (relatively) independent activity. That conception of the person is used in close connection with the holistic method of justification, and is one of the primary ways in which citizens imagine their humanity for political purposes.

We must now extend this aspect of the view. As we have said, laws and political principles are made by humans. So the political conception of the person as maker of law is still the Aristotelian conception we articulated in Chapter 3. But since the capabilities view does not run together the two questions of justice (who makes the principles, and for whom the principles are made), it now needs a different political conception of the creature as subject of justice. The fact that the human maker of principles is imagined as a needy, often dependent animal being prepares the way for that extension. People who see themselves in this way, and who do not pride themselves on an allegedly unique characteristic, are more likely than is the contractarian to see themselves as making principles for an interlocking world that contains many types of animal life, each with its own needs, each with its own dignity. Thus the conception of the creature as a subject of justice is exactly that: the conception of a world in which there are many different types of animals striving to live their lives, each life with its dignity. It is not a single conception at all, because the plurality of forms of life is very important to the whole idea.

vi. Species and Individual

What should the focus of these commitments be? It seems that here, as in the human case, the focus should be the well-being and dignity of the individual creature. The capabilities approach attaches no importance to increased numbers as such; its focus is on the well-being of existing creatures, and the harm that is done to them when their powers are blighted. Of course creatures cannot flourish in isolation, and thus for animals, as for humans, the existence of suitable groups and communities is an important part of the flourishing of individuals.

What about the continuation of species? Here my answers are tentative, and I am sure that they will not satisfy many thinkers about ecology. Further work clearly remains to be done in this area. But as of now I believe that the continuity of species would have little moral weight as a consideration of *justice* (though it may certainly have aesthetic significance, scientific significance, or some other sort of ethical significance), if species were becoming extinct in ways that had no impact on the well-being of individual creatures. But species are becoming extinct, typically, because human beings are killing their members and damaging their natural environment. Thus, damage to species occurs through damage to individuals. I believe that this individual damage should be the focus of ethical concern within the capabilities approach. Biodiversity as such may be a good, but what sort of good it is, and what its relation may be to political justice, seem to be questions best left for another inquiry. If I am right about what makes something a question of *justice,* rather than some other sort of question, animals are subjects of justice to the extent that individual animals are suffering pain and deprivation.

Should an endangered species get enhanced consideration for its individual members, as is now done when members of endangered species get special protections for their habitats? There are times when something analogous to this happens in the human case. The Amish parents who were plaintiffs in *Wisconsin v. Yoder*, asking for permission to withdraw their children from the last two years of compulsory public education, said that their free exercise of religion was threatened by the danger that their entire way of life might cease to exist.[36] That was why those particular individuals had a free exercise claim. Through this argument they won a special concession in the education of their children. In a similar way, I think that one might justify a special attention to endangered species as a way of showing concern for the reproductive capabilities and the flourishing generally of the individual members of that species. Enhanced attention to habitat and reproductive environment is necessary, not so much for the sake of future individuals who are not yet born, but in order to continue the way of life that existing individuals are living. At any rate, this would be the focus of ethical concern where basic justice is in view. To the extent that we adopt a just savings principle in the human case—a topic on which I believe Rawls has written convincingly[37]—we may adopt an analogous principle, as well, for the animal case. Such a focus on individuals does not rule out the idea that other principles, whether aesthetic or ethical or scientific, might dictate a concern for the continuity of species as a good in its own right.

The view, then, is individualistic in making the living creature, not the group or the species, the basic subject of justice. But there is another type of individualism that we must now consider: namely the view known as "moral individualism," the view that species membership in itself is of no moral relevance and that all moral relevance lies in the capacities of the individual.

Almost all ethical views of animal entitlements hold that there are morally relevant distinctions among forms of life. Killing a mosquito is not the same sort of harm as killing a chimpanzee. But the question is, what sorts of differences are relevant for basic justice? Singer, following Bentham, puts the issue in terms of sentience. Animals of many kinds can suffer bodily pain, and it is always bad to cause pain to a sentient being. If there are nonsentient or barely sentient animals—and it appears that crustaceans and mollusks, as well as sponges and the other creatures Aristotle called "stationary animals," are such animals—there is either no harm or only a trivial harm done in killing them. Among the sentient creatures, moreover, there are some who can suffer additional harms through their cognitive capacity: a few animals can foresee and mind their own death, and others will have conscious, sentient interests in continuing to live that are frustrated by death. The painless killing of an animal that does not foresee its own death or take a conscious interest in the continuation of its life is, for Singer and Bentham, not bad, for all badness, for them, consists in the frustration of interests, understood as forms of conscious awareness.[38] Singer is not, then, saying that some animals are inherently more worthy of esteem than others; he is simply saying that, if we agree with him that all harms reside in sentience, the creature's form of life limits the conditions under which it can actually suffer harm.

Tom Regan, who defends a rights-based view of animal entitlements,[39] refuses to admit differences of intrinsic value within the group of animals he considers, which includes all mammals who have reached the age of one year. All these, he holds, have intrinsic value, and intrinsic value is not a matter of degree. Nonetheless, he, too, gives conscious awareness a large place in his account of intrinsic value; his argument that all mammals who have reached one year have it is a large part of the support he provides for the claim that they do all have intrinsic value.

James Rachels, whose view has elements of both Utilitarianism and Aristotelianism,[40] holds, like Singer, that the complexity and level of a creature's form of life make a difference when we think what forms of treatment are and are not permissible. But the harms he considers do not all reside in sentience, as they do for Singer: thus, he is prepared to count certain forms of constraint on free movement, say, as harmful whether or not the animal is aware of them as bad or limiting, or has conscious interests in free movement. But he is like Singer in his more general account of the *way* in which the complexity of forms of life matters. It is not that some creatures are more wonderful or admirable per se, from some detached point of view in the universe. (That may be what Aristotle believed.) Instead, the level of complexity of a creature affects what can be a harm for it. What is relevant to the harm of pain is sentience; what is relevant to the harm of a specific type of pain is a specific type of sentience (for example, the ability to imagine one's own death). What is relevant to the harm of diminishing freedom is a capacity for freedom or autonomy. It would make no sense to complain that a worm is being deprived of autonomy, or a rabbit of the right to vote.

To summarize, moral individualism of the type espoused by Singer and Rachels makes two claims that we must now assess: first, the claim that differences of capacity affect entitlements not by creating a hierarchy of worth or value, but only by affecting what can be a good or a harm to a creature; second, the claim that species membership itself is of no significance in affecting what can be a good or harm to a creature—only the capacities of the individual count.

The first claim is powerful, and the capabilities approach can easily agree with it. We should not follow Aristotle in saying that there is a natural ranking of forms of life, some being intrinsically more worthy of support and wonder than others. Considerations of intrinsic worth might have ethical significance of some other kind in some comprehensive conceptions of the good life. It seems plausible for a comprehensive ethical view to judge that some activities and pleasures are "higher" and some "lower," some lives richer and some more impoverished; that it is better to live as a chimpanzee than to live as a worm, were that choice of lives a coherent thought experiment. But it seems dubious that these considerations should affect questions of basic justice and the political principles with which we frame an approach to those questions.

Here, then, we should agree with Rachels, putting his point in a slightly different way. Because the capabilities approach finds ethical significance in the unfolding and flourishing of basic (innate) capabilities—those that are evaluated as both good and central—it will also find harm in the thwarting or blighting of those capabilities. More complex forms of life have more and more complex (good) capabilities to be blighted, so they can suffer more and different types of harm. We can agree with Rachels that nothing is blighted when a rabbit is deprived of the right to vote, or a worm of the free exercise of religion. Level of life is relevant not because it gives different species differential worth per se, but because the type and degree of harm a creature can suffer varies with its form of life.

Is there a threshold beneath which the blighting of capabilities is not a harm? It seems minimally bad to kill a mosquito, because it appears that a mosquito does not feel pain. It is easy for Singer to explain this conclusion; it is more difficult for the capabilities theorist to do so, since the good resides in opportunities for flourishing, not in sentience alone. Why isn't the mosquito's ability to continue living one of the capacities that it is bad to cut off? Here I believe that the capabilities approach should admit the wisdom in Utilitarianism.[41] Sentience is not the only thing that matters for basic justice; but it seems plausible to consider the possession of sentience as a threshold condition for member-

ship in the community of beings who have entitlements based
on justice. If we abstract from the harm that mosquitoes do to
other animals (I shall consider this below), there would seem to
be something wanton and unpleasant about devoting a lot of
energy to killing mosquitoes. Harmless insects of similar capacities should not be unnecessarily killed. But is this a matter of basic justice, a matter that political principles should be framed
about? I believe that we have enough on our plate if we focus for
the time being on sentient creatures.

Given the fact that pleasure and pain are not the only things
of intrinsic value for the capabilities approach, the approach,
strictly speaking, should not say that the capacity to feel pleasure
and pain is a necessary condition of moral status. Instead, we
should adopt a disjunctive approach: if a creature has *either* the
capacity for pleasure and pain *or* the capacity for movement
from place to place[42] *or* the capacity for emotion and affiliation
or the capacity for reasoning, and so forth (we might add play,
tool use, and others), then that creature has moral standing. Science fiction reminds us that there are intelligent creatures who
lack the ability to feel pleasure and pain. So does religion: God,
in many traditional views, is a rational being who lacks sentience.
But nature as we know it is not like science fiction or theology.
All the creatures that have one of the other salient capabilities
mentioned above also have the capacity to feel pleasure and
pain. Aristotle reminds us that this is no accident: for sentience
is central to movement, affiliation, emotion, and thought. We
may, however, admit the science fiction possibility for theoretical
purposes.

Now let us turn to the second claim. For the Utilitarians,
and for Rachels, the species to which a creature belongs has no
moral relevance. Utilitarian writers are fond of comparing apes
to young children and to human beings with mental disabilities.
The capabilities approach, by contrast, with its talk of character-

istic functioning and forms of life, seems to attach some significance to species membership as such. I argued in Chapter 3
that the species to which Sesha belongs has moral relevance in
describing what capabilities society should extend to her, either
directly or through guardianship.

We should admit, first of all, that we need to know a great
deal more than we presently do about the capacities of animals.
Second, we should admit that there is much to be learned from
reflection on the continuum of life. Rachels' study of Darwinism
and its ethical implications shows us in a very convincing way
that the world is not the way the Stoics, and the Judeo-Christian
tradition, see it, with human beings sharply set off from the rest
of nature.[43] Capacities crisscross and overlap; a chimpanzee may
have more capacity for empathy and perspectival thinking than a
very young child, or an older autistic child. And capacities that
humans sometimes arrogantly claim for themselves alone are
found very widely in nature: Rachels gives a telling account of
Darwin's important essay on the practical intelligence of the
flatworm. Such reflection helps us to see ourselves more correctly and less arrogantly. It helps us to see reason as an animal
capacity whose dignity is not opposed to animality, but inherent
in it. It helps us to see compassion and altruism as characteristics
that extend broadly in nature, rather than special outgrowths of
a God-given moral nature.[44]

On the other hand, it seems wrong to conclude from this examination that species membership is morally and politically ir-
relevant. A child with severe mental impairments is actually very
different from a chimpanzee, though in certain respects some of
her capacities may be comparable. Her life is lived as a member
of the human community and not some other community; it is
there that she will either flourish or not flourish. The possibilities of flourishing in that community are defined around species
norms. Sesha and Jamie do not have the option of going off

and living in a nonlinguistic community of primates; for this reason, their disabilities with respect to linguistic capacity must be addressed by society: in Jamie's case, by specially designed education and physical therapy; in Sesha's, through relations of guardianship. Moreover, the fact that their disabilities create impediments to species-typical ways of flourishing creates a moral imperative for society: such impediments should be treated and cured, where possible, even if the treatment is expensive. Such issues are obscured by the facile comparison of Sesha and Jamie to chimpanzees. For chimpanzees, language use is a frill, constructed by human scientists; their own characteristic mode of flourishing in their own community does not rely on it. For Sesha and Jamie, some access to language, preferably through one's own development, but, where that is not possible, through guardianship, is essential to a dignified life. Each can flourish only as a human being. They have no option of flourishing as happy chimpanzees.

Arthur's case adds a fresh dimension to the problem. Arthur used to have less social capacity than some chimpanzees, according to experiments on perspectival thinking. There is no nonhuman animal that is even closely comparable to Arthur, whose linguistic and mathematical capacities are very high. Moral individualism appears to suggest that for normative purposes we treat Arthur as a *sui generis* being, not really fitting into any kind; we should simply develop the mixed capacities he has, not making any special effort in any one area. But in fact, Arthur will flourish, if he does, as a human being; and that fact means that special efforts must be made to develop his social capacities. It is clear that without such efforts he will not form friendships, wider social relationships, or useful political relationships. Such a lack matters for Arthur, because the human community is his community. He has no option to go off and search somewhere in the universe for a community of intelligent aliens with minimal social capacity (such as Mr. Spock). Humans expect certain things of him, and so education must nourish those capacities, even if it is very expensive to devise such forms of education. The relevance of the species norm is that it defines the context, the political and social community, in which people either flourish or do not. So they need to have support in order to attain the core capabilities that form part of that species norm, as politically defined.

In short, the species norm (duly evaluated) tells us what the appropriate benchmark is for judging whether a given creature has decent opportunities for flourishing. The same thing goes for nonhuman animals: in each case, what is wanted is a species-specific account of central capabilities (which may include particular interspecies relationships, such as the traditional relationship between the dog and the human), and then a commitment to bring members of that species up to that norm, even if special obstacles lie in the way of that.

Take Bear for example. Bear was the highly intelligent and loving German Shepherd who lived for eight years in the home of Cass Sunstein and Ellen Ruddick-Sunstein. When Bear began to age, his hips began to fail. He was not in pain, but he could not move as he formerly could; increasingly, he had to drag his hind quarters along. Because he was not in pain, moral individualism probably would not have recommended any special treatment for Bear. His family thought otherwise, providing him with a newly engineered dog wheelchair that supported his hindquarters, making it possible for him to roll his body along by walking on his front legs. Bear is analogous to Jamie and Sesha: each needs unusual types of support in order to attain, as much as possible, a species-specific norm of flourishing. Mobility is a key part of flourishing for dogs, in a way that it is not for sponges. Having access to movement was an essential part of a life with dignity for Bear. Thinking of the characteristic functioning and interactions of dogs helps us to see where unusual support for individuals with disabilities is needed.

To say this does not entail that humans should always take on the task of supporting all the animal capabilities in this direct, and somewhat interventionist, way. For dogs, however, with rare exceptions, there is no option to flourish in an all-dog community; their community is always one that includes intimate human members, and so it is obvious that human support for their capabilities is morally permissible and in some cases required. Moral individualism says too little to guide us in such matters.

vii. Evaluating Animal Capabilities: No Nature Worship

In the human case, the capabilities view refuses to extract norms directly from some facts about human nature. We should know what we can about the innate capacities of human beings, and this information is valuable in telling us what our opportunities are and what our dangers might be. But we must begin by evaluating the innate powers of human beings, asking which ones are the good ones, and the ones that are central to the notion of a decently flourishing human life, a life with human dignity. Thus not only evaluation but also ethical evaluation are put into the approach from the start. Many things that are found in human life are not on the capabilities list. The political conception does not have the job of fostering greed or making sure that crime and brutality get a chance to flourish, although all these activities are surely based in human powers. The conception of flourishing is thoroughly evaluative and ethical; it holds that the frustration of certain tendencies is not only compatible with flourishing, but actually required by it.[45]

There is a danger in any theory that alludes to the characteristic flourishing and form of life of a species. This is the danger of romanticizing nature, or suggesting that things are in order as they are, if only we humans would stop interfering. This danger looms large when we turn from the human case, where it seems inevitable that we will need to do some moral evaluating, to the animal case, where evaluating is elusive and difficult, if it can be done at all. Inherent in at least some environmentalist writing is a picture of nature as harmonious and wise, and of humans as wasteful overreachers who would live better were we to get in tune with this fine harmony. This image of nature is already very sensibly attacked by John Stuart Mill in his essay "Nature," which points out that nature, far from being morally normative, is actually violent, heedless of moral norms, prodigal, full of conflict:

> In sober truth, nearly all the things which men are hanged or imprisoned for doing to one another, are nature's every day performances. Killing, the most criminal act recognized by human laws, Nature does once to every being that lives; and in a large proportion of cases, after protracted tortures such as only the greatest monsters whom we read of ever purposely inflicted on their living fellow-creatures. If, by an arbitrary reservation, we refuse to account anything murder but what abridges a certain term supposed to be allotted to human life, nature also does this to all but a small percentage of lives, and does it in all the modes, violent or insidious, in which the worst human beings take the lives of one another. Nature impales men, breaks them as if on the wheel, casts them to be devoured by wild beasts, burns them to death, crushes them with stones like the first Christian martyr, starves them with hunger, freezes them with cold, poisons them by the quick or slow venom of her exhalations, and has hundreds of other hideous deaths in reserve, such as the ingenious cruelty of a Nabis or a Domitian never surpassed.[46]

We may add that nature does these unpleasant things not only to human beings, but also to other animals, whose relationship to one another, and to the natural environment, is hardly harmonious.

Nor is Mill's view of things merely a product of his human-focused perspective. It lies at the heart of much modern ecological thinking. To quote from a leading expert in environmental protection, Daniel Botkin:

> There has been a revolution in environmental sciences. At the heart of this revolution is a shift from the old idea of the constancy of Nature which is a part of the ancient myth of the Balance of Nature. Briefly stated, the Balance of Nature myth has three basic features: First, Nature, undisturbed by human influences, achieves a permanency of form and structure that persists indefinitely. Second, this permanent condition is the best condition for Nature: best for other creatures, best for the environment, and best for humans. Third, when disturbed from this perfect state, Nature is capable of returning to it. The idea of the Balance of Nature is deeply rooted in our history, civilization, and religions . . . Unfortunately, the Balance of Nature myth is not true. During the past 30 years, this has been demonstrated as part of the revolution in environmental sciences.[47]

Botkin goes on to support this claim in many ways, arguing, *inter alia,* that many of the natural ecosystems that we admire as such actually sustain themselves to the extent that they do only on account of various forms of human intervention. He concludes that we cannot just leave nature alone and expect it to manage itself; instead, we must have precise information about each species, and a precise sense of what our goals should be, supported with good normative arguments. In the process, he argues, we should not repudiate human changes as if they are by definition bad: for they just might be what would make an ecosystem survive.

These issues take us well beyond the entitlements of animals, which are our focus. They do tell us, however, that a no-evaluation view, which extracts norms directly from observation of animals' characteristic ways of life, is probably not going to be a helpful way of promoting the good of animals. Instead, we need a careful evaluation of both "nature" and possible changes. Respect for nature should not and cannot mean just leaving nature as it is, and must involve careful normative arguments about what plausible goals might be. It makes sense to begin with the best studies we can devise of what animals do when left to their own devices, for how else are we to understand how they conceive their own flourishing, or how they pursue flourishing, whether they conceive it or not? But that is the beginning, not the end, of evaluation.

In the case of humans, the primary area in which the political conception inhibits or fails to foster tendencies that are pervasive in human life is the area of harm to others. Animals, of course, pervasively cause harm, both to members of their own species and, even more often, to members of other species. These harm-causing capabilities are of two sorts. In one sort of case, an animal directly attacks and kills another, often for food; let us call this the case of the predator. In another case, some characteristic activity of the animal causes harm to other species (bearing disease, killing crops), even though the animal is just going about its life without hostile intent or even hostile behavior; let us call this the case of the mosquito.

In both of these cases, the capabilities theorist will have a strong inclination to say that the harm-causing capabilities are not among those that should be protected by political and social principles. But to say this—if we preserve the general conception of core capabilities that we employ in the human case—

would require us to judge that these capabilities, and the associated functionings, are not central to the ability of the creature to live a flourishing and dignified life as the sort of creature it is. This judgment, however, is difficult to make, if we are giving subjective experience any role at all in saying what a creature's flourishing is. The capabilities approach is not Utilitarian, and does not hold that all good is in sentience; nor does it extract norms directly from human desire or preference. Instead, it uses a freestanding moral argument to support its claims about the connection between capabilities and a life with human dignity. But desire is not utterly repudiated: the approach (in the human case) does use the results of the best informed-desire approaches as a cross-check on the capabilities list, on the assumption that no view that systematically frustrates human desire can be stable over time.[48] If we apply this approach to other species, it will be difficult to maintain that a creature who feels frustration and pain at the inhibition of its predatory capacities is living a flourishing life. A human being can be expected to learn to flourish without homicide and, let us hope, even without most killing of animals. But a lion who is given no exercise for its predatory capacity appears to suffer greatly, and there is no chance that education or acculturation would remove this pain.

Here the capabilities view may, however, distinguish two aspects of the capability in question. The capability to kill small animals, defined as such, is not valuable. Basic political principles can omit it, and even inhibit it. But the capability to exercise one's predatory nature, avoiding the pain of frustration, may well have value, if the pain of frustration is considerable. Zoos have learned how to make this distinction. Noticing that they were giving predatory animals insufficient exercise for their predatory capacities, they had to face the question of the harm done to smaller animals by allowing these capabilities to be exercised. Should they give a tiger a tender gazelle to crunch on?

The Bronx Zoo has found that it can give the tiger a large ball on a rope, whose resistance and weight symbolize the gazelle. The tiger seems satisfied. People with predatory house animals (cats especially) are familiar with such stratagems. (Competitive sports probably play a related role in human life.) Wherever predatory animals are living under direct human support and control, these solutions seem the most ethically sound.

As for the case of the animal that is not aware of killing anything, but whose normal activities spread disease or kill plants: some of these animals are beneath the threshold of sentience, nor do they have any of the other abilities that figure in our disjunctive account of moral standing; so we should not mind greatly if killing them is the way to protect ourselves and others. On the other hand, if it is possible to sterilize them and prevent spread that way, rather than through killing, it seems all the better to do that. With animals above the threshold of sentience, rats for example, it seems to me that here, too, we may admit the wisdom in Utilitarianism and say that the primary goal should be painless humane killing, if there has to be killing—and there might have to be, to prevent the spread of disease or damage to human children and other animals. On the other hand, once again, sterilization and other nonviolent methods are morally preferable.

Apart from the issue of harm to others, it seems best for humans not to engage in too much second-guessing of animal capabilities, but to try to observe what each creature actually considers important, on the basis of what it does. The distortions that make preference-based approaches highly undependable in the human case are the result of socialization in complex human societies, with their hierarchies and their codes of what is fitting and proper. Although we do find such adaptive preferences in the lives of animals who live in a context of pervasive human influence, they are likely to be less common in other animal lives.

Part of respect for other species is a willingness to look and study, learning the internal rhythms of an animal community and the sense of value the way of life expresses.

viii. Positive and Negative, Capability and Functioning

In the human case, there is a traditional distinction between positive and negative duties that it seems important to criticize. Traditional moralities hold that it is wrong to harm another by aggression or fraud, but that letting people perish of hunger or disease is not morally problematic, even though a more equitable distribution of social resources could solve these problems. We have a strict duty not to commit bad acts, but we have no correspondingly strict duty to stop hunger or disease or to give money to promote their cessation.[49]

The capabilities approach calls into question both this positive/negative distinction and the distinction between matters of justice and matters of material aid that typically underlies it. All the human capabilities cost money to support. This is just as true of protecting property and personal security as it is of health care, just as true of the political and civil liberties as it is of providing adequate shelter. As we saw in Chapter 5, the capabilities approach criticizes the approach to human rights that defines rights in terms of "negative liberty" alone, and also the distinction between "first-generation" and "second-generation" rights that is often linked to the "negative liberty" conception of political rights. The state that protects capabilities has affirmative tasks in every area, and in every area these jobs require money, which typically must be gathered through taxation that is to some extent redistributive. Both the distinction between state action and noninterference and the distinction between justice and material aid need to be criticized if we are to make progress. Even the concept of redistribution, which I have just employed, needs to be called into question, since it rests on the prior determination that people own the unequal amounts they have. Many views of ownership in the history of philosophy, from Grotius to Mill, have called this judgment into question, saying that the part of a person's holdings that is needed to support other members of a society (or world, in the case of Grotius) are actually owned by the people who need them, not by the people who are holding on to them.

In the case of animals, however, there might appear to be room for a positive/negative distinction that makes some sense. It seems at least coherent to say that the human community has the obligation to refrain from certain egregious harms toward animals, but that it is not obliged to support the welfare of all animals, in the sense of ensuring them adequate food, shelter, and health care. Fulfilling our negative duties would not be enough to ensure that all animals have a chance to pursue flourishing in their own way, but it might be that nothing more is morally required of us: the species themselves have the rest of the task of ensuring their own flourishing. We might further defend such a conclusion on the grounds that we would just mess up the lives of animals if we tried to be benevolent despots of the world. More adequately, we could defend it by saying that the very idea of a benevolent despotism of humans over animals, supplying their needs, is morally repugnant: the sovereignty of species, like the sovereignty of nations, has moral weight. Part of what it is to flourish, for a creature, is to settle certain very important matters on its own, without human intervention, even of a benevolent sort.

There is much truth in this imagined argument. And certainly, if our political principles simply ruled out the many egregious forms of harm to animals, they would have done quite a lot. But the rebuttal, and the distinction between negative and positive duties that it suggests, cannot be accepted in full. First of all, large numbers of animals live under humans' direct control: domestic animals, farm animals, and those members of wild species that are in zoos or other forms of captivity. Humans have direct responsibility for the nutrition and health care of these animals, as even our defective current systems of law acknowledge.[50] Animals in the "wild" appear to go their way unaffected by human beings. But of course that can hardly be so in many cases in today's world. Human beings pervasively affect the habitats of animals, determining opportunities for nutrition, free movement, and other aspects of flourishing. Even a person who wanted to deny that we had responsibilities to animals in the "wild" before this century ought to grant that our pervasive involvement with the conditions of animal flourishing gives us such responsibilities now.

Moreover, as Botkin points out, human intervention is actually necessary to maintain "the balance of nature" in many cases. Preserving species, for example, requires human action, even when the threat to the species is not human in origin. Should human beings fail to protect animals in ways that are available, unless and until a clear determination is made that the problem the animals are facing is human in origin? In many cases it clearly is; often, however, the factors involved are so numerous that it is difficult to tell. Thus, while we may still maintain that one primary area of human responsibility to animals is that of refraining from a whole range of bad acts (to be discussed in section x), we cannot plausibly stop there. We have the ability to make countless choices that spoil or preserve the habitats of animals. In many cases, too, we have the power to save animals who might otherwise die of disease or the aftereffects of a natural disaster. It seems implausible to think that we have no duties of material aid in such cases; the only question should be how extensive they are, and how to balance them against appropriate respect for the autonomy of a species. This question is very similar in form to the question of foreign aid, and must, like that question, be dealt with cautiously, with delicate balancing of the various factors involved. As in the foreign-aid case, the best form of aid is a form that preserves and enhances autonomy, rather than increasing dependency. It would be a bad result if all animals ended up in zoos, completely dependent on human arrangements.

In the human case, one way we respect autonomy is to focus on capability, not functioning, as the legitimate political goal. But we also insisted that for children, and in some cases for people with lifelong mental disabilities, it was appropriate to aim at functioning instead, or to leave choice-making to a guardian. In general, paternalistic treatment is appropriate wherever the individual's capacity for choice and autonomy is compromised. This principle suggests that paternalism is usually appropriate when we are dealing with nonhuman animals. That conclusion, however, should be qualified by our previous endorsement of the idea that species autonomy, in pursuit of flourishing, is part of the good for nonhuman animals. Can the two principles be coherently combined, and, if so, how should this be done?

I believe that they can be combined, if we adopt a type of paternalism that is highly sensitive to the different forms of flourishing that different species pursue. It is no use saying that we should just let tigers flourish in their own way, given that human activity ubiquitously affects the possibilities for tigers to flourish, and, indeed, to live at all. This being the case, the only decent alternative to complete neglect of tiger flourishing is a policy that thinks carefully about the flourishing of tigers and what habitat that requires, and then tries hard to create such habitats. (In this way, the decent treatment of actual living tigers does turn out to be bound up with the preservation of species.)

In many cases, the intelligent and careful use of zoos and animal parks may well be part of a policy aimed at giving members of these species decent lives. Many animals will do better in an imaginative and well-maintained zoo than in the wild, at least in present conditions of threat and scarcity. Especially when Country A cannot affect the behavior of Country B toward its animals, or ensure their flourishing in their natural habitat in Country B, zoos established in Country A may serve an invaluable function. Zoos, when well designed, can also build interspecies friendship by promoting education of young human beings. The long-term goal of policy should always, however, be preservation of at least some part of the creature's original habitat, and there is no way of doing this without consistent human intervention.

Domestic animals raise special problems. There is a romantic view of domestic animals that goes like this. These animals are being held prisoner by humans, and treated as mere property. The best thing for them would be simply to let them go to live in the wild as nature intended. The 2002 movie *Spirit* is one example of this fantasy: the wild horse bursts every barrier on the way to his freedom, and is happy only when he is running in the hills along with his fellow wild horses.

In reality, however, there are many species of animals for whom no plausibly flourishing existence in the wild is possible, given that they have evolved over millennia in symbiosis with human beings. Dogs, domestic cats, and most breeds of horse are in this situation, and many farm animals and some birds as well. Such animals should surely not be treated like mere objects for humans' use and control: their own flourishing and their own ends should be held constantly in view. But to say that is not to say that we ought simply to let them run off without human control. The morally sensible alternative is to treat them as companions in need of prudent guardianship, but endowed with entitlements that are theirs, even if exercised through guardianship. In other words, they may be treated as we currently treat children and many people with mental disabilities, who have a large menu of rights and are in that sense far from being "mere property," although those rights must be exercised through human guardianship. (It seems to me that there is nothing evil about exchanging guardianship of animals through buying and selling, provided that their rights are duly protected in this way.)

The romantic fantasy also suggests that animals should not be made to do things that humans want them to do. This, too, is a delicate issue. The corresponding romantic fantasy about children has by now been thoroughly refuted, in the sense that we now know children will not learn in schools that allow them to choose what they want to learn. Children do not even toilet train themselves. We generally feel that it is culpable neglect not to toilet train, and in countless ways to discipline and educate, our children, since flourishing life requires possibilities for choice and excellence that are opened up only by compulsory education. A good education is sensitive to the individuality of the child, and is not rigid and above all not cruel or humiliating; but it does have goals and standards, and exacting though respectful discipline is often appropriate in leading children toward those goals. Why should we think differently about nonhuman animals? Most domestic animals profit from some training and discipline. Many, in addition, are capable of fine feats of athletic excellence if they are given the appropriate training. Surely cruel forms of training should be condemned, and the circus described in my case from Kerala does sound extremely cruel. But it does not seem to follow from this that horses should not be taught to jump hedges and fences, or to perform dressage, or to race; or that dogs capable of complicated feats, such as the border collie, should not be trained to be able to manifest those excellences. Here again, an intelligent, species-sensitive paternalism seems to give the right result. Such a paternalism will ponder the nature of each animal's flourishing, thinking of the characteristic achievement not only of species, but of breeds, and will design an education, and a whole form of life, suited to those opportunities for excellence.

The capacities and personality of the individual animal must also be considered. Should the aging hunter-jumper be turned out to pasture? This is not a simple question. It is similar to the question whether an aging athlete should keep on doing the sport he or she is good at. No sensible answer is possible in the abstract: Martina Navratilova is one case, but there are many other cases. It is condescending to animals (as it is to aging humans) to assume that lazing around the pasture is their only good. In most cases, some sort of continued activity is better than lazing around, even when the animal cannot initiate the requisite sort of activity entirely on its own.

An intelligent, respectful paternalism cultivates spaces for choice. Animals are centers of activity, and no treatment is respectful that does not allow them to initiate activity on their own in some ways and to some degree. Any physical situation that is too confining is inimical to flourishing, as is any routine that does not allow play and uncoerced social interaction. Once again, the touchstone should be a respectful consideration of the species norm of flourishing and a respectful attention to the capacities of the individual.

In this difficult matter of control and freedom the capabilities approach, suitably extended, offers possibilities for the support of animal flourishing that are greatly superior to those offered by Utilitarianism, with its single-minded focus on pain and pleasure (or the fulfillment of conscious interests). Consideration of the species norm helps us to craft forms of paternalism that are respectful of animal needs, even when those needs are plural, qualitatively nonhomogeneous, and not necessarily present to the animal's consciousness.

I have said that nonintervention is not a plausible choice for human beings, in a world where human choices ubiquitously affect animal lives. Some forms of affirmative protection are required. What implications should this observation have for the question of harm, as we have raised them in the previous section? It is one thing to say that a tiger in a zoo should not be given a gazelle to eat: but what about the tiger in the wild? Should humans police the animal world, protecting vulnerable animals from predators?

In one sense, this seems absurd. And yet to the capabilities approach, as to Utilitarianism, what happens to the victim is the key issue, not who does the bad thing. The death of a gazelle after painful torture is just as bad for the gazelle when torture is inflicted by a tiger as when it is done by a human being. That does not mean that death by tiger is as blameworthy; obviously it is not. But it does suggest that we have similar reasons to prevent it, if we can do so without doing greater harms. The capabilities approach is entitlement-based and outcome-oriented. One way of preventing gruesome deaths of animals at the hands of other animals is to put all vulnerable animals (or, alternatively, all predators) in protective detention, so to speak. But this alternative surely does greater harms, by closing off the very possibility of flourishing in the wild. So the question must remain a very difficult one, especially given that death by predation may be more gruesome than death by hunger or disease. It seems plausible that we have less responsibility to protect gazelles than we do to protect domestic dogs and cats, since we are the guardians of the latter and they have evolved in symbiosis with us. But where we can protect gazelles without the type of massive intervention that would be harm-producing, perhaps we should do so. The problem is that the needs of the predatory animal must also be considered, and we do not have the option of giving the tiger in the wild a nice ball on a string to play with.

One very complicated question in this area is that of control-

ling animal populations by the introduction of "natural predators": for example, an overpopulation of elks is controlled by the
introduction of wolves. Is this method actually better than hunting? Humans may be able to preserve moral purity, but the elks
may die a more painful death. Nor is the alternative—allowing
the population to expand without limit and then to die off for
lack of nutrition—one that promises good deaths for elks. Once
again, any nonviolent method of population control (for example, by sterilization) is to be preferred to a violent method. But if
such methods are not available, it would appear that the most
painless death is to be preferred. R. M. Hare's cautious support
of carefully controlled human predation seems plausible, and it
certainly is not tantamount to the endorsement of hunting as
sport in its current form, where animals are hunted without regard to overpopulation, and both agonizing fear and painful
death are inflicted.[51]

Whatever we say about this difficult case, it shows us once
again that the positive/negative distinction cannot be maintained in anything like its classical form. Humans are intervening in animals' lives all the time, and the question can only be
what form this intervention should take. An intelligently respectful paternalism is vastly superior to neglect.

ix. Equality and Adequacy

Some writers on animal rights, in particular David DeGrazia in
his impressive book,[52] have pressed the question of equal consideration: Do animals' interests count on a par with those of humans? We have already said that animals have different interests
from those of humans, and that those interests affect what can
be a harm for an animal. Thus the denial of the right to vote is
not a harm for nonhuman animals, or the denial of the freedom
of religion. But that does not yet answer DeGrazia's question.

Answering the equality question is crucial for Utilitarians (among whom I number DeGrazia, although his form of Utilitarianism is much more subtle and multivalued than many), since Utilitarians produce an account of social welfare by aggregation, and thus must know how much each life and each interest within a life counts. The capabilities approach has to some extent a very different structure. Because it is a threshold-based approach, it focuses on adequacy rather than equality, in the human case as well as the animal case. That is, we specify a minimum threshold, below which justice has not been done. As I have frequently noted, the approach does not yet take a stand on how far it would be imperative to pursue equality of wealth and income above the threshold; thus it is a partial rather than a complete theory of justice even with regard to the items that it does discuss. Up to a point, then, the capabilities approach simply does not run into DeGrazia's question. What is minimally just is the securing to animals of each of the group of core capabilities (to be specified), up to some minimum threshold. For humans as for animals, conflicts may occur; and conflicts may also occur among the species. But if the threshold has been correctly set, any failure to secure a capability at a minimum level is a failure of justice, and we should work for a world in which those conflicts will not occur. I shall return to that question in section xi.

In Chapter 5, however, I argued that there are some capabilities in the human case that have not been *adequately* secured unless they have been *equally* secured. The freedom of religion, the political liberties, and access to education all fall within that class, or so I argued. I argued that the core idea of the approach is not simply the bare idea of human dignity but, instead, the idea of *equal* human dignity; and I argued that some inequalities in capability compromise that equality. Concerning other capabilities, such as housing rights and employment rights, adequacy rather than equality is the appropriate social goal, since those capabilities do not have an intrinsic connection to dignity. Now we must ask: Are there animal capabilities that are like political liberty for humans, that is, they cannot be adequately secured unless they are secured on a basis of equality? And is this equality within the species only, or does adequacy require equality across the species?

The reason why we insisted on equality in certain areas, in the human case, was a concern with equal dignity and equal respect. Unequal voting rights or unequal religious liberties signal a society's failure of equal respect for persons, in a way that unequal housing, within the constraints of adequacy, probably does not. The reason why these capabilities are intrinsically connected to equal dignity pertains to ideas of nonhumiliation and reciprocity that seem peculiarly human; and of course those capabilities in general are important only for humans. It is difficult to imagine a nonhuman animal analogue, in which the unequal distribution of a capability compromises equal respect and reciprocity. I am inclined to think that the urgent issues of animal entitlement pertain more to adequacy than to equal distribution. If the minimum threshold of health protection or decent working conditions is correctly set, that is all that justice requires, although the threshold should be ample.

We have not, however, confronted the large question: Should the idea of dignity, in the case of nonhuman animals, be understood as an idea of fully equal dignity? Even if specific entitlements are conceived in terms more of adequacy than of equality, there is still this abstract question to consider, and considering it does seem to matter. It is really two questions: Should dignity within each species be understood as equal dignity, and should the dignity of creatures across the species line be understood as fully equal dignity? The former question seems less pressing, and an affirmative answer does not pose any difficult problems. The implications of the latter question for situations of conflict are obvious.

Because the capabilities approach has such a different structure from DeGrazia's approach, the abstract question about equality does not play such a fundamental role for us as it must for him. He must think of a social calculus that aggregates the interests of all creatures, so he must therefore think all the time, and from the very start, about how much each creature shall count in this calculus. Since our focus is, instead, on bringing each creature up above a capability threshold specific to each species, not on aggregating, then in many contexts the approach can simply avoid this question, which appears very threatening from the point of view of establishing an overlapping consensus. The questions we need to face concern particular capabilities for particular creatures. Where those questions are concerned, it would appear that a high threshold of adequacy is the right approach. On the other hand, since many thinkers hold that human interests always take precedence over animal interests in case of conflict,[53] a position that appears to deny equal dignity across species, we need to have something to say about this issue.

It seems that there is no respectable way to deny the equal dignity of creatures across species. On the other hand, it is also clear that an overlapping consensus on a basic minimum of capability for animals, difficult already, will be made far more difficult if we supply it with such a foundation. So I would like at this point to treat the question of equal dignity as a metaphysical question on which citizens may hold different positions while accepting the basic substantive claims about animal entitlement that will subsequently be laid out here. Where humans are concerned, the idea of equal dignity is not a metaphysical idea, but a central element in political conceptions that have long been prevalent in modern constitutional democracies. Asking people to agree to it does not involve asking them to disregard central elements in their religious or other comprehensive doctrine. Things are different across species, I believe: an idea of cross-species dignity is not a political idea that can readily be accepted by citizens who otherwise differ in metaphysical conception. It is a divisive metaphysical idea, in contradiction with many religious ideas of the soul, and so forth. So let us simply say that the idea of equal cross-species dignity is an attractive idea, indeed from many points of view a compelling idea, but that we do not need to rely on it in our political overlapping consensus. We may rely, instead, on the looser idea that all creatures are entitled to adequate opportunities for a flourishing life.

x. Death and Harm

So far we have avoided a large question: What sort of harm is death for animals of different types, and what harm is done by killing, for animals of different types? Utilitarians typically hold that painless death is not a harm to an animal, because animals cannot have conscious interests in the future such that these interests are frustrated by painless killing. Thus Bentham opposed all forms of cruelty but permitted the painless slaughter of animals for a useful purpose. R. M. Hare, similarly, holds that it is permissible to slaughter certain sorts of animals for food, so long as the slaughter is genuinely painless: thus he will buy fish from his local fishmonger, who conks the fish soundly on the head with a mallet, but he would not eat fish caught in the usual painful way.

One problem with these Utilitarian arguments is that they may be wrong about the interests of animals. Some animals probably do have a sense of their life as a narrative extended over time, to at least some degree. Any animal with memory (as opposed to rote repetition) is likely to have such a sense. So it would seem that death is a harm to those creatures, though it will often be a lesser harm than continuing to live in pain and decrepitude. People's treatment of animals whom they love, whether dogs or cats or horses, usually displays appropriate judgment about the harm of death and the related harm of killing: that is, killing seems morally appropriate when the alternative is a painful or undignified life (such as a life with incontinence, which animals feel as shameful and embarrassing), but it is not to be chosen simply for the human's convenience, any more than we should kill our aged parents to avoid the inconvenience of caring for them. Probably the euthanizing of aged animals is more often permissible than the euthanizing of humans: humans who are not severely demented have a right to consent to any such procedure, and humans also have more life interests that are compatible with physical pain and decrepitude; thus a human might find worth living a painful and diseased life that for an animal would not be worth living.

But there are many animals concerning whom Bentham and Hare are probably correct: they have conscious interests, but these interests do not extend into the future in such a way as to give them temporally extended projects of a type that sudden death would frustrate. So what about the killing of such animals for food? And what about the humane killing of animals for other reasons, such as the killing of rats to prevent health problems for human or other animal populations, or the painless predation of animals who would otherwise starve to death in the wild or be torn apart by other animals? Are Bentham and Hare correct that a painless death is not a harm for such animals and that a humane form of slaughter is consequently not harmful?

The capabilities approach has a more difficult time reaching this conclusion than the Utilitarian view, since we recognize many goods and bads that do not consist in forms of sentient awareness. The ability to move around freely, for example, may be valuable for an animal even if the animal does not feel its absence as a pain. The ability to have loving and supportive relationships with other animals and humans can be a good, even if the animal, raised in isolation, is not aware of the deprivation or pained by it. So what we need to ask is a different question from the Utilitarian question: it is, whether there are centrally valuable forms of capability, in such animal lives, that are cut short by sudden painless death. If so, then it is a harm to inflict such a death.

We have already concluded that painless death can be nonharmful, if the alternative is life with pain or decrepitude. We have also concluded that it is not a morally significant harm to kill a nonsentient creature.[54] But most animals who are killed for food are sentient, and they are typically killed in their prime or even in their youth, well before the alternative is life with pain and decrepitude. We can admit that a large part of the harm we currently do to animals raised for food consists in the ways we treat them during their lives without conceding that the painless death of such an animal, after (let us suppose) a flourishing freeranging life, is no harm at all.

There are many different cases here. The level of capacity a creature has affects what can be a harm for it. More complexly sentient animals can suffer more and different harms than less complexly sentient creatures. Think of a cow and a shrimp. It seems likely that the cow can suffer many harms, at death, that the shrimp cannot: deprivation of a social network, deprivation of varied pleasures of moving and eating, deprivation of mobility. A shrimp probably does not even feel pain; certainly, it has a restricted range of functions and little awareness of those functions. Unlike the Utilitarian approach, the capabilities approach, not being entirely focused on sentience, can still see some harm in the termination of a minimally sentient life; but the harm seems less grave, since sentience is extremely important, and the shrimp does not have one of the other major life functions either (like our science fiction case of the nonsentient but thinking being). The infliction of pain on a sentient being is a particularly grave harm. The termination of many and varied functionings is also a grave harm. Neither of these seems to be present in the case of the shrimp. Hare's fishmonger is a more complicated case, since fish, by his own account, have sentience of a sort. Thus, even if the death is painless there is deprivation of positive good, namely opportunities for enjoyment and movement, given that the fish is not likely to be killed on the brink of old age and decrepitude. The capabilities theorist will take this deprivation more seriously than the Utilitarian. Nonetheless, the harm of painlessly killing a fish seems a different sort of harm from the harm of killing a cow, and at least possibly less grave.

These are very slippery issues. We should admit that we are likely to be self-serving here, and biased toward our own form of life. Nonetheless, it would appear that the Utilitarian is partly right: the prevention of suffering, both during life and at death, is of crucial importance always. As for painless death, that can involve a harm, but the harm seems to vary with the nature of the creature in question, and it may often be a less grievous moral harm than the harm of inflicting suffering.

Where animals are killed to stop harm that they would otherwise do (killing rats in cities, for example), we can say once again that the harm of killing varies with the form of life involved, and in the case of a rat the harm is not comparable to the harm of killing a healthy dog; a rat has many fewer interests and capabilities to be frustrated—although we have said that this does not mean that its life is per se less valuable. Nonetheless, to the extent that a different solution to the problem is available, such as sterilization, that is clearly morally preferable, in a way relevant to the moral content of principles of political justice; even pain-less killing of a relatively simple animal like a rat inflicts some harm.

xi. An Overlapping Consensus?

The capabilities approach is a form of political liberalism: it relies on the idea that an overlapping consensus of the reasonable comprehensive doctrines can emerge over time to support and sustain the political conception. To show this, and thus to justify the conception, we do not have to show that the consensus exists at present; but we do need to show that there is sufficient basis for it in the existing views of liberal constitutional democracies that it is reasonable to think that over time such a consensus may emerge. Because the political conception rests not on metaphysical theories but on judgments that are ethical all the way down, it is important that they be the sort of judgment that citizens can share.

When we turn to animals, we must face two difficult questions: first, who takes part in this consensus? And second, is it reasonable to hope that the rights of animals can, over time, become the object of an overlapping consensus?

Who takes part? By appropriating the idea of overlapping consensus, the capabilities approach converges, to at least some extent, with social contract views, since it is at this point that the idea of reasonable agreement, crucial to such views, plays a role in our own approach. It seems obvious that the actual parties to such an agreement must be humans, and it also seems obvious that even hypothetically we should not try to imagine what animals would "reasonably" agree to. That question is just as fantastic as the question we have already rejected, the question what contract they would make in a state of nature. What we can, however, ask is: What would a guardian appointed to protect the entitlements of such creatures reasonably agree to, on their behalf? Thus the solution of trusteeship, which is not satisfactory if the framers of the contract are identified with the primary subjects of justice, as in contractarian approaches, seems to be one that, in a limited way, a theorist who rejects that conflation is entitled to use.

The fact that the members of the consensus are in that sense all human does not mean that animals are not direct subjects of the theory of justice. They are. It does mean, however, that the agreement of humans plays a special role in justification, for the stability of the conception can be guaranteed only if we can show that it is supported by a family of reasonable comprehensive doctrines. The comprehensive doctrines in question will be those held by humans, plus those that they may impute (through imagination) to those that they represent: that is, their own good-faith estimate of a conception of the good for each type of animal.

The whole idea of a justification that looks for a reflective equilibrium and uses the idea of overlapping consensus is an anthropocentric idea. The holism in ethics that Rawls and I share may be contested at this point by a reasonable Benthamite, who will insist that what justifies changes in our treatment of animals is not the coherence of a family of human theories and judgments, even bolstered by reasonable agreement and overlapping consensus; it is, instead, a fact utterly external to the human point of view, namely animal suffering. This challenge raises profound metaethical issues that go beyond the arguments of this book. They also go beyond my current understanding. I believe that we have good reasons to work toward a holistic justification of the Rawlsian sort; but we do need to think further about how the perceptions and experiences of other sentient creatures enter into the account of what justification is, and I have not solved that problem to my own satisfaction.

Can we hope for an overlapping consensus on the entitlements of animals? I see two problems: one concerning the animal conceptions in their relation to one another, another concerning human conceptions. First, then, even in fiction and through trusteeship, can we imagine an animal supporting a decent life for species to which it is hostile? Would the trustee of the tiger rightly impute to it a conception that supports decent life for a gazelle? Nature is not just, and species are not all nice. We cannot expect that they will become nice, or supportive of the good of their enemies. I think, however, that this is not such a severe problem for the political conception, since at this point the trustee can just say, the tiger's conception is unreasonable insofar as it seeks the death of gazelles, and I, as trustee, shall advance it politically only insofar as it is reasonable. The stability of the political conception is not at stake here: if we do not persuade the tigers to change their mind, so to speak, we can always control them.

The real stability problem is the human problem. Most of the existing religious and secular comprehensive doctrines are miles away from the positions being defended here. Hindu, Jain, and Buddhist traditions contain many elements of what I recommend, as did early Platonism. But Christianity, Judaism, Islam, and most people's secular comprehensive doctrines rank the human species metaphysically above the other species and give the human secure rights to the use of animals for many purposes.

Even in these traditions there are prohibitions on cruelty and ideas of moral trusteeship, such as those advanced by Baumgartner in the book that Kant criticized. Nor is an ampler recognition of animal entitlements ruled out, I believe, by anything basic in these religions: it is just not insisted on. In fact, it would seem, if we focus on the foundational texts, that the case for overlapping consensus here is much more promising than the case for overlapping consensus concerning the equality of the sexes. The core texts of each major religion all pronounce on matters of sexual subordination in ways that cause problems for liberal reform. Even so, to a great extent this reform has taken place, and the religions have altered their understandings to support this political consensus. By contrast, religious texts do not say, typically, that one *must* or *should* wear fur or leather, or that one *should not* be a vegetarian. That space is left open, and there are conscientious supporters of animal rights in every major religion. Certainly, the cruel treatment of animals, whether in the food industry or in other areas of life, is very hard to square with the approaches to animals in key religious texts, as Baumgartner seems to have noted. By expressing the core idea of the extended capabilities approach in terms of a threshold of capability, and by leaving aside the difficult metaphysical question of equality, I hope to have shown that we can advance the approach in a strong form without putting at risk any of the core metaphysical commitments of the major religions. We must continue to emphasize that the principles we are advancing are political and not metaphysical: they are expressed in a practical (albeit moral) form that is metaphysically abstemious, intended not to conflict with key metaphysical doctrines of the major religions.

In practical terms people have not yet taken the direction that Bentham thought they would, when he wrote that the oppression of animals would eventually seem as morally heinous as slavery. People frequently do not even want to think about the issue seriously, because they like meat, they feel they need it, and they are also convinced that human lives are being prolonged by research with animal subjects. It is clearly incumbent upon the supporter of animal entitlements to provide answers to the questions such people have, about how human life will be supported. But eventually, as people acquire more information about the treatment of animals and gain the ability to make more informed consumer choices, it seems reasonable to expect that opposition to cruel practices will increase, and that some, if not all, of what I tentatively recommend can become the object of an overlapping consensus.

Recent developments in animal law in Europe are very encouraging in this regard, particularly the tough new law passed in Austria in May 2004, which bans cages for poultry, the use of wild animals in circus acts, and a variety of invasive practices such as clipping ears and cropping tails. Germany is phasing out the mass farming of caged chickens by 2006; Italy is considering a law that forbids sending horses to the slaughterhouse when their competitive life is over. Tougher penalties for cruelty to animals are being adopted across Europe. If all this can happen in nations predominantly Christian, there is reason to think that other religions, often more metaphysically supportive of animal life, will also be able to join the overlapping consensus.

xii. Toward Basic Political Principles: The Capabilities List

It seems premature to map out any definite content for our political principles in this area; and yet we cannot go further without content. So let us see whether we can use the human basis of the capabilities approach to map out, in a highly tentative and general way, some basic political principles that can guide law and public policy in dealing with animals.

The core of the approach, as we have said, is that animals are entitled to a wide range of capabilities to function, those that are most essential to a flourishing life, a life worthy of the dignity of each creature. Animals have entitlements based upon justice.

The entitlements of animals are species-specific and based upon their characteristic forms of life and flourishing. Nonetheless, let us see to what extent we can use the existing core of the capabilities list to sketch out directions for political principles. Even though the more concrete specification of each capability will lead ultimately to a plurality of lists, it seems that the big general categories on the list offer good guidance.

1. *Life*. Utilitarian approaches focus only on sentience, and thus give animals no entitlement to life except to the extent that the interest in continuing life is one of their conscious interests. In the capabilities approach, all animals are entitled to continue their lives, whether or not they have such a conscious interest, unless and until pain and decrepitude make death no longer a harm. This entitlement is less robust when we are dealing with insects and other nonsentient or minimally sentient forms of life. The gratuitous killing of such creatures is still wrong, and perhaps law should in some cases prevent it (as, for example, the killing of butterflies for school projects). But when there is a plausible reason for the killing (preventing harm to crops or people or other animals, preventing pain, even gaining necessary or useful food), no entitlement based on justice has been violated.

With sentient animals, things are different. All these animals have a secure entitlement against gratuitous killing for sport. Killing for luxury items such as fur falls in this category, and should be banned. So, too, should all cruel practices and painful killings in the process of raising animals for food. On the other hand, intelligently respectful paternalism supports euthanasia for elderly (and younger) animals in irreversible pain. In the middle, as we saw, are the very difficult cases, involving painless killing, whether for food or to control populations. It seems wise to focus initially on banning all forms of cruelty to living animals and then moving gradually toward a consensus against killing at least the more complexly sentient animals for food. One of the most useful steps we can take would be to insist on clear labeling of all meat as to the conditions in which the animals were raised. Practices vary widely, and consumers lack adequate information on which to base ethically responsible choices. Demivegetarians who press this search for information may advance the goals of public policy at least as well as vegetarians.

A further advantage of the capabilities approach over Utilitarianism emerges here. Unlike the Utilitarian, we do not have to perform complicated and indeterminate calculations of welfare in order to know whether an entitlement has been violated. If people lose jobs in the meat industry, that is no part of our concern, as it must be for the Utilitarian: for they have no entitlement to jobs that exploit and tyrannize. Animals, by contrast, do have entitlements, and it is on these that our policy toward them should focus.

As for painless predation to control populations, this may often be preferable to other deaths that elks would die, such as starving or being torn apart by wolves. That does not mean, however, that no harm is done by painlessly killing a creature in its prime; so if we can work for a future in which our menu of choices includes some harmless options, such as sterilization, so much the better.

2. *Bodily Health.* One of the most central entitlements of animals is the entitlement to a healthy life. Where animals are directly under human control, it is relatively clear what policies this entails: laws banning cruel treatment and neglect; laws banning the confinement and ill treatment of animals in the meat and fur industries; laws forbidding harsh or cruel treatment for working animals, including circus animals; laws regulating zoos and aquaria, mandating adequate nutrition and space. Many of these laws already exist, although they are not well enforced.[55] The striking asymmetry in current practice is that animals raised for food are not protected in the way domestic animals are protected. This asymmetry must be eliminated. In general, humans

are guardians of the animals who live with them, and laws governing permissible treatment can be closely modeled on laws dealing with parental responsibility to children.

3. *Bodily Integrity.* Under the capabilities approach, animals have direct entitlements against violations of their bodily integrity by violence, abuse, and other forms of harmful treatment—whether or not the treatment in question is painful. Thus the declawing of cats would probably be banned under this rubric, on the grounds that it prevents the cat from flourishing in its own characteristic way, even if it may be done in a painfree manner and cause no subsequent pain.[56] Other mutilations that simply make the animal more beautiful to humans are similarly inappropriate.[57] On the other hand, forms of training that, though involving discipline, equip the animal to manifest excellences that are part of its characteristic capability profile would not be eliminated. Again, the fact that the horse is at first annoyed by the bridle is not a negative thing in the capabilities approach, any more than is the annoyance of human children at compulsory schooling. It can be justified by its role in promoting adult flourishing and capability.

The positive side of this entitlement, in the human case, is having opportunities for reproduction and sexual satisfaction. What should we say about this in the animal case? Other things equal, it would seem good to protect this capability for animals; but the castrating of certain male animals (horses, dogs, cats) seems (on the basis of long experience) to be compatible with flourishing lives for those animals, with diverse forms of activity and no suffering—and often lives of less violence toward other animals, some of which typically results in pain and injury to the male animal himself. Whereas castration of a violent human seems utterly inappropriate, a "cruel and unusual punishment," the castration of a nonhuman animal seems very different—because of these animals' lesser capacity for character change and choice. One cannot tell a dog inclined to aggression to change and behave differently; so castration may in many cases be the course most appropriate to its own flourishing and that of other animals. These cases have to be carefully scrutinized, and justified on a case-by-case basis.

In other instances, sterilization, while not particularly affecting the life of the individual animal, may create better lives for future animals by preventing overpopulation and consequent shortage and neglect. Is this just using one animal as a means for the good of others? That would be a grave point against such policies if the sterilization of, say, a female dog or cat produced a life incompatible with flourishing and the form of dignity characteristic of that animal. I am inclined to think that it does not. The enforced sterilization of human beings is objectionable because it is a violation of an entitlement to certain types of freedom and choice that are particularly important in human life.[58] I am inclined to think that such considerations are not central in the flourishing of animals.

4. *Senses, Imagination, and Thought.* For humans, this capability creates a wide range of entitlements: to appropriate education, to free speech and artistic expression, to freedom of religion. It also includes a more general entitlement to pleasurable experience and the avoidance of nonbeneficial pain. By now it ought to be rather obvious where the latter point takes us in thinking about animals: toward stringent laws regulating the harsh, cruel, and abusive treatment of animals, and ensuring their access to sources of pleasure, such as free movement in an environment that is such as to please their senses.[59] It also means a ban on hunting and fishing for sport, which inflict painful deaths on animals. The freedom-related part of this capability has no precise analogue, and yet we can come up with appropriate analogues in the case of each type of animal, by asking what choices and areas of freedom seem most important to each.

Clearly, this reflection would lead us to reject confinement and to regulate the places in which animals of all kinds are kept for spaciousness, light and shade, and the variety of opportunities they offer the animal for a range of characteristic activities.[60] One of the greatest defects of most zoos has been their boringness, which constitutes a cruel assault on animals' opportunities for flourishing. Again, the capabilities approach seems superior to Utilitarianism in its ability to recognize such entitlements: for few animals will have a conscious interest, as such, in engaging in a variety of activities or living in a nonboring environment.

Some animals also have entitlements to suitable education. A border collie who is not trained has been abused, and the same is true of many breeds of horses. All domestic animals, like children, are abused if they are not toilet trained, that is, shown a way to dispose of their wastes, since animals connect cleanliness with the absence of shame.

Animals "in the wild" are entitled to an environment that is the sort in which they characteristically flourish: so protecting this capability also means protecting animal environments.

5. *Emotions.* Animals have a wide range of emotions. All or almost all sentient animals have fear. Many animals can experience anger, resentment, gratitude, grief, envy, and joy. A small number—those who are capable of perspectival thinking—can experience compassion.[61] Like human beings, they are entitled to lives in which it is open to them to have attachments to others, to love and care for others, and not to have those attachments warped by enforced isolation or the deliberate infliction of fear. We understand well what this means where our cherished domestic animals are in question. Oddly, we do not extend the same consideration to animals we think of as "wild." Until recently, zoos took no thought for the emotional needs of animals; and animals being used for research were often treated with gross carelessness in this regard, being left in isolation and

confinement when they might easily have been given a decent emotional life.[62] Some very famous animal experiments are sullied by similar neglect: the experiment in which infant monkeys were deprived of maternal holding, only to end up emotionally disturbed; Martin Seligman's experiments with dogs, which induced in them a state of "learned helplessness" analogous to depression.[63] The difficult question of research will be taken up in the next section. But these are at least *prima facie* examples of entitlement violations in the area of emotion.

6. *Practical Reason.* This is a key architectonic entitlement in the case of human beings. It pervades and informs all the others, making their pursuit fully human. There is no precise analogue in the case of nonhuman animals. In each case we need to ask to what extent the creature has a capacity to frame goals and projects and to plan its life. To the extent that this capacity is present, it ought to be supported, and this support requires many of the same policies already suggested by Capability 4: plenty of room to move around, opportunities for a variety of activities.

7. *Affiliation.* In the human case, this capability has two parts: an interpersonal part (being able to live with and toward others), and a more public part, focused on self-respect and non-humiliation. It seems to me that the same two parts are pertinent for nonhuman animals. Animals are entitled to opportunities to form attachments (as in Capability 5) and to engage in characteristic forms of bonding and interrelationship. They are also entitled to relations with humans, where humans enter the picture, that are rewarding and reciprocal rather than tyrannical. At the same time, they are entitled to live in a world public culture that respects them and treats them as dignified beings. This entitlement does not just mean protecting them from instances of humiliation that they will *feel* as painful. The capabilities approach here extends more broadly than Utilitarianism, holding that animals are entitled to world policies that grant them politi-

cal rights and the legal status of dignified beings. Whether or not they are able to comprehend that status, it shapes a world in which they are seen and treated differently.

Being from the first an evaluative approach, the capabilities approach does not protect all forms of affiliation that animals actually have with one another. We have already mentioned the obvious instances of destructive interspecies behavior. What about intraspecies harms? This is a very complicated issue. On the one hand, there are some harms that we can straightforwardly oppose and prevent, such as assaults on infants by parents, and harsh policies toward sick, disabled, or elderly species members. Whether among domestic animals or "in the wild," human beings are obliged to intervene to prevent these abuses. But what about hierarchy and inequality? Animal cultures are full of humiliation of the weak by the strong and of sometimes violent competition for sexual advantage. Animals do not always, or even commonly, pursue the human capability of "being able to be treated as a dignified being whose worth is equal to that of others." It seems clear that humans cannot intervene to change all that, especially "in the wild," without greatly upsetting the economy of species life. Probably this is a case in which we must say that only the most egregious harms to weaker species members must be prevented, and other forms of hierarchy may be tolerated, though they will not be protected as central animal capabilities. Human dealings with animals, at least, should be regulated by respectful attention to each species member, and the idea that each is worthy of a flourishing life.

8. *Other Species.* If human beings are entitled to "being able to live with concern for and in relation to animals, plants, and the world of nature," so, too, are other animals, in relation to species not their own, including the human species, and the rest of the natural world. This capability, seen from both the human and the animal side, calls for the gradual formation of an

interdependent world in which all species will enjoy cooperative and mutually supportive relations. Nature is not that way and never has been. So it calls, in a very general way, for the gradual supplanting of the natural by the just.

9. *Play.* This capability is obviously central to the lives of all sentient animals. It calls for many of the same policies we have already discussed: protection of adequate space, light, and sensory stimulation in living places, and, above all, the presence of other species members.

10. *Control over One's Environment.* In the human case, this capability has two prongs, the political and the material. The political is defined in terms of active citizenship and rights of political participation. For nonhuman animals, the important thing is being part of a political conception that is framed so as to respect them, and is committed to treating them justly. It is important, however, that animals have entitlements directly within the conception, even if a human guardian must go to court, as with children, to vindicate those entitlements. On the material side, the human form of the capability includes certain sorts of protection for property rights and employment rights, including the right to form unions and the free choice of occupation. For nonhuman animals, the analogue to property rights is respect for the territorial integrity of their habitat, whether domestic or "in the wild." The analogue to work rights is the right of laboring animals to dignified and respectful labor conditions.

Are there animal capabilities not covered by this list, suitably specified? If so, we will discover them over time, as we work further both on the general level and on the species-specific level.

In general, the capabilities approach suggests that each nation should include in its constitution or other founding statement of principle an inclusion of animals as subjects of political justice, and a commitment that animals will be treated as beings entitled to a dignified existence. The constitution might also spell out some of the very general principles suggested by this capabilities list. The rest of the work of protecting animal entitlements will be done by suitable legislation and by court cases demanding the enforcement of the law, where it is not enforced. If animals are indeed granted entitlements, they will have standing to bring a suit (argued by a guardian), a right they do not currently have.[64]

At the same time, many of the issues covered by this approach cannot be dealt with by nations taken in isolation, but can be addressed only by international cooperation. So we also need international accords committing the world community to the protection of animal habitats and the eradication of cruel practices.

xiii. The Ineliminability of Conflict

In the human case, we often face the question of conflict between one capability and another. But in the human case, if the capabilities list and its threshold are suitably designed, we ought to say that the presence of conflict between one capability and another is a sign that society has gone wrong somewhere.[65] We should focus on long-term planning that will create a world in which all the capabilities can be secured to all citizens. Thus, the conflict displayed in Sophocles' *Antigone,* between civic order and the free exercise of religion, is removed (in the Hegelian sense *aufgehoben*) by the creation of societies that honor each individual's free exercise of religion as a part of what constitutes the political sphere and its basic values. If parents face a conflict between life-sustaining food and the education of their children, in the sense that only sending their children to work all day will enable the family to survive, that again is a sign that society is not well designed. Even in very poor regions, intelligent planning can make it possible for people to live healthy lives and also to educate their children. (The Indian state of Kerala, a relatively poor state, has achieved 99 percent literacy for both boys and girls in adolescence through flexible school hours and other creative policies.)

In discussing the capabilities of human beings, I have argued that the threshold of each capability should be set with an eye to the other capabilities. In framing the education capability, for example, it is sensible to ask what we can expect to deliver compatibly with delivering all the other capabilities. On the one hand, the threshold of each should not be set in a utopian or unrealistic way: so we must ask what combination we can hope to deliver to people under reasonably good conditions. On the other hand, we should not set our sights too low, deferring to present bad arrangements. Thus it would have been wrong to conclude that universal primary and secondary education of children is not a good goal for a just public policy, on the grounds that right now it is not feasible in some badly managed states.

The world we live in contains persistent and often tragic conflicts between the well-being of human beings and the well-being of animals. Some bad treatment of animals can be eliminated without serious losses in human well-being: such is the case with the use of animals for fur, and the brutal and confining treatment of animals used for food. The use of animals for food in general is a much more difficult case, since nobody really knows what the impact on the world environment would be of a total switch to vegetarian sources of protein, or the extent to which such a diet could be made compatible with the health of all the world's children. In this case, it appears that the best solution might be to focus initially on good treatment during life and painless killing, setting the threshold there, at first, where it is clearly compatible with securing all the human capabilities, and not very clearly in violation of any major animal capability, depending on how we understand the harm of a painless death for various types of animals. Even that threshold is utopian at present, but it seems to be realistically utopian.

Such a Hegelian approach, however, cannot solve all problems. One problem that will have to be faced is the issue of cost. If health care for animals (even those that live directly under human control) requires lowering the threshold for human health care, how should we think about these trade-offs? I believe that we should think about the whole set of capabilities together when facing such questions, rather than thinking that health costs must always be traded off against health costs. There are very likely to be other costs not associated with fundamental entitlements that could be trimmed way back before we would have to cut anyone's health care. That is the sort of question that each nation needs to consider for itself when setting the thresholds of all the major capabilities. We have not yet even begun to deliberate well about such questions, and I believe it is premature right now to say what the precise result of such deliberations would be. But surely support for luxury items would be our first target. If, for example, people stopped driving SUVs, there would be many gains, not the least of which would be decreased spending on gasoline, which would free up money to be used in other ways, connected with fundamental entitlements— and health would be the gainer, on both sides.

The most obvious unresolved area of conflict is the use of animals in research. On the one hand, research using animals remains crucial to medical advances, both for humans and for other animals. It also gives us crucial information about many other topics, from depression to the nature of attachment. Such research cuts short the lives of animals prematurely, and often inflicts other harms upon them.

A lot can be done to improve the lives of research animals without stopping useful research. As Steven Wise has shown, primates used in research often live in squalid, lonely conditions while they are used as medical subjects. This situation of course is totally unnecessary and morally unacceptable, and could be ended without ending the research. Some research that is done is unnecessary and can be terminated: for example, the testing of cosmetics on rabbits, which has been bypassed without loss of quality by some cosmetics firms. But much important research with major consequences for the life and health of human beings and other animals will inflict disease, pain, and death on at least some animals, even under the best conditions.

We should admit, then, that there will be an ineliminable residue of tragedy in the relationships between humans and animals. Research that should be allowed to promote human health and safety will continue to inflict the risk of disease, pain, and premature death on animals. As a matter of ideal entitlement theory, this research is morally bad. As a matter of current implementation, I do not favor stopping all such research immediately. What I do favor is: (a) asking whether the research is really necessary to promote a major human or animal capability; (b) focusing on the use of less complexly sentient animals where possible, on the grounds that they suffer fewer and lesser harms from such research; (c) improving the conditions of research animals, including palliative terminal care when they have contracted a terminal illness, and supportive interactions with both humans and other animals; (d) removing the psychological brutality that is inherent in so much treatment of animals in research;[66] (e) choosing topics cautiously and seriously, so that no animal is harmed for a frivolous reason, without a good chance of an important benefit; and, finally, (f) a vigorous and publicly funded effort to develop experimental methods (for example, computer simulations) that do not have these bad consequences.

Above all, my approach favors constant public and philosophical discussion of these issues, together with an acknowledgment that such uses of animals in research are tragic, that they do in some cases violate basic animal entitlements. This sort of public acknowledgment is far from useless, even in the non-Hegelian world we share with animals. First of all, it states what is morally true, and thus acknowledges the dignity of animals and our own culpability toward them. Second, it reaffirms dispositions to behave well toward them where no such urgent exigencies intervene. Finally, it prepares us for a world in which at least some of the pertinent research could in fact be done in other ways, for example through the use of computer simulations. It informs us that we should actively seek such a world, and take advantage of any progress toward it to cut back on the abuse of animals.

xiv. Toward a Truly Global Justice

It has been obvious for a long time that the pursuit of global justice requires the inclusion of many people and groups who were not previously included as fully equal subjects of justice: the poor; the lower classes; members of religious, ethnic, and racial minorities; more recently, women. Classic liberal approaches in the social contract tradition were designed to deal with these inequalities, and they dealt with them, for the most part, very well. Their most unsatisfactory aspect, with regard to this traditional list of the disadvantaged, was their failure to scrutinize sufficiently the distribution of opportunities and benefits within the family, and to consider the family itself a site where justice is either done or not done.

More recently, it has become evident that another large and heterogeneous group of citizens demands full and equal justice: people with physical and mental impairments, temporary or lifelong. Classic social contract doctrines, even Rawls's very subtle and morally sensitive such doctrine, cannot adequately handle these problems of justice for and to the disabled, or the related problems of care for dependents that the existence of disabled and elderly people in our societies creates. The capabilities approach seems well placed to offer a fruitful way forward.

It has also been clear for some centuries that the pursuit of global justice requires political philosophy to depart from the paradigm of the self-sufficient nation-state and to think what justice may require of nations in their dealings with one another. Since the late twentieth century it has been obvious that an adequate treatment of international and cosmopolitan justice must address not only the traditional topics of war and peace, but also the topics of economic justice and material redistribution. Traditional social contract doctrines cannot solve these problems very well, and even Rawls's brave and fascinating approach does not adequately do so. Once again, I have suggested that the capabilities approach offers a useful way forward, and I have argued that only an outcome-oriented approach can adequately confront the bewildering and rapidly changing world scene, with its variety of constantly shifting institutional forms.

But a truly global justice requires not simply looking across the world for other fellow species members who are entitled to a decent life. It also requires looking, both in one's own nation and around the world, at the other sentient beings with whose lives our own are inextricably and complexly intertwined. Traditional contractarian approaches to the theory of justice do not and, in their very form, cannot confront these questions as questions of justice. Utilitarian approaches have boldly done so, and they deserve high praise for bringing abuses to light and promoting the beginnings, at least, of an adequate ethical awareness. But in the end, that approach is too homogenizing—both across lives and with respect to the heterogeneous constituents of each life—to provide us with an adequate theory of animal justice. The capabilities approach, which begins from an ethically attuned wonder before each form of animal life, offers a model that does justice to the complexity of animal lives and their strivings for flourishing. Here I have offered only a sketch of what this approach might ultimately say. But even a sketch is a step forward, on the way to a fully global theory of justice.

7

THE MORAL SENTIMENTS AND THE CAPABILITIES APPROACH

> When we consider how ardent a sentiment, in favourable circumstances of education, the love of country has become, we cannot judge it impossible that the love of that larger country, the world, may be nursed into similar strength, both as a source of elevated emotion and as a principle of duty.
>
> —John Stuart Mill, "The Utility of Religion"

The social contract tradition has one big apparent advantage over the approach to basic justice that I have just defended. Namely, it does not require extensive benevolence. It derives political principles from the idea of mutual advantage, without assuming that human beings have deep and motivationally powerful ties to others. This parsimonious starting point looked like a large advantage to most thinkers in the tradition because they were skeptical about the moral sentiments. Hobbes believes that the most powerful sentiments are egoistic and that other sentiments are too weak to motivate conduct stably and consistently. Kant is certainly pessimistic about the desires and inclinations, and his doctrine of "radical evil" suggests that envy and aggression are likely to be large problems in any society. Although he does consider it possible for people to obey the moral law without constraint, he believes that consistently moral behavior to others probably will not happen on a large scale unless people join churches of the right sort, which turns out to mean a type of church that has never yet existed. Locke has a much more optimistic view about the sentiments, but he, too, appears to be skeptical about their potential to produce action in accordance with just political principles. At any rate, his own derivation of the social contract relies on mutual advantage rather than benevolence, despite his emphasis on the latter in his account of duties in the state of nature. Finally, Hume—who, though not a contractarian, is a major source for modern contractarianism and one of the most astute moral psychologists in the tradition—believes that benevolent sentiments will not on the whole prevail in society, unless greatly aided by conventions and laws based on the idea of mutual advantage.

Rawls is in a more complex position, because the Veil of Ignorance builds moral impartiality into the foundations of political principles, in a way that corresponds, he says, to a standpoint of impartiality ("purity of heart") that a real person can take up at any time, though usually we do not. Moreover, in his account of the Well-Ordered Society considerable attention is devoted to the education of sentiments that will underwrite the political conception, making it stable over time. Although Rawls came to have some doubts about the particulars of this section of *A Theory of Justice* by the time of *Political Liberalism,* thinking that too much had been based on a single comprehensive doctrine of the good, he nonetheless advanced a political psychology even in that book, and emphasized its importance, arguing that society needs some public cultivation of sentiment if it is to remain stable.

The capabilities approach demands a great deal from human beings. It demands a great deal more from them than classical theories of the social contract, and somewhat more than Rawls demands of citizens in the Well-Ordered Society, although Rawls's demands are already very substantial. The solution to our three unsolved problems requires people to have very great sympathy and benevolence, and to sustain these sentiments over time. As in Rawls's case, institutions will play a large role in making benevolence stable and, indeed, in articulating an adequately definite conception of what benevolence requires. But institutions do not come into being unless people want them, and they can cease to be if people stop wanting them, something that the demise of New Deal–style social democracy in the United States has shown all too clearly.

Is the capabilities approach then hopelessly unrealistic? Only time and effort will answer this question. But we may begin an answer by pointing to a large defect in the classical theorists' treatment of the moral sentiments: their lack of attention to cultural variation and the role of education. Hobbes, Locke, Kant, and even Hume seem to hold that the repertoire of sentiments of which a group of citizens is capable is pretty well fixed; at the margins, societies may influence things, as when Hume's imagined society teaches people to attach sentiments to the usefulness of justice, and as when Kant's rational religion gains more adherents, motivating people to support the moral law. But on the whole these thinkers do not seem to think that there is much scope for large-scale personal change, or for social efforts supporting such changes. Kant does think we can hope for peace, in part because it is to the advantage of all; but he does not think that we can hope for a benevolence that supports basic life opportunities for all the citizens of the world, or even for all in a given nation. This lack of moral ambition is surprising, given that all these thinkers are surrounded by, and in some cases adherents of, a Christian culture that prominently advocated spiritual reform and self-change in respect of benevolence and other basic sentiments.

Indeed, the only classical social contract thinker who devotes sustained attention to the malleability of the moral sentiments, their susceptibility to cultivation through education, is Rousseau, whose *Emile* attributes much current injustice to a perverse sentimental education and then proposes an education, based upon compassion, that would support social justice. The fourth book of *Emile* is an immensely fertile starting point for further reflection on this problem; along with Adam Smith's *Theory of the Moral Sentiments* and John Stuart Mill's essay "The Utility of Religion," it is one of the truly insightful texts about the problem of forming sentiments that will support radical social change in the direction of justice and equal dignity.

Rawls follows Rousseau in believing that a just society can do a great deal to educate sentiments that support its principles. His perceptive discussion of the moral sentiments in both *TJ* and *PL* shows that he thinks of emotions as intelligent attitudes that can be socially shaped, and that can take society's principles as objects, if appropriately taught to do so. So his theory is almost as ambitious, *ex post,* as mine: the stability of the just society depends on its ability to inculcate the right attitudes and sentiments in people, such that they will support very extensive changes in the existing distribution of goods. Of course, since Rawls is doing ideal theory rather than proposing a transition to a real new system, he does not speak in terms of supporting radical change. If, however, we try to imagine how anything close to his ideal were ever to come into being, the transition would obviously require extensive efforts of sentimental education.

By now, psychology has told us clearly that many aspects of our emotional life are socially shaped, and can be otherwise. Even sentiments as apparently "hard-wired" as disgust have strong components of parental and cultural teaching.[1] Anger, grief, fear—all these are socially shaped with respect to their choice of objects, their modes of expression, the norms they express, the beliefs about the world they embody, and even the concrete varieties of them that a given society will contain.[2] We may not be in the situation that John Stuart Mill thought we were in, when he suggested that young children are rather like blank slates, and that any sentiments the society wants can be successfully inculcated in them. Surely Mill's associationist psychology (borrowed from his father, James Mill) was exceedingly naïve, neglecting both evolutionary bases for the emotional life and also the way in which the developmental process begun in infancy shapes the emotional repertoire. So Mill's conclusion, namely that people can be taught to think that the happiness of all the world's people is a part of their own happiness, was reached too quickly, without enough grappling with recalcitrant aspects of human psychology.

Nonetheless, in the area of compassion and benevolence, what Mill believed is at least to some extent true: the surrounding culture can make a great deal of difference to the emotions people experience, and to their efficacy. C. Daniel Batson's important work on altruism has shown that people who hear the story of another person's plight vividly presented, with the salient aspects dramatically underlined, will experience compassion and form projects of helping as a result.[3] Our basic equipment would appear to be more Rousseauian than Hobbesian: if we are made aware of another person's suffering in the right way, we will go to his or her aid. The problem is that most of the time we are distracted, not well educated to understand the plights of other people, and (what both Rousseau and Batson emphasize in different ways) not led, through an education of the imagination, to picture these sufferings vividly to ourselves. We may add a point much stressed by Rousseau, though not by Batson: people often have insufficient awareness of their own human vulnerability, if they have been brought up to believe that they are privileged, or even self-sufficient and invulnerable.

How far could the public education of a liberal society cultivate sentiments that would complement and support the capabilities approach? And how could this education be arranged, in a society whose principles abhor indoctrination and restrictions on freedom of expression?

It seems that the extension of benevolence is at least possible, and that people's conceptions of what they owe to self and others are actually very fluid, responding to social teaching. It is clear, for example, that the general public culture of the United States teaches many things that militate against benevolence: that the poor cause their poverty, that a "real man" is self-sufficient and not needy, and many other pernicious fictions that abound in our popular culture. On the other hand, some pernicious sentiments in the public culture of the United States have also been undermined over time, by criticism and replacement of the conceptions and beliefs that inform them. Thus, racial hatred and disgust, and even misogynistic hatred and disgust, have certainly diminished in our public culture, through attention to the upbringing of children and their early education. The careful attention to language and imagery that some pejoratively call "political correctness" has an important public purpose, enabling children to see one another as individuals and not as members of stigmatized groups. To some extent, these beneficial changes are under way in public ways of speaking and teaching about people with disabilities. The inclusion of children with disabilities in classrooms alongside other children assists this movement yet further, making it evident to children that a child with a disability is a distinctive individual, capable of a wide range of human sentiments and activities.

In these and other ways, a liberal society may foster, and make central, conceptions of the person and of human relations that support its basic political principles. Although it should not suppress contrary views, it can give the supportive views prominence in public education and public rhetoric—as when Franklin Delano Roosevelt portrayed poor Americans as citizens with dignity, beset by catastrophe, rather than as lazy good-for-nothings; as when Martin Luther King Jr. portrayed in moving terms a future of racial equality and world citizenship; as when advocates for people with disabilities represent the complexity and variety of such lives, and their capacities for love and achievement.

If the capabilities approach is ever to be realized in the world, such examples must be understood and followed. A society aspiring to justice in the three areas I have discussed must devote sustained attention to the moral sentiments and their cultivation—in child development, in public education, in public rhetoric, in the arts. I have not shown that the extension of sentiment required by the normative project of this book is possible. And I have certainly not shown *how* it is possible. This silence stems not from the feeling that there is nothing of interest to say about these questions, or that they cannot be answered. It stems, rather, from the decision to make these questions the topic of another book.[4]

Even though I have not yet shown that the realization of justice as I construe it is possible, I do believe that my argument here removes one obstacle to seeing it as possible. For it establishes that a particular picture of who we are and what political society is has for some time imprisoned us, preventing us from imagining other ways in which people might get together and decide to live together. If we take for granted the fact that mutual advantage is the only cement for a liberal political culture, we will speak cynically about "utopian" projects such as those that I propose in the three frontier areas of justice. I have shown, however, that this picture has a specific historical origin and has never been the only picture available. We should by now be able to see that it is a picture, as Hobbes and Locke knew well that it was, rather than a realistic description of what people are and must be. Seeing it as a picture, we are in a position to ask what that picture does for us, how fully it expresses us, and whether we want to choose that picture or some other to articulate our aspirations for political society.

In this way, the answers to large philosophical questions have practical significance.[5] They shape our sense of what is possible, giving us terms in which to name ourselves and our political relationships. The social contract picture, fertile and admirable in so many areas, limits us in our approach to the three unsolved problems that I believe to be frontiers of justice for our future. While we should not dismiss the best such theories, we should and can use philosophical argument to open the windows of our imaginations. Without imaginative courage we are likely to be left with public cynicism and despair before the very large challenges that these three areas pose. But with some new pictures of what may be possible we can at least approach these frontiers and think creatively about what justice can be in a world that is so much more complicated, and interdependent, than philosophical theory has often acknowledged.

NOTES

1. For a detailed account of my position on political justification, see Nussbaum (2000a), chap. 2; and (2004d).

2. See Nussbaum (2000a), chap. 4.

3. In Chapter 1 I shall argue that Locke's theory actually avoids some of the problems that beset Rawls, but only because Locke has a hybrid theory, with a strong commitment to prepolitical natural rights and to natural duties of benevolence.

4. For my own appropriation of this Rawlsian/Aristotelian notion, see Nussbaum (2000a), chap. 2; and (2004d).

1. SOCIAL CONTRACTS AND THREE UNSOLVED PROBLEMS OF JUSTICE

1. Hobbes (1651/1991), chap. 13. Hobbes is probably influenced, however, by Epicurus and Lucretius (see especially Lucretius, *De rerum natura* 5). On the history of social contract theories in antiquity, see Goldschmidt (1977).

2. Locke (1679–80?/1960), *Second Treatise,* chap. 2 para. 4, chap. 8 para. 98. Unless specified by the roman numeral I, all references to Locke are to the *Second Treatise.* The *First* and *Second Treatises* are of disputed date, but Peter Laslett has argued convincingly that they were composed much earlier than was previously thought; see Locke (1679–80?/1960), 15–135, esp. 66–79.

3. Not all the exponents of the tradition speak of their project in terms of the idea of political justice. Since I shall be focusing on Rawls's version of the tradition, which, of course, centrally does so, I hope the reader will forgive the anachronism.

4. What else is included in "and so on" is of course one of the points of contention within the tradition. For Rawls, as we shall see, race and sex are very important parts of the list, but physical and mental disabilities cannot be. See Chapter 2.

5. I shall argue, however, that the historical tradition does not em-

ploy Rawls's idea of "pure procedural justice" but starts, instead, from a robust account of natural rights or entitlements.

6. Hobbes, of course, does not use it in that way; although he had a deep influence on the liberal tradition, he himself is not a liberal; see section iv.

7. A footnote states that Hobbes's version, great though it is, presents special problems.

8. It is interesting that in *TJ* 11 n. 4, listing the texts that are his primary historical antecedents, Rawls mentions Locke's *Second Treatise* and Rousseau's *Social Contract* but, instead of Kant's political writings, his "ethical works beginning with *The Foundations of the Metaphysics of Morals.*"

9. One sign of this: in one class discussion (around 1976) of education theorist Lawrence Kohlberg's account of the stages of moral awareness, alleged Piagetian developmental stages through which children pass as they mature—in which social contract doctrines represent Stage Four, Utilitarianism Stage Five, and Kantianism Stage Six—Rawls said that it followed from Kohlberg's views about moral development that he (Rawls) could not criticize Utilitarianism, as he plainly had, since he was by definition at a lower developmental stage, and criticism, for Kohlberg, requires having moved through the stage one is criticizing. I remember being surprised that Rawls placed himself in Stage Four rather than in Stage Six.

10. For the usage of "impairment," "disability," and "handicap," see Chapter 2, note 5.

11. Hobbes did not omit women, and he is in many respects a surprising exception on matters of sex. Kant omits quite a few more people, since his independence condition requires property and leads to the positing of a distinction between "active" and "passive" citizenship: see section iv.

12. See Nussbaum (2000a), chap. 4.

13. This all became much worse in the nineteenth century, as Michel Foucault documents for the case of insanity; before that, exclusions were less severe, and many people with substantial disabilities were able to play significant roles in public life. Consider Julius Caesar, who suf-

fered from epilepsy; the emperor Claudius, whose mobility was severely impaired and who had other disabilities of uncertain nature; the philosopher Seneca, who suffered from many chronic and disabling ailments, as he records, and who yet was regent of the empire. No doubt one could find examples in other times and cultures to parallel these.

14. Charles Dickens, here as elsewhere, is in the vanguard of criticism with his complex portrait of Mr. Dick in *David Copperfield:* see Cora Diamond, "Anything but Argument?" in Diamond (1995). We should also mention Wilkie Collins, radical here as elsewhere: in *No Name,* a woman with severe mental impairments provides the novel with its moral center.

15. For this way of putting things, I am indebted to Barbara Herman.

16. I am developing an account of this tradition in Nussbaum (forthcoming).

17. Cf. also *TJ* 17, where he states that contract theories, his own included, "leave out of account how we are to conduct ourselves toward animals and the rest of nature . . . We must recognize the limited scope of justice as fairness and of the general type of view that it exemplifies. How far its conclusions must be revised once these other matters are understood cannot be decided in advance"; and *TJ* 512, which states that "we should recall here the limits of a theory of justice," mentioning that the theory of justice gives no account of right conduct toward beings who lack the capacity for a sense of justice. This would appear to include not only nonhuman animals, Rawls's immediate subject, but also human beings with severe mental disabilities.

18. Nussbaum (2000a).

19. Gauthier (1986).

20. This phrase is not always used in contexts in which the social contract is described, but the ideas involved do appear to be central to the thinking of Locke and Kant, as well as to Hume's very different theory.

21. Among the leading figures in the tradition, Locke appears the most concerned with finding historical parallels to the various elements of the state of nature; but he does this in order to demonstrate that it is not unrealistic, not because he thinks literal historical truth is an important feature of the approach.

22. Locke (1679–80?/1960), chap. 8 para. 95.

23. Kant, "Theory and Practice," in Kant (1970), 74.

24. Ibid. This section of Kant's essay is subtitled "Against Hobbes," another reminder that we should not pretend that Hobbes belongs to this tradition in any simple way—although one should also insist that Hobbes's own account of rights in the state of nature is complex.

25. Hobbes (1651/1991), chap. 13.

26. Locke (1679–80?/1960), chap. 2 para. 4.

27. Smith (1776/1784/1981), 28–29; Rousseau (1762/1979), bk. 4.

28. Locke (1679–80?/1960), chap. 8 para. 95.

29. Hobbes (1651/1991), chap. 14.

30. For Cicero's view, see Nussbaum (1999b).

31. Pufendorf's *On the Law of Nature and Nations* was published in 1672, his *On the Duty of Man and Citizen According to Natural Law* in 1673.

32. For an excellent sorting out of these tensions, see Green (2003).

33. See Simmons (1992), who argues that Locke's idea is consequentialist in form.

34. I have deliberately not taken a stand on debates about the role played by God in Locke's argument; for a valuable treatment, see Simmons (1992).

35. *Some Thoughts Concerning Education*, 31. See the excellent discussion of the latter point in Simmons (1992), 44.

36. In the *Treatise* Hume criticizes philosophers who overemphasize this characteristic, saying that they are "as wide of nature as any accounts of monsters, which we meet with in fables and romances."

37. Although Kant does not explicitly mention this category, he speaks of "generally anyone who must depend for his support (subsistence and protection), not on his own industry, but on arrangements by others." This class must include all people with severe mental impairments, and many with severe physical impairments as well, given the conditions of his day. Does the proviso that the state make it possible to "work up from this passive status to an active status" suggest that the state should make elaborate accommodations for people with impairments, so that

they can indeed be economically productive? A modern Kantian might so use the text; but the idea is clearly far from Kant's own thinking.

38. For an excellent discussion of some of the important distinctions within this tradition, see Stark (2000).

39. Not only the Veil of Ignorance but also the Formal Constraints of the Concept of Right (*TJ* 130–136) are important here.

40. One might conjecture that Rawls's dialogue with neoclassical economists shaped this aspect of his theory. He was very concerned to convince economists, and those influenced by them, that a theory with a commitment to fairness could be rigorously and convincingly grounded. Perhaps this argumentative context explains the concession he makes, in the initial framing of the choice situation, to classical portrayals of contract. Later Rawls's polemical focus shifted, and he was especially concerned to convince religious believers that a pluralistic liberal society could be plausibly grounded; but he never rejected or significantly changed the formative elements of *TJ*.

41. Scanlon (1998) uses the term "contractualism."

42. It has been suggested that Fichte anticipates the approach, though I do not claim to know.

43. See also Nussbaum (2000a), chap. 2.

44. Barry (1995).

45. Rawls uses the terms "political liberalism," "overlapping consensus," and "comprehensive conception" in *PL*.

46. For one compelling argument about this, see the regional comparisons in Drèze and Sen (1995) and (1997).

47. *TJ* 156–173, discussing average utility and its difficulties.

48. See Nussbaum (2000a), chap. 2.

49. Nozick (1974), 42–45.

50. Marx (1844/1978), 88, 91; translation modified.

51. Stability is clearly one such value, but stability is already incorporated in the justification of the capabilities list itself, since I argue that we can justify any account of core political commitments only by showing that it can remain stable: see Nussbaum (2000a), chap. 2.

52. In Nussbaum (1995b) I make this argument in detail for affiliation and practical reason.

53. See Chapter 3 and Nussbaum (2003b).

54. See, for example, Nussbaum (2000a), chap. 1.

55. See also Nussbaum (2003b).

56. See my discussion of this issue in Nussbaum (2000a), chap. 1.

57. See Nussbaum (2000f), replying to a defense of functioning by Richard Arneson.

58. Here I am speaking only of Rawls's own procedure within *TJ*. He also offers a quite distinct account of the procedure through which one scrutinizes, Socratically, all theories and one's own "considered judgment," attempting to reach "reflective equilibrium" (*TJ* 40–43). This is not a pure procedural account, and is much closer in method to my own account; see Nussbaum (2000a), 2, for the use of a Rawlsian method of justification inside the capabilities approach.

59. I do not use the Rawlsian terminology here, because I think it is confusing. He contrasts his own "pure procedural justice" with "perfect procedural justice" (the cake division) and "imperfect procedural justice" (the criminal trial). But really, it seems misleading to call either of these procedural theories. So I prefer to call them outcome-oriented theories, as is plainly Rawls's intent.

60. There is a further distinction in Rawls's discussion, between "perfect" and "imperfect" outcome-oriented accounts of justice. The cake division illustrates the former, since we can reliably achieve the correct result; the criminal trial illustrates the latter. The capabilities approach seems likely to deliver only an imperfect justice, simply because no institutions we can imagine would guarantee all citizens all their rights all the time—though we presumably build in remedies for those whose rights have been abridged.

61. Rawls addresses this concern with his overarching account of justification aiming at reflective equilibrium: for the outcome (and the procedure) will be checked against our considered judgments, as will the other theories we consider.

62. Obviously this isn't quite right, since the cook might have cooked it too long, etc.

63. See Nussbaum (2000a), chap. 2.

64. Although only Hume uses the word "artificial," all the classical

social contract theorists seem to believe that we can imagine human beings living a full and recognizable human life without political society.

65. On Aristotle's conception of friendship and shared ends, see Sherman (1989).

66. See Nussbaum (2001a), chaps. 6 and 8. The latter discusses the relationship of compassion to the capabilities approach.

67. See Chapter 7 and Nussbaum (2003c).

68. Sex equality, however, cannot be adequately addressed without a thoroughgoing critique of the family, which no theorist in this tradition has been willing to undertake, for reasons that are probably not just accidentally linked to their espousal of the contract doctrine. See further in Chapter 2, and, for a detailed account, see Nussbaum (2000a), chap. 4. Inequalities resulting from sexual orientation prove resistant to bargaining theories for two very different reasons: because addressing them requires a radical critique of the family in its current form, and because the presence in society of gays and lesbians, who do all right with respect to income and wealth but are the worst off with respect to the social bases of self-respect, puts great pressure on Rawls's theory of the primary goods and his use of income and wealth to index relative social positions. See Chapter 2.

2. Disabilities and the Social Contract

1. See Kittay (1999). My portrait of Sesha here is from the time described in that book.

2. He also has numerous physical disabilities, prominently including a group of very severe food allergies.

3. This is a picture of Art in 2000; as we shall see, things have changed a lot since then.

4. In Bérubé (1996); my portrait of Jamie derives from that description.

5. A note on terminology: in the disability literature, "impairment" is a loss of normal bodily function; a "disability" is something you cannot do in your environment as a result; a "handicap" is the resulting competitive disadvantage. I shall try to observe these distinctions in

what follows, although the line between impairment and disability is difficult to draw, particularly when the social context is not held fixed but is up for debate. As I shall argue, we cannot prevent all disability: for some impairments will continue to affect functioning even in a just social environment. What we ought to do is to prevent handicap with regard to basic entitlements.

The literature typically distinguishes between "mental illness," which is taken to be primarily an emotional disorder, and "cognitive impairments" or "intellectual disabilities," which are taken to involve reason only and not the emotions. I believe that this division is misleading: core cases of mental illness, such as schizophrenia, involve cognitive as well as emotional impairments; "cognitive impairments" such as autism and Asperger's prominently involve the emotions. Moreover, if one holds, as I do, that emotions involve cognition, one will not want to use language that encourages people to separate them. For all these reasons I use the term "mental impairment" and "mental disability" to cover the terrain occupied by both "cognitive" disabilities and "mental illnesses": it corresponds to "physical impairment" and "physical disability" (although of course it does not imply that the mental impairments do not have a physical basis).

6. Locke is the source for the first phrase, Rawls for the second (*PL* 20, 21, 183, and elsewhere): see the discussion in section ii, and, on Locke, see Chapter 1.

7. Once again, I speak only of theories that think of the point of the contract as mutual advantage.

8. Things were not always this way: institutionalization began at the time of the Civil War in the United States, somewhat earlier in Europe and Britain.

9. For a remarkable example of political advocacy by two men with Down syndrome, see Levitz and Kingsley (1994) and Levitz (2003).

10. On the general issue of respect for care labor, see Ruddick (1989), citing a 1975 U.S. government study that rated different types of work in terms of the "complexity" and skill they involved. The best score was awarded to the job of surgeon. Among the worst scores were those allotted to the jobs of foster mother and nursery school teacher,

who were grouped together with the "mud mixer helper" and the person who shovels chicken offal into a container.

11. The term "normals" is from Goffman (1963); on his theory of stigma, see Nussbaum (2004a).

12. According to the Women's Bureau of the U.S. Department of Labor, as of May 1998 an estimated 22.4 million households—nearly one in four—were providing home care for family members or friends over the age of fifty. For these and other data, see Harrington (1999).

13. Just as the increasing life span means that, even given the increased incidence of divorce, the average marriage lasts longer than it did in the nineteenth century, the increasingly disabled time of old age will soon exceed what used to be the average life span.

14. On the distinction, see *JF*, discussed in section vi; Rawls, in turn, draws on Daniels (1985).

15. This is a major theme in recent feminist work: see especially Kittay (1999); Folbre (1999) and (2001). Earlier influential work in this area includes Fineman (1991) and (1995); Ruddick (1989); Tronto (1993); Held (1993); West (1997). For two excellent collections of articles from diverse feminist perspectives, see Held (1995) and Kittay and Feder (2002).

16. See also United Nations Development Programme (1999), 77–83, which argues that in developing as in developed countries, such unpaid work is a major source of disadvantage to women, and increasingly so in the new global economy, which in many cases has replaced home-based work by work outside the home.

17. The parties in the Original Position have the same conception of well-being, defined in terms of primary goods. They know that the people they represent have diverse conceptions of the good. Some such comprehensive conceptions may of course include other-related interests and attachments, but since the parties make the contract without awareness of their own particular conceptions, those interests cannot enter into their concerns as they make it.

18. Here, interestingly, it is not terribly clear whether we are to think of these capacities acontextually (as freedom from grave impairment) or against the background of some generalized context (as freedom from

grave disability within some "normal" human context). The classical contract thinkers did not envisage the extent to which changes in social context could affect the relationship between what I call impairment and what I call disability.

19. Like Kant's political theory.

20. Locke (1679–80?/1960), chap. 8. Locke, however, as we have seen, gives benevolence a large role in his account of the parties; to that extent his theory escapes some of the objections I shall be making.

21. Gauthier (1986), 18, speaking of all "persons who decrease th[e] average level" of well-being in a society.

22. Ibid., n. 30; see epigraph.

23. And disability? Once again, it is not terribly clear whether impairments are imagined against an idea of the general circumstances of human life, and thus as generating disabilities in that generalized context.

24. Indeed also in the history of Indian political thought, the only nonwestern tradition sufficiently known to me for me to comment: see Nussbaum (2002a).

25. See Nussbaum (2000a), chap. 4.

26. See Sen (1990); Agarwal (1997).

27. See Okin (1989); concerning Rawls's restatement of his position in IPRR, see Nussbaum (2001a), chap. 4. The family is ultimately treated as a voluntary institution, analogous to a church or a university, which political justice regulates on the outside only.

28. See Nussbaum (2000a), chap. 4; (2000c).

29. See also *PL* 51: in the Original Position, he says, the Reasonable is modeled by the informational constraints, which are kept clearly separate from the account of the rationality of the parties, that being connected to their interest in pursuing their own diverse conceptions of the good. See also *PL* 103–105: citizens in the Well-Ordered Society possess two moral powers: a capacity for the sense of justice and a capacity for a conception of the good. The capacity for forming and being guided by a conception of the good is modeled in the Original Position by the rationality of the parties; the capacity for the sense of justice by the rough symmetry among the parties and by their informational con-

straints. Thus it would seem that they map onto the Rational and the Reasonable as elsewhere defined.

30. Rawls justifies the claim that this question is fundamental by pointing to its centrality in the tradition of liberal political thought (*PL* 22). Such an argument may perhaps suffice to establish its importance, but it can hardly establish that other questions, neglected by the tradition, are not equally important.

31. Eva Kittay has argued in an excellent discussion (1999, 88–99; and also 1997) that there are five places in Rawls's theory where he fails to confront facts of asymmetrical neediness that might naturally have been confronted: (1) his account of the Circumstances of Justice assumes a rough equality between persons; (2) his idealization of citizens as "fully cooperating," etc. puts disability and dependency to one side; (3) his conception of social cooperation, again, is based on the idea of reciprocity between equals and has no explicit place for relations of extreme dependency; (4) his account of the primary goods, introduced, as it is, as an account of the needs of citizens who are characterized by the capacity to be "fully cooperating," has no place for the care needs of many real people; (5) his account of citizens' freedom in terms of being a self-authenticating source of valid claims (e.g., *PL* 32) omits any freedom that might be enjoyed by someone who is not like that.

32. See Sen (1980); other good accounts of the approach are in Sen (1993), (1995), and (1992), especially chaps. 1, 3, and 5.

33. See *TJ* 440–446.

34. It is true that at *PL* 7 Rawls considers the possibility of adding a prior principle (prior even to the basic liberties) stipulating that "citizens' basic needs be met, at least insofar as their being met is necessary for citizens to understand and to be able fruitfully to exercise those rights and liberties." He does not pursue that issue; nor does he show how this principle would be derived in the Original Position. But even if a principle of that sort should be added, it would hardly amount to an "ample social minimum" in the sense required either by my theoretical approach or by modern nations that think about distribution in this way: for a citizen may be fully able to exercise political rights and liber-

ties while being at a very low level with respect to health, education, employment rights, access to property, and so forth. The rural voters in India who determined the outcome of the election of May 2004 were such citizens: active, effective participants in democracy, exercising their basic liberties at a high level of commitment and effectiveness. Nonetheless, nobody could say that they enjoyed an "ample social minimum": indeed, this was just what their dissatisfaction was about.

35. In terms of the definitions used in the disability literature, these defects are not, strictly speaking, impairments, because they are not a "loss of normal bodily function." What I want to capture here, though, is the idea that we all have bodily limits and weaknesses that bring limitation and even pain.

36. TenBroek (1966).

37. Pregnancy leave is an exception, but this can easily be justified on grounds of efficiency, given the large number of female workers and their productivity.

38. On the difference, see, for example, Epstein (1992), 480: "Whereas there is normally little if any private reason for a common carrier or a public accommodation to *want* to discriminate on grounds of race or . . . sex, the same cannot be said of the ADA [Americans with Disabilities Act], which requires major expenditures with respect to trains, buses, airports, and all other forms of public facilities, to be financed out of general revenues rather than specific charges levied on disabled persons." Epstein holds that antidiscrimination laws for race and sex are unnecessary, and that the market will solve the problem.

39. Gauthier (1986), 18 and n. 30.

40. Epstein (1992), 481.

41. Rawls's discussion of Sen at *PL* 183 ff. does not explicitly distinguish the two cases, but the argument plainly applies in similar ways to both.

42. This is my reading of the cryptic discussion of Sen at *PL* 183 ff.

43. See Kittay (1999), 77: "Dependency must be faced from the beginning of any project in egalitarian theory that hopes to include all persons within its scope." The concrete stratagems adopted to address

issues of disability (laws mandating wheelchair ramps, laws such as the Individuals with Disabilities Education Act) could well be left until this stage; but the fact that citizens experience such needs for care must be recognized from the start, and a commitment made to address these concerns.

44. See Bérubé (1996) for a detailed account of these expenses.

45. Mill (1850/1988), 86.

46. Sorabji (1993).

47. The pertinent passages are well discussed in Regan (1983), 177–185.

48. Another way of putting this, common in discussions of Kant, is to say that for Kant the most relevant genus under which we classify the human being is that of Rational Being; our fellow genus-members are the angels and any such further rational beings there may be. Within this genus, we are the animal species: the animal rational, then, rather than the rational animal. This problem is exacerbated, of course, by Kant's focus on some aspects of our humanity and not others as what particularly constitute its worth and dignity.

49. See *LHE*, esp. 253–290.

50. See Kittay (1999), 93.

51. See *TJ* 505: "Presumably this [the emphasis on the two moral powers] excludes animals; they have some protection certainly but their status is not that of human beings."

52. Scanlon (1999), 177–187. I am very grateful to Scanlon for correspondence that makes the complexity of his approach to these cases clear.

53. Once again, it is very important to stress that this is Rawls's project, not Scanlon's, and that Scanlon does not recommend applying it in this way.

54. Or, in the case of *PL*, are trustees for citizens who have similar powers and abilities.

55. See, for example, *TJ* 135, where finality is a formal condition on political principles; and 175–178, in the argument for the two principles where it is made clear that the agreement "is final and made in per-

petuity" and that "there is no second chance" (176). Rawls's opposition to intuitionism focuses on this issue; see, for example, *TJ* 35–36.

56. Kittay (1999), 102–103.

57. Kittay expresses sympathy with this proposal as well.

58. I did not understand this in Nussbaum (2000c).

59. See Nussbaum (2000a), chap. 1; and (2000c).

60. *JF* 168–176. Although this book is the latest in date of publication, it is not clear that it actually forms the latest stage in Rawls's thinking; it seems to be based largely on lecture notes from the 1980s; see Samuel Freeman's comment in *Fordham Law Review* 72 (2004), 2028 n. 19.

61. This language was actually in the theory from the beginning: for example, at *TJ* 90–95, comparisons for the purposes of the Difference Principle are made in terms of "expectations of primary social goods" (92). But the insight is used to solve the temporary-disability problem only in this late work.

62. Thus Alan Gewirth's Kantian theory of human rights, though it lacks the structural problems of social contract theories, nonetheless has difficulty with issues of disability, as it also does with issues of animal entitlement, because of its highly Kantian understanding of the human, as I shall discuss further in Chapter 5; see Gewirth (1978) and (1996).

63. Scanlon (1999), 168; and see the report of objections from Frances Kamm and Judith Jarvis Thomson at 391 n. 21, where Scanlon appears to grant that suffering (for example) has independent significance and is what explains why acts causing it would reasonably be rejected.

64. Ibid., 170.

65. Scanlon in correspondence also asserts this point.

66. In correspondence.

67. Thus it is not surprising that in speaking of the goals of international development Scanlon defends a view that he calls a "substantive good" or "substantive list" theory; see Scanlon (1993).

68. Barry (1995), chap. 2.

69. Ibid., 60 and 272 n. 28.

70. "In effect" because in *PL* the account of the good is closely liked to the Kantian account of the person.

3. Capabilities and Disabilities

1. This practical assessment is of only limited value, however, since the various constitutional traditions do not elaborate on the notion of human dignity, and thus are indeterminate between a Kantian rationalistic interpretation and my more inclusive interpretation—unless we construe the judgment of the Kerala High Court, in the animal case to be examined in Chapter 6, as a definitive interpretation of article 21 of the Indian Constitution. (The question is unresolved.)

2. Nussbaum (2000a), chap. 2.

3. See Nussbaum (2001a), chaps. 6–8.

4. Sen (1980).

5. Once again, we need to bear in mind that Rawls has already established the lexical priority of liberty. But this priority should not make us content, for two reasons: first, liberty itself is thoroughly dependent on economic distribution and redistribution, so the whole strategy of settling matters of liberty before going on to economic matters is problematic; second, there are numerous capabilities not covered by Rawls's list of liberties, for which income and wealth are not good proxies: Rawls's own good of self-respect, for one, as well as capabilities for health, education, mobility, and so forth.

6. For my detailed argument with Sen on this point, see Nussbaum (2003a).

7. See Nussbaum (2000d).

8. Obviously enough, the capabilities might be individuated in more than one way; there should be no dogmatism about the precise form the list takes, so long as its content is preserved.

9. In Norway, while out hiking in the forested areas of some foothills near the coast, I came upon a busload of disabled elderly people who had been brought up there to enjoy the forest trails. Their wheelchairs were being unloaded, and they were being wheeled along in the crisp mountain air.

10. Sesha has now moved out of her family's home into a group home; the change was very exhilarating to her.

11. Arneson (2000).

12. See Nussbaum (2000a), chap. 1.

13. See *TJ* 48–51 and Nussbaum (2000), chap. 2, on my own use of Rawls's method.

14. Larmore (2003).

15. See Nussbaum (2000d).

16. Similar is Aristotle's way of defining each virtue: in doing so he considers the implications for accounts of other virtues.

17. See Nussbaum (1995b).

18. Thus I modify some statements made in articles in the 1980s and 1990s, which might have been read to suggest that if any one of the capabilities is totally cut off, the life is no longer a human life.

19. On chance and justice, see Buchanan et al. (2000). On the social and the natural, see the discussion of Rawls's social and natural primary goods in Nussbaum (2000a), chap. 1. Just as Rawls defines justice in terms of the "social basis of self-respect," which may of course have other determinants, so too I define the relevant task in the areas of health, imagination, and so forth: to provide the social conditions of these capabilities. I understand "social," however, somewhat more broadly than Rawls does, since I include the structure of the family in the account of what is "social." Thus, insofar as failures in capability derive from some aspect of the family structure that is within the domain of law to restructure, thus far it is the job of the state to promote a more adequate structure.

20. Whether this restriction of information should be allowed where children are concerned raises very difficult issues, which I discuss in Nussbaum (2000a), chap. 4. I here discuss only adults who have chosen, against the background of adequate education and exit options, to live in such a community.

21. These others may of course exist inside a pluralistic democratic society, and their choices will be protected; but their view will not count as one of the reasonable comprehensive views, since it does not express respect for the different views of their fellow citizens.

22. This strategy is similar to Rawls's at *PL* 139 and elsewhere. Once again, I accept the basic structure of his political liberalism.

23. See McMahan (1996).

24. As McMahan correctly notes, that is the position implicit in some of my earlier articles on this point.

25. Thus, *pace* McMahan, my "species norm account" is not required to say that the anencephalic child is the worst-off human because it is the furthest from the species norm (see McMahan [1996], 12–13). I agree that it would be wrong to say that this child is more unfortunate than a child with Sesha's capabilities. But I think we need not give up on the idea that a species norm can do at least some work for us without leading to this conclusion; for surely it would be only dogmatism to insist that the life of such a child is a human life, whereas Sesha's is clearly such a life.

26. The chronology here is not unilinear: much longer ago, blindness and deafness were so common that there may have been less marginalization of people with these conditions.

27. See tenBroek (1966).

28. Goffman (1963), 5 ff.

29. Ibid., 15.

30. Of course this raises issues of personal identity; but I defer those for another occasion. Here I think I am in agreement with McMahan's "Individual Possibilities Account": we judge the standard of good or bad fortune for someone by looking to the best life with which she "could have been natively endowed" (14). Thus he agrees that a child with Sesha's level of disability is unfortunate, even though a nonhuman animal with a similar level of cognitive ability would not be unfortunate.

31. See Levitz and Kingsley (1994); Levitz (2003).

32. See, for example, *In re Nelda Boyer*, 636 P. 2d 1085, 1091 (Utah 1982): "Although the powers conferred upon a guardian may be very broad, the court is authorized to tailor the powers of a guardian to the specific needs of the ward . . . The process should be individualized and based upon careful consideration of the particular needs for supervision." For this reference I am grateful to Leslie Francis.

33. Herr (2003), 431.

34. Ibid., 435.

35. Herr (2003).

36. Ibid., 445.

37. This material, like the account of Israeli and German law, is drawn from Herr, Gostin, and Koh (2003).

38. Herr (2003), 431–438. For other support services and a detailed discussion of the definition of "persons with disabilities," see ibid., 438–439.

39. Ibid., 441–442.

40. Herr, Gostin, and Koh (2003), vi.

41. Francis and Silvers (2000), xix.

42. *Watson v. Cambridge,* 157 Mass. 561 (1893). Watson was said to be "unable to take the ordinary decent physical care of himself"; *State ex Rel Beattie v. Board of Education of the City of Antigo,* 169 Wisc. 231 (1919). The Supreme Court of Wisconsin upheld the exclusion of Beattie. Beattie was apparently not mentally handicapped, but his case nonetheless typifies the stigmatizing that often affects the lives of the mentally handicapped.

43. 343 F. Supp. 279 (1972). The court, however, lightened the plaintiffs' burden, holding that they had established a constitutional claim even under the less stringent rational basis test: in other words, they did not need to show that education is a fundamental right in order to make their equal protection claim. The plaintiffs' contention that the exclusions violate both due process and equal protection prevailed.

44. 348 F. Supp. 866 (D.C.C. 1972) at 876. Technically, because of the legally anomalous situation of the District, they held that it was a due process violation under the Fifth Amendment and that the equal protection clause in its application to education is "a component of due process binding on the District."

45. 397 U.S. 254 (1969) at 266.

46. Ibid. at 264–265.

47. We can hear here an echo of the dignity-related aspect of Locke that I mentioned in Chapter 1, which is connected to his theory of natural rights and is not included in modern forms of contractarianism.

48. Today the terms "impairment" and "disability" are typically used to describe the presocial condition of such children, so to speak; the

term "handicap" is used to describe their socially disadvantaged situation.

49. I wish to thank John Brademas, one of the authors of this legislation, for very helpful discussion about the background and history of the law.

50. 473 U.S. 432 (1985) at 449.

51. Ibid., 446, 450, 449.

52. A related issue, however, was raised in an equal protection case from the previous year, *Palmore v. Sidoti,* 466 U.S. 429 (1984). The case concerned the custody of a child whose mother, who had been awarded custody, remarried, to an African-American man. The child's father sought custody, citing the prejudice the child would encounter from being part of a stigmatized family. Because the case concerned race, it involved not the rational basis standard but strict scrutiny. However, the Court's analysis was pertinent: it said that law must refuse to turn private prejudice into systematic public disadvantage: "Private biases may be outside the reach of the law, but the law cannot, directly or indirectly, give them effect." This part of *Palmore* was cited by the Court in *Cleburne* in connection with the judgment that "the city may not avoid the strictures of [the Equal Protection] clause by deferring to the wishes or objections of some fraction of the body politic" (473 U.S. 448).

53. The same approach was used in *Romer v. Evans* (2000), the famous case in which Colorado's Amendment 2, which denied local communities the right to pass laws protecting gays and lesbians from discrimination, was declared unconstitutional. Again, this law was held not to have a rational basis, and to rest on mere "animus" against an unpopular group.

54. 875 F. 2d 954, 960 (1st Cir. 1989), cert. denied 493 U.S. 983 (1989). For this case and for a valuable discussion of the zero-reject policy, I am indebted to Ladenson (2004). A valuable discussion of the entire issue is in Minow (2002), 80–86.

55. Both in 1975 and in 1997 the federal government was authorized to pay up to 40 percent of each state's excess cost of educating

children with disabilities; as of 2004, no more than 16 percent has ever been appropriated. During Senate consideration of reauthorization of the law in the spring of 2004, the bipartisan Harkin-Hagel Amendment proposed a gradual increase in funding over the next six years to reach the 40 percent mark. Because it did not include offsetting cuts to pay for the increases it would have required, it was in violation of budget rules, and the 60 votes needed to waive such rules were not forthcoming: the amendment fell 4 votes short of passage. The Senate did, however, authorize by 95–1 a competing amendment that would authorize, but not require, discretionary funding increases to reach the 40 percent mark by 2011.

56. See Kelman and Lester (1997). They quote a special educator from Mississippi: "Are there kids who fall through the cracks? Yeah . . . I think that every year we just keep doing it. We're going to reevaluate to see if we can't fit that discrepancy somewhere. 'Did we get it yet? Has he fallen far enough behind in achievement now that we can make him eligible for special ed?' . . . I think that somehow, someday we're going to all have to say this is our kid, what we need to do is educate this kid. Whether it's the regular ed teacher taking him into a group for a certain subject or whether it's special ed or Chapter One or whomever, it's necessary" (100).

57. This is Kelman and Lester's conclusion, on the basis of their extensive study of IDEA as applied to learning-disabled children.

58. Of course this is just a part of the larger issue of child care; but it encompasses most of the issue of elder care, because most elderly people require care only insofar as they have one or more disabilities.

59. See Nussbaum (2000a), chap. 4.

60. Kittay (1999).

61. See the appendix to Nussbaum (2002c).

62. As of 1986, 46 percent of working women in Sweden were employed part-time, and women took fifty-two days of leave for every day taken by a man; Williams (2000), 51, with references.

63. On this issue see Ehrenreich (2001).

64. See Nussbaum (2000a), chap. 1.

65. See my criticism of Sen on this point in Nussbaum (2003b).

66. See Nussbaum (1998).

67. Kittay (1999), chap. 1. Part III, on political strategies, is titled "Some Mother's Child."

68. For passages that focus on the need of the individual for choice and independence, see, for example, ibid., 34–35, 53, 98, 192 n. 32.

69. Ibid., chap. 5.

70. See ibid., chap. 6.

71. Eva Kittay, personal communication, March 2003.

72. Bérubé (1996), 264; Levitz and Kingsley (1994).

73. Bérubé (1996), 264.

4. Mutual Advantage and Global Inequality

1. All data in this paragraph are from United Nations Development Programme (2003), 237–240. Data are listed as from 2001. Sierra Leone never got above 40 years in life expectancy, even before the advent of HIV/AIDS, but in the past year its life expectancy has declined from 38.9 to 34.5 years, largely from that cause. The United States overall ranks number 7 in the weighted Human Development Index, behind Norway, Iceland, Sweden, Australia, the Netherlands, and Belgium. It is twenty-fifth in life expectancy, behind most of the generally high-ranking nations, but also behind Costa Rica, Malta, Singapore, and Hong Kong.

2. See discussion in Nussbaum (2000a), introduction. For education, see Nussbaum (2004b).

3. See also *LP* 4: "This idea of justice is based on the familiar idea of the social contract."

4. Kant (1797/1999), 343, 307 (Akademie pagination).

5. Kant says, rightly, that "Law of Nations" is a misnomer: it ought to be "Law of States" (in his Latin, *ius publicum civitatum*).

6. See also "Idea for a Universal History," where Kant speaks of the "barbarous freedom of established states" (Kant [1970], 49); "Theory and Practice," where he speaks of a "state of international right, based upon enforceable public laws to which each state must submit by analogy with a state of civil or political right among individual men" (ibid.,

92); *Perpetual Peace,* where he speaks of the "lawless condition of pure warfare" between states, and continues, "Just like individual men, they must renounce their savage and lawless freedom, adapt themselves to public coercive laws" (ibid., 105). (All translations from these works are from Kant [1970]. Pages are given as in that edition, which does not include the Akademie pagination.)

7. Ibid., 104.

8. To some extent this thin focus is explained (not, I think, justified) by Rawls's subsequent focus on the issue of conscientious objection, to which the discussion of international law is a preliminary.

9. Although, as we shall see, consideration is also given to reasonable nonliberal peoples, the purpose of this consideration, Rawls emphasizes, is to "assure ourselves that the ideals and principles of the foreign policy of a liberal people are also reasonable from a decent nonliberal point of view" (*LP* 10).

10. Here he cites Sen (1981). But he misdescribes Sen's conclusion. Sen does hold that a free press and political democracy are extremely important ingredients in famine prevention, but he does not hold that they are always sufficient. Moreover, his analysis applies only to famine and not to undernutrition, poor health due to undernutrition, and so on.

11. Rawls introduces the term "comprehensive conception" in *PL* to distinguish the political conception from citizens' religious and secular overall conceptions of the meaning of life, ethical requirement, and so forth.

12. As Fred Kniss has argued (1997), even the Mennonites, often cited as an example of a small and homogeneous religion, have numerous and intense disagreements about basic elements of the conception of the good.

13. See, for example, *TJ* 264–265: "We want to account for the social values, for the intrinsic good of institutional, community, and associative activities, by a conception of justice that in its theoretical basis is individualistic. For reasons of clarity among others, we do not want to rely on an undefined concept of community, or to suppose that society is an organic whole with a life of its own distinct from and superior to

that of all its members . . . From this conception, however individualistic it may seem, we must eventually explain the value of community."

14. Who are the "burdened societies"? Rawls's lack of realism shows up once again in the thin specification of this concept. These societies are said to "lack the political and cultural traditions, the human capital and know-how, and, often, the material and technological resources needed to be well-ordered" (*PL* 106). This statement is very vague. For some extremely interesting further remarks about economic assistance, see the letter by Rawls in Rawls and Van Parijs (2000).

15. This is clear because Rawls refers to the Universal Declaration, saying that his group of rights includes articles 3 to 18 (although it really cannot include the full version of article 7, equality before the law) but excludes the rights enumerated in the subsequent articles of the Declaration.

16. This stipulation also limits the degree of ignorance the parties can have in the Original Position.

17. See Stiglitz (2002), who describes a notorious photograph in which a French representative of the IMF stands with arms crossed over a seated Indonesian leader, in a posture of high colonial condescension, delivering the wisdom of the rich nations and their agencies.

18. An initial problem in assessing Rawls's theory in this area is its historical vagueness. Rawls has nothing to say about actual hierarchical societies in the contemporary world. (His fictional example derives from the Ottoman Empire.) In "LP," as in earlier writings, Rawls presents his own liberal principles as grounded in a specifically "Western" heritage, and characterizes liberalism itself as "Western," even as based on "Western individualism." In the book, references to the West are dropped in favor of a schematic distinction between liberal and non-liberal societies. But Rawls still seems to be thinking primarily of Western democracies, not of India, Bangladesh, and so forth. The omission of these societies is striking when we arrive at the principle of toleration, for if the rationale for his uncritical attitude toward the "decent hierarchical societies" involves the idea that they have a different set of historical traditions and cannot plausibly have been expected to be liberal, that rationale is undercut by the fact, if it were to be acknowledged,

that many nonwestern nations have adopted liberal constitutions. (Of course the very distinction between "Western" and "nonwestern" is itself a Western construct, and not a very useful way to think about these varied societies with their heterogeneous traditions.) Moreover, the core ideas of Rawls's political theory are known to have deep roots in other political traditions: India, for example, had a well-developed and politically effective idea of religious toleration long before Europe; see Sen (1997). To the extent that Rawls justifies his relaxed treatment of certain nonliberal societies by appeal to differences in history, then, these claims are not, and cannot be, borne out.

19. For this language, see *PL* 144–145: "the political conception is a module, an essential constituent part, that in different ways fits into and can be supported by various reasonable comprehensive doctrines that endure in the society regulated by it."

20. *LP* 65 stipulates that the right to property is part of the basic list of human rights, but Rawls is careful to avoid insisting on equal property rights.

21. See *LP* 65 n. 2: "this liberty of conscience may not be as extensive nor as equal for all members of society: for instance, one religion may legally predominate in the state government, while other religions, though tolerated, may be denied the right to hold certain positions."

22. See *LP* 71: "all persons in a decent hierarchical society are not regarded as free and equal citizens, nor as separate individuals deserving equal representation (according to the maxim: one citizen, one vote)."

23. This is the standard term in "LP." In *LP* it is replaced by the term "decent consultation hierarchy."

24. *LP*'s requirement of "formal equality . . . (that is, that similar cases be treated similarly)" (65) notoriously does not suffice for nondiscrimination, since some allegedly relevant difference between women and men can always be produced: see "Difference and Dominance," in MacKinnon (1987). In describing Kazanistan, Rawls states that minorities are not "subjected to arbitrary discrimination," but that very phrase allows that some types of discrimination are merely arbitrary and others justified by a difference.

25. For a longer version of this argument, see Nussbaum (2002b).

26. Cf. *TJ* 27, 29, 185–189.

27. In his formulation, none, since the society is assumed to be closed.

28. Isn't it time to declare a moratorium on the use of the word "individualism," with its multiple ambiguities? If it means egoism (psychological or ethical) or even a belief that self-sufficiency is best, few Western thinkers have held such views. If it means that each person should be treated as an end, many Western thinkers have held this view (as have many "nonwestern" thinkers), but it seems to be a good view to hold; and we would be unlikely to see "the notion that each person is an end" used as a term of abuse, as if just to bring it up made argument unnecessary. See "The Feminist Critique of Liberalism," in Nussbaum (1999a).

29. See again Agarwal (1994).

30. See my treatment of Grotius in Nussbaum (forthcoming). So expressed, the view sounds like a comprehensive doctrine, and Grotius does not distinguish between political and moral autonomy, as I (with Rawls) would like to do. So my version of the Grotian argument would say, instead, that by giving themselves laws, human beings assert a political autonomy that can be agreed to be important even by citizens who differ about the value of a comprehensive moral autonomy.

31. See Agarwal (1994). Laws vary from state to state and from religion to religion. Christian property law (which gave daughters one-fourth the share of sons) has been declared inapplicable to Christian women in Kerala; but in many states Hindu property law still contains large inequalities, giving women smaller shares and in some cases tying property to jointly owned family consortia in such a way that a woman who leaves a family cannot extricate and separately control her share. Subsequent work by Agarwal has shown a high correlation between land ownership and the ability to resist domestic violence: so this issue is of consequence for more than one capability.

32. See Nussbaum (2003c).

33. Catharine MacKinnon developed similar ideas very convincingly in "Women's 9/11," a Dewey Lecture delivered in October 2004 at the University of Chicago Law School.

34. A pillar of educational policy under the BJP government was the

rewriting of national textbooks to bring them into line with the view of history and culture held by the Hindu right; Education Minister M. M. Joshi was one of the most vehement partisans of a Hindu-supremacist vision of society. This unfortunate policy is being reversed under the new government.

35. On these matters, see further Nussbaum (2001b).

36. Rawls never quite says that a fuller set of norms cannot be justified, but he does suggest that it is for this reason that we should focus not on the entirety of the Universal Declaration but only on a few urgent rights.

37. Beitz (1979); Pogge (1989).

38. Pogge (1989), 247.

39. There are questions of chronology here, but Scanlon was working on his theory for many years before the publication of his book, and had published crucial parts of it in article form; moreover, Pogge could have made a move in that direction independently, for example by announcing that he was keeping the Kantian element in Rawls's theory but rejecting its social contract component and its allegiance to Hume's Circumstances of Justice.

40. See Drèze and Sen (2002), 257–262.

41. Pogge (2002).

42. Hobbes's own approach, however, is more complex, since he recognizes at least some role for justice and moral obligation in the state of nature, although he also holds that these concerns will be impotent: see Chapter 1.

5. Capabilities across National Boundaries

1. O'Neill (1996).

2. Shue (1996); Jones (1999).

3. O'Neill's duty-based approach, similarly, makes at least implicit reference to need, for example in its assumption that violence and deception are bad; for, as Aristotle said, such things would not be bad for gods, who would have no need of promises, contracts, etc.

4. See the excellent treatment of this example in Wood (1999).

5. For a longer discussion, see Nussbaum (1999b).

6. Nussbaum (2000a), chap. 2.

7. Chapter 6 contains a much more detailed critique of Utilitarian approaches, in the context of animal entitlements. As will become obvious, some of these objections to Utilitarianism were influentially expressed by Rawls, though not by him alone.

8. Singer (1972); Murphy (2000).

9. See Nussbaum (2000a), chap. 2 and references there.

10. I leave aside Mill's multivalued Utilitarianism, which lies much closer to the position that I defend.

11. See Nussbaum (2000a), chap. 2 and discussion of Sen and Elster there.

12. *San Antonio Independent School District v. Rodriguez,* 4ll U.S. 1 (1973).

13. See generally Nussbaum (2000a), chap. 4.

14. See Nussbaum (2003b).

15. I am exceedingly grateful to Charles Larmore for pushing me to confront this question, and for his suggestions about how it might be confronted.

16. Cf. Justice Marshall's dissenting opinion in *San Antonio,* 4ll U.S. 70 (1973).

17. See Frankfurt (1988) and (1999).

18. Dworkin (2000), chap. 7. Dworkin directs this criticism against Sen, although Sen has never said that equality of capability is the right social goal; he says only that to the extent that society pursues equality as a social goal, equality of capability is the right space within which to make the relevant comparisons.

19. Income and wealth are not on the list at all, since they are not capabilities; thus the frequently discussed issue of equality in income and wealth is touched on only indirectly, through commitments concerning the central capabilities.

20. For a longer account of this point, see Nussbaum (2003b).

21. See Nussbaum (2000a), chap. 1.

22. See Nussbaum (2000a), where I do use Rawlsian ideas in connection with nations around the world. For criticism of this use of Rawls,

see Barclay (2003) and my reply in Nussbaum (2003d). I develop these issues further in a short book on *PL* under contract to Columbia University Press.

23. See Sen (1997).

24. See Maritain (1951) and (1943).

25. See Glendon (2001).

26. See Stiglitz (2002), who, however, does not challenge the idea of mutual advantage explicitly enough.

27. See Murphy (2000).

28. See Green (2002).

29. In one form, this family of objections is eloquently pressed in Williams (1973).

30. See also Nagel (1991).

31. This distinction is sometimes run together with the public/private distinction, but it is not the same. Many comprehensive doctrines are shared and public (in the sense that they are part of civil society); and the political sphere itself takes on the protection of central capabilities of women and children in the family, an area traditionally deemed private.

32. I am grateful to Iris Young for pressing me to take on this question.

33. See Nussbaum (2000a), chap. 3, for some general balancing principles, with regard to religion, that can be adjusted to guide the nation-state relation.

34. Nussbaum (2004b).

35. The announcement by Great Britain in late September 2004 that it would pay off around 20 percent of the debt of the poorer nations is a hopeful beacon, and a creative way of using aid in a nondominating fashion.

36. See, for example, Stiglitz (2002) and Friedman (2002).

37. Conversation with François Bourguigon, April 2002.

38. See Pogge (2002).

39. In several cases, for example, the norms of sex equality in CEDAW have been held to be binding on nations that have ratified it,

in a way that has affected the outcome of legal disputes and also generated new legislation.

40. See Nussbaum (2000a), chap. 4; and (1999a), chap. 2.

41. Thus I take a stand against child marriage and marriage without consent: not against arranged marriage, when practiced with a person over some reasonable legal age of consent, who has options, is not coerced, and consents to the arrangement in question.

42. For a comparison of India and Western traditions in this regard, see Nussbaum (2002a).

43. See Nussbaum (2004a).

44. Cf. Stiglitz (2002), xii, analyzing the failings of international development policies: "What was at issue . . . is a matter of *ideas,* and conceptions of the role of the government that derive from these ideas."

6. BEYOND "COMPASSION AND HUMANITY"

1. The incident is discussed in Pliny, *Natural History* 8.7.20–1; and Cicero, *Ad Familiares* 7.1.3. See also Dio Cassius, *History* 39, 38. See the discussion in Sorabji (1993).

2. I shall often refer to other animal species this way; my use of the word "animals" should be understood as a shorthand for the longer and more accurate term.

3. See Sorabji (1993). He blames much of our later obtuseness on Stoicism, without, to my mind, sufficiently appreciating the force of Judeo-Christian sources, which influenced which Greek views were likely to gain a hearing.

4. Hobbes and Locke say nothing interesting about animals, so the Kantian tradition is the only evidence for what classical social contract theory says about this.

5. These lectures, edited from student notes, were probably given between 1775 and 1780; *Groundwork* was published in 1785, the second *Critique* in 1788, *Metaphysics of Morals* (with its account of the social contract) in 1797–98.

6. Kant (1963), 239–240.

7. For a history of such arguments in the eighteenth century, particularly in Britain, see Lee (2002), which also discusses the influence of Hogarth's engravings. Lee also examines modern psychological findings on the question, and concludes that there is at least some evidence in favor of the "cruel habits" claim.

8. A more extensive consideration of duties to animals in the context of a Kantian moral theory is in Gewirth (1978), which goes further than Rawls by suggesting that animals have certain limited rights in virtue of their similarity to humans.

9. Are these duties supposed to be part of the political realm? This is unclear, because *TJ* is less clear than *PL* about the distinction between political principles and comprehensive moral doctrines. I tentatively conclude that for Rawls these duties are part of a comprehensive moral doctrine, and not the part that forms a portion of the "overlapping consensus" in the political realm; thus, in the terms of *PL,* he would not feel free to form political principles on the basis of his beliefs about them.

10. See the analysis in Nussbaum (2001a), chap. 6. This part of the analysis is uncontroversial, recapitulating a long tradition.

11. When Rawls contrasts "the love of mankind" with "the sense of justice," (*TJ* 190 ff.) he states that the love of mankind is more comprehensive and prompts us to actions of supererogation as well as justice. In terms of this contrast, I am suggesting that at least some of our duties to animals are not merely supererogatory, but are requirements generated by animals' legitimate moral entitlements.

12. See Sen and Williams (1982).

13. Bentham (1789/1823/1948), 1: "the standard of right and wrong" is "fastened to their throne."

14. Singer (1980), 12. See the good analysis in Regan (1983), 206–208.

15. Singer (1980), 238.

16. See Nussbaum (2000e).

17. This may mean simply that there is none clearly better: thus consequentialism can admit incomplete rankings, as it must if it is to include plural and incommensurable goods.

18. See Nussbaum (2000a); *PL;* Larmore (1996).

19. Not all forms of Utilitarianism require that actors choose as consequentialists. Sidgwick's indirect Utilitarianism urges that ordinary people should usually abide by conventional virtue, and that only a few experts should use the Utilitarian calculus. This version of Utilitarianism seems defective on account of its lack of publicity. Rule Utilitarianism, which urges actors to follow rules that can be given a Utilitarian justification, does not have this defect, but it has another: there is no reason for such an agent to follow the rule in a case in which he knows that the Utilitarian calculus gives a different result. So rule Utilitarianism seems to collapse into act Utilitarianism, with provision made for the use of rules in situations of imperfect information.

20. See also Nussbaum (2000a), chap. 2.

21. Seligman (1975).

22. Coetzee (1999), 21.

23. See Nussbaum (2004c).

24. I do not comment here on the issue of plants or of the natural world in general, although I do think that the capabilities approach can be extended to deal with these issues.

25. *Parts of Animals* 645a26–27. Aristotle goes on to say that it is not possible to look without disgust at the blood, bones, etc. of which the human body is made; he seems to find wonder in the contemplation of form and structure alone. Here he stops short of what his own view suggests, an embracing of all of life, including its material stuffs.

26. See my detailed discussion of Rawls's view, and my own, in Nussbaum (2000a), chap. 2.

27. On this see Richardson (1994).

28. In *TJ* Rawls thinks of the deliberation as carried out by each individual person, in a Socratic fashion; in *PL* he adds a requirement of communal endorsement; see Chapter 5.

29. Narrative fiction is frequently valuable in such an exercise: see Nussbaum (1990), (1995a).

30. See Okin (1989).

31. See Lee (2002).

32. Proust (1954), 105.

33. See my discussions of this idea in Nussbaum (1995a).

34. Coetzee (1999), 45.

35. Thus Rawls, Sidgwick, and Aristotle, all with very different theories, have used it.

36. 406 U.S. 205 (1972).

37. See *PL* 20, 244, 273–274.

38. Singer (1980).

39. Regan (1983), 240–241.

40. Rachels (1990). See my discussion in Nussbaum (2001c).

41. See DeGrazia (1996), 226 ff.

42. Here we should probably exclude one-celled creatures that appear to have the capacity for locomotion. I focus here on locomotion in its Aristotelian sense, in which it involves the ability to become aware of a good thing at a distance, to desire that good, and to move toward it in consequence.

43. Rachels (1990); and see the excellent treatment of these issues in DeGrazia (1996).

44. See de Waal (1996). Similar is David Hume's attempt to get his reader to consider human and animal rationality and emotion together, as related species of a general capacity.

45. I argue that this is also Aristotle's approach, in Nussbaum (1995b). Whether that argument is accepted or not, it shows what my own approach is.

46. Mill (1850/1988), 28–29.

47. Botkin (1996), 26–27.

48. Nussbaum (2000a), chap. 2.

49. See my critique in Nussbaum (1999b). Several of the essays in Sunstein and Nussbaum (2004) discuss current legal arrangements and their problems.

50. See Sunstein (2004).

51. See Hare (1999).

52. DeGrazia (1996). I am also grateful to DeGrazia for excellent comments on a draft of this material when it was presented as a Tanner Lecture.

53. See, for example, Gewirth (1978).

54. Here we must supply the caveat mentioned above: if there should be a creature that is not sentient, but has one of the other central life functions, such as thinking, affiliation with others, and so on, then the killing of such a creature would also be problematic; but in the real world we do not find such cases.

55. As mentioned above, the new animal rights law enacted by Austria in May 2004 requires chickens to be free to run around, bans lions and tigers in circuses, and institutes a wide range of other protections for both domestic and nondomestic animals.

56. The declawed cat cannot climb or jump (well), both of which seem to be important ingredients in its characteristic form of life. The lion who cannot tear a gazelle and is given a ball instead can still rip things to shreds and is able to move in a nonmutilated way; so the two cases do not appear to be symmetrical. Even to the extent that they are, cats are declawed only because people want to protect their rugs and furniture, whereas forbidding lions access to gazelles saves gazelles from excruciating pain.

57. The new Austrian law bans clipping dogs' ears and tails.

58. See Sen (1999).

59. Again, the new Austrian law points the way, requiring that all farm animals be allowed to roam freely for at least three months in the year.

60. Austria's law bans keeping puppies and kittens in cramped, airless conditions in pet shops.

61. On all this, see Nussbaum (2001a), chap. 2.

62. See Wise (2000), chap. 1.

63. On the monkeys, see Nussbaum (2001a), chap. 4; on the dogs, Seligman (1975).

64. See Sunstein and Nussbaum (2004).

65. See Nussbaum (2000d).

66. Does this mean banning experiments whose very topic is psychological brutality, such as those of Seligman and the attachment research reported by Bowlby? It seems so—although the illumination we have derived from Seligman's work is very great, as is its fruitfulness for constructing better modes of treatment for both humans and other ani-

mals. We will have to observe the same constraints that we already observe for psychological research on human subjects.

7. THE MORAL SENTIMENTS AND THE CAPABILITIES APPROACH

1. See Nussbaum (2004a), discussing psychological research on disgust.

2. Nussbaum (2000a), chap. 3.

3. Batson (1991); see discussion in Nussbaum (2001a), chap. 6.

4. *Capabilities and Compassion,* under contract to Cambridge University Press.

5. Here I consciously imitate the end of Rawls's introduction to the paperback edition of *PL*.

REFERENCES

Agarwal, Bina. 1994. *A Field of One's Own: Gender and Land Rights in South Asia*. Cambridge: Cambridge University Press.

―――― 1997. "'Bargaining' and Gender Relations: Within and Beyond the Household." *Feminist Economics* 3: 1–51.

Amundson, Ron. 1992. "Disability, Handicap, and the Environment." *Journal of Social Philosophy* 23: 105–118.

―――― 2000a. "Biological Normality and the ADA." In Francis and Silvers (2000): 102–110.

―――― 2000b. "Against Normal Function." *Studies in History and Philosophy of Biological and Biomedical Sciences* 31C: 33–53.

Arneson, Richard J. 2000. "Perfectionism and Politics." *Ethics* 111: 37–63.

Asch, Adrienne, Lawrence O. Gostin, and Diann Johnson. 2003. "Respecting Persons with Disabilities and Preventing Disability: Is There a Conflict?" In Herr, Gostin, and Koh (2003): 319–346.

Barclay, Linda. 2003. "What Kind of Liberal Is Martha Nussbaum?" *Sats: Nordic Journal of Philosophy* 4: 5–24.

Barry, Brian. 1995. *Justice as Impartiality*. Oxford: Clarendon Press, 1995.

Batson, C. Daniel. 1991. *The Altruism Question: Toward a Social-Psychological Answer*. Hillsdale, N.J.: Lawrence Erlbaum Associates.

Becker, Lawrence C. 2000. "The Good of Agency." In Francis and Silvers (2000): 54–63.

Beitz, Charles. 1979. *Political Theory and International Relations*. Princeton: Princeton University Press.

Bentham, Jeremy. 1789/1823/1948. *An Introduction to the Principles of Morals and Legislation*. New York: Hafner. (The text is based on the 1823 edition.)

Bérubé, Michael. 1996. *Life as We Know It: A Father, a Family, and an Exceptional Child*. New York: Pantheon.

Botkin, Daniel. 1996. "Adjusting Law to Nature's Discordant Harmonies." *Duke Environmental Law and Policy Forum* 7: 25–37.

Brock, Dan W. 2000. "Health Care Resource Prioritization and Discrimination against Persons with Disabilities." In Francis and Silvers (2000): 223–235.

Buchanan, Allen, Dan W. Brock, Norman Daniels, and Daniel Wikler. 2000. *From Chance to Choice: Genetics and Justice.* New York: Cambridge University Press.

Coetzee, J. M. 1999. *The Lives of Animals,* ed. Amy Gutmann. Princeton: Princeton University Press. Coetzee's Tanner Lectures: pp. 15–69.

Daniels, Norman. 1985. *Just Health Care.* Cambridge: Cambridge University Press.

——— 2000. "Mental Disabilities, Equal Opportunity and the ADA." In Francis and Silvers (2000): 255–268.

DeGrazia, David. 1996. *Taking Animals Seriously: Mental Life and Moral Status.* Cambridge: Cambridge University Press.

de Waal, Frans. 1996. *Good Natured: The Origins of Right and Wrong in Humans and Other Animals.* Cambridge, Mass.: Harvard University Press.

Diamond, Cora. 1995. *Realism and the Realistic Spirit.* Cambridge, Mass.: Bradford Books. Reprint edition.

Drèze, Jean, and Amartya Sen. 1995. *India: Economic Development and Social Opportunity.* Oxford: Oxford University Press.

———, eds. 1997. *Indian Development: Selected Regional Perspectives.* Oxford: Oxford University Press.

Drèze, Jean, and Amartya Sen. 2002. *India: Development and Participation.* Oxford: Oxford University Press.

Dworkin, Ronald. 2000. *Sovereign Virtue: The Theory and Practice of Equality.* Cambridge, Mass.: Harvard University Press.

Ehrenreich, Barbara. 2001. *Nickel and Dimed: On (Not) Getting By in America.* New York: Metropolitan Books.

Epstein, Richard. 1992. *Forbidden Grounds: The Case against Employment Discrimination Law.* Cambridge, Mass.: Harvard University Press.

Fineman, Martha A. 1991. *The Illusion of Equality.* Chicago: University of Chicago Press.

———— 1995. *The Neutered Mother, the Sexual Family and Other Twentieth Century Tragedies.* New York: Routledge.

Folbre, Nancy. 1999. "Care and the Global Economy." Background paper prepared for United Nations Development Programme (1999).

———— 2001. *The Invisible Heart: Economics and Family Values.* New York: New Press.

Francis, Leslie Pickering, and Anita Silvers, eds. 2000. *Americans with Disabilities: Exploring Implications of the Law for Individuals and Institutions.* New York: Routledge.

Frankfurt, Harry G. 1988. "Equality as a Moral Ideal." In Frankfurt, *The Importance of What We Care About: Philosophical Essays.* Cambridge: Cambridge University Press. Pp. 134–158.

———— 1999. "Equality and Respect." In Frankfurt, *Necessity, Volition, and Love.* Cambridge: Cambridge University Press. Pp. 146–154.

Friedman, Benjamin. 2002. Review of Stiglitz (2002). *New York Review of Books,* August 22.

Gauthier, David. 1986. *Morals by Agreement.* New York: Oxford University Press.

Gewirth, Alan. 1978. *Reason and Morality.* Chicago: University of Chicago Press.

———— 1996. *The Community of Rights.* Chicago: University of Chicago Press.

Glendon, Mary Ann. 2001. *A World Made New: Eleanor Roosevelt and the Universal Declaration of Human Rights.* New York: Random House.

Goffman, Erving. 1963. *Stigma: Notes on the Management of Spoiled Identity.* New York: Simon and Schuster.

Goldschmidt, Victor. 1977. *La doctrine d'Epicure et la droit.* Paris: Vrin.

Green, Michael. 2002. "Institutional Responsibility for Global Problems." *Philosophical Topics* 30 (2002): 79–96.

———— 2003. "Justice and Law in Hobbes." *Oxford Studies in Early Modern Philosophy* 1: 111–138.

Grotius, Hugo. 1625/1646/1925. *De Iure Belli ac Pacis Libri Tres/*

On the Law of War and Peace. 2 vols. Vol. 1: Latin text; vol. 2: translation. Trans. Francis W. Kelsey. Oxford: Clarendon Press. (The text is based on the 1646 edition.)

Hare, R. M. 1999. "Why I Am Only a Demi-vegetarian." In Jamieson (1999): 233–246.

Harrington, Mona. 1999. *Care and Equality.* New York: Knopf.

Held, Virginia. 1993. *Feminist Morality: Transforming Culture, Society, and Politics.* Chicago: University of Chicago Press.

———, ed. 1995. *Justice and Care: Essential Readings in Feminist Ethics.* Boulder: Westview.

Herr, Stanley S. 2003. "Self-Determination, Autonomy, and Alternatives for Guardianship." In Herr, Gostin, and Koh (2003): 429–450.

Herr, Stanley S., Lawrence O. Gostin, and Harold Hongju Koh, eds. 2003. *The Human Rights of Persons with Intellectual Disabilities.* Oxford and New York: Oxford University Press.

Hobbes, Thomas. 1651/1991. *Leviathan.* Ed. Richard Tuck. Cambridge: Cambridge University Press.

Holton, Richard, and Rae Langton. 1999. "Empathy and Animal Ethics." In Jamieson (1999): 209–232.

Hume, David. 1739–40/1978. *A Treatise of Human Nature.* Ed. L. A. Selby-Bigge. 2d ed. revised by P. H. Nidditch. Oxford: Clarendon Press.

——— 1777/1975. *Enquiries Concerning Human Understanding and Concerning the Principles of Morals.* Ed. L. A. Selby-Bigge. 3d ed. revised by P. H. Nidditch. Oxford: Clarendon Press.

Jamieson, Dale, ed. 1999. *Singer and His Critics.* Oxford: Basil Blackwell.

Jones, Charles. 1999. *Global Justice: Defending Cosmopolitanism.* Oxford: Oxford University Press.

Kant, Immanuel. 1797/1999. *Metaphysical Elements of Justice.* Ed. and trans. John Ladd. Indianapolis: Hackett.

——— 1963. *Lectures on Ethics.* Trans. L. Infield. Indianapolis: Hackett.

———— 1970. *Kant: Political Writings.* Ed. Hans Reiss. Cambridge: Cambridge University Press.

Kavka, Gregory S. 2000. "Disability and the Right to Work." In Francis and Silvers (2000): 174–192.

Kelman, Mark, and Gillian Lester. 1997. *Jumping the Queue: An Inquiry into the Legal Treatment of Students with Learning Disabilities.* Cambridge, Mass.: Harvard University Press.

Kittay, Eva Feder. 1997. "Human Dependency and Rawlsian Equality." In *Feminists Rethink the Self.* Ed. Diana T. Meyers. Boulder: Westview. Pp. 219–266.

———— 1999. *Love's Labor: Essays on Women, Equality, and Dependency.* New York: Routledge.

Kittay, Eva Feder, and Ellen K. Feder, eds. 2002. *The Subject of Care: Feminist Perspectives on Dependency.* Lanham: Rowman and Littlefield.

Kniss, Fred. 1997. *Disquiet in the Land: Cultural Conflict in American Mennonite Communities.* New Brunswick, N.J.: Rutgers University Press.

Ladenson, Robert T. 2004. "The Zero-Reject Policy in Special Education: A Moral Analysis." Manuscript cited by permission of the author.

Larmore, Charles. 1996. *The Morals of Modernity.* Cambridge: Cambridge University Press.

———— 2003. "Public Reason." In *The Cambridge Companion to Rawls.* Ed. Samuel Freeman. New York: Cambridge University Press: 368–393.

Lee, Jadran. 2002. "Bentham on Animals." Ph.D. diss., University of Chicago.

Levitz, Mitchell. 2003. "Voices of Self-Advocates." In Herr, Gostin, and Koh (2003): 453–465.

Levitz, Mitchell, and Jason Kingsley. 1994. *Count Us In: Growing Up with Down Syndrome.* New York: Harcourt Brace.

Locke, John 1679–80?/1960. *Two Treatises of Government.* Ed. Peter Laslett. Cambridge: Cambridge University Press.

MacIntyre, Alasdair. 1999. *Dependent Rational Animals: Why Human Beings Need the Virtues.* Chicago: Open Court.

MacKinnon, Catharine. 1987. *Feminism Unmodified.* Cambridge, Mass.: Harvard University Press.

Maritain, Jacques. 1943. *The Rights of Man and Natural Law.* New York: Scribner's.

——— 1951. *Man and the State.* Chicago: University of Chicago Press.

Marx, Karl. 1844/1978. *Economic and Philosophical Manuscripts of 1844.* In *The Marx-Engels Reader.* Ed. Robert C. Tucker. New York: Norton. Pp. 66–125.

McMahan, Jeff. 1996. "Cognitive Disability, Misfortune, and Justice." *Philosophy and Public Affairs* 25: 3–35.

Mill, John Stuart. 1850/1988. "Nature." In *John Stuart Mill: Three Essays on Religion.* Amherst, N.Y.: Prometheus Books. Pp. 3–65.

——— 1869/1988. *The Subjection of Women.* Ed. Susan M. Okin. Indianapolis: Hackett.

Minow, Martha. 2002. *Making All the Difference: Inclusion, Exclusion, and American Law.* Ithaca: Cornell University Press.

Murphy, Liam. 2000. *Moral Demands in Ideal Theory.* New York: Oxford University Press.

Nagel, Thomas. 1991. *Equality and Partiality.* New York: Oxford University Press.

Nozick, Robert. 1974. *Anarchy, State, and Utopia.* New York: Basic Books.

Nussbaum, Martha C. 1995a. *Poetic Justice: The Literary Imagination and Public Life.* Boston: Beacon.

——— 1995b. "Aristotle on Human Nature and the Foundations of Ethics." In *World, Mind, and Ethics: Essays on the Philosophy of Bernard Williams.* Ed. J. E. G. Altham and Ross Harrison. Cambridge: Cambridge University Press.

——— 1998. "The Good as Discipline, the Good as Freedom." In *Ethics of Consumption: The Good Life, Justice, and Global Stewardship.* Ed. David Crocker and Toby Linden. Lanham, Md.: Rowman and Littlefield. Pp. 312–341.

—— 1999a. *Sex and Social Justice.* New York: Oxford University Press.

—— 1999b. "Duties of Justice, Duties of Material Aid: Cicero's Problematic Legacy." *Journal of Political Philosophy* 7: 1–31.

—— 2000a. *Women and Human Development.* Cambridge: Cambridge University Press.

—— 2000b. "Is Privacy Bad for Women? What the Indian Constitutional Tradition Can Teach Us about Sex Equality." *Boston Review* 25 (April–May): 42–47.

—— 2000c. "The Future of Feminist Liberalism." Presidential address delivered to the Central Division of the American Philosophical Association. *Proceedings and Addresses of the American Philosophical Association* 74: 47–79. Reprinted in Kittay and Feder (2002): 186–214.

—— 2000d. "The Costs of Tragedy: Some Moral Limits of Cost-Benefit Analysis." *Journal of Legal Studies* 29: 1005–36. Reprinted in *Cost-Benefit Analysis: Legal, Economic and Philosophical Perspectives.* Ed. Matthew D. Adler and Eric A. Posner. Chicago: University of Chicago Press. Pp. 169–200.

—— 2000e. "Comment on Thomson." In Judith Jarvis Thomson, *Goodness and Advice.* Tanner Lectures. Ed. Amy Gutmann. Princeton: Princeton University Press. Pp. 97–125.

—— 2000f. "Aristotle, Politics, and Human Capabilities: A Response to Antony, Arneson, Charlesworth, and Mulgan." *Ethics* 111: 102–140.

—— 2001a. *Upheavals of Thought: The Intelligence of Emotions.* Cambridge: Cambridge University Press.

—— 2001b. "India: Constructing Sex Equality through Law." *Chicago Journal of International Law* 2: 35–58.

—— 2001c. "Animal Rights: The Need for a Theoretical Basis." Review of Wise (2000). *Harvard Law Review* 114: 1506–49.

—— 2002a. "Sex Equality, Liberty, and Privacy: A Comparative Approach to the Feminist Critique." In *India's Living Constitution: Ideas, Practices, Controversies.* Ed. E. Sridharan, Z. Hasan, and R. Sudarshan. New Delhi: Permanent Black. Pp. 242–283.

———— 2002b. "Women and the Law of Peoples." *Philosophy, Politics and Economics* 1: 283–306.

———— 2002c. "Long-Term Care and Social Justice: A Challenge to Conventional Ideas of the Social Contract." In World Health Organization, *Ethical Choices in Long-Term Care: What Does Justice Require?* Geneva. Pp. 31–66.

———— 2003a. "The Complexity of Groups." *Philosophy and Social Criticism* 29: 57–69.

———— 2003b. "Capabilities as Fundamental Entitlements: Sen and Social Justice." *Feminist Economics* 9 (July/November): 33–59.

———— 2003c. "Compassion and Terror." *Daedalus,* winter: 10–26.

———— 2003d. "Political Liberalism and Respect: A Response to Linda Barclay." *Sats: Nordic Journal of Philosophy* 4: 25–44.

———— 2004a. *Hiding From Humanity: Disgust, Shame, and the Law.* Princeton: Princeton University Press.

————. 2004b. "Women's Education: A Global Challenge." *Signs* 29: 325–355.

———— 2004c. "Mill between Aristotle and Bentham." *Daedalus,* spring: 60–68.

———— 2004d. "On Hearing Women's Voices: A Reply to Susan Okin." *Philosophy and Public Affairs* 32: 193–205.

———— Forthcoming. "Grotius: A Society of States and Individuals under Moral Law." In *The Cosmopolitan Tradition.* New Haven: Yale University Press.

Okin, Susan Moller. 1989. *Justice, Gender, and the Family.* New York: Basic Books.

O'Neill, Onora. 1996. *Towards Justice and Virtue: A Constructive Account of Practical Reasoning.* Cambridge: Cambridge University Press.

Pitcher, George. 1995. *The Dogs Who Came to Stay.* New York: Penguin.

Pluhar, Evelyn B. 1995. *Beyond Prejudice: The Moral Significance of Human and Nonhuman Animals.* Durham: Duke University Press.

Pogge, Thomas. 1989. *Realizing Rawls.* Ithaca: Cornell University Press.

―――― 2002. *World Poverty and Human Rights: Cosmopolitan Responsibilities and Reforms.* Cambridge: Polity.

Proust, Marcel. 1954. *A la recherche du temps perdu.* Vol. 1: *Du côté de chez Swann.* Paris: Gallimard.

Pufendorf, Samuel. 1673/1991. *On the Duty of Man and Citizen According to Natural Law.* Ed. James Tully. Trans. Michael Silverthorne. Cambridge: Cambridge University Press.

Rachels, James. 1990. *Created from Animals: The Moral Implications of Darwinism.* New York: Oxford University Press.

Rawls, John. 1971. *A Theory of Justice.* Cambridge, Mass.: Harvard University Press.

―――― 1980. "Kantian Constructivism in Moral Theory." *Journal of Philosophy* 77: 515–571.

―――― 1993. "The Law of Peoples." In *On Human Rights: The Oxford Amnesty Lectures 1993.* Ed. Stephen Shute and Susan Hurley. New York: Basic Books.

―――― 1996. *Political Liberalism.* Enl. ed. New York: Columbia University Press.

―――― 1999. *The Law of Peoples with "The Idea of Public Reason Revisited."* Cambridge, Mass.: Harvard University Press.

―――― 2000. *Lectures on the History of Ethics.* Ed. Barbara Herman. Cambridge, Mass.: Harvard University Press.

―――― 2001. *Justice as Fairness: A Restatement.* Ed. Erin Kelly. Cambridge, Mass.: Harvard University Press.

Rawls, John, and Philippe Van Parijs. 2003. "Three Letters on *The Law of Peoples* and the European Union." *Revue de philosophie économique* 7: 1–20.

Regan, Tom. 1983. *The Case for Animal Rights.* Berkeley: University of California Press.

Richardson, Henry S. 1994. *Practical Reasoning about Final Ends.* Cambridge: Cambridge University Press.

Rosenthal, Eric, and Clarence J. Sundram. 2003. "Recognizing Existing Rights and Crafting New Ones: Tools for Drafting Human Rights Instruments for People with Mental Disabilities." In Herr, Gostin, and Koh (2003): 467–501.

Rousseau, Jean-Jacques. 1762/1979. *Emile: or On Education*. Trans. Allan Bloom. New York: Basic Books.

Ruddick, Sarah. 1989. *Maternal Thinking*. Boston: Beacon.

Scanlon, Thomas. 1993. "Value, Desire, and Quality of Life." In *The Quality of Life*. Ed. Martha C. Nussbaum and Amartya Sen. Oxford: Clarendon Press. Pp. 185–200.

——— 1999. *What We Owe to Each Other*. Cambridge, Mass.: Harvard University Press.

Seligman, Martin. 1975. *Helplessness: On Development, Depression, and Death*. New York: W. H. Freeman.

Sen, Amartya. 1980. "Equality of What?" In *Tanner Lectures on Human Values*. Ed. S. M. McMurrin. Salt Lake City: University of Utah Press. Reprinted in Sen 1982: 353–369.

——— 1982. *Choice, Welfare and Measurement*. Oxford: Basil Blackwell.

——— 1985. *Commodities and Capabilities*. Amsterdam: North-Holland.

——— 1990. "Gender and Cooperative Conflicts." In *Persistent Inequalities*. Ed. Irene Tinker. New York: Oxford University Press. Pp. 123–149.

——— 1992. *Inequality Reexamined*. New York: Russell Sage.

——— 1993. "Capability and Well-Being." In *The Quality of Life*. Ed. Martha C. Nussbaum and Amartya Sen. Oxford: Clarendon Press. Pp. 30–53.

——— 1995. "Gender Inequality and Theories of Justice." In *Women, Culture and Development*. Ed. Martha C. Nussbaum and Jonathan Glover. Oxford: Clarendon Press. Pp. 259–273.

——— 1997. "Human Rights and Asian Values." *New Republic*, July 14/21: 33–40.

——— 1999. *Development as Freedom*. New York: Knopf.

Sen, Amartya, and Bernard Williams. 1982. "Introduction." In *Utilitarianism and Beyond*. Ed. Amartya Sen and Bernard Williams. Cambridge: Cambridge University Press. Pp. 1–21.

Sherman, Nancy. 1989. *The Fabric of Character: Aristotle's Theory of Virtue*. Oxford: Clarendon Press.

Shue, Henry. 1996. *Basic Rights.* 2d ed. Princeton: Princeton University Press.

Silvers, Anita. 1998. "Formal Justice." In Silvers, Wasserman, and Mahowald (1998): 13–146.

——— 2000. "The Unprotected: Constructing Disability in the Context of Antidiscrimination Law." In Francis and Silvers (2000): 126–45.

Silvers, Anita, David Wasserman, and Mary B. Mahowald. 1998. *Disability, Difference, Discrimination.* Lanham, Md.: Rowman and Littlefield.

Simmons, A. John. 1992. *The Lockean Theory of Rights.* Princeton: Princeton University Press.

Singer, Peter. 1972. "Famine, Affluence and Morality." *Philosophy and Public Affairs* 1: 229–244.

——— 1975. *Animal Liberation.* New York: Avon Books.

——— 1980. "Animals and the Value of Life." In *Matters of Life and Death: New Introductory Essays on Moral Philosophy.* Ed. Tom Regan. New York: Random House. Pp. 28–66.

——— 1999a. Response to Coetzee. In Coetzee (1999): 85–92.

——— 1999b. "A Response." In Jamieson (1999): 269–335.

Smith, Adam. 1776/1784/1981. *An Inquiry into the Nature and Causes of the Wealth of Nations.* Ed. R. H. Campbell, A. S. Skinner, and W. B. Todd. 2 vols. Indianapolis: Liberty Fund. (The text is based on the 1784 edition, which can be regarded as Smith's final version.)

Smuts, Barbara. 1999. Response to Coetzee. In Coetzee (1999): 107–120.

Sorabji, Richard. 1993. *Animal Minds and Human Morals: The Origins of the Western Debate.* Ithaca: Cornell University Press.

Stark, Cynthia. 2000. "Hypothetical Consent and Justification." *Journal of Philosophy* 97: 313–334.

Stiglitz, Joseph. 2002. *Globalization and Its Discontents.* New York: Norton.

Sunstein, Cass R. 2004. "Can Animals Sue?" In Sunstein and Nussbaum (2004): 251–262.

Sunstein, Cass R., and Martha C. Nussbaum, eds. 2004. *Animal Rights: Current Debates and New Directions*. New York: Oxford University Press.

tenBroek, Jacobus. 1966. "The Right to Be in the World: The Disabled in the Law of Torts." *California Law Review* 54: 841–919.

Tronto, Joan. 1993. *Moral Boundaries: A Political Argument for an Ethic of Care*. New York: Routledge.

United Nations Development Programme. 1999. *Human Development Report 1999*. New York: Oxford University Press.

—— 2000. *Human Development Report 2000*. New York: Oxford University Press.

—— 2001. *Human Development Report 2001*. New York: Oxford University Press.

—— 2002. *Human Development Report 2002*. New York: Oxford University Press.

—— 2003. *Human Development Report 2003*. New York: Oxford University Press.

Wasserman, David. 1998. "Distributive Justice." In Silvers, Wasserman, and Mahowald (1998): 147–208.

—— 2000. "Stigma without Impairment: Demedicalizing Disability Discrimination." In Francis and Silvers (2000): 146–162.

West, Robin. 1997. *Caring for Justice*. New York: New York University Press.

Williams, Bernard. 1973. "A Critique of Utilitarianism." In J. J. C. Smart and Bernard Williams, *Utilitarianism: For and Against*. Cambridge: Cambridge University Press. Pp. 77–150.

Williams, Joan. 2000. *Unbending Gender: Why Family and Work Conflict and What to Do about It*. New York: Oxford University Press.

Wise, Stephen. 2000. *Rattling the Cage: Toward Legal Rights for Animals*. Cambridge, Mass.: Perseus Books.

Wood, Allen. 1999. *Kant's Ethical Theory*. Cambridge: Cambridge University Press.

INDEX